A Highland History

A Highland History

by the Earl of Cromartie

Dedicated to my Comrades of the 4th Battalion
The Seaforth Highlanders; to my son John Ruaridh;
and to the Men and Women of Ross and Cromarty.
Tìr nam Beann 's nan Gleann 's nan Gaisgeach.

 The Gavin Press

First Edition 1979

Published by The Gavin Press, Berkhamsted, Hertfordshire

ISBN 0 905868 03 X

Printed in Great Britain by T & A Constable, Ltd, Edinburgh

CONTENTS

Illustrations

Maps   Endpapers

Contents

INTRODUCTION

The story of the Province of Ross, its three Earldoms, Ross, Seaforth and Cromartie; its people, and the part they have played in the History of Scotland.

This book was planned and written by me while a prisoner-of-war in Germany. It could not, of course, be quite completed under those unpleasant circumstances as for this purpose access to certain books and contemporary documents was necessary, and these were far away. Information has been collected from many sources; such as National, Clan, and Local Histories, Letters, Diaries, Biographies, and a Manuscript History of Clan Mackenzie by Sir George Mackenzie, Viscount Tarbat 1st Earl of Cromartie, written by him during the 17th century. Whenever possible I have made use of contemporary papers, charters and letters, including the Cromartie Papers in the possession of my own family; the Munro Papers and Balnagown (Ross) Documents; all of which cover a period from the 13th century to the present day; likewise Church and Burgh Records. When tradition and legend—in Scotland often surprisingly reliable—are quoted, the fact is indicated. I owe debts of gratitude to many writers both ancient and modern, as well as others who have helped me in various ways; some few of these are mentioned in the acknowledgements.

Before starting this account of an historically very important section of Scotland, it is desirable to state briefly my aims. I have tried to tell some of the story about the area which once formed the Province, Mormaerdom, and Earldom of Ross. This naturally entails frequent references to the two neighbouring Earldoms of the north, Sutherland and Caithness which together formed the Province of Cat, to the great Province of Moray further south, and to the Western Isles.

At the same time I have endeavoured to link up the whole with national events in which the Highlands played such an important part; an aspect too often misrepresented and distorted by historical writers of the 19th and early 20th centuries. The Whig bias of the 18th and 19th centuries produced a very unreal picture of the Celt and the Highlands, which was further obscured by racial myths—since largely disproved—which tended to perpetuate barriers between Highlander and Lowlander in Scotland. These barriers we know existed but from comparatively recent times, and their cause was mainly religious and not racial difference.

The Gaelic was spoken in the greater part of the southern Lowlands till a late date, letters of 1725 referring to this language as being 'lately universal in many parts of . . . the Lowlands,' but gradually it gave way to the 'Scots' of Lothian which spread as the language of commerce, though in Fife, Gaelic remained the predominant language till the end of the 17th century. The racial position of Lothian differs from that of the rest of Scotland. As this area holds a mixed population of both Goidelic and Brythonic Celts and many Angles of the old post-Roman Kingdom of Northumbria who to some degree replaced the original Celtic population, by whom, however, they were finally conquered in A.D. 1018, when Lothian became part of the Kingdom of Scotland, the population remaining primarily Angle in blood, though nevertheless good Scots.

The Highland Area was not a vast desert peopled by savages playing no part in the cultural development of Scotland, neither were the inhabitants continually engaged in clan feuds to the exclusion of all else. Territorial squabbles were common to all mediaeval Britain, their severity and duration depending on the power, or lack of it, in the central governments. Both before and after the Reformation education for the Highlands was in precisely the same position as for the rest of Scotland. No country in Europe organized universal education till a very recent date and in this Scotland led the way, but during the Middle Ages, the children of the Chiefs, Barons, Gentlemen, and the Seannachies, as well as all intended for the Church, were able to receive the same amount of learning as their counterparts further south.

During the centuries prior to the Reformation, first the settlements of the Celtic Church, then the Roman Catholic Cathedrals and Religious Houses conducted our schools, the north being very adequately served in this respect. From these beginnings the Grammar and Parish schools managed jointly by the Church and Burgh Councils sprang up, of which we have records that prove that they were already functioning in the 15th century; and that in spite of wars and civil disturbance the work of these same schools continued after the Reformation. Difficulty of communication was common to all the British Isles and the mountains of the north aggravated this, especially in winter, so that it became a common practice for Highland gentlemen to band together and employ a tutor for their children.

The once popular theory of the replacement of the Celtic Nobility by Norman Houses during the 12th and 13th centuries also needs drastic revision. For instance, the mighty House of Douglas, eventual holders of five Earldoms and the greatest family of Scotland, were Celtic, probably descended from the Mormaers of Moray. In fact, the great Celtic families were very far from extinct and with few exceptions those Norman and French Knights who did settle in Scotland were there as guests, not conquerors as in England, so that many of them made good marriages with Celtic heiresses, and they and their descendants as a result became good Scots—just as a Scot, Scandinavian or an Englishman can become a good American. On the whole this mixture was of considerable benefit to the nation as it introduced some useful organization without unduly upsetting the Celtic customs and culture, or the essential and accepted leadership of the Celtic noble families; this disaster was to come about many centuries later. Within the boundaries of the old Earldom of Ross several families including the Chiefs of Clans Fraser and Chisholm are descended from such a union.

The Norman admixture was usually satisfactory for various important reasons: firstly the form of feudalism which they introduced was greatly modified by Celtic custom and law; while secondly the Celt was inclined to the modern view that the woman, far from being the personal property of her husband, was a separate entity with equal rights and was every bit as capable of transmitting to her children the family strain and pride of race. The fact that these Normans were the lineal descendants of the Norsemen who for so long had ruled great areas of northern and western Scotland may have helped, especially as many Highland families such as the Earls of Caithness and the MacLeods of Dunvegan and Lewis were themselves, to a high degree, of Norse descent.

Finally, I make no apology for my attempt to describe something of the, so-called, pre-historic background. The Highlanders may be 'Children of the Mist', but they had, also, a great number of more solid forefathers and mothers who all played a vital part in their evolution. For this reason the first two chapters have had to cover a larger canvas than the Province of Ross or even Scotland. This glance at certain historical facts may help to provide a more realistic basis from which to start our story, as well as warn the reader against expecting either a certain type of 'Romantic story of the Highlands' or a re-hash of the 'stuff' served up to us as 'Scottish History'—when indeed it was served at all—at our various schools.

Note: Usually the present-day spelling has been used for personal and place names as prior to the 19th century variations were infinite, e.g. Crumbarthy—Crumertie—Cromertie—present practice: Cromarty for Firth, town and county and Cromartie for the personal title.

COMPARATIVE TABLE OF SCOTTISH AND ENGLISH KINGS

Pictish–Caledonian	Scottish A.D.	Dalriadic–Scots–Kingdom of Argyll	A.D.	English
Drust, the son of Erp				
Talorc, the son of Aniel	451			
Nechtan Morbet, the son of Erp, built Church of St. Brigit at Abernethy	455			
Drust Gurthinmoch	480			
		Fergus, the son of Erc	503	
		Domangart, the son of Fergus	506	
Galanau Etelich, or Galanan Errlech	510			
		Comgal, the son of Domangart	511	
Dadrest	522			
Drust, the son of Girom	523			
Drust, the son of Wdrest with the former	524			Many Saxon, Angle and British–Brython petty kingdoms
Drust, the son of Girom	529			
Gartnach, the son of Girom	534			
		Gavran, the son of Domangart	535	
Gealtraim, or Cailtraim, the son of Girom	541			
Talorc, the son of Muircholaich	542			
Drust, the son of Munait	553			
Galam, with Aleph	554			
Galam, with Bridei	555			
Bridei, the son of Mailcon	556			
		Conal, the son of Comgal	557	
		Aidan, the son of Gavran	571	
Gartnaich, the son of Domelch, or Donald	586			
Nectu, or Nechtan, the nephew of Verb	597			
		Eoacha'-Bui, the son of Aidan	605	
Cineoch, or Kenneth, the son of Luthrin	617			
		Kenneth-Cear, the son of Eoacha'-Bui	621	
		Ferchar, the son of Eogan, the first of the race of Lorn	621	
Garnard, the son of Wid	636			
		Donal-Breac, the son of Eoacha'-Bui	637	
Bridei, the son of Wid	640			
		Conal II, the grandson of Conal I	642	
		Dungal reigned some years with Conal II		
Talorc, their brother	645			
		Donal-Duin, the son of Conal	652	
Tallorcan, the son of Enfret	657			
Gartnait, the son of Donnel	661			
		Maol-Duin, the son of Conal	665	
Drust, his brother	667			
Bridei, the son of Bili	674			
		Ferchar-Fada, the grandson of Ferchar	681	
Taran, the son of Entifidich	695			
Bridei, the son of Dereli	699			
		Eoacha'-Rinevel, the son of Domangart, and the grandson of Donal-Breac	702	
		Ainbhcealach, the son of Ferchar-Fada	705	
		Selvach, the son of Ferchar-Fada reigned over Lorn from 706 to 729		
Nechtan, the son of Dereli	710			
		Duncha Beg, reigned over Cantyre and Argaill till 720		
		Eocha' III, the son of Eocha'-Rinevel, over Cantyre and Argaill	706	

Pictish–Caledonian	Scottish A.D.	Dalriadic–Scots–Kingdom of Argyll	A.D.	English	
Drust and Elpin	725	from 720 to 729; and over			
Angus I, MacFergus, the son of		Lorn 729 to 733. Defeated by			
Urguist, the greatest Pictish		Angus I			
monarch	730	Dalriada under Pictish rule			
		Muredach, the son of			
		Ainbhcealach	733		
		Eogan, the son of Muredach	736		
		Aodh-Fin, the son of			
		Eoacha' III	739		
Bridei, the son of Wirguist	761				
Cinioch, or Kenneth, the son of					
Wredech	763				
		Fergus, the son of Aodh-Fin	769		
		Selvach II, the son of Eogan	772		
Elpin, the son of Wroid	775				
Drust, the son of Talorgan	779				
Talorgan, the son of Ungus or					
Angus	784				
Canaul, the son of Tarla	786				
Constantine I, the son of Urguist,					
founded church of Dunkeld	791				
		Eoacha'-Annuine IV, the son			
		of Aodh-Fin	796		
Angus II, the son of Urguist.					
Introduced veneration of St.					
Andrew and possibly use of				Eegberht of Wessex, but	
Saltire as National emblem	821			overlord of others to	
		Dungal, the son of Selvach II	826	South of Forth i.e.	802
				Lothian	–839
Drust, the son of Constantine		Alpin, the son of Eoacha'-			
and Talorgan, the son of		Annuine IV. m. heiress of			
Wthoil	833	Pictish Royal House	833		
Uuen, the son of Ungus	836				
Wrad, the son of Bargoit	839			Aethelwulf, son of	839
Bred, or Briudi	842			Eegberht	–858

Union of Pictish and Dalriadic Thrones

House of Alpin

Kenneth I, son of Alpin	843–860	Aethelbald	858–860
Donald I, his brother	860–863	Aethelberht	860–866
Constantine II, son of Kenneth I	863–877	Aethlred	866–871
Aedh, brother of Constantine	877–878		
Cyric—with Eocha, nephew of Aedh	878–889		
—with Donald II, son of			
Constantine	889–900	Aelfred, the Great 4th son of Aethelwulf	871–900
Constantine III, son of Aedh	900–943	Eadward, son of Aelfred	901–925
		Aethalston, son of Eadward	925–940
		Eadmund, son of Eadward	940–946
Malcolm I, son of Donald II	943–954	Eadred, son of Eadward	946–955
Indulf, son of Constantine III	954–962	England divided—3 sons of Eadmund	
		over Wessex–Northumberland–Mercia	955–959
Duff, son of Malcolm I	962–967		
		United by Edgar of Northumberland	959–975
Colin, son of Indulf	967–971		
Kenneth II, Mac MacLchaluin, brother			
of Duff. Succeeded to throne of			
Brython Kingdom of Cumbria, and			
routed Danes at Luncarty	971–995	Eadward, son of Eadgar	975–979
Constantine IV, son of Colin	995–997		
Kenneth III, son of Duff	997–1005	Aethelred, The Unready, step-brother	
		of Eadward	979–1016
Malcolm II, son of Kenneth II. Final		*Danes conquer England*	1015
defeat of Danes. Victory of Carham		Edmund Ironside	1016–1017
gains Lothian	1005–1034	Cnut the Dane. Scots gain Lothian by	
		victory at Carham	1017–1035

House of Dunkeld

Duncan I, son of Bethoc dtr. of Malcolm II			
by Crinan of Dunkeld—Lay Abbot and			
powerful Pictish leader. Killed during or			
after Torfness	1034–1040	England divided by Cnut's sons	
		eventually re-united by Cnut's son	
House of Moray and Ross		Harold	1035–1040
MacBeth, son of Donada dtr. of Malcolm II			
by Findlaec of Ross. Killed Lumphanan	1040–1057	Aarthacnut of Denmark and West Saxons	1040–1042

Return of Saxon House
Edward Atheling, The Confessor, m. dtr.
of St. Stephen, King of Hungary. His
dtr. Margaret m. Malcolm III of
Scotland; their son David I was heir to
four Royal houses. The Scots dynasty of
over six centuries; the Saxon almost as
old; the Pictish older still; and House of
of Cumbria or Strathclyde (Brython)

Scottish		English	
Lulach, stepson of MacBeth and son of Gruoch, grand-dtr. of Gillecomgan of Moray. Killed	1057–1058	and the blood of three more: Kings of Hungary, Denmark and Hohenstaufen Emperors	1042–1066
		Harold, son of Earl Godwin	1066
House of Dunkeld restored			
Malcolm III, Ceann Mor, son of Duncan I. m. (1) Ingibjorg of Norway, (2) Margaret, dtr. of Edward the Confessor. Killed at siege of Alnwick	1057–1093	*House of Normandy* William I, Duke of Normandy	1066–1087
		William II, Rufus, son of William I	1087–1100
Donald III, Bane, brother of Malcolm III. Succession by Tanistry. Ruled with Edmund, son of Malcolm and Margaret	1093–1097		
Duncan II, son of Malcolm III and Ingibjorg. Killed	1094		
Donald III, restored with Edmund. Murdered	1094–1097		
Edgar, son of Malcolm III and Margaret	1097–1107		
		Henry I, m. Matilda dtr. of Malcolm III of Scotland	1100–1135
Alexander I, brother of Edgar, m. Sibyl, natural dtr. of Henry I of England	1107–1124		
David I, brother of Alexander I, m. Matilda, Countess of Huntingdon in her own right	1124–1153		
		Stephen, Usurper. Henry's sister's son. Anarchy in England. Scots back Matilda and her small son	1135–1154
Minority.	1153–1160	*House of Plantagenet*	
Malcolm IV, grandson of David I, and son of Prince Henry of Scotland, the son of David I and Ada, dtr. of Earl of Surrey	1160–1165	Henry II, grandson of Henry I	1154–1189
William I, The Lion, brother of Malcolm IV. Probably first to use the Lion Rampant as Royal Standard. m. Princess Ermengarde	1165–1214		
Alexander II, son of William I. m. (1) Joan, dtr. of King John. (2) Mary, dtr. of Ingelram de Coucy of Picardy	1214–1249		
Minority. Wards—Earl of Menteith; Durward the Justiciar; Walter Comyn; Robert de Ros of Wark Castle, a kinsman of Alexander III; Bishop Gamelin	1249–1258	Richard I, son of Henry II	1189–1199
Alexander III, son of Alexander II. m. (1) Princess Margaret, dtr. of Henry III of England. Victory of Largs ends Norwegian domination in Hebrides. m.		John, brother of Richard I	1199–1216
(2) Yolette de Dreux	1258–1286	Henry III, son of John	1216–1272
House of Norway Margaret, minority. Maid of Norway, dtr. of Margaret dtr. of Alexander III by Erik II of Norway, died sp. Six guardians included—James the Steward; Black John Comyn of Badenoch; Bishop of St. Andrews; Wishart Bishop of Glasgow	1286–1290		
Interregnum	1290–1291		
House of Balliol John, 5th in descent from David I	1291–1296	Edward I, son of Henry III	1272–1307
Interregnum	1296–1306		
House of Bruce Robert I, 6th in descent from David I. Born 1274. Victor of Bannockburn, 1314. m. (1) Isobel of Mar (2) Mary of Ulster	1306–1329		
		Edward II, son of Edward I	1307–1327
		Edward III, son of Edward II	1327–1377
Minority. Guardians of the Kingdom. (1) Randolph Earl of Moray (2) Earl of Mar			

Scottish		English	
(3) Andrew de Moray and Avoch			
(4) Douglas			
(5) Robert Stewart			
(6) Randolph's son	1329–1341		
David II, son of Robert I by Mary of Ulster. m. (1) Princess Joanna, dtr. of Edward II (2) Margaret Lady Logie	1341–1371	Beginning of 100 Years War	1338
First House of Stewart			
Robert II, son of Marjorie Bruce, b. 1316. dtr. of Robert I and Isobel of Mar, by Walter Stewart of Scotland. m. (1) Elizabeth Mure (2) Euphemia of Ross	1371–1389	Richard II, grandson of Edward III Peasant Revolt, led by Wat Tyler	1377–1399 1381
Regency. Robert Earl of Monteith and Fife. Robert II's second son	1389–1390		
Robert III, son of Robert II, died 1406. m. Annabella Drummond	1390–1406		
Regency. (1) Robert, Duke of Albany	1406–1420		
(2) Murdoch, Duke of Albany	1420–1424	Henry IV, cousin of Richard II Henry V, son of Henry IV Henry VI, son of Henry V	1399–1413 1413–1422 1422–1461
James I, son of Robert III. m. Lady Joan Beaufort dtr. of Earl of Somerset, the son of John of Gaunt, 3rd son of Edward III. Assassinated at Perth	1424–1437		
Minority. Guardians—Queen Joan; Douglas; Crichton; Livingstone; Bishop Kennedy	1437–1449		
James II, son of James I. m. Mary of Gueldres. Killed by bursting cannon at Siege of Roxburgh	1449–1460		
Minority. Guardians—The Queen; Bishop Kennedy; Sir Alexander Boyd	1460–1469	End of 100 Years War Start of the Wars of the Roses Edward IV, cousin of Henry VI	1453 1455 1461–1483
James III, son of James II. m. Princess Margaret of Denmark and Norway	1469–1488	Edward V, murdered in Tower Richard III, Duke of Gloucester. Uncle of Edward V *Tudors* Henry VII whose m. to Elizabeth of York ended the Wars of the Roses	1483 1483–1485 1485–1509
James IV, son of James III. m. Margaret Tudor. Killed at Flodden	1488–1513	Henry VIII, son of Henry VII	1509–1547
Minority. Earl of Angus; Albany	1513–1528		
James V, son of James IV. m. Mary of Lorraine dtr. of Duke of Guise	1528–1542		
Minority. Queen Regent, Mary of Guise	1543–1560	Edward VI, son of Henry VIII Lady Jane Grey Mary, daughter of Henry VIII Elizabeth I, daughter of Henry VIII	1547–1553 1553 1553–1558 1558–1603
Mary I, Queen of Scots, daughter of James V. m. (1) Dauphin of France (2) Darnley (3) Bothwell	1561–1567		
Second or Lennox House of Stewart Minority. Regents—(1) Earl of Moray, assassinated 1570 (2) Earl of Lennox, shot (3) Earl of Mar	1567–1583		
James VI, son of Mary I and Henry Stewart, Lord Darnley. m. Princess Anne of Denmark. Succeeding to dual Crown in 1603. His daughter Elizabeth m. Frederick, Count Palatine, afterwards King of Bohemia, and their daughter Sophia m. the Elector of Hanover and was mother of George I of England	1583–1603		

UNION OF CROWNS

James VI of Scotland and I of England	1603–1625
Charles I, son of James VI and I. m. Henrietta Maria of France, dtr. of Henry IV. Great Rebellion	1625–1649
Charles II—in Scotland—son of Charles I. m. Catherine of Portugal	1649–1651
Oliver Cromwell, Protector	1651–1658
Richard Cromwell, Protector	1658–1659
Charles II restored	1660–1685
James VII of Scotland and II of England, brother of Charles II. m. (1) Anne Hyde, dtr. of Earl of Clarendon (2) Princess Mary of Modena	1685–1688

House of Orange

Mary II, dtr. of James VII and II by 1st marriage, and William II of Scotland and III of England, her husband	1989–1702

House of Lennox Stewarts restored—of United Kingdoms
Anne, sister of Mary II. m. Prince George of Denmark. All progeny died young   1702–1714
House of Hanover
George I, great-grandson of James VI and I. m. Princess Sophia Dorothea of Brunswick and Zell   1714–1727
George II, son of George I. m. Princess Caroline of Anspach   1727–1760
George III, son of Frederick Prince of Wales who died 1751, the son of George II and Princess
   Augusta of Saxe-Coburg. m. Princess Charlotte of Mecklenburg-Strelitz   1760–1820
George IV, son of George III. m. Princess Carolina of Brunswick sp.   1820–1830
William III of Scotland and IV of England, brother of George IV. m. Princess Adelaide of Saxe-
   Meiningen sp.   1830–1837
Victoria, niece of William III and IV, and daughter of Duke of Kent, 4th son of George III. m.
   Prince Albert of Saxe-Coburg-Gotha   1837–1901
House of Saxe-Coburg-Gotha later Windsor
Edward I of Scotland and VII of England, son of Victoria and Prince Albert. m. Princess Alexandra of
   Denmark   1901–1910
George V, son of Edward I and VII. m. Mary, daughter of Duke of Teck   1910–1936
Edward II of Scotland and VIII of England, son of George V. Abdicated   1936
George VI, brother of Edward II and VIII. m. Lady Elizabeth Bowes-Lyon, daughter of the Earl of
   Strathmore and Kinghorne   1936–1952
Elizabeth I and II, daughter of George VI. m. Prince Philip, Duke of Edinburgh, son of Prince Andrew
   of Greece and Princess Alice of Battenberg   1952–

CHAPTER I

PREHISTORIC ANCESTORS—ARRIVAL OF THE IBERIANS

A Chronological Table—continued at the commencement of each chapter—of some events important in Scottish History, and happenings elsewhere in the World.

Eolithic Age 3rd Ice Age Early Palaeolithic Period Old Stone Age 200,000 B.C.	Ape-Men—Early man. Discovery of art of chipping flint. Wood and bone worked. Covers most of Europe.
Chellean Age	Extinct Men (sub-human), the uncles not forefathers of Homo-Sapiens. 100,000 years of flint knapping. Food, raw and putrid flesh, roots and fruit. Cave dwellings.
100,000 B.C. Acheulean Age	50,000 years, improving flints, same diet. Cave dwellings.
50,000 B.C. Mousterian Age Late Palaeolithic Period	Neanderthalers etc. Fire discovered. Cave dwellings. Ceremonial burial—skin—clothing.
25,000 B.C. Aurignacian Age (Reindeer Age) 4th Ice Age 20,000 B.C.	True Men. Cro-Magnards etc. Art of drawing discovered. Trinkets and statuettes. Antler implements. Body painting with red ochre. Cave dwellings. Scotland Covered.
Solutrean Age 15,000 B.C.	Bone whistles—needles invented. The horse may have been domesticated. Cave dwellings.
Magdalenian Age	Bows and arrows—fish-hooks—buttons—pins—tubes (bone) of paint—Fine Art— Early huts.
Transition Period 12,000 B.C. Azilian Age Mesolithic Culture (till 3000 B.C. in Britain)	A few colonists arrive in Scotland late during this period—rafts and boats invented. Weaving and possibly rollers (early wheels) and possibly writing.
8000 B.C. Neolithic or New Stone Age	This age introduces agriculture, the milking of cows, domestication of dogs, dew-ponds, potting, gold, religious buildings and stringed instruments, but Britain remains almost untouched by these advances till c. 3000 B.C.
c. 8000 B.C.	Dawn of Sumerian and Egyptian Civilization.
c. 5000 B.C.	Appearance of true Egyptians.
4236 B.C.	The oldest known practical Calendar produced in Egypt.
c. 4000 B.C.	Aegean Civilization Established.
3733 B.C. Bronze Age	The Pyramids built during the IVth Dynasty.
Megalithic Period	Metal-smelting. Tin, copper, antimony etc. Bone studs—trumpets, tea-pots (in China). The use of bronze did not start in Britain much before 2000 B.C.
c. 3000 B.C.	Arrival of Iberian people in the British Isles who replace the Mesolithic hunters and food-gatherers.
c. 2750 B.C.	Sargon I founds Akkadian-Sumerian Empire. Oldest civilized map of the World engraved showing Babylon at centre.
c. 2500 B.C.	First of five Chinese Emperors recorded. Peak of Minoan, Crete, Civilization lasting till destruction by very early Achaean Greeks of Celtic origin, in 1400 B.C.
c. 2400 B.C.	First Babylonian Empire.

The scene opens about 20,000 B.C. in an uninhabited Scotland from which the ice mantle of the fourth and most recent glacial age has retreated north leaving in its wake bare tundra, to be followed many years later by a landscape covered with birch, willow, and aspen scrub. Then after another great lapse of time the climate became drier and generally more Continental while Scotland clothed herself with great forests of Caledonian Pine which grew up to an altitude of 3,000 feet. Later to the lower levels came hazel scrub, then oak, ash, elm and alder, followed by beech, the presence of the alder tree indicating a change to damper conditions, which in time became so pronounced that many of the forests got water-logged, fell and rotted, forming the great peat deposits which for so long have provided the Highlands with fuel.

Climatic fluctuations continued till a drier regime caused a second afforestation period which, however, failed to restore timber to Caithness, Orkney and Shetland; quantities of birch reappeared showing a further change of climate probably resembling, or even being worse than, that of our own day. In many areas the land sank beneath the sea, but later in the north there came a re-elevation, exemplified by old raised beaches and some caves at the Sutors of Cromarty which, originally excavated by the waves, now lie 15 to 25 ft. above sea level. This upheaval cannot have been a lengthy process as whales were left stranded five miles north of Stirling.

South-east Britain was still attached to the continent of Europe by a land bridge over which a few Mesolithic food gathering people had followed the retreating ice to hunt the fast disappearing mammoth and woolly rhinoceros. In south Britain they found and replaced the old Palaeolithic people being joined, as time went on, by other food-gatherers from the continent. The Mesolithic folk do not seem to have arrived in Scotland till sometime during the Late Stone Age, a period lasting from 12,000 to 3000 B.C.

Little is known of our first colonists, but they were short, long-headed people with square jaws, narrow set eyes, and a very primitive way of life. By the time the majority of these people arrived, Britain had become an island and the earliest men of whom in Scotland we find traces are the Azilian strandloopers who arrived by sea, in their dug-out tree-trunk canoes, from southern France. They and the Mesolithic forest folk from the north European plain made their homes on the sea-shore and lived by fishing and hunting the elk, red deer, roe, wild pig and aurochs with the help of their dogs, using simple tools and weapons, bone harpoons and small flint blades, arrow-heads known as microliths often found amongst the large heaps of shells which can yet be seen along our western coasts, and in such Kitchen Middens as those near Dingwall, Munlochy and Fortrose where a flint factory was situated supplying a number of families on the Black Isle. The size of these shell-heaps is evidence of the importance of shell-fish in their diet, which was augmented with wild vegetable food and berries. Their dwellings were the sheltering sand-dunes, simple huts, or caves like those of Inchnadamph in Sutherland.

Thousands of years later their small flint microliths became known as 'Elf Bolts', once credited with magical and healing powers for ailing cattle if put in their drinking water, but also as weapons of offence against the same cattle in the hands of an antagonistic fairy or witch. Perhaps the traditional 'Island of the Pygmies' off Lewis had some connection with these early inhabitants, as stories of the 'little people' lingered in this area till A.D. 1600.

The immense tracts of the Caledonian Forest became the home of many animals which had migrated from Europe before the submergence of the land bridge, whose descendants in many cases are still with us: the red deer, whose ancestor was of much larger proportions, roe, grouse, badger, martyn, wild cat and the ptarmigan of the high tops. The great elk, northern lynx, wild horses, reindeer, great auroch, eagles, beavers, bears and wolves dwelt for long ages in our land till at length they died out, some like the lynx comparatively soon, others more recently, the elk surviving till Roman times, the reindeer till c. A.D. 900 in Caithness while several places claim the last wolf and in Sutherland there stands a memorial commemorating the occasion when a wolf was killed in Glen *Loth* c. A.D. 1700 by a hunter, Polson.

It is not known to what extent the Mesolithic people influenced later populations, but traces of their industry cover a period of 3000 years in the British Isles; they appear to have been very conservative, altering their habits but little; however, a big change was on its way the origin of which may have been about 7000 years ago.

Owing to constant renewal of the soil by the River Nile, people were able to stay put along its banks, relinquishing the nomadic existence necessitated by the impoverishment of the soil in other places. The Nile Valley, as also that of the Tigris, Euphrates and Indus produced great and flourishing cities at an early date; the populations grew forcing outwards the semi-nomadic farmers on their fringes so that these dispossessed folk were forced to move and search for new lands. From the eastern Mediterranean zone they moved west, absorbing in their progress their distant relations the old Mesolithic communities in the same way as the latter had replaced and absorbed the Upper Palaeolithic peoples long ages before, finally reaching Britain about 3,000 B.C. These Neolithic Colonists are usually known as Iberians whose culture can be traced through southern France, the Iberian Peninsula (Spain), and back to Egypt. They are, perhaps, the first race who materially effected the divers racial strains which go to make up the Highland and Lowland Scot of our own day.

Their language is unknown but belonged to the Hamitic group and it may have resembled Basque, which has no connection with any language of modern Europe. The Hamitic Races were originally the dark whites of North Africa and included the Ancient Egyptians— Aegean Civilization and their offshoots the Philistines and Etruscans who were the survivors from Crete after the Minoan destruction by early Greeks 1400 B.C.—and lastly the Berbers.

It had taken these first farmers some 2500 years to reach the shores of Britain, but when they eventually crossed from southern Europe they brought with them already formed a culture far in advance of that possessed by the Mesolithic peoples, who were primitive in the extreme and in fact seem to have lacked the fine artistic ability shown by their very early Palaeolithic predecessors, whose wonderful animal studies may yet be seen in their cave dwellings at Dordogne in France. During the last twenty years scientific research has greatly increased our knowledge of these very ancient Britons, though still they remain shadowy, as the sole sources of information are their pottery, weapons, and archaeological remains.

Early groups settled in Sussex and Wessex, where they constructed fortified camps and from a hill in Wiltshire their culture has been named Windmill Hill. They were great cattle breeders, having introduced long-horned cattle which they may have crossed with the native wild cattle of the British Isles. Sheep, goats and pigs were raised, and they cultivated wheat of at least two varieties, short-eared club wheat, and the primitive emmer and small spelt, using a digging stick or antler horn; they introduced the saddle quern for grinding their corn, and developed the mining of flint, an industry they took over from their Mesolithic precursors. Their religion, connected with the Sun, either as a god in itself or else symbolizing the supreme power, included fertility rites and the burying of their dead in long barrows.

Traces of the Windmill Hill Culture have been found in the Hebrides and as far north as Orkney, but this culture was only one outpost of the Neolithic civilization, and other groups of the same kind arrived by sea and slowly replaced the Mesolithic people of Scotland and Ireland. In these two countries there appeared considerable variations in their cultures when compared to that of the Windmill Hill groups which occupied south Britain, so that the northern development is known as the Unstan or Pentland Culture.

At some period of Neolithic history a great religious movement affected all the peoples of the Mediterranean coasts, spread to the Atlantic and through all the British Isles even reaching the Baltic, probably by way of Scotland. What this 'Reformation' set out to teach we do not know, but the results were remarkable, huge and elaborate tombs being constructed as family vaults for collective interment of the dead with a single ritual common to the whole vast area. It is probable that these tombs were built as the family vaults of a caste who combined the duties of priest and chief in their respective areas, who at their burial were accompanied by offerings of food, vases, ornaments, leaf-shaped arrow and axe-heads of flint and stone maces.

In Scotland we find two predominant branches of this Megalithic Religion, both of which came by way of Ireland from the Iberian Peninsula without touching south Britain. The great horned cairns of the Clyde-Carlingford group were introduced by groups of settlers from northern Ireland into the west of Scotland between the Solway Firth and Lorn, thence spreading through the Hebrides, being particularly prominent in the islands of Skye and Lewis. The fine pottery found in these graves shows an artistic affinity not only with the Iberian Peninsula, but also with the early Minoan Civilization in Crete.

The spread of this Megalithic religion may to some degree have been caused by the search for the Isles of the Blest beneath the setting sun, *Tir nan Óg*, and followed the natural sea routes round western Scotland. The more strictly orthodox Passage Graves of the Boyne Culture, first introduced from Spain to the Sligo Bay area in Ireland, followed the same sea route becoming the dominant sect on both sides of the Pentland (Pictland) Firth: north in Orkney, Shetland and south in Caithness, Sutherland and Ross where chambered tumuli still exist in considerable numbers, many still intact as at the Blackstand near Cromarty. On the Isle of Skye and in Lewis both denominations of the Megalithic religion existed side by side, apparently without friction—a state of affairs seldom found in more recent and civilized ages. The most famous monument of this dim age survives at Callernish in Lewis, consisting of a large stone circle which surrounds a round cairn containing a cruciform chamber.

A well-known Passage Grave exists at *Rudh'an Dunain* in Skye. A round cairn 78 ft. across was surrounded by a peristalith of upright blocks with dry stone masonry in between them. The peristalith was constructed to form a forecourt at the entrance to a passage leading into the vault and through an ante-chamber into two further chambers, the last being polygonal, $7\frac{1}{4}$ ft. in diameter and about 7 ft. high. Beyond this area of divided but friendly loyalties, the Pentland culture held sway, dominated by the Passage Tombs, with their corbelled domes and hidden chambers—the vaulted ceilings of which were constructed by the same method; but here we find an early example of Scottish individuality in a modification of tradition to the segmented cists of Caithness type which are represented by some hundred cairns mostly on the mainland of the three northern counties though penetrating into Moray. But in north-west Scotland, for geological reasons, the Passage Graves often vary from the much larger Caithness types where the stone is so suitable for dry stone building, so that we frequently find orthostatic building, the corbelled roofs being replaced by huge horizontal lintels.

By 2000 B.C.[1] the trade and culture of the Middle East was having repercussions on the British Isles by way of Ireland, where the first Irish metallurgists were busily making flat axes of bronze and copper halberds. Trade grew and soon spread outside Ireland, as is demonstrated by Boyne trade routes, which are clearly blazed, not only by their Passage Graves beautifully constructed and decorated with spiral

Note 1. Recent discoveries along the Danube and carbon dating now reveal that advanced metallurgy reached Ireland much earlier.

patterns, but also by the weapon dumps at their trading posts. The two main trade routes serving Scotland ran from Galloway to Lothian; and from Clyde up Loch Fyne to the Firth of Lorne, thence up the Great Glen to the Beauly-Moray Firth. This route is well marked by finds of weapons, jet necklaces and collective tombs, which at the head of the Beauly Firth assumed characteristics of their own, now classified as the Beauly Culture, that spread to the Spey Valley and the area defined by the later recumbent stone circles of Aberdeenshire and Moray. So much for the early religious aspect which played so great a part in the evolution of our civilization.

The economy of all the Megalithic groups was the same as that of all Neolithic Britain. We do not get a clear picture of these early folk but know that they were possessed of an advanced civilization, being physically a dark squat race of long-headed people of medium or short stature, who depended primarily on pastoral pursuits, the mainstay of which was the breeding of their long-horned cattle. In the north where arable land was sour and scarce, being mountainous, or covered by forests as yet uncleared, and undrained quaking bogs, the raising of stock was to an even greater degree the main occupation, helped out by hunting and fishing. Flint in the Highlands of Scotland was extremely scarce, and like their forerunners the Mesolithic folk, the Iberians were forced to practise the strictest economy, every flint being used till it was so worn down as to be unserviceable, while stone usually took its place for their axe-heads.

They lived in houses which in many respects would compare more than favourably with dwellings inhabited by some of our city slum-folk of the 20th century A.D. The discoveries at Skara Brae in Orkney where an entire settlement, long covered by sand-dunes, was exposed after a gale have produced classic examples of domestic architecture of Neolithic type, while due to the absence of trees in this area all their building was of Caithness flag-stone and so has survived. Each individual house was built to the same pattern, in shape a parallelogram with rounded corners and, as in the great Caithness tumuli, partly roofed by corbelling—the external measurements of the house being about 20 ft. × 18 ft. and the internal 14 ft. × 12 ft. The entrance was very small, being only 4 ft. high, probably for warmth and the exclusion of draughts rather than prowling beasts; even the door was a stone slab secured with a bar of stone or whalebone.

Inside conditions were by no means uncomfortable especially when viewed by the imaginative eye of a prisoner-of-war in Germany; on either side of the room were two or three beds enclosed by stone slabs which held in place the mattress of heather, while at the head and foot of each bed were stone bed-posts which supported a canopy of skins, the personal belongings of the family being kept above their beds on shelves built into the wall. In the centre of the room on a square hearth burned a peat fire, and small boxes made of thin stone slabs with carefully luted joints were let into the floor containing liquids, we know not of what kind, perhaps the lost 'Heather Ale' the secret of which was to baffle the Roman invader and eventually the Caledonians, both Iberian and Celtic, themselves. The well-made and decorated household pottery was arranged on a two-shelved stone dresser which stood against the back wall. Opening off this main room were two or three cells some of which were used as storerooms, others as privies which were drained and connect up with a regular drainage system of built sewers running under and draining the whole settlement. The houses were grouped in regular clusters connected by paved alleyways which were all roofed over, one building being used as a communal workshop.

These people lived a self-sufficient life typical of their Neolithic kind, importing nothing from outside, using skins for their clothing, fashioning their weapons from stone, and their needles and bodkins from bone. The hafts of their stone axes, in the absence of wood, being of deer antler, a custom handed down by the Mesolithic folk of pre-Neolithic times. To light their fires they used instead of Iron Pyrites, Nodular Haematite which they also crushed to form a red pigment for artistic purposes. Their taste for decoration is shown, not only by the beads and pendants of their women, usually made of bone or boars' tushes, but also in the triangles, zigzags, and lozenges carved or engraved on the walls of the dwelling-rooms, a style of art inherited from Atlantic patterns. From the household middens we learn something of their diet and discover that owing to their inability to winter many calves in this and similar areas they were able to help out fish and limpet dishes with large quantities of veal.

This type of culture covered all north-east Scotland, but was very similar to that in the west where, in like manner, every occupied glen would be dominated by the great family vault of the Priest-Chief. Gradually the remnants of Mesolithic groups would have been absorbed into the Neolithic societies of this kind; in Ross a flourishing community on the Hill of Tulloch above Dingwall has left traces which include a very well made flint adze. Side by side with these farmers lived the de-tribalized metallurgists of Boyne culture who probably belonged to a priestly caste and implemented their farming by a highly developed commerce centred at the trading posts along their regular trade routes.

Their super-tombs contained burial furnishings of a far more exotic order, such as amber beads, probably from Jutland, bronze and gold ornaments made by the Irish Iberian smiths, though as yet such articles were comparatively scarce, but soon this commerce was to

gain great impetus from some new arrivals, who were to create the
first industrial boom in the British [Pretanic] Isles, and finally break
down the self-sufficient economy of the Neolithic Age, as well as cause
some increase in the population, which during the period in which the
great tombs were being built by our Iberian ancestors may not have
exceeded three or four hundred people over all Scotland.

CHAPTER II

NEW ARRIVALS—THE CELTS, AND THE CLASH WITH ROME

Chronological Table

c. 2000 B.C.	Start of Bronze Age in Britain through agency of the Iberian metallurgists.
c. 2000 B.C.	Arrival of the Beaker People in Scotland, probably the first Celts of the Goidelic branch. They mixed with Iberian race finally being absorbed and producing a hybrid race. Later another influx of Goidelic Celts arrived and eventually *Gaidhlig* (Gaelic) influenced by the Iberian language became the tongue of all the British Isles.
c. 1600 B.C.	'New Empire' Egypt.
c. 1550 B.C.	The Phoenician cities of Tyre and Sidon flourish. By this date the east Mediterranean had been charted by Minoans.
c. 1450 B.C.	Hittites take Nineveh.
1412 B.C.	Start of the reign of Amenhatep III in Egypt of XVIIIth Dynasty. With this Pharaoh started the New Religion which recognized a personal approach to a Supreme God. After his death in 1376 this belief was adopted by his son and heir Akhenaten IV but was soon suppressed by a reactionary Priesthood who had become corrupted since the early days of Egyptian history.
1400 B.C.	Destruction of Minoan (Crete) Civilization by early Greeks the Achaeans of Celtic origin.
1317 B.C.	Ramases II rules in Egypt—Moses—Complete survey of Nile lands carried out; Map-making now an art of long standing.
1000 B.C.	Homer.
c. 960 B.C.	Solomon starts reign in Israel.
800 B.C.	Founding of Carthage by Phoenicians.
753 B.C.	Rome built on older Etruscan site.
750 B.C.	Late Bronze Age established in south Britain, arriving somewhat later in Scotland.
c. 700 B.C.	Gautama Buddha—First transcription of The Iliad.
610 B.C.	Birth of great philosopher and scientist Anaximander.
606 B.C.	Capture of Nineveh by Chaldeans and Medes and founding of Chaldean Empire.
600 B.C.	Probable circumnavigation of Africa by Phoenicians.
586 B.C.	Israelites into captivity at Babylon by Nebuchadnezzar.
585 B.C.	Thales of Miletus 'The father of philosophy', credited with introducing Egyptian geometry into Greece.
551 B.C.	Confucius born.
540 B.C.	Pythagoras born.
539 B.C.	Cyrus took Babylon and founded Persian Empire.
c. 500 B.C.	Iron Age arrives in south Britain—Hecataeus makes map of known world.
490 B.C.	Battle of Marathon.
484 B.C.	Herodotus born.
480 B.C.	Thermopylae and Salamis.
470 B.C.	Hanno's Voyages.
466 B.C.	Pericles—Aspasia.
460 B.C.	Democritus, great scientist. For long both Indian and Chinese philosophers had held advanced scientific theories. A common body of doctrine may have spread east, and west via Egypt and Babylon from the great Indus civilization which flourished in the third millennium B.C.
450 B.C.	World's first large canal of 1000 miles between Hangchow and Peking.
440 B.C.	Hippocrates.
427 B.C.	Plato born.
c. 400 B.C.	Arrival of Brythonic Celts into south Britain, bringing Iron manufacture with them. Some had probably arrived prior to this, possibly about 600 or 500 B.C.
388 B.C.	The Celts of Gaul under Brennus sack the still feeble City of Rome.
380 B.C.	Birth of Eudoxus at Cnidus, the father of scientific mechanics.
332 B.C.	Egypt submits to Alexander the Great and founding of Ptolemaic dynasty and Empire. Establishment of lecture theatres, laboratories and libraries for study of every department of science at Alexandria; dissection and vivisection carried out and an observatory, a zoo, and botanical garden created.
330 B.C.	Aristotle.
325 B.C.	The Greek scientist Pytheas makes a voyage round our western coasts.
323 B.C.	Death of Alexander the Great. Euclid born.
c. 300 B.C.	Iron Age arrives in Scotland.
c. 300 B.C.	Settlement from Gaul by groups of La Tene Celts, probably Brythonic, in certain areas of Scotland.
290 B.C.	Etruria mastered by Rome, after being weakened by Celtic attacks in the north.
287 B.C.	Birth of Archimedes of Syracuse, the greatest mechanical engineer of the ancient world.
264 B.C.	First Punic War, Rome v Carthage. Asoka began rule in India.
c. 250 B.C.	Ctesibius invents liquid fire-thrower and water organ.
218 B.C.	The Gauls help Hannibal against Rome.
214 B.C.	Great Wall of China begun.
c. 200 B.C.	Eratosthenes of Alexandria produces the most accurate map of world, as yet, largely from the records of Pytheas.
c. 150 B.C.	Settlement by groups of broch-building Celts in Caithness, Sutherland and Western Isles. Probably Brythons from S. France and Spain via Cornwall. British Isles mapped by Ptolemy.
146 B.C.	Destruction of Carthage.
102 B.C.	Marius utterly defeats Germans at Aix.
c. 100 B.C.	Birth of Julius Caesar.
55 B.C.	Caesar conducts a short and abortive expedition to south Britain in an endeavour to sever the link between the Celts of Gaul and the Celts of Britain where lay the headquarters of the powerful Druidical Hierarchy.
53 B.C.	Revolt of Gaul led by the great and noble Vercingetorix, the last great figure of independent Gaul.

Chronological Table

51 B.C.	Pacification of Gaul by Rome.
47 B.C.	Great library of Alexandria containing 700,000 volumes completely destroyed by fire.
44 B.C.	Julius Caesar assassinated.
	[Early B.C. dates are very approximate and the period of division into Goidelic and Brythonic speaking Celts is unknown.]
A.D.	
A.D. 20	Conchobar MacNessa King of Ulster. Queen Medb (Maive) and her husband Ailill rule in Connaught.
A.D. 30	Crucifixion.
A.D. 78	Roman occupation of south Britain (till A.D. 410). Building up of Caledonian Confederation of Tribes.
A.D. 81	Battle of Mons Graupius, Romans under Agricola defeat Caledonians. Roman fleet sails round British Isles.
A.D .119	IXth Roman Legion wiped out by Caledonians, shortly followed by Emperor Hadrian's abortive expedition into Caledonia. Lollius Urbicus builds Antonine Wall between Forth and Clyde, destroyed after 40 years. Periods of fighting and revivals of trade between Caledonians and Roman Britain.
A.D. 130	Birth of Galen.
c. A.D. 150	Hero constructs a reaction turbine.
A.D. 180	Caledonians drive Romans south of Hadrian's Wall. Punitive expedition follows under Severus, reaching the Moray Firth but is soon compelled to retire again behind the restored Wall of Hadrian.
A.D. 200	Conn Ced-cathach founds the Middle Kingdom (Meath) and begins the High Kingship of Tara in Ireland.
A.D. 274	Gaul again joined to Rome by Aurelian.
A.D. 297	Alliance made between the Caledonians (Picts) of *Alba* (Scotland), and the Scots of Ireland.
A.D. 306	Constantine the Great, Emperor of Rome.
A.D. 312	Constantine supported by Gallic Christians enters Rome.
A.D. 314	Three British Bishops accompanied by a Presbyter and Deacon, attend Council of Arles.
A.D. 355	Julian commands the Gallic Army and makes Paris the seat of Roman Government.
A.D. 367	Allies overrun Hadrian's Wall and invade south Britain.
A.D. 377	Niall of the Nine Hostages High King of Ireland till A.D. 405.
A.D. 383	Hadrian's Wall finally destroyed and overrun by Caledonians (Picts) who invade Roman Britain to south of the River Thames.
A.D. 387	Birth of St. Patrick, probably at Dumbarton; in 432 he was to begin his mission to Ireland.

About 2000 B.C. there arrived in Scotland the Beakers, so called from the shape of their pottery, a people already making inroads over southern Britain. They were in the main a round-headed race, though among them were some long-headed types probably due to an admixture of European 'Battle Axe' folk. It is probable, or at any rate possible, that these Beakers were the original Goidelic Celts of the Indo-European family, but we can say with certainty that they were a branch of aristocratic farmer-warriors who had spread over the southern and middle part of Europe from Asia Minor to the North Sea.

Their outstanding characteristics were domineering habits, organizing ability and great appreciation of metal weapons which, however, on their arrival in Britain consisted only of copper daggers, bows and arrows and a wrist guard made from a stone plaque. It is unlikely that they were present in great numbers, but they imposed their overlordship on the Neolithic groups throughout the British Isles, and finally through their descendants on Ireland as well. In time they mingled with the Iberians and in some areas of southern Britain eventually absorbed them, but in Scotland were themselves, more often, finally absorbed by the older race.

They were more pastoral than the older Britons, introducing a new breed of cattle, the Celtic shorthorn, but because of nomadic habits their dwellings were of a more perishable kind, and so have left little trace. Yet their funerary ritual, though less elaborate than that practised by the Megalithic Age, had much in common. They constructed the recumbent circles and round barrows so marked in the north-east hump of Scotland, the stones of their sanctuaries often being decorated with 'Cup and Ring Marks', while the straight edges of the recumbent stones may have provided an artificial horizon for astronomical calculations and calendrical regulation. Their religion was closely akin to the Megalithic Boyne denomination, both sometimes practising cremation; the main difference lay in the Beaker introduction of individual instead of collective burial.

In the Aberdeen-Buchan-Moray area the Beaker folk must have settled in greater numbers and consequently have influenced the racial type to a more marked degree. These people established throughout all Britain a uniformity of culture unknown to previous ages, and not repeated till Rome organized south Britain; also they were the builders, or originators, of such sanctuaries as Avebury and Stonehenge, which are comparable to cathedrals while the smaller circles which covered Britain were the parish churches. Both the Megalithic and Bronze periods have left their mark in many parts of Ross while Beaker pottery has been found near Beauly, Redcastle, Evanton and Edderton.

Remains of stone circles abound. In the Dingwall area alone ten remain and they can be traced on the banks of the Skiach, at Ussie, and Swordale where there are also hut circles—the single or double low wall of stone or earth which enclosed single or groups of skin huts, and above Assynt (Novar), while the most complete stone circle stands on top of the Mulbuie. Below the hill now called the Cat's Back (*Druim a' Chait*), but whose proper name is *Cnoc an Eagalis* (the Hill of the Church), is another of these circles, while at the old Kirk of Fodderty and at *Muir* of Ord can be seen a number of ancient cup-marked monoliths.

The orientation of Stonehenge and other circles stresses the importance of the mid-summer sunrise, suggesting that the Solstice was observed by these people as a great religious festival which, as a traditional custom at least, lingered on till modern times, and will be further discussed when we look into the Celtic Druidical Religion.

As a ruling caste the Beakers accumulated wealth so that their life was surrounded by more material comfort than had been the lot of the great tomb builders, and as their wants increased trade with the Irish craftsmen from across the sea grew enormously under their control, so it may be said that the Bronze Age had arrived in Scotland even though stone and flint were still in general use. The tombs of this period show a new plenty in luxury articles, both imported and home-made, such as jet, bone, or amber buttons which followed the fashion of all the Atlantic peoples; the Celtic pins and brooches were not yet the mode.

The Irish smiths and Cornish tin miners, both Iberian, were becoming the source from which a World market was being supplied, a fact proved by the finding of their bronze halberds, flat axes, awls and daggers scattered all over Europe, the construction of the daggers showing that the tradition inspiring the Irish metallurgists was Egyptian. These weapons together with sheet-gold work are found buried with their Beaker purchasers who themselves manufactured little or nothing, but bought from Irish traders or resident metallurgical craftsmen who had imported moulds and worked with Scottish gold and metals.

As already indicated, these Beakers were a relatively small governing class, widely distributed over southern Britain and Scotland so that, in many areas, their numerical inferiority led to their absorption and the re-emergence of the older race, particularly in the Highlands of Scotland. In southern Britain the Beakers of Wessex were replaced by a new ruling group of Celts probably with connections in north central rather than Atlantic Europe.

But over all Britain north of the Thames the Beaker-Iberian fusion produced the Food Vessel people who not only brought forward the Beaker culture and organization, but also inherited the metallurgical, commercial traditions, and ritual of the Iberian Megalith builders. This combination of the characteristics of their farmer-warrior-trader forbears produced a very considerable advance in the general standard of living. The Food Vessel folk—so-called on account of their distinctive funerary pottery containing food for the dead—crossed to Ireland where they became the predominant race, and if the Beakers were not the first Goidelic Celts in Britain, they are presumably the first part Celts to enter that country. The Food Vessel pottery is distinctive and they continued to make full use of the Irish metallurgical experts for their weapons and jewellery.

This race still held to the Atlantic fashion of buttons and belt clasps made of jet orlignite, while they adorned themselves with gold-panelled, crescent-shaped collars, and their womenfolk with basket-shaped ear-rings of gold or bronze, the pattern of which is derived by way of Spain from Egypt, their type being depicted in Egyptian paintings of New Kingdom period. From Ireland weapons and jewellery which included golden ribbon Torques, several of which have been found in Ross, were exported to Europe reaching as far as Poland, while from northern Scotland surplus metallurgical products went from the Moray Firth to the Baltic in exchange for amber.

Some of their burial cairns are large, though they do not compare with Neolithic tumuli; other graves are flat or the mounds conceal stone crescents or circles of boulders often assuming in Ross a D shape, while between Achterneed and Swordale, on the lower slopes of Wyvis are numerous burial cairns but all of them small in size and may be of later date. Actual food vessels have been unearthed near Chanonry, Redcastle, Dingwall and Edderton. The symbolic art of the Boyne culture was developed, sometimes attempting to reproduce the divinity, but more often using on their monuments cup and ring marks such as are found on stones near Lemlair, Achterneed, and in Kintail. Coffin burials start with these Food Vessel people and their hollow tree-trunk coffins are sometimes shaped to represent a boat, probably a connection with Egypt and the belief that the first stage to the next world entailed a voyage by water.

This race is clearly a mixture, both long and round heads abound though an intermediate type is the most usual, likewise their culture is hybrid and in the west they are found buried in the older collective tombs. The Goidelic-speaking Celtic chiefs who had supplanted the Beaker lords of Wessex, c. 1400 B.C., developed a high standard of material civilization; the native population expanded with the result that migrants of Peterborough tradition, modified by their Beaker rulers, spread from south Britain as far as Caithness. Their presence in Ross is attested by the discovery at Chanonry on the Black Isle of a Cinerary Urn, and an Encrusted Cinerary Urn from an Urnfield or cemetery at Alness.

The Scottish Urnfields or cemeteries, are a natural evolution of Urn burial and should not be confused with the later Urnfield Celts who invaded south Britain and get their name from the very large cemeteries which exist as far north as Scarborough. These Urn folk introduced a new modification in burial rites by placing the ashes of their cremated dead inside an Urn which they buried, usually plugged and inverted, in a variety of different places such as a Cist grave of stone slabs, shallow depressions in the ground, or in tumuli of Beaker, Food Vessel or older origin. Sometimes Urn burials are found within, usually older, stone circles, and in Scotland as far north as Ross, within more or less debased versions of the true Bell-Barrow of southern Britain; apart from this they followed the usual Bronze Age custom of including food and ornaments for the use of the dead in the next world.

These Celts produced a uniformity of culture over all the British Isles so far as burial rites and funerary pottery are concerned, but they did not replace the Food Vessel people whose own tongue may well have been the Goidelic Celtic language, but if this is not so, the newcomers were strong enough to impose their Goidelic, probably influenced by the older speech on all the peoples of south Britain, Scotland—whose mainland population during the Beaker-Food Vessel period may have been as low as 2500—and finally Ireland whose cultures they incorporated with their own. Their influence can be traced over a very long period as is proved by the presence of a cordoned Urn found in a grave at Edderton in Ross, together with La Tène glass beads, the latter being of a much later age (c. 300 B.C.), in fact the Cinerary Urns were current for about 1200 years. Their warriors were often armed with stone battle-axes and maces; while both in Scotland and in Ireland bronze oval-bladed razors have been found, which belonged to these people. Stock-breeding and hunting still played a primary part in their economy, though the Urn folk were not nomadic but cultivated the improved long eared common wheat, six-rowed barley and flax, the digging-stick or a *cas-chrom* (hand plough) being used. An addition to personal ornament introduced by them are the segmented fayence beads of Egyptian type similar to some found in a tomb at Abydos and dated by a scarab of Amenhotep III 1412–1376 B.C., but of still more practical use was their practice of excellent weaving.

Usually their dwellings were huts built of perishable material, either isolated or in village groups to some extent fortified and with refuges called Soutterains or Earth-houses, which consisted of long sub-terranean and curved galleries 2 ft. by 2 ft. lined with stone slabs and leading into a chamber often roofed by corbelling; these were primarily intended for the concealment of women and children.

The work of the Iberian metallurgists—still an exclusive society within the tribes—was reaching a very high standard around 750 B.C., the smiths of this period being in close touch with their brother crafts-men across the Bay of Biscay. Both the Urn and Food Vessel people were now able to buy decorated axes, advanced halberds, gold lunulae and earrings, torques of types current in Greece and Cyprus between 1500–1300 B.C., as well as rapiers the pattern of which was suggested by the longer weapons of Mycenaean Greece of 1600 B.C. During this period the British Isles were the scene of a general revolution in the Bronze industry which was to continue unabated till the introduction of Iron some hundreds of years later.

One of the signs of this advance was not only the greater service-ability of weapons and metal tools—the use of the latter still confined to the metal workers—but the fact that much time was spent on the ornamentation of these things, while in addition there appears a tremendous increase in the numbers of socketed axes, spear-heads with leaf-shaped blades, and the rapiers, turned out by the manu-facturers. But of yet greater moment was the introduction of a sword with a slashing edge and carried in a scabbard, showing not only a new development in weapons, but also in the method of fighting, a departure from the old system, which like other changes, owed its origin to the Mediterranean civilizations, where such swords were current in the Aegean 1500 B.C.

Further advances appeared in metallurgical technique, and large sheets of metal were now shaped and decorated, the peak of this type of bronze work in Britain being contemporary with that in Phoenicia and Assyria, though of course the Orient had been familiar with this metal-work before 3000 B.C. Yet another victory gained during this epoch by the western goldsmiths was their discovery of the use of solder, and so great had the demand for metal now become that Irish copper had to be supplemented by supplies from as far north as Shetland. The merchant artificers during this busy period made their circuits in caravans, exchanging new tools for scrap and using gold rings for currency; it is even possible that their transport included horse-drawn waggons as at this period is found the first evidence, in the British Isles, of vehicles and the domestication of the horse.

Lead also was in use, for the first time in our Islands, though the Megalith builders of Spain had known it. The greatest advance, which soon came to pass, was that tools for all workers became available, so that carpentry went ahead producing such commodities as two-piece tubs and wooden shields. Cauldrons made of beaten bronze rivetted together, double-edged knives for domestic use, sickles, and round targes of hammered bronze for the rich warrior, became plentiful, with the consequent raising of the standard of life, and it is interesting that both in Greek and in Celtic law the cauldron figured as a standard of wealth, these articles being far more common to Ireland and Scotland than to south Britain. As evidence of this advance in Ross the hoard found at Poolewe produced among other things a cauldron, again at Adabrock in Lewis were found two axes, a socketed hammer, a socketed gauge, a tanged chisel, a riveted spear-head, two bifid razors, two whetstones, beads of gold, amber and glass, also a broken bronze vessel, while from Point of Sleat, Skye, and the Wester Ord hoard in Easter Ross come two curved knives.

So far as Scotland was concerned the late Bronze Age was still flourishing in 500 B.C. and it is quite possible that some bronze weapons were still in use when the Romans made their abortive attempts to subdue Caledonia. The Celtic fashion of pins very slowly began to replace buttons, and then took the form of disc pins ornamented with compass drawn circles and gold-foil, the two-piece safety pins being peculiar to Scotland and Ireland.

From the prehistoric village of Jarlshof in Shetland comes the first authenticated record of stall-dung being collected and used for manure, while at last signs appeared of a well balanced mixed farming with light plough tillage replacing scratch agriculture and pastoralism. At least this was true of the lowlands of south Britain where this agricultural revolution was caused by the advent of two new Celtic invasions of peasant cultivators known as Urnfield Folk who had been expanding in eastern central Europe since about 1200 B.C. moving west in search

B

of new lands and metals, eventually mixing with Middle Bronze Age people whom they met round the Alps and Upper Rhine. They then crossed to southern Britain and Cornwall where their irregular square Celtic fields can still be traced, but like their earlier kinsmen they bred the Celtic shorthorn, sheep and horses, introducing improvements to the textile industry exemplified by their importation of spindle whorls and loom weights into Britain; the second invasion by these people absorbed the first, reaching as far north as Scarborough.

By 800 B.C. the economic working of iron was being practised round the Alpine regions and in Central Europe; this was to change the face of western Europe as for the first time satisfactory tree-felling tools were produced, as well as more efficient weapons, and the Celtic peoples who developed this more advanced economy are classified as the Hallstatt Culture. They crossed the Channel sometime between 600 and 400 B.C. absorbing their Urnfield kinsmen, and establishing various cultures in southern Britain. Gradually they spread over that area building villages and forts, while they developed the first Iron industry, though for a long period the old bronze workers were still kept busy. It is probable that these Hallstatt folk were the first Brythonic-speaking Celts who were starting to replace completely the Goidel-speaking Celts in south Britain.

With them came further changes: they tilled the ground with a two-ox light plough, used pit silos for grain storage which now included oats and rye, and introduced the manufacture of salt. Their dwellings were open villages, lone steadings or hill forts when necessary. In their dress they preferred the pin to the button for their garments, following a fashion common to all central Europe, but their household pottery differed little from Bronze Age patterns.

These Brython Celts never reached Ireland but they become the predominant people of south Britain, later, to some extent influencing southern and eastern Scotland, especially Aberdeenshire where Brythonic place-names are common. In Ireland and parts of Scotland—e.g. Kinellan in Ross—are found the *Crannog*, lake dwellings, built on artificial islands, which were constructed on rafts, weighted to sink to the bottom of the loch where they were secured by piles. These damp but safe dwellings, which continued in use into historic times, are probably evidence of an early immigration of Iron Age folk who brought this *Crannog* architecture from the Alpine Regions; but in Ireland as in Scotland these early Iron-using Celts were completely absorbed by the Goidelic-speaking residents.

The period which follows introduced the Iron Age to Scotland, but it is marked by turbulence and strife to a far greater degree than the previous Bronze Age, a process that unfortunately was to get progressively worse, the advance in civilization being marked by ever bigger and better wars. The Celts of France, Switzerland and central Europe were in close touch with Greece and Etruria; to start with these contacts were commercial, via the Alpine passes and down the Rhône Valley to the Greek settlement at Marseilles. The trade in metal, amber, slaves, and furs produced surplus wealth which enriched the Gallic chiefs, who spent their riches on Mediterranean imports such as wine, and table services of Greek and Etruscan metal-ware. Etruria provided the model for their light two-wheeled chariots and foreign artisans taught classical metallurgy to the Celtic craftsmen, at the same time introducing many household conveniences.

In 400 and 300 B.C. these Celts spread to the Danube Basin and invaded Italy, south France, Spain and Britain, our invaders c. 300 B.C. being the younger sons of the great Gallic chiefs and their junior tenantry. Eastern Yorkshire was occupied by a section of these La Tène interlopers known as The Marnian Charioteers, connected with the Champagne district of Gaul, and of Arras Culture. In course of time this rich and warlike aristocracy were to found a Celtic School of Art in Britain, which, though inspired by 5th-century Greece, had developed along its own Celtic lines.

The group which chose Scotland for its goal have been described as belonging to the Abernethy Culture, who have left numerous traces in many parts of our land and these La Tène farmer-adventurers were similar to the Charioteers and probably Brythonic; bands of them landed round the Firths of Tay and Moray, eventually spreading across Scotland. They were not welcomed, so promptly entrenched themselves in mighty hill-top fortresses whose huge stone ramparts 10 to 20 feet thick only partially followed the contour of the site. The two facing walls of roughly squared blocks were tied at intervals by balks of timber set at right angles and horizontal to the faces, while the interspace was filled with timbers, laid parallel to the faces, and with rubble. There are many forts of this type in Ross, one of the most clearly defined being situated on the summit of Knock Farrol, or more correctly *Cnoc Farralaidh* which means the hill of the high projecting stone building.

Now these forts, strong as they were, possessed one fatal weakness, of which either chance or enemy action took full advantage. Sooner or later most of the forts fell a victim to fire and such was their construction that they resembled kilns generating great heat which might bring down the face and did melt the rubble core, forming vitrified masses in which the stones are fused together, hence their nomenclature of Vitrified Forts. There is, however, another school of thought which considers that the vitrification was part of the constructional plan.

Within these walls were hut villages complete with a well which often had to be of considerable depth to reach water. It is probable that during times of peace a proportion of the fort people built their huts alongside their fields, which would be dominated by, and not far from the fort.

The geography of the west coast had since Megalithic times forced certain modifications in the social structure, so that here a smaller fort or *dun*[1] was more usual, and it held the Chief's household only, while his clan dwelt in and cultivated the glen dominated by the *dun*, breeding their cattle, some sheep and a few pigs, and grinding their cereals in the saddle quern. Many of these small but solid castles resemble closely the Irish cashels, and though they existed in very great numbers in the west, e.g. Kintail, they are also numerous in the east, e.g. Black Isle, Nigg and Beauly. As on the east, metal and textile industries were carried on but on a lesser scale as the groups were smaller and more isolated, though an advanced type of smelting furnace was discovered in a cave near *Rudh 'an Dunain*, Skye.

These La Tène invaders in Scotland, being primarily adventurers, had shed much of their European culture, so instead of high-grade pottery made by the skilled craftsmen they had left behind, the warrior families used only coarse clay cooking pots and wooden bowls, but they still used bronze or iron brooches to fasten their cloaks, wore jet rings as pendants, armlets and finger-rings of bronze like their folk at home. Most of their tools and weapons were of iron and the old commercial system provided their new lords with their bronze ornaments and bulbous spear-butts.

These invaders spreading from the east had reached our western coasts by 200 B.C. but gradually they were absorbed into the general race. They had introduced iron, a more intensive agriculture, and forest clearance into Scotland, but unfortunately they also brought in what was to become a Celtic habit of internecine warfare.

We have now reached an age when it is possible to find references to the Celtic people in Classic literature, and Book VIII of the Aeneid, first recorded in writing about 600 or 700 B.C., describes them thus: 'Golden their flowing hair, their dress of gold, their cloaks are striped and shining.' These colours and stripes did not originally differentiate between the tribes, but was a distinctive emblem of rank and position: servants had one colour, farmers who were free-men two, officers three, chieftains five, Druids and poets six, and the *Ard Righ* (High King) seven. Tartan, though worn at a very early date, does not appear as a definite clan distinction till much later in history when, because of administrative neglect, the system of semi-independent clans was again evolved, and the larger tribal unit under a *Mormaer* (Provincial Governor), which grew up after the shock of the Roman invasions, disappeared.

Note 1. The Gaelic word *dun* is applied to any type of fort or castle.

From many another source comes other information regarding the characteristics of our Celtic forefathers especially those of Gaul, though many descriptions are clouded by the usual bias which in all ages too often describes peoples who are valiantly fighting against the imposition of a foreign yoke as rebels, at the same time studiously avoiding, or wilfully misinterpreting, facts that prove that the justice of the cause lay with the so-called rebels. Both Rome and the Anglo-Saxon, ancient and modern, have shared to a high degree this un-generous and very unattractive trait, far less nauseating was the old Viking attitude of quite bare-faced and unabashed conquest, piracy and robbery.

S. W. Kitchen, M.A., in his History of France (1873) gives a very good description of the Celtic character of a time preceding and during the Roman conquest of Gaul which is worth recording here in his own words: 'An eminently intelligent race: open to every impression, touched by heroism and greatness, by intellect and genius; a people of rare sensibility.' He goes on to say that: 'Theirs was a frank and open disposition scorning subterfuge: if they lied it was through vivacity and heedlessness, rather than of set purpose. They knew nothing of strategy and despised it: a fierce onslaught straight forward, summed up their tactics . . . they had a vigorous imagination; and their poetry was full of feeling, and dealt with nature and man, love, war, and the world unseen, in strange proportions; Ossian's poems . . . have the true Gallic spirit.'

Merlin, Arthur, Guinevere and the like—though retouched by the fashions of a later chivalry—are yet true Celtic figures, embodying the real characteristics of the race. Theirs, too, is the sense of honour, taking the form of passionate bravery, bitter feuds; they were fearless even against the powers of nature, despised death in battle, even slew themselves, if their Chieftain perished, on his funeral cairn. To them rather than to the German, belongs the sense of chivalry. Theirs the 'Round Table, the Gawains and Lancelots, the round table at which all were equal and none could quarrel for the higher or lower seat.' The writer goes on to show the weaknesses that so often proved their undoing, how their very intelligence made them too independent in thought to be able to resist over long periods their less imaginative and more bovine foes.

Effective combination had become transitory in Gaul by the time Rome started her invasions as by then the one binding force, the great Druidical hierarchy and system, had been weakened in that country by the Celtic nobles who had become spoilt by riches gained from trade with the Latin countries, and had turned their free tribesmen into slaves. Again the individual was often 'too greedy of glory, apt to boast, and too sensitive as to praise or blame,' while the strong clannish feeling always made effective national effort difficult. . . . 'His sensibility, imaginativeness and quickness gave to him the genius of oratory,' a characteristic still noticeable both in the more purely Celtic areas as well as in France where the strong Celtic strain has become so predominant over the more Teutonic peculiarities introduced by their Frankish and other German conquerors during the Dark Ages. With the removal of supreme control from the powerful and educated Druidical Hierarchy, Gaul passed from the greatest Celtic Epoch and her numerous chiefs and princes gave themselves up to tribal disputes, and carrying the racial love of display to inordinate lengths in the splendour of apparel, horse, furniture and arms.

But time was yet to pass before the Celts of south Britain were to be destroyed in their turn through contact with Rome, as in those Islands lay the headquarters of the Druidical system as yet unweakened by outside influences. Infusion with the older inhabitants of Scotland greatly influenced the physical type of Scottish Celt, frequently producing a dark, or often red-haired people as well as the fair, they were tall and of magnificent physique, though the dark squat Iberian type still formed a considerable part of the population.

The Phoenicians who traded along the western coasts after 500 B.C. were probably the first to spread some account of our far-off land which about 325 B.C. was described in some detail by the Greek Arctic explorer Pytheas. Further Celtic Iron Age invasions arrived in south Britain, a number of them travelling by the Atlantic route and settling in Cornwall, while at Glastonbury a new very advanced culture of that name was founded lasting from about 150 B.C. to A.D. 43 when it was destroyed by the Celto-Teutonic Belgae, the people who introduced the heavy-wheeled plough and potters' wheel into Britain.

There was still one more B.C. immigration to arrive in Scotland before the sum total was complete, though we shall see the final one in A.D. 503 when the Goidelic Scots arrived from Ireland to found a kingdom in Argyll. The new arrivals were the Broch-building Celts, probably Brythonic, a section of the invaders in south-west Britain who continued up our western coasts, leaving in their wake a number of small single-walled *duns* of fine masonry scattered about the Hebrides and western Scottish mainland, each of which was the fortified home belonging to the local chieftain. Many of these forts are sited, usually near the sea, on hill-tops or promontories and their single walls follow the hill contours, though lower sites were quite frequently chosen.

These chieftains followed the usual economy, farming, hunting and fishing, but piracy and reiving seem to have played an increasingly important part indicating a big increase in population over areas none too fertile. The main home of these people became the Outer Hebrides,

Skye, Lewis, Sutherland, Caithness, Orkney and Shetland, an area cut off by sea or lying to the north of La Tène influence. In these parts their castle architecture assumed the form of the weird but magnificent Broch and traces of 425 of them still exist within these boundaries, clearly demonstrating the density of the population at this period.

These double-walled, circular all-stone towers, sometimes reaching a height of sixty feet, must have been quite impregnable unless taken by trickery. The structure rose from a broad base of solid masonry 12 to 15 ft. thick. Both the inner and outer walls though nearly vertical inside were steeply battened externally, while at the top the open space between the inner and outer wall was roofed with flag-stones. Similar stones were used to tie the walls and form four or five galleries which ran round the circumference of the Broch between the twin walls. These floors were reached by stone stairs which starting from ground level rose clockwise within the walls eventually giving access to the narrow roof. Within the circumference of the double wall the area was open to the sky except for a verandah running round the tower 6 ft 8 in. above ground level; here all the cooking was done, there being ample space as the internal diameter ranged from 25 to 35 ft. Within the massive base were several circular chambers opening onto the central yard; one of these covered the small entrance and from it the door-keeper operated the door bar, while a second acted as a vestibule to the stairway.

The Broch usually stood within a strongly fortified stone enclosure inside which were grouped the round or oval huts of the clansmen and such of the older population who left their wheel-houses to join with the new lords.

All the best agricultural land was dominated by these strongholds, while older groups of wheel-houses with soutterains attached were also used by these intensive farmers who grew barley and brewed beer. The Bronze Age Wheel-House consisted of a walled area, circular or oval 25 ft. to 38 ft. across, this space being divided into a number of voussoir-shaped rooms by radial walls arranged like the spokes of a wheel. The radials stop short 6 to 12 ft. from the middle of the wheel leaving a space 15 to 25 ft. in diameter; this court may have been open to the sky, but the rooms were roofed by corbelling. These houses were situated in groups.

From the Glastonbury Culture they obtained and introduced the first flat rotary querns, new textile appliances as well as dice, ornamental and weaving combs, while to aid their maritime exploits they built artificially protected anchorages for their boats, the sea-going curraghs and small coracles—long used for tidal, river and loch transport. It is probable that these people would have improved the practice of basketry for which the Iron Age was justly famous in classical times, a fact mentioned by both Juvenal and Martial, and supported by the Latin word Bascauda being derived from the Celtic word *bascaid*.

Before the advent of Rome, groups of these Broch people spreading from the North had colonized areas south of the river Oykel, eventually reaching districts as far distant as Lothian and Galloway. Their culture may be said to have survived in degenerate form till as late as A.D. 700 though by A.D. 200, their absorption by the original Caledonians was probably complete.

It is probable that a considerable number of Iron Age peasants originally came north with the Broch Chiefs as iron became plentiful as compared with the amount available during the La Tène domination. Once again the Hill of Tulloch features as the home of a community during this period; no traces of Brochs exist but evidently weaving was carried on as instruments known as Whorls for fulling cloth have been discovered. This industry, still carried on in this area at the present day, was not confined to the east; a similar instrument made of Torridon sandstone was recently picked up in far Kintail.

The only traces of Brochs on the mainland of Ross lie in the northeast, these being five miles south of the Oykel and Dornoch Firth in the parish of Kincardine, but in the west they lie outside the boundaries of mainland Ross, to the north in Assynt and to the south Glenelg, which indicates that Ross remained the farthest north La Tène sphere till natural fusion took place. About 75 B.C. south-east Britain attracted some new settlers who brought the first Teutonic influence into what was to be England; these new folk were in blood half Celtic and half German, being named by Julius Caesar the Belgae.

Britain as a whole was now a Celtic country, but in the highland zones especially in Scotland, people of Bronze Age culture still remained unmixed though they had adopted the more advanced methods of agriculture, metallurgy and textile work introduced by Iron Age immigrants. Some of the La Tène Celts had moved south and appear to have settled as far off as north Wales and the midlands of south Britain, while the brilliant craftsmen, employed by their kinsmen the Marnian Charioteers of east Yorkshire, have left samples of their work, horse trappings, hand mirrors, weapons and jewellery, in south-west Scotland as well as Wales and Ulster.

When the Romans appeared in south Britain in A.D. 78 what was to be Scotland and England were divided among some thirty great tribes. North of the Forth and Clyde was Goidelic in speech as was Ireland and the Isle of Man; England and Wales were Brythonic. The southern lowlands of Scotland held a mixture probably with a Goidelic majority, but after the evacuation of south Britain by the Romans and its gradual subjection by the Anglo-Saxon, Clydeside and south-west Scotland were to become largely Brythonic in blood; this change being due to an influx of refugees who fled north to avoid a life of slavery under their new conquerors.

In central Goidelic Scotland, an area which lay, roughly, within the modern counties of Perth, part of Argyll and Inverness, dwelt a great tribe called by the Romans, Kaledonioi; soon this name came to be used by them to describe the whole area in Britain which they failed to conquer—Caledonia. The first serious engagement against the might of Rome took place A.D. 84 at Mons Graupius, the exact location of which is unknown, but it may have been near Forfar or Brechin. The tribes now formed into the Caledonian Confederacy led by Galgacus and armed with long iron broadswords with no points, spears and war chariots, were defeated, temporally, by Agricola, but soon after the Romans withdrew to the Tyne-Solway line, abandoning their new Forth-Clyde positions.

Scotland's population had greatly increased. The Caledonian Army at Mons Graupius mustered 30,000 according to Tacitus, and allowing for the historian's exaggeration, archaeology has proved the presence of dense populations in most of the areas chosen for settlement. Caledonians were excellent fighters but considered it effeminate to wear much defensive armour, which put them at a disadvantage against the well-armoured and highly disciplined legions; however about A.D. 119 they rose and wiped out the 9th Legion. The great Emperor Hadrian himself commanded the relieving expedition which accomplished little, and retired south to where he was building the Great Wall between Newcastle and Burgh-on-Sands. Lollius Urbicus tried once again to establish the forward policy of the Forth-Clyde line by building the Antonine Wall, but it lasted only forty years during which it was subject to constant attacks.

In A.D. 180 the Romans were soundly beaten by the Caledonians and driven south of Hadrian's Wall. To restore the situation levies were raised from all parts of the Roman Empire and an invasion of Caledonia started under the command of the gouty Libyan Emperor Severus, after he had repaired the devastation wrought on Hadrian's Wall and the Roman forts as far south as York. This expedition probably reached the shores of the Moray Firth, but it failed, if we exclude the perpetration of the indiscriminate destruction of forests etc. by fire which characterize the efforts to establish the Pax Romana in Caledonia. Julius Septimus Severus worn out by the strain of constant guerrilla warfare returned to die in York A.D. 211, and within a year or two the new forts north of the Tay were abandoned and Rome was back behind the Tyne-Solway Wall. The Caledonian tribes were well led, Fingal, according to tradition, being one of their successful leaders; while their Confederations were beginning to approximate to Nations.

At this period the Romans begin to refer to those north of the Wall as Picts, which was simply the collective name for the tribes, predominantly Celtic, though it is probable that a diminishing number of the earlier short and swarthy inhabitants of our country still lived unmixed in out of the way areas such as the northern and central Highlands would provide; the Iberian type, to this day, is by no means extinct in Britain, being present in Cornwall as well as the other Celtic zones. Caledonia was known to the Picts as *Alba* and many centuries were to pass before Scotia or Scotland was to become the more usual name. The Scots of those days lived in Ireland; they also were predominantly Goidelic Celts and in A.D. 297 they and the Picts formed an alliance which seventy years later triumphed over the Wall. The Roman Count Theodosius, to some extent, restored the situation by driving back the Picts and Scots who had made deep inroads into south Britain. A Roman fleet reached Orkney, but this was the last effort, the restored Wall was overrun by the Caledonians and finally abandoned by A.D. 383 and the sack of Rome by Alaric in A.D. 410 found the Caledonians or Picts a free people still.

Before leaving the Roman phase it is of interest to consider what effect this foreign domination in the south had on the unconquered Caledonians or Picts, north of Hadrian's Wall. On Rome's abandonment of imperialistic designs against Caledonia long periods of armed neutrality ensued during which a very active trade grew up, or revived, between Roman Britain and the Picts, the two chief trading routes overland following up both coasts and crossing the Wall at the Solway and Newcastle toll-gates. The principal commodities going north were Rhenish pottery, glass, brooches, coins, bronze work and ironmongery, which penetrated as far as the Broch folk of Caithness, Orkney and the Hebrides, the bronze Roman lamp having actually been copied in stone. In return, cattle, leather, furs, gold, oysters, pearls, wild animals for the circus and perhaps some slaves, came south from every part of *Alba*.

But apart from a revived trade the north remained untouched by Roman influence, which in the light of future events was fortunate for *Alba*.

Equally so was this the case from an artistic point of view: Roman life with its efficiency and decidedly material outlook had the most disastrous effects on the gifted and brilliant artist-craftsmen among the southern Brythonic Celts, who being Celts, and, at that time, quite disinterested in classic architecture or town-planning except under compulsion, lost their flair for abstract and symbolic art under the mass production methods introduced by Rome; and, though a revival did occur after the Roman exodus, yet it never attained its pre-conquest excellence. In Caledonia Celtic Art, exemplified by pottery, metal work, jewellery and stone carving, survived and developed, following its own northern style which showed a feeling for mass which is absent from the delicate and fine-drawn work of the southern Celts whose ruling passion in art was subtlety of line.

The Celtic language was one of the Indo-European family of languages which at the beginning of our era covered an area extending from India to north Scotland. The existing Celtic languages fall into two distinct groups: Goidelic (Scots, Irish and Manx Gaelic) and Brythonic (Welsh, Breton and Cornish). A convenient method for describing the difference between the two is that taking the Indo-European 'QU', Goidelic preserves the guttural sound; while Brythonic labializes it, changing 'qu' to 'p'. The antiquity of the cleavage is unknown since hardly any written record survives of Celtic speech before 300 B.C. but it is thought likely that the cleavage took place in Europe and that Goidelic and Brythonic were brought to the British Isles as two differentiated languages. In the text of this book Gaelic words are in italic.

As has been mentioned Pict was the collective name for the peoples of Caledonia. In Chapters III, IV and V it is used to differentiate between them and the Irish Scots who in A.D. 503 colonized and founded the Kingdom of Dalriada or Scotia, in what is now Argyllshire. Eventually, in certain areas, a fusion of the two closely related peoples took place, a circumstance largely brought about by the severing of all lines of communication with Ireland by the Norwegian invasions after A.D. 750, while a further bond was created by the amalgamation of the Pictish and Scottish Royal Houses in A.D. 843.

It should be remembered that these Scots formed but a small proportion of the general community in *Alba*, so that the once held theory that they replaced the native Pictish or Caledonian population is untenable. Some indication of the localities where the Picts remained more or less undisturbed by the Dalriadic relations, can be got from place names and an interesting difference in custom, which is pointed out by Professor Calder: In Pictish usage a River gives its name to the Loch, if any, from which it issues, to the Strath or Glen through which it flows, and to the spot where it enters the Sea or another river. In the Irish Gaelic (*Erse*) usage the river does not necessarily do any of these things.

CHAPTER III

THE PICTISH KINGDOM OF *ALBA*—THE TRIBES OF ROSS AND THEIR CONVERSION TO CHRISTIANITY

Chronological Table

A.D. 397	Founding of first Celtic Church in Scotland by St. Ninian.
c. A.D. 400	Though probably prior to this date, compilation of *Tain Bó Cualnge* which set down in Pagan times events in Ireland c. A.D. 20. Among the many characters are Queen Medb (Maive) of Connaught, her husband Ailill, Conchobar (Connor), MacNessa King of Ulster, MacRoth one of the Queen's heralds, etc.
A.D. 407	Beginning of German settlement in Gaul.
A.D. 476	Empire of Rome destroyed. Conquest and settlement of south Britain by Angles and Saxons in progress.
c. A.D. 500	Celtic Chronicles of Gildas—probably an ecclesiastic of Strath Clyde. Century of the great Welsh Bard Taliesin.
A.D. 503	Irish, or Dalriadic, Goidelic Scots found a Kingdom in Argyll.
A.D. 529	The Emperor Justinian closes the Philosophical Schools of Athens, as a result experimental and progressive science suffers a severe check; but the quest for knowledge in western Europe is kept alive by the diligence of the Arabs via their great school at Baghdad.
A.D. 563	Founding of Second Celtic Church by St. Columba.
A.D. 570	Muhammad born. Gildas the Celtic Chronicler died.
A.D. 574	Columba attends synod of Drumceatt in Ireland, where the position of the Bards is discussed; these poets and historians of the Nations, both Pictish and Scottish, had survived the introduction of Christianity but shortly before the Synod they had been suppressed owing to their expensive habits. The *Ollamh* or Chief Poet kept a retinue of 30 while each Anrad or ordinary poet retained 15. All could claim free board and lodging from the tribes. Columba, himself no mean Bard, reorganized them at this Synod but on a less lavish scale. To these Bards we owe a great debt. One of the best genealogical tables of the Kings of *Alba* is contained in a poem, the Albanic *Duan*, officially recited in full for the last time at the coronation of King Malcolm III *Ceann Mór* in 1057. They produced a system of elaborate metric poetry, survivals of which still exist, which influenced early modern Gaelic poetry and through it Scottish and to some extent English poetry.
A.D. 597	St. Columba died. St. Augustine lands in Kent.
A.D. 651	St. Cuthbert enters Melrose Abbey, transferred to Lindisfarne 664, dies as Bishop 687.
A.D. 673	Birth of Bede.
A.D. 674	Birth of Adamnan 9th Abbot of Iona, author of Life of St. Columba. Died 704.
A.D. 685	Great victory of Pictish King Bruidhe destroys the invading army from Northumbria under King Ecgfrid, at Nechtansmere.
A.D. 711	Moslem Army from Africa invades Spain.
A.D. 748	Death of Gaelic Bard Rumann; The Song of the Sea is attributed to him.

With the disappearance of the Roman Legions and Governors from south Britain the unfortunate Brython Celts south of Hadrian's Wall found themselves without efficient leaders and quite unable to cope effectively with the invasions of Pict and Saxon which quickly followed. The great Wall of Hadrian was down, for the last time; the Caledonians, sometimes joined by the poorer and latterly oppressed southern Celts, swept south to within sight of Roman London and beyond it, thus repeating their exploits of A.D. 367, but this time without their Irish (Scots) allies. In despair the Brython leaders tried a policy of appeasement with the Saxon, c. A.D. 449, which though it forced the withdrawal of the Picts ended in a worse disaster.

The new masters of England reinforced by fresh pagan hordes turned on the Brythons, but that they did not go down without a struggle, and were for a time successful we know, though vaguely, from the Arthurian legends, and Celtic Chronicles (*Gildas*) and later the Anglo-Saxon Chronicle by Bede, which describe the Celtic revival under Ambrosius Aurelianus and the great victory of Mons Badonis fought sometime between A.D. 490–516. Gradually, however, the Celts were pressed back onto the highland zones of south Britain and the five as yet un-conquered Brython kingdoms which existed between Cornwall and north Wales.

About 547 the Angle ruling house in the Humber area was coming to the fore and beginning to force a way into Celtic Northumberland with-out, however, displacing the Brython population to the same extent as elsewhere. The Kingdom of Northumbria grew apace, eventually in-cluding the district north of Hadrian's Wall and River Tweed, now known as Lothian. The Brythons who stayed in the Anglo-Saxon areas usually became slaves, gradually being absorbed into the new com-munity; to avoid this fate many fled into south-western Scotland and Cumberland-Westmorland, where they built up the Brython Kingdom of Strathclyde or Cumbria.

Between A.D. 500–600, a Pictish kingdom came into being, formed from two Pictish kingdoms—one being north the other south of the Grampians, a division referred to long before A.D. 500. This produced some measure of organization within *Alba*, which was divided up into great Provinces under governorship of the *Mormaers*, the highest title of Celtic nobility which is referred to by Tacitus in the 1st century A.D. The original Pictish provinces numbered seven, being ruled by the seven *Mormaers* (*Righs* or Local Kings, known in Gaul as Rigs or Rix—in Latin Rex—and old Norse Rikir), who elected the *Ard Righ* or High King, to whom they gave allegiance, if they felt so inclined. The pro-vince was known as a coicidh, the home of two or more *mortuaths* or great tribes, each sub-divided into a single tribal unit known as the *tuath* (clan) under a chief.

The number seven had some mystic significance, occurring fre-quently and till a late date as in the *Ard Righ's* Council of the Seven *Mormaers*—later Earls—even though from time to time, with the ad-dition or loss of lands, the actual number of these governors varied, provincial marches changed and new provinces came into being. During the early Pictish kingdom, Ross and Cromarty would appear to have been included in the great Province of *Ce* in which Moray and Ross each formed a sub-district of the whole, which consisted of Ross and Cromarty together with parts of what are now Elgin, Nairn, Inverness, Banff and Argyll.

Ptolemy in his map has given names to the thirteen great tribes of *Alba*. In the northern part the Karnones occupied a wide area which included western Ross with the exception of *Coigach*, and from this great tribe are descended the Clans of Anrias (Ross); *Coinnich* (Mac-kenzie); *Mathan* (Matheson), though the later chiefs of this last clan may have been of Norse descent; while further south the *Siol Alpin* with all its offshoots was evolved from this same *mortuath*.

It is indeed probable that the Clan Mackenzie did not originate from their western territories but from an area around Beauly and it is from the Aird and Black Isle that the MacRaes and MacLennans later joined them. The reason for this is evident, they supported MacBeth and later Donald III Bane, Malcolm *Ceann-mor*'s brother, in the dynastic disputes; indeed Donald was an ancestor of the Mackenzie Chief. By this time William the Lion became King of Scots during the middle of the 12th century and had gained control of the north. He persuaded the Mackenzies, possibly by some show of force, to remove themselves to Kintail, where they were less likely to engage in any further rebellion and where they could also act as a buffer to the Viking power in the Hebrides. This they were quite used to doing, as it must be remembered that the Norse were constantly raiding from north of *Muir* of Ord, and Dingwall was held by them for many years. During the 12th and 14th centuries several smaller clans or setts from Kintail joined themselves to the Mackenzies.

The Kairinoi occupied the lands of *Coigach*, Assynt, Edderachylis and Durness, and were the ancestors of Clan Nical, fated to be supplanted during the 14th century by Clan Leod of Lewis, a branch of the Kreones in western Inverness which area at some early date formed the province of *Garmoran*, from where Clan Leod under their Norse descended chiefs spread to Skye, Harris and Lewis during the 14th century, by which time the Chief MacNical also would have been able to claim a Scandinavian ancestor. In Lewis they may have dispossessed MacNicals who, according to tradition, had made their homes in this island for three centuries, having themselves replaced the MacSweens in the 10th century.

The Kanteai dwelt in eastern Ross and Moray, etc.; from them came the *Siol* O'Cain which branched into Clan Munro in Ross, Mac-Millans, and according to Skene, Clans Chattan and others south of the Moray Firth. In addition there are others in Easter Ross connected with the Kanteai *mortuath*, though they may not exist in sufficient numbers to form a clan, among them the most famous name is probably Mac-Beth, that of the old *mormaers* of Ross, and a family also closely connected with Moray. With this name are equated others such as :—MacBean and Beaton, while as MacCullach—MacLulaich a name associated with the *mormaers* of both Ross and Moray, the MacCullachs of Tarrel, Plaids, etc. also are probably derived from the same great tribe.

In central *Alba* the Kaledonioi were to break up into the great Clans of the west, including Clan Donald who eventually formed an Island Kingdom of their own and played such an important part in Scotland generally and Ross in particular. To the north of Ross were three tribes inhabiting the Province of Cat now known as Caithness and Sutherland, but, as we shall see, by the 10th century Strathnaver and Caithness were conquered by the Norwegians and so disappeared from the provinces of the Celtic kingdom of *Alba*. In their stead the province of Arrigaithel came into being, consisting of what, between A.D. 503–843, had been the Dalriadic (Dal Riáta) kingdom of Irish Scots in Argyll proper, with an additional area stretching from Ardnamurchan, the extreme northern limit of this kingdom, to Loch Broom in Ross. Although Dalriada did not extend further north than Ardnamurchan its boundaries were not constant, their position depending on whether the Pictish or Scottish kingdom was in the ascendant.

With certain minor adjustments, we find that the Pictish province or *mormaerdoms*, almost exactly correspond in location to the later Celtic earldoms into which they evolved, and it must have been at an early date that Ross and Cromarty became a separate Province with a *mormaer* of its own, though the Moray connection remained throughout history being perpetuated to-day in the combined Scottish Episcopal diocese of Moray and Ross.

Some few years before the evacuation of south Britain by the Romans, there was born in the Principality of Galloway, St. Ninian or Ringan, the founder of the first Celtic Church in Scotland and a contemporary of St. Patrick who carried Christianity from Scotland to Ireland, which already had some Christian connections. During his youth he was taken, possibly as a hostage, to Rome and thence to Tours where he became a pupil of the soldier Bishop St. Martin. In 397 St. Ninian returned to his home where he founded his first monastery and church of *Candida Casa* or Whithorn, from which centre he and his missionaries set out to preach the Gospel of Christ throughout *Alba* where forty churches and chapels were founded by him or dedicated to him by his disciples. We know that the southern Picts who occupied an area south of the Grampians were converted by him, but when we come to consider our own area north of the Grampians the position is less clear and violent differences of opinion exist among the authorities both ancient and modern on the subject.

The Venerable Bede in his none too reliable Anglo-Saxon Chronicle written long after the event mentions only the southern Picts and in addition it does not appear that St. Columba, when he visited Inverness, found much trace of christianity at the Court of Bruidhe, the Pictish King of all *Alba*. Yet against this stands a continuity of legend and the fact that there are at least thirteen St. Ninian dedications north of the Grampians, some such as *Fearn* in eastern Ross and Dornoch in Sutherland being very closely associated with this saint, neither do the Pictish crosses in eastern Ross resemble in every respect those of the Irish or Columban variety.

Again the apparent absence of any signs of christianity at the Court of Bruidhe is not a conclusive argument; apostasy both before and after occurred in many places and in addition it is impossible to dismiss entirely the argument that Columba, great Saint as he was, was also a great Irish Scot and very politically-minded so that he and his disciples, for political and prestige reasons, may have given less than their due to any vestiges of the first Celtic Church north of the Grampian Mountains. The belief in the Ninian connection which has always existed in the north-eastern Highlands is far too firmly grounded to dismiss lightly, so that it is more than probable that even if Ninian himself did not come north his disciples did and founded a few missionary centres which may of course only have succeeded in converting areas in their immediate neighbourhood.

Few, if any, of his simple foundations remain visible, but a shrine and settlement dedicated to St. Martin once stood on Isle Martin, *Coigach*, and may have been in existence prior to the Columban establishment, while at Mid-*Fearn*, near Ardgay, perhaps St. Ninian himself or one of his missionaries founded a monastic settlement—of brethren often known as Culdee—the word Culdhee meaning a servant of God—during an expedition north into Sutherland where a similar establishment was planted at Dornoch c. A.D. 400. The ruined church of Nonikiln above Alness appears to have been among those dedicated to St. Ninian, and it is not impossible that in eastern Ross the Ninian missionary establishments remained for a long period unaffected by the later Columban influence which is far more in evidence over Wester Ross.

The Celtic Religion, which Ninian's monks began to replace, was somewhat involved but by no means evil, possessing a high moral code and valuable principles of conduct, a fact admitted by the Classical writers and St. Columba himself. It inherited much from the Mediterranean civilizations especially the Egyptian, Grecian, and probably Phoenician; the Druids seem to have been very enlightened men, combining the functions of priest and magistrate, their relation to the Celtic tribes being closely analogous to that in which the Brahmans of India, the Magi of Persia and the Priests of Egypt stood to their people, while it is significant that there is no recorded instance of any Christian missionary of either the Ninian or Columban church suffering death or persecution for his faith, neither was there any hindrance placed on their work, rather was it welcomed.

Certainly St. Donan, a contemporary of Columba's, was murdered together with fifty-two monks on the Island of Eigg by a certain queen, but the reason appears to have had nothing to do with religious affairs, and the deed was perpetrated by pirates.

The God Belenos—the Bright One, 'The life of everything'— symbolized by the Sun was the supreme deity and it was in his honour that the Mayday Beallteine fire was kindled rather than the Phoenicean Baal's, with whom, however, there was some affinity; with Mayday started the Summer of the Celtic year and it is from this ancient Pagan festival that some relics have lingered into our own day, the other main festival being *Samh'n* held on Hallow-eve when the 'fire of peace' was kindled, while the appearance of the full moon especially the sixth day was also observed. There were, in addition, lesser gods such as the Celtic Sea God *Manannan MacLir*, while each river had its goddess, such as Nessa, and burn its attendant nymph and sometimes a water horse or bull.

Other divinities of the ancient Gael were Lugaidh Lamhfhada, the god of Light, Art and Science, who combined some of the attributes of Apollo and Mercury, though the former was himself represented by the Celtic Grannus; several gods of war; various goddesses including an important goddess of fertility sometimes known as Anu, but by whatever name, obviously equated with Artemis and Diana. Little is known of the religious ceremonies though it seems that the Druids used some form of cornu or horn, possibly as a call to prayer, held in the sacred grove where stood the stone circle, or at their high places on some hill-top, the spot marked by a cairn and where the 'fire of God' would be lighted to welcome the returning sun.

Transmigration and Reincarnation were among their firm beliefs and the idea that somewhere in the west over, or sometimes under, the sea lay the Isles of the Blest, land of the ever young, the *Tir nan Òg* of the other world. The references to the perfectly logical belief in re-incarnation as held by all the ancient Celts are numerous, Caesar in Book VI of De Bello Gallico writes: 'As one of their leading dogmas they inculcate this; that souls are not annihilated, but pass after death from one body to another, and they hold that by this teaching men are much encouraged to valour, through disregarding the fear of death.'

Diodorus of Sicily referring to the Druids, wrote as follows: 'Among them the doctrine of Pythagoras had force, namely, that the souls of men are undying, and that after a fixed number of years they begin to live again, the soul passing into another body.' Again Valerius Maximus says of the Druids that they, 'would fain have us believe that the souls of men are immortal. I should be tempted to call these breeches-wearing gentry fools, were not their doctrine the same as that of the mantle-clad Pythagoras.' This early reference to the Trews is interesting and it is probable that the breeches mentioned may have originated with the pre-Celtic Iberians as the Celt of antiquity more often wore the ankle or knee-length tunic with deep flowing sleeves over which was draped the many coloured mantle.

One more example from the Classics will suffice; from Lucan (The Pharsalia) we get yet another light on Celtic belief; 'From you we learn that the destination of man's spirit is not the grave, nor the Kingdom of the Shades. The same spirit in another world animates a body and, if your teaching be true, death is the centre, not the finish, of a long life' (meaning a round of many lives). 'Happy the folk upon whom the Bear looks down, happy in this error, whom of fears, the greatest moves not, the dread of death. . . . For who were coward enough to grudge a life sure of its return.'

The priests, though probably literate, left nothing in writing regarding their tenets and ceremonies as everything was handed down orally but we find this Druidic Triad, Three necessities of Transmigration—

> the least of all things, whence a beginning;
> the substance of all things, whence progress;
> and the formation of all things, whence individuality.

Our closest link is through the Bards, themselves closely linked to the Druidical hierarchy, such as the great Welsh poet of the 6th century A.D. Taliesin, a devout Christian with knowledge of the Scriptures, who brings out this strong belief in much of his poetry in which he recalls former sojourns passed in many different parts of the world. It is not therefore surprising to find that the mythology and folk tales of Scotland and Ireland are full of references to reincarnation, a belief once common to the whole civilized world and by no means dead today. Much later in history we find the great Scottish philosopher of the 18th century, Hume, stating that metempsychosis is the only system of immortality 'that philosophy can hearken to.'

About A.D. 432 the Teutonic barbarian hordes had started to run amok over Europe and it was Ninian's missionaries, followed by Columba's, who from Iceland to the Danube kept alive Christianity and learning through the Dark Ages, while about this same time the symbolic stone sculpture of the Picts, quite distinct from the later Irish or Columban work, was introduced into Ireland from Scotland. The Teutonic heathens in south Britain, to all intents and purposes, ousted the Christian religion from the areas they had seized which included Lothian as part of the Angle Northumbrian kingdom.

A further attempted expansion of this kingdom to areas north of the Forth was to be frustrated in 685 by the overwhelming victory of the Pictish King Bruidhe at Dunnichen, or Nechtans Mere, in Angus. The capital of the Pictish monarchy and the residence of the *Ard Righ* was near Inverness, the 'town' probably consisting of circular wood and turf huts grouped around the stockaded *dun* of the King, and this capital remained here till the end of the 6th century when it was moved to Abernethy on the Tay.

In A.D. 503 the Irish Princes and brothers, Fergus, Erc and Loarn founded the Kingdom of Dalriada or Scotia in Argyll, but these colonists were hardly foreigners as they not only belonged to the same branch of the Celtic race, but almost certainly used a very similar speech, and had similar customs. They were Christians—thanks to St. Patrick—a missionary from the kingdom of Strathclyde in south-west Scotland—and fifty years later the Abbey of Iona was founded by one of them named St. Oran.

In 563 the great statesman and scholar St. Columba arrived from Ireland to join his kinsman the King of Scots, and was made Abbot of Iona. The writings of St. Adamnan, Columba's biographer, give us some idea of this saint's inexhaustible energy. We find him visiting Inverness in the dual role of missionary and ambassador; firstly to enquire into certain backsliding in the direction of a Druidical revival under the Archdruid Broichan, and secondly to persuade the Pictish King Bruidhe to abandon his claim to suzerainty over Dalriada. In both these tasks he was successful, being a past-master in diplomacy and not averse to using trickery to impress the superstitious Pict, so that in 574 Aidan was crowned King of Scots by Columba at Iona, seated on the *Lia-fàil*—Stone of Destiny—which now rests below the coronation throne in Westminster Abbey.

The traditional story of the *Lia-fàil* is very romantic despite the fact that the science of Geology would seem to disprove its more remote history, which reports it to be the very stone on which Jacob rested his head the night he wrestled with the angel at Bethel. From there is was conveyed to Egypt whence it was brought to Spain by Gathelus—legendary founder of the Scottish (Irish) nation, who had married Scota, daughter of the Pharaoh Ramases II, who ruled in Egypt c. 1317 B.C.; this Princess, it is said, had been influenced by the preaching of Moses. From Spain the stone was taken by the legendary Hiberus to Ireland and placed on the Hill of Tara, becoming the coronation throne of the Irish *Ard Righs*. In A.D. 503 King Fergus moved it again to his new kingdom of Dalriada where later it was built into the wall of Dunstaffnage Castle, there it remained till transferred to the Church of Scone by King Kenneth, ruler of the United Picto-Scottish Kingdom, in A.D. 850. Up to the year 1296 all our kings were crowned seated on this stone, then it was stolen by Edward I of England, placed in West-minster Abbey and dedicated to Edward the Confessor. But eventually the old prophecy was fulfilled that where the stone should be a King of Scottish blood should reign—namely James VI and I in 1603 and his descendants of to-day.

It was during St. Columba's visit to Inverness that the, or a, Loch Ness Monster made its first recorded appearance; also of considerable interest is the fact that the Pictish king reigning at that time (and again in 685) had a non-Celtic name—Bruidhe—in which case his family may well have been of pre-Celtic origin, the names of the chiefs who were with him, recorded by Adamnan, are on the other hand Gaelic.

Before long Columban settlements began to spring up all over the country, bringing fresh life into the first Celtic Church founded by Ninian. In Ross grew up the settlements of Rosemarkie on the Black Isle, founded by St. Moluag, a contemporary of Columba's and Abbot of Lismore, who died in 577 after founding many churches in the Highlands and till the Reformation this place was to remain the ecclesiastical capital of Ross; Kilmuir Easter; also the famous Abbey of Applecross—*Comraich Ma Ruibha*—founded in 673 by St. *Maol Rubha*, the red-headed Abbot, once of Bangor in Ulster. This Saint also founded churches at Lochcarron in the west, Contin, and Ferintosh, the two latter being in east Ross, where he was killed by Danish pirates near the farm of Coulnagower on April 21st, 721 at the age of 80 years 3 months and 9 days, while returning from a visit to the Black Isle, after fifty-one years' work at Applecross.

A story is told of the Red Priest that just before dying he expressed a wish that four 'red men' of Applecross should be summoned to carry back his mortal remains for burial, but the people of the Black Isle neglected to carry out these instructions, wishing to keep the body of this famous saint nearer home. However, when they attempted to lift the coffin they found it immovable until the original orders were complied with, when the four red men found the body so light that the journey back was accomplished with only two halts! One of which was at Press Maree Contin. His grave is marked by two round stones though it is said that a more imposing stone of red granite was sent by a daughter of a King of Norway, but that it was broken up when the modern manse was built.

A Girth or Sanctuary six miles in circumference, formerly marked by stone crosses, surrounded the Abbey behind which lies *Eilean nan Naomh*—the Holy Isle. For many centuries a piece of earth from within the girth was carried for protection in battle and on journeys. From this place the Columban missionaries spread all over the north-west and islands, erecting their little beehive cells and chapels from which they ministered to the people, and in Lewis alone Martin Martin, who in 1703 made a close study of the Hebrides, mentions twenty-five Columban chapels as well as others on its lesser islands: the Shiants, the two Berneras and Colmkill, St. Flannan of the Flannan Islands; St. Kilda and St. Ronan's chapel on North Rona. The small buildings of the Celtic church blossomed out in every district of Ross; between Nigg, *Muir* of Ord and Cromarty there exist about thirty sites of old Celtic churches. Others were situated at *Morangie* outside Tain, *Cladh Churadain* near Assynt, Novar, connected with Rosemarkie and dedicated to St. Curidan, one of the signatories of Adamnan's Law promulgated in 697 prohibiting the use of women as combatants in warfare; *Cladh mo Bhrigh*, two miles east of Dingwall; Brahan which included Fodderty, and Kinettas at Strathpeffer.

St. *Bride* or Brigit 'the greatest woman of the Celtic Church' belongs to pre-Columban times, of St. Ninian and St. Patrick, whose shroud she is said to have woven. But there is a still older *Bride* or Brigit, the Celtic goddess of a time B.C. and she also was a loveable character, a goddess of hearth, home and plenty, as well as poetry and music through her grandson, so the prestige of the goddess undoubtedly enhanced the reputation of the saint, in *Alba*. To St. *Bride* is dedicated the old Church of Logiebride (Logie Wester) the burn *Allt Bride* being close by, the old burying ground situated on a mound once an island of the River *Conan* that probably began its career as a burial cairn with some form of dedication to the pagan *Bride*; the ruins of a cell also dedicated to St. *Bride* still exist near *Conan* Station. Further west at Garve a church was erected to the memory of St. Fionn while churches in Kintail and Loch Alsh bore the name of the Saints Comgan, his sister Kentigerna and her son Fillan c. 715. The same type of missionary from Iona had carried back Christianity to northern England, St. Aidan having converted the Angles of Northumbria, becoming Bishop of Holy Isle and Lindisfarne. These men, together with the faith, introduced the flourishing Celtic culture of the time and by mid 7th century this had spread south as far as the Thames where it came in contact with the Continental church, reintroduced into Kent by St. Augustine.

The differences between the Celtic and Latin Churches were less doctrinal than administrative, though the Celtic Church tended to retain a greater simplicity, while it is a disputed point whether or not celibacy of the priesthood was enforced; each recognized the other, but whereas the Continental church had grown up in the Empire on a diocesan basis, the Celtic church of *Alba* and Ireland had created a system more suitable for a people organized in loose tribal confederacies. After the Synod of Whitby in 664 the Celtic Church began very slowly to conform more closely with the parent body. Colman, the Abbot of Lindisfarne leader of the Celtic Church party in the date of Easter controversy at this Synod was both outvoted, and outwitted by his Roman Church opponent; thus was the seed sown for the eventual but slow extinction of the Celtic Church system, though it lingered on into the 13th century or even later. Colman himself returned to Iona where it seems probable that he was sent to minister to the Picts of Easter Ross in the parish of Tarbat where in later years around his church, grew up the little town of Portmahomack, in the Gaelic *Port-ma Chalmag* the Port of my own little Colman. Certain of the Pictish carved stones and crosses of this area show an unusual Saxon influence, probably introduced by him.

At the beginning of this chapter we saw how the Provinces were governed by the *mormaers* (great officers) owing allegiance to the *Ard Righ*, either Pictish or Scottish, the systems being similar, and after 843 to the High-King of the combined kingdoms. With the fusion of Pict and Scot into one nation, the name Scotia very slowly replaces *Alba* or *Alban*, though centuries later the change of name was still causing a certain amount of confusion among chroniclers.

The *mormaers* constituted the highest nobility but during the 12th and 13th centuries were to adopt the Continental title of Earl or Comites; the next in order of Celtic nobility was the *maor* (officer) senior chieftain of a clan or sept and steward to the *mormaer*, and *tòiseach* (this Gaelic name meaning: front, van, origin or source); also a senior Chieftain and often the military leader of the clan and both held land, some part of the province the equivalent of the later Scottish Barony; it is interesting that in documents up to the 18th century the Barony of Milntown (New Tarbat) is referred to as the *maordom*. These two Crown offices had long been hereditary, the officers being responsible to their kinsman the King for the administration of Justice, which duty they carried out by appointing district judges known as Brieves [*Breitheamh*] to administer the Brehon Law. In time of war they were required to aid the King with all their forces, so that generally speaking, they were the government in their respective areas, the King's Council, and collectors of taxes, fulfilling the duties of Earl, Justiciar, Sheriff, Steward, etc., though as yet they were not called by these alien titles. Sometimes the *Maors* of the 10th and 11th centuries adopted the Saxon title of Thane—Cawdor being one example and references to the Thanes of Ross another—though the office remained distinct from the Saxon Thanage.

It was not until the focal point of political activity became fixed south of the Forth that the *Mór-Tuaths* split up into their more localized *Tuath* (Clan) and Sept units, having as their chief some noble of the tribe, the *Mormaer-Maor* (*Tòiseach*) or lesser chieftain, all of whom were inevitably closely related. Although for centuries these noble offices had been hereditary this did not imply invariable succession by the eldest son as in the Continental feudal sense, for by the ancient Celtic Law of Tanistry the most suitable person—the Tanist—succeeded, provided he was a member of the particular ruling family. Illegitimacy was not in itself a bar, but the degree of relationship to which the office could descend was strictly regulated, a 5th degree connection with the late incumbent being the outside limit. In other words, blood relationship was essential but latitude was permitted in the choice of individual. The man selected to fill the important post of chief of a clan or chieftain of a sept was chosen during the lifetime of the old chief— usually the aspirant's father—and after the choice was made he was known as the Tanist.

The qualifications, apart from the strict rule which laid down that the tanist must be within the 5th degree of blood relationship to the chief, were as follows: He must be, 'the most experienced, the most noble, the most wealthy, the wisest, the most learned, the most truly popular, the most powerful to oppose, the most steadfast to sue for profits and (be sued) for losses.' In addition, he was supposed to be free from personal blemishes, and deformities and of fit age to lead his clan or sept in battle. To support the dignity of chief or chieftain a proportion of the clan or sept lands were attached as an appendage to the office. This land with the *duns* (castles), and fortified residences upon it went to the new chief, though his private heritage might be split up (gavelled) amongst his progeny.

This law of succession applied equally to the Royal House, which although admirable in conception, had the great disadvantage of providing opportunities for dynastic disputes and consequent civil strife. But Tanistry did avoid minorities, the frequency of which in the Royal House, after the 12th century, was the curse of Scotland, or at least one of them. For long the succession to the Pictish throne went to a male but by female descent, possibly a pre-Celtic carry-over started by an Iberian heiress marrying a recently arrived Celt, a fashion later to be repeated by certain Celtic heiresses marrying Normans.

During the early Christian period the Pictish kingdom grew in power and started to expand especially under the great Pictish King Angus MacFergus 731–761 who dominated the Dalriadic Scots; Brython Celts of south-west Scotland; and the Angle kingdom of Northumbria, where certain areas had remained all along in occupation of both Brython and Goidel Celts. The Cymry (Brython Celtic speech) of the south-west gave way to Goidel Gaelic which became the language of all *Alba* though to a much lesser extent in Lothian.

The culture of this period as expressed in sculpture represents both the Celtic and older Iberian love of symbolism. The work can be divided into three groups, the first having its roots buried in an age long before the advent of Christianity, and lasting till about A.D. 600. In these early examples the stone is neither shaped nor dressed but very cleverly and artistically decorated with spiral, interlace and fret patterns while the symbols, always rigidly conventional, consist of such combinations as the rod, sun disc and crescent moon, all of which are connected with both Celtic and Iberian mysticism, though their exact meanings are unknown. The system of this art is the same over all Pictish *Alba* where it can be traced from Shetland to Galloway in the far south-west as also through every island of the Hebrides. The much defaced 'Dingwall Stone,' once built into the fabric of the Church but rescued during the 19th century, is an example of this class of sculpture.

The second group appeared approximately between the years A.D. 600–A.D. 1000, co-eval with the Pictish Chronicle of the Brechin culdees, The Book of Deer. Here the slabs of stone are roughly tooled and shaped bearing in most cases the Celtic Cross which sometimes may have been superimposed on older carved stones at the same time; on these human and animal figures are excellently portrayed, the sculpture now being in relief instead of incised, while the whole stone is covered with, more or less, complex ornamentation.

The Eagle Stone or *Clach'n Tuindeain*, the stone of the turning at Strathpeffer has been thought to be of this period, though as it is incised and carries no cross it may well be of an earlier date, it was moved from its original position in the 15th century and set up some 600 yards further to the north-east at Nutwood to commemorate the battle fought by MacKays, Mackenzies and Munros against a force of the MacDonalds that formed the northern column of the Army on its way to Harlaw from the west under Donald Lord of the Isles in 1411; by chance it displayed an Eagle, the heraldic emblem of Munro of Foulis whose clan played such a prominent part in the engagement.

Fine examples of the Pictish crosses exist at Edderton—not far from the site of the St. Ninian foundation—as well as in the Parish of Tarbat: at Nigg, Shandwick, Hilton—this stone now being in the Edinburgh Museum—and at Rosemarkie on the Black Isle. On the western coast as at Applecross the crosses are more closely linked with the Irish Columban variety.

The third group dates from about A.D. 1000 till the extinction of pure Celtic sculpture, in southern Scotland by the 13th century and in the north by the Reformation; the main change in these later examples is the disappearance of the symbols from the slabs, leaving the cross in relief and richly decorated. Examples of Celtic stone carving that come within this group are to be seen in the 13th century Cathedral of St. Clement at Rodil, Harris, and in the ancient church of Aignish in Lewis where the 15th century MacLeod effigies are pure Celtic in design and execution even though they do not compare in merit with much of the older work.

Ogham—the old Celtic alphabet—is found on many stones of the pre-Christian era, north of Forth and Clyde, one having been found on Badentarbat Beach, *Coigach*; but this method of writing because of its Pagan connections was unpopular with the early Church so that it was replaced by a Celtic form of the Roman script. Some description of the people who did this work has already been given, but it is possible to catch a few more glimpses of their way of life.

The great Caledonian Forest still covered much of the land, though it was fast decreasing as new areas were brought under cultivation, stock increased, while more and more fuel was needed for smelting and metal work. Many species of tree familiar to us now were not to appear for many a century yet, but, besides the ubiquitous Scots pine and birch of the higher levels, the rowan flourished, endowed with qualities dangerous to witches and bogles generally. The more sheltered straths and lower lands grew oak, beech, hazel and ash which was much in demand for arrow-shafts; the yew and holly grew among the woods, but the only fruit trees seem to have been the gean and crab-apple, and of course the numerous berries.

Large areas of the valleys such as the Straths formed by the rivers Peffrey and Conon were sodden marshes, haunted by wild fowl; thus they remained till drained by men in the 18th and 19th centuries. Here would be found the alder, aspen and certain of the willow tribe, from which the useful creels and baskets would be made. The people lived in communities either in round conical huts made of earth, clay, wattle or dry stone, and it is likely that some of the old wheel-houses were still in use; the majority of these villages would be grouped about a circular *dun*, in some areas the fort might be a broch, in others a stockaded fort, built of whatever material was available locally, in these strongholds dwelt the chieftain with his family and entourage. The old soutterains were still used as store-rooms and possibly as places of retreat for anyone who failed to find accommodation in the *dun* during an alarm.

Since the advent of Christianity there would certainly be a small church in the vicinity, the ruins of such, Columban foundations, exist at Laide, which lies south of Gruinard Bay; at Eoropie in Lewis; as well as at Aignish near Stornoway where are interred the remains of nineteen chiefs of *Siol* Torquil, the MacLeods of Lewis. At such places as Rosemarkie, *Fearn*, Applecross, and Annait in Skye there existed the religious centres, first perhaps the monastic settlements of St. Ninian then those of St. Columba. They were very simple in construction, the living quarters of the brethren consisting of individual beehive cells, in the first instance of wattle and wood but eventually replaced by stone buildings of identical shape; the whole settlement being surrounded by a dry stone wall forming an enclosure in which the monks erected a refectory for their meals, taken in common; a barn, stable and byre, usually a water mill and bakery, a kiln for drying corn, and always a separate building for any guests who might turn up.

Their little stone church was as simple as the other buildings, thatched with heather and with a sacristy opening on one side wherein was housed the much venerated Monastic Bell together with any sacred relics. The congregation at a well attended service could not all have found room in the church, seldom little bigger than an oratory, so that they assembled outside under the shadow of the great Pictish or Columban Cross. Later to many of these buildings were added slim round towers for use as a place of refuge from the raiding Norwegians in the west and Danes in the east. The attacks of the latter were eventually to be frustrated by the decisive victories at Luncarty by King Kenneth III at the end of the 10th century, and on the coast of Moray in the first decade of the 11th century by King Malcolm II, but the Norsemen were to gain an Island kingdom in the west which lasted for 400 years.

The settlements of the Celtic Church were often located in some spot that in pre-Christian days had been sacred to the Druidical faith so that nearby would be their sacred well, now transformed into a Holy Well dedicated to some Saint of the Christian Church. The ruler of this monastic community was the Abbot who, in many cases, was also a Bishop though as in the case of Columba himself ordained a Presbyter, and head of the Columban Church this was not an invariable rule, but the Bishops of the Celtic Church though ranking above the Abbot in ecclesiastical position were subject to his conventual rule though this did not imply any usurpation of the Bishop's functions. The Abbot's dwelling stood a little apart from the others, though he led the same unostentatious life, clad like his junior bretheren in an undergarment of white covered by a woollen overall of the natural wool colour and reaching down to his sandal-shod feet, these sandals were always removed before eating. The Celtic tonsure differed from that of the priests in the Continental church, their hair being shaved back to the line of the ears.

The Abbacy was hereditary, being retained within the family of the founder, and latterly it became a lay office—our present Queen being able to trace her ancestry to a lay Abbot of Dunkeld through his Stewart, House of Bruce, and House of Dunkeld forbears, as can the families of Ross and Mackenzie to the Abbots of Applecross. Under the Abbot were various officials responsible for both clerical and secular duties; the fearleighinn or reader was in charge of education; the schibhneoir or scribe copied the scriptures, some of their work, for example, The Book of Kells, being of unequalled beauty in any age; the *deoir*—from which comes the name Dewar—was in charge of the relics of his monastery and this office was generally hereditary.

The Diseartach, or hermits, were culdees who retired for a period of meditation and prayer to some lonely spot such as *Eilean a' Cleireach* (Priest Island) of the Summer Isle group, *Eilean Mourie* on Loch Maree, and *An Uaimh Shiante* (the Holy Cave) at Torridon Bay, while the other members of the community went out into the country founding and serving their numerous local churches, though the title of *sagairt* or priest does not appear till late in the history of the Celtic Church.

Through the great forests roamed the red deer, still a mighty beast but changing from his European ancestors, and gradually assuming the unique character of the present-day breed as the forest areas grew smaller, though in the main his home as yet lay among the pines and other trees which clothed so much of *Alba*; but the time was approaching when he must adapt himself to the almost treeless forests of a later day. With the exception of the wild boar, large numbers of wolves, a few bears and reindeer, the animal life was much the same as may yet be found around Ben Wyvis and the highlands of Ross and Cromarty, so that hunting was still a very important source of food supply. Considerable commerce in hides and ornaments existed with Ireland, while the poets and harpers visited each other's country carrying news and spreading the stories of their homeland.

The mythology of *Alba* is inextricably mixed up with that of Ireland leaving but a few tales which can be said to belong wholly to the Pictish people. Both Pict of Caledonia and Scot of Ireland can claim the stories of the *Fionn*-cycle, as professional warrior bands under such leaders as Diarmid existed in both countries, and are known to have harried Roman Britain under *Fionn* Cumhaill c. A.D. 364. The Cuchulainn-cycle of tales, in *Alba*, deal mainly with Deirdre, her husband Naoise and the sons of Uisneach; while many stories are the Celtic versions of Greek mythology.

Soon after A.D. 750 new complications entered into the lives of both Pict and Scot when the Viking galleys appeared round our coasts. At the start they came as raiders and pirates but, before the century was out, stayed to colonize in Caithness, Orkney, Shetland and the Hebrides. Caithness, part of Sutherland and the major part of our western seaboard between Durness and Clyde suffered from their raids so that the Celtic population in certain areas such as Caithness tended to withdraw, temporarily, to the high but free hinterland from where for centuries the fight was carried on. The Hebrides eventually came completely under the sway of the Norsemen, but here as elsewhere, the Gael after generations of struggle reimposed his civilization and language on the Scandinavian who has left few visible remains but numerous place-names, and in certain areas such as Lewis a heritage of great sailors.

CHAPTER IV

THE COMING OF THE NORSEMEN AND THE FIRST DYNASTIC REBELLIONS IN MORAY AND ROSS

Chronological Table

A.D. 771   Karl the Great (Charlemagne) King of France.
A.D. 780   Commencement of Viking inroads into north and western *Alba*.
A.D. 786   Haroun al Raschid Abbasid, Caliph of Baghdad till 809.
A.D. 795   Iona and Lambay in Skye sacked by Vikings.
A.D. 800   Rise of Holy Roman Empire. Compilation of The Book of Kells in Ireland.
A.D. 814   Death of Charlemagne.
A.D. 840   Robert the Strong ancestor of the Capet Kings of France allies himself with Charles the Bald who gives him the job of defending the area between Seine and Loire against the Normans. By his side fought Tertullus 'the Rustic' of Gallic peasant origin who became seneschal of Anjou and founded the House of the Counts of Anjou and the Plantagenets of England.
A.D. 843   Union of Pictish and Scottish Kingdoms.
A.D. 850   Relics of St. Columba removed by King Kenneth MacAlpin to Dunkeld.
A.D. 852   Norse occupy Dublin and Waterford.
A.D. 868   Buddhist Sutra printed as also Chinese 'Court Gazette'.
A.D. 911   Rolf the Ganger established in Normandy.
A.D. 912–   Reigns of Abd-er-Rahman and peak of Golden Age in Arab-Spain. The Arab (Moorish) occupation
A.D. 961   in Spain produced the most enlightened civilization in Europe at that period of history.

     While Christendom existed in a state of semi-barbarism, with the nobles more or less permanently engaged in cutting each other's throats and the poor living a life of slavery—called serfdom—in complete squalor, the Arabs in Spain were founding great colleges open to scholars of all the world regardless of creed or race, the only rule being that complete religious toleration should be practised by Christian, Mahomedan and Jew, any bigotry being sternly checked.

     Very great strides were made in medical and other sciences while a standard of social justice, equally applicable to their well-cared-for slaves, was reached many hundreds of years in advance of the remainder of Europe.

     In like manner it is necessary to arrive at very modern times before the peoples of Europe can compare their sanitation, building, and way of life with these Arabs in Spain who had introduced at this early date an educational system for all their population. In spite of the attitude of the Church some of this culture penetrated into Christian Europe before the decline and eventual destruction of this Empire took place.

A.D. 971   Brython Kingdom of Strathclyde added to Scotland.
A.D. 1015   Danes conquer England.
A.D. 1018   Great victory of Carham brings Lothian, part of the kingdom of Northumbria and predominantly Angle, into the Scottish kingdom.
A.D. 1040   Beginning of dynastic struggle in Moray and north.
A.D. 1066   Capital of Scotland moved from Scone to Dunfermline, and flight of Saxon Royal family from William the Conqueror to Scottish Court. England conquered by Normans.
A.D. 1079   In Persia Omar Khayyam devises a calendar considerably more accurate than the Gregorian calendar which is in use to-day.
A.D. 1095   First Crusade.
A.D. 1097   Edinburgh becomes Capital of Scotland.
A.D. 1116   Dynastic risings in Moray, Ross and south-west Scotland till 1130.
A.D. 1138   Scots support Queen Matilda of England and her small son against King Stephen who had usurped the Crown of England.
A.D. 1147   Second Crusade by Louis VII.
A.D. 1150   Church of Rome gains ascendancy over Celtic Culdee Church. The Book of Leinster MS. written in Ireland.

In 795 the Columban Settlements of Iona and Lambay in Skye were sacked and till A.D. 900 bitter fighting took place in the north and west to stem the Viking invasions. But by the end of the 9th century Orkney, Shetland, Caithness and the Hebrides were all paying skät (tribute) to Harald Fairhair King of Norway who appointed Norwegian Jarls as governors of the conquered areas, which included the Isle of Man. However, for only three generations in Orkney and Caithness were the Jarls pure Scandinavians, they found the Pictish women very attractive as did their followers.

Note Alpin King of the Scots of Dalriada died in 843 and was succeeded by his son Kenneth I MacAlpin who also inherited the throne of the Picts through his mother Princess and heiress of the Pictish Royal House. The capital became Scone. From now on King of Scots is used to denote King of the United Kingdom of Picts and Scots in Scotland.

There is a story told concerning one of the earlier Viking raids on the east coast: a certain Rover was accompanied by his daughter, a blonde of great beauty and charm who was seen by a Pictish chieftain, the leader of a pastoral clan who had their homes somewhere on the slopes of Ben Wyvis, perhaps by the upper waters of the Peffrey. It may have been a case of love at first sight, though on the other hand, collusion seems probable as our hero succeeded in getting possession of his love while 'driving off' cattle from the Rover's pied à terre at Ardullie. The Scandinavians, somewhat incensed, followed up the party, a fight ensued resulting in the recapture of the girl. But she must have had words with her father as she succeeded in bringing him round to a different view of the situation, so that the outcome was a pact of friendship between the opponents and a wedding.

The Vikings took to themselves Celtic wives and settled at Ledvarigid to the west of Dingwall, from whence the descendants of these men came out to play their part under Finlaec, *Mormaer* of Ross, in checking the later Norwegian invasions from the north, until the murder of Finlaec in 1023. It is to the Norse Sagas, the products of Viking energy and Celtic culture, that we must turn for any detailed account of our northern area during this period. It is only from them that a reasonably clear picture emerges of Caithness, Sutherland, Ross and Moray, up to the opening years of the 13th century.

Harald Fairhair did not win his western kingdom of the Isles without meeting serious opposition from the Viking pirates already operating in these areas. Through the agency of Thorstein the Red, who was killed by the Picts c. 900, and Ragnvald Möri-Jarl of Norway, he gained the far north, making Ragnvald the first Jarl of Orkney and part of Caithness,[1] but he in turn passed the position on to his brother Sigurd I. Further west in the Hebrides, Harald had the assistance of Ketil Flatneb so was able to dispose of such turbulent spirits as Onund Tree-foot—he had lost a leg in battle—who decided that Iceland was a more healthy spot. He was joined later by old Ketil himself who wearying of submission and good behaviour had become obstreperous which soon resulted in his own flight.

Sigurd I pushed south gaining a large part of Caithness and the seaboard of Sutherland as far as the river Oykel where he met a *Mormaer* of Ross, Malbridge, a name equated with *Malbeatha* and MacBeth, of the Buck Tooth, c. 890. For some time northern Ross became a battle-ground, neither side gaining any decisive victory till Malbridge accepted a challenge of personal combat together with forty warriors from each side. The combatants arrived mounted but Sigurd had 'pulled a fast one' having mounted two men on each horse; in spite of the trick the fight had to proceed. The battle was desperate, continuing

Note 1. See Appendix I a. for Jarls and Earls of Orkney-Caithness.

till the gallant *Mormaer* together with his forty followers lay dead on the field. Sigurd in his triumph beheaded the corpses of his foes tying the gruesome trophies to the saddle-bows, and taking as his share Malbridge's head. The Vikings' triumph was short-lived, the Buck Tooth was yet to have the final say; on the ride north Sigurd felt a sudden stab in the thigh, a mere scratch as it turned out, from his victim's tooth, but the wound turned septic, Sigurd died of blood poisoning and was buried at Dornoch. The conquests in north and west quickly fell away, and Sigurd leaving no son, the succession fell on two of Ragnvald's sons, Hallad who found the job beyond him so returned to Norway, and his half-Pictish brother Turf Einer who succeeded to a diminished territory.

During this period the south of Scotland was subjected to frequent and destructive raids by the Vikings who had settled in Ireland but in 937 an alliance was made to combat an invading force from England. A united army of Vikings, Scots and Welsh under the Scottish King Constantine III met this force at Brunanburgh in Cumbria, but suffered a defeat, largely due to the lack of liaison between the varied units of the allied force. As was customary right through the Middle Ages and described in some detail by Froissart, many of the Scots force would have arrived at the scene of battle mounted on their small horses which the Celt generally rode without stirrups with his legs very far extended and forward towards the horse's head. The horse furniture consisted of a brass bit and sliding reins, the saddle made up of the normal tree but varying in that the seat was a 2 ft. long and 1 ft. broad plane table covered with blanketing, the whole being secured to the horse, not with girths but by a breast-plate and crupper, with a surcingle in the middle.

By 971 the Brython kingdom of Strathclyde (Cumbria), already in Picto-Scottish hands, had become officially part of the kingdom of Scotland as had northern Lothian with the important fort of *Dun Eideann* (Edinburgh), an old Brython fortress.

Toward the end of this century the north again comes into the picture. Thorfinn I 'Skull Splitter' the son of Turf Einer, married Grelaud, the daughter of Duncan the Pictish *Mormaer* of Caithness, so adding once again a large area of Caithness to his Jarldom. The latter part of his life must have been troubled as a wicked adventuress Ragnhild proceeded to marry and murder in turn his three eldest sons; she must have possessed no ordinary charm as she captured as her fourth husband the next son, Jarl Ljotr. The life of this man was short because although he escaped death at the hands of his wife and another brother Skuli whom he killed, he fell in battle against MacBeth *Mormaer* of Ross in 963, the same year in which his father 'Skull Splitter' died. The sixth brother Hlödur (Lewis) succeeded but did not make the mistake of marrying Ragnhild, instead he chose as his wife an Irish Princess and died quietly in his own bed in 980, leaving a son Sigurd II 'The Stout' already a rising power in the land. This Jarl tried to create a Scandinavian block consisting of the settlements in Ireland, Man, the Isles, and the north. He partially succeeded, but was frustrated in 1014 at the Battle of Clontarf in Ireland, where a combined Irish-Scottish army under Brian Boru, High King of Ireland, routed the Danes and Norwegians.

Sigurd was killed leaving a young son Thorfinn II 'The Mighty'. Now this boy was a grandson of Malcolm II King of the united Picto-Scottish kingdom who had given his daughter in marriage to Sigurd the Stout probably with the idea of creating a counterweight to balance the great power of the northern *Mormaers*-Finlaec MacRuaridh (MacBeth) of Ross, the father of Shakespeare's MacBeth, and Mael-brighde of Moray, Finlaec's brother or cousin, and subsequent murderer in 1023. The young Thorfinn was allowed therefore to succeed to Caithness and Sutherland, being created an Earl by Malcolm though kept at Court till his sixteenth birthday. Four years later there was fought one of the two crucial battles of Scottish history: the victory of Carham in 1018 wiped out the Northumbrian kingdom carrying Scotland's boundaries to the Tweed, where they have since remained.

By the early 11th century the Norwegian area in the Western Isles was becoming the home of a mixed race with Norse fathers and Celtic mothers, known as the Gall-Gael. On the east coast the Norse dominion stretched along the seaboard to Dornoch and the Oykel. In these parts Norwegian had become the predominant language, remaining so in Lewis till 1200, but through the influence of the Celtic mothers Gaelic eventually returned to replace the Norse tongue in east and west, though less completely in Caithness, Orkney or Shetland.

The Celtic Church was still a separate organization from the Roman establishment, but it was losing some of its austere simplicity as it grew richer. In the Columban monasteries the Abbot was now, more often than not, a layman who did not take the priest's vows, though holding the title and revenues of Prior or Abbot.

The first Lay Abbots—or Co-Arbs—who succeeded to, or took over the temporal possessions of, the consecrated Abbots were usually members of the real cleric's own family so that Scottish clericalism tended to become the monopoly of an hereditary aristocracy. The forbears of the Earls of Ross were the Lay Abbots of Applecross, and there is every reason to suppose that they were connected closely with the old MacBeth *Mormaers* of Ross. This is not proven by written record, but their policy and actions in Scotia's fight against the Norsemen not to mention their territorial position in the west makes the assumption a likely one.

The power of the new Bishops appointed by Rome was growing at the expense of the Abbot, however, while the ecclesiastical capital already changed from Iona to Dunkeld in 808, had been moved after 906 to St. Andrews where lay the relics of this Saint, the veneration of St. Andrew having been introduced by a Pictish King Angus who had taken for his emblem the Saltire—the Cross of St. Andrew. The Norwegians who for long stuck to Odin, Thor and their fierce warrior religion, had embraced Christianity somewhat reluctantly, during the 9th century and were, to some extent, supervised by the See of Trondhjem.

The Norsemen when they first arrived had found the small Celtic horse and still smaller Shetland pony; with the former they crossed their own sturdy dun ponies which produced the Highland Garron, still used on the croft and until very recently as the mount of the Lovat Scouts. Oats, barley, rye and wheat were the main crops, the open fields being divided into communal parcels or ridges, a system which survived into the 18th century and in some places till late in the 19th century. Oxen not horses drew the plough, and although Scotland was primarily a cattle country, the long fine wool of the small sheep was beginning to create a weaving industry. The forests were still extensive and there is a very old legend which describes how a young man of Ross, having been on the losing side during a skirmish with Vikings near Dingwall, decided to remove himself and his old father with the utmost speed to *Coigach*; he took the old man on his shoulders and ran, without stopping, a matter of some fifty miles.

During the whole of this stupendous cross-country run the youth was passing through dense forest, and by the time he reached *Loch Lurgan* in *Coigach* he was feeling thirsty so decided on a drink; what was his dismay on lifting the old man from off his shoulders, to find that only the legs were left, the top half of father having been swept off by branches during their flight through the forests. The legs not being of much use without the rest, were thrown into the *Loch*, which ever since has been called *Lurgan*, the Loch of the Shanks. Now apart from being an amusing story, its chief interest lies in indicating the extent to which trees still covered the land, as supposing the warrior's route to have been Strath Peffer—the *Bealach* between Big and Little Wyvis—Garbat—Strath Vaich—*Geàrrie Mór*—Ullapool—Strath Caniard—*Lurgan*; the only woods of any size that exist to-day are those of Castle Leod, Braemore and Leckmelm, hardly sufficient even to scalp father.

By the end of Malcolm II's reign the Celtic kingdom was established to all intents and purposes within its present boundaries, though on several subsequent occasions there was a fair chance that the boundary might have been fixed on the Humber and not the Tweed. Norsemen still held the Islands, but their hold on the mainland was weakening, but Thorfinn II, his Earldom confirmed by Olaf 'The Saint', King of Norway, had formed the Islands into a kingdom, and ruled from Shetland to Dublin, owing allegiance to Olaf's son, King Magnus Barefoot, though this allegiance was apt to be vague.

The next big event in the north is the start of the Moray Rebellions and the advent into History of their cause, the somewhat shadowy figure made famous by Shakespeare, MacBeth, *Mormaer* of Ross and later Moray. The historical background of this magnificent tragedy was gathered from the none too reliable Holinshed which, though it in no way detracts from the merit of the play, has given to this great Highland *Mormaer* an undeservedly bad character. MacBeth was the hereditary *Mormaer* of Ross, an area which held the important forts of Dingwall guarding the only land route from north to south, and the *dun* dominating the harbour of Cromarty on the Black Isle. At some period of his life he married Gruoch a lady of Royal descent and the widow of Gillecomgan the *Mormaer* of Moray, so that through her MacBeth became *Mormaer* of this great province as well. It is by this second title that he is more often known, though Shakespeare incorrectly refers to him as a Thane which as we have seen was only equivalent to a *Maordom* or Barony.

Now King Malcolm II who had died in 1034, had bequeathed the throne of Scotland to his eldest grandson, 'the gentle' Duncan, but by the old Celtic custom of the Royal succession alternating between different branches of the family, MacBeth, a younger grandson, considered that he had the better right; indeed it is possible that he had; added to this, his wife the Lady Gruoch had herself dynastic claims, being directly descended from King Malcolm I and Kenneth III. The *Mormaer* of Ross and Moray[1] had the support of the greater part of Scotland, including the powerful, semi-independent Celto-Viking Jarl, and Earl of Orkney-Caithness Thorfinn II, King Malcolm's other tall, black-haired grandson, his participation being due to King Duncan's reversal of his grandfather's policy of appeasement with his grandson by claiming tribute for the Earldom of Caithness. During the early part of Duncan's six-year reign there is no record of any move by MacBeth, who in all probability remained quietly at home administering his huge Provinces, but building up his resources, while carefully avoiding any suspicion of open collusion in the violent action being taken by his northern cousin.

Thorfinn raided and plundered central and southern Scotland, till finally the King created his own nephew Mumtan Earl of Caithness in 1040 and sent him north with an army which appears to have met with defeat in Sutherland, though the Jarl retired to Caithness to meet the double threat of a Royal fleet and Mumtan with another

Note 1. See Appendix I. b/1 for table of *Mormaers* of Ross and Moray.

army. The fleet was defeated off Durness, its retreat being followed up
to the Moray coast, Thorfinn meanwhile sending his foster father and
right-hand man Thorkel Fostri to deal with the Royal army; Mumtan's
headquarters in Thurso were surprised and burnt with the unfortunate
man inside.

The King in person raised yet another army to deal with Thorfinn
and the rival claimant to the throne, MacBeth, who had now openly
showed his hand, Duncan marched north, the opposing armies meeting
at Torfness. The actual location of this place is disputed; some consider
it to have been at Burghead in Moray, others who have equally valid
reasons, choose a strategically more likely spot, namely, the two bottle-
necks on the only north and south route. The two defiles in question
were formed by the lower slopes of Ben Wyvis and the Hill of Tulloch
on the northern flank of the Strathpeffer valley, which closed the north
side, while on the south stretched the Cromarty Firth and marshland
at this period reaching some two miles further west to Milnain
[Inchrory]. The second defile covered by the fort at Dingwall was
formed by the Firth and marsh, this time to the north, while south lay
the barrier ridge of the Cat's Back, Knockfarrel and *Coil na Righ* (The
King's wood). Below these hills the battle of Torfness may have been
fought and here or nearby King Duncan may have received the death
wound which carried MacBeth, *Mormaer* of Ross and Moray, to the
throne of Scotland.

Ross and the *dun* at *Inbherpefferon*, whose name was now changed
to Tingavollr—the meeting-place of the 'Thing' or Council (Dingwall),
became an appanage of Thorfinn, while numerous Scandinavians
founded homes on the Black Isle and *Baile Dubhthaich* changed its
name, at least among Scandinavians to Teinn (Tain). In the West,
Ullapool—Olaf's place, probably named after St. Olaf, King of
Norway—became a Norse settlement, and the Viking galleys rode at
anchor in the fine anchorage of Tanera *Mór*, called by these foreigners
Hawrary Mor.

Although the Norse, or part Norse, domination of Ross did not last
many years it was sufficient to introduce a Scandinavian strain into
Easter Ross, and has left numerous place-names over the whole
Province, many of the names ending in Dale such as Ulladale, are of
Norse origin, as is Scatwell from Skatvöllr which means a place paying
tribute, but *Dail*—pronounced dal— is also a Gaelic word meaning the
same thing, dale or field, therefore not every name ending in dale is
derived from old Norse.

Thorfinn returned to Caithness on the accession of MacBeth and
married Princess Ingibjorg of Norway, the happy event being followed
by serious trouble with his newphew Ragnvald, a Jarl in Orkney,
where Thorfinn narrowly escaped being trapped and burned with his

young wife, but lived to return and annihilate his foes which made him sole Jarl of Orkney, Shetland and Earl of Caithness and Sutherland, drawing tribute from Ross, the western seaboard and Hebrides. This remarkable man then visited King Magnus of Norway—late backer of Ragnvald—made friends with him and his heir Harald Hardrada, then proceeded on a journey to Denmark, Germany and Rome, to which city MacBeth accompanied him, according to tradition. While in Rome the Viking was absolved from various sins by the Pope and got his nominee, Thorolf, elected Bishop of Orkney. Thorfinn on his return to Orkney built the Minster of Christchurch, and governed his domains to the satisfaction of all, dying, unlike so many of his race, in his bed in 1057.

The King MacBeth ruled wisely and well for seventeen years, a popular monarch in Scotland and a liberal supporter of the Church, the centre of civilization and learning. Eventually the late King Duncan's son Malcolm III defeated and slew MacBeth at the battle of Lumphanan, but before ascending the throne, had also to defeat and kill Lulach, MacBeth's stepson who had been crowned at Scone claiming right of Royal descent from his mother. The new King Malcolm III surnamed *Ceann Mór*, followed MacBeth and Lulach in 1058, reigning for thirty-five years. He has been accused by some for introducing feudalism to Scotland and generally upsetting the old established order. Let us glance briefly at facts. The general confusion and barbarism in Europe and the absence of any strong central authority had caused peoples for self-protection to form themselves into a socio-military organization, called the feudal system which spread outwards from France.

England had almost ceased to exist; in 1066 the English dynasty was driven out by Duke William of Normandy, the majority of Anglo-Saxon nobles replaced by Norman Seigneurs and the native clergy by Norman clerics, while England's official speech became French.

Malcolm with his very astute second wife Princess Margaret, who with her sister, her brother the Saxon heir Edgar Atheling, and other refugees, had fled to Dunfermline the Scottish capital, realized that change was in the air, and that unless kingdoms kept up with universal change they stagnated and died. By the introduction of a modified feudalism they brought Scotland into line with the rest of Europe. Scotland did not die, though as is inevitable with change certain excellent characteristics of the old Celtic world were lost, while Queen Margaret increasingly made use of Edinburgh as the Royal residence. As we shall see the dynastic troubles were by no means at an end, but it is as well to remember that the rebellions in Moray and Ross were dynastic and not popular uprisings against a new way of life which for very many years was hardly apparent.

Ceann Mór's early years had been spent establishing his rule in the north, being greatly helped in this by his first wife the beautiful Ingibjorg, Thorfinn's widow, who gave him possession of that vital strong point Dingwall Castle. The family of Munro of Foulis are said to have taken the side of Malcolm during this early struggle by the Crown against the warring claimants to the throne allied to the Norsemen of Caithness, which is borne out by the fact that the next head of this family and clan, Hugh died, c. 1126, firmly established in the lands of Ferindonald between Dingwall and Alness with the addition of Logie Wester and Findon.

The position of a *Mormaer* of Ross at this juncture is a mystery, but it is not impossible that any near relation of the last ruling MacBeth would have backed the wrong horse; perhaps the Lay Abbot was this relative and in what place could he be safer than on his Abbey lands of Applecross. It is from this district, in the early 13th century, that a powerful figure Fearchar, 'the son of the Priest'—Lay Abbot—walks straight into a leading position in the history of Scotland and Ross.

For one generation the Earldom of Ross was to be added to the MacHeth House of Moray in the person of Malcolm MacHeth, the younger brother of Earl Angus of Moray. This Malcolm was created Earl of Ross c. 1160 by King Malcolm IV, after spending twenty-seven years as a prisoner-of-war in Roxburgh Castle for his participation in the Moray rebellion led by his brother, which ended in the forfeiture of the Earldom of Moray and the death of Angus in the bloody battle of Stracathro in 1130. The superior of the lands held by the Baron of Foulis is stated in the clan history to have been this Malcolm of Moray.

At the end of *Ceann Mór's* reign in 1093 the last major adjustment to Scotland's southern marches occurred, William II 'Rufus' King of England, by his capture of Carlisle deprived Scotland of Cumberland. Three years of dynastic dispute followed during which Donald III 'Bane', *Ceann Mór's* brother and an ancestor of the Mackenzies of Kintail, reigned at intervals, making himself very popular by sending back to England, or liquidating, the excessive number of Anglo-Saxons who had followed Queen Margaret into Scotland, but with Norman help Edgar the fourth son of Malcolm and Margaret slew King Donald and came to the throne of Scotland. Edgar reigned for only ten years and moved, finally, the capital from Dunfermline to Edinburgh, which as fountain head of the administration was inconveniently far away from the homes of the people who had been instrumental in constructing the kingdom, and who in the future were frequently called upon to save the very existence of that kingdom.

From now on begins the gradual break up of the great Celtic Provinces into semi-independent clan (*tuath*) areas, the central administration was becoming involved in a different political sphere to the eventual detriment and neglect of great areas of the Scottish nation. In 1097 Magnus Barefoot, King of Norway, had reduced the Isles to obedience and brought the Island Princes to heel, when necessary by strong arm methods, but the mainland no longer owed allegiance to Norway, though the Earl of Caithness and Sutherland remained independent of both kingdoms for a while yet.

Magnus after his expedition to the Hebrides adopted for himself and many of his followers the Celtic dress which is described in Magnus Berfaet's Saga of 1093 as: consisting of a short kyrtle or tunic, and a mantle while, as his nickname implies, the legs below the knee were bare, a garb showing little change from that of the 6th and 7th centuries, and common to all Scotland as is shown by the seals of the Scots' monarchs of this period which depict them attired in a similar fashion. The dress of the governing class from pre-Roman times, was to all intents and purposes the same in Scotland as in Ireland. The mantle or cloak fastened with a brooch, and the linen or silk leine or tunic, often embroidered and of rich design. These two principal garments differed but little from the peplos and chiton of the Greeks and the sagum and tunica of the Romans. The other form of dress was a jacket and close-fitting trews, the latter usually coming to the ankles and being secured under the instep, though there are early stone engravings showing short trews reaching only to just below the knee. It is quite likely that this latter costume belonged to the pre-Celtic peoples and it is not till later in history that we find the assimilation of the jacket and trews into the dress of the nobles.

The period covered by the reigns of Edgar and his successor Alexander I have left no record of events in Ross, but that of David I 1124–1153 was of immense moment to Ross and indeed to the whole Celtic kingdom, therefore it is important to get a clear picture of certain events which are usually portrayed as sweeping changes, not only in law and custom but also in personnel.

Certain Normans, heartily sick of the state of anarchy which existed in England under the usurper Stephen, or unsuccessful themselves at brigandage, came north as guests, where many of them married Celtic heiresses, and through these ladies, who in Scotland shared equality with their menfolk having equal rights of inheritance, they gained the support of their people, on whom the safety and prosperity of the family ultimately depended. These knights brought with them a new system of organization such as the registration of land tenure by Charter, but the vital difference between the feudal system of Scotland and that of France or England, which influences the whole of our history, is usually overlooked by the majority of those who write about or refer to Scottish history. In England the Norman feudal system was imposed on a conquered people, forcibly ousting many of the laws, and, to a lesser degree, the customs of the Angle and Saxon, whereas in Scotland it became interwoven with the existing system of the Celtic personal headship of the tribe, clan and sept. This applied equally in southern (lowland) Scotland as in the Highlands, where the Chief or Lord was not only the holder of land for himself, but was responsible for the maintenance of a free people's territorial rights, that is the clan lands which were inalienable; he remained essentially the leader of the people.

With the absorption of certain Norman ideas during the 12th century the usual Barons' Courts of Justice were instituted but they were merged with the Sabaid from 'Sab' a Prop—which continued to exist for centuries, and in these assemblies the voice of the clansmen was heard and respected. Every individual of the clan, however humble his position, had his place of honour as a member of the community; while his personal dignity and rights in the clan were fully established. Serfdom, except for prisoners of war, but even for them lasting only for a limited period, was never practised in the Highlands; while it existed for only a short time in the southern lowlands; where, however, it was revived by a measure passed in the 17th century applicable to colliers and salters, it lasted till 1775. The latter part of David's reign was happy and prosperous, while perhaps the most significant feature of the social life of Scotland in the middle ages was the absence of any parallel to the peasant risings of France and England in the 14th century.

King David completed the establishment of diocesan episcopacy, among others creating in 1124 the Bishopric of Ross with its Cathedral, Church and headquarters known as Chanonry by Rosemarkie and Fortrose, the first two bishops being named MacBeth, followed by Simeon.[1] Caithness with Sutherland also became a see, but not till the expulsion of the Norwegians did the Island of Lewis come into this scheme when it was included in the Diocese of the Isles.

Dingwall, like Tain and the little 'towns' of Ross consisted largely of wooden buildings, some of which would have owed their origin to Thorfinn's regime, and it is probable that King David was responsible for the first stone dwelling in Dingwall when he caused to be erected a Lazar House for lepers situated near the Royal Castle at the Peffrey estuary; even the Castle at this period was, in the main, a timber and earth rampart edifice.[2]

The title of *mormaer* had disappeared being replaced by earl, and we begin to come across the usual Norman-French judicial and fiscal titles; but in most cases the men leading the country were of the original Celtic, sometimes Celto-Norman, families, the hereditary leaders of

Note 1. For Roll of Bishops see Appendix II.
Note 2. For consecutive account of Dingwall Castle see Appendix III.

the Pictish and Scottish peoples. Had this not been the case, nothing would have induced the Celtic people of Scotland to have followed their lead with a loyalty and courage unsurpassed in history, not only during success, but rising to its grandest heights in disaster and desperate causes.

CHAPTER V

THE RISE OF THE O'BEOLANS EARLS OF ROSS AND THE FRESKINS OF MORAY AND SUTHERLAND

Chronological Table

A.D. 1156   Dynastic rebellion in Moray and Ross lasting till 1175.
A.D. 1169   Maurice Fitzgerald, the descendant of Gerald of Windsor who married Princess Nesta, daughter of the Welsh King Rhys killed in battle against the Normans, and 'Strongbow' Richard FitzGilbert Earl of Pembroke, go to Ireland to help Dermot of Leinster. Henry II of England alarmed at their power, blockades them with the help of 30 Norse galleys from the Isle of Man and the Hebrides.
A.D. 1174   King William 'The Lion' captured by English and imprisoned at Alnwick.
A.D. 1175   Death of Rury O'Connor last native King of Ireland.
A.D. 1189   Third Crusade headed by Emperor Frederick Barbarossa.
A.D. 1202   Fourth Crusade.
A.D. 1204   Latins take Constantinople.
A.D. 1206   Albigensian Crusade. Founding of University of Paris.
A.D. 1211   Final phase of rebellions in Moray and Ross ending 1235.
A.D. 1214   Birth of Roger Bacon.
A.D. 1215   Magna Carta.
A.D. 1224   Bishop Bricius Douglas transfers his H.Q. from Spynie to Elgin.
A.D. 1228   Fifth Crusade under Frederick II.
A.D. 1230   Completion of 140 new churches in Scotland including Elgin Cathedral; choir and undercroft of Glasgow Cathedral; St. Giles, Edinburgh; Beauly Priory; *Fearn* Abbey; Dornoch Cathedral.
A.D. 1233   Death of Alan last Prince of Galloway; he left no male heir.
A.D. 1248   Fifth Crusade under St. Louis to Egypt.
A.D. 1253   Earl of Buchan and Coadjutor Fergus, Justiciar for northern Scotland.
A.D. 1258   Scottish treaty with Welsh, who had fought under Prince Llewellyn with success against Henry of England, in 1257. Trade as well as military clauses were included.
         Coming of Galloglasses to Ulster under Donald Oge O'Donnell, who married Catriona MacSweeney, a descendant of the Suibhne of 1034. He became overlord of Tyrconnell, Sligo and Fermanagh. The power of these mail-clad professional warriors of the Gall-Gael checked for good the Norman advance into north west Ireland and they remained till the 16th century the most formidable element in Irish warfare.
A.D. 1259   A year of famine, storms and bad harvest. Boll of flour cost 4/-.
A.D. 1261   Latin Empire of Constantinople ends.

The first phase of the Moray rebellions, which had so intimately affected Ross, had ended with the forfeiture of the Earldom of Moray in 1130,[1] while many of the leading Pictish families were forced to leave that province and settle in Strathnaver, north-west Sutherland, where they formed the nucleus of Clan Morgan (Mackay), and while others founded famous houses in southern Scotland, particularly Fife.

The second phase opened with Donald MacHeth, son of Malcolm of Moray Earl of Ross, who this time took no part, opposing King Malcolm IV, basing his claim on descent from MacBeth's stepson Lulach. Donald did not last long as he was captured and imprisoned in 1156, but the result was by no means confined to Moray and was carried on by Somerled of the Isles,[2] the Celto-Norwegian King of the Hebrides.

This ancestor of Clan Donald was to inaugurate an Island principality which could challenge the Kingdom of Scotland, so that his descendants for centuries remained a threat to the Scottish Kings; meanwhile this widespread revolt continued for five years till a peace was patched up with Somerled.

Note 1. For table of Earls of Moray, see Appendix I b/1.
Note 2. For table of Lords of the Isles and MacDonalds, see Appendix I c/.

During the preceding reign Henry II of England had evicted large numbers of Flemish merchants, who had been welcomed in Scotland where they settled in the East coast towns, particularly Berwick, the Fife towns and Aberdeen. At these centres they soon built up a trade with the northern countries of Europe, which for long surpassed that of England, the intake of goods into Berwick exceeding that of London. From their advent begins the development of the Scottish Burghs, which played such an important part in the national and cultural development of our country. The country north of the Forth and Clyde was still the core of the Kingdom, the town of Inverness, grouped around its castle, being larger and of more importance than Edinburgh as yet, while the future division between Highlands and Lowlands was not yet apparent, and did not come about till much later when religion and not racial difference was the main cause.

In 1165 William I, 'the Lion', came to the throne of Scotland, and nine years later was faced with yet another rebellion in the north led by Donald Bane MacWilliam, who claimed the crown as the son of Duncan II and grandson of Malcolm III and Queen Ingibjorg.

King William marched an army into Ross in 1179, where Donald had secured the Royal Castle of Dingwall, subdued that strongpoint and caused to be built two new Royal Castles, Eddirdovir (Redcastle) on the Black Isle, and Dunskaith at Nigg, on the North Sutor of Cromarty, the revenues for the latter being provided by the Ferry tolls and some land, which in the 15th century endowed a prebend in Tain's Collegiate church. The King was aided on this expedition by Donald Munro, the third Baron, and the builder of the first tower of Foulis, but the trouble lasted for six years, till at last Prince Roland of Galloway, on 31st July 1187, surprised a party of rebels outside Inverness, among them MacWilliam himself, who was killed in the skirmish.

Some years later Harold Maddadson Earl of Caithness[1] egged on by his ambitious wife Gormflaith, the sister of Earl Malcolm MacHeth of Moray and Ross, tried to gain possession of those districts in Ross which had been subject to her brother. But the expedition commanded by his son Thorfinn III was soundly beaten by the King, and driven back over the River Oykel, closely pursued by the Lion who subdued Sutherland and Caithness until finally Harold was cornered in his stronghold at Thurso. Seeing the position was hopeless the Earl offered Thorfinn III as a hostage for future good behaviour, but failed to deliver him up according to his agreement, at Nairn, instead appearing himself, upon which he was at once forwarded to Edinburgh Castle where he was incarcerated till Thorfinn turned up to take his father's place.

Note 1. For Earls of Caithness, see Appendix I a/–.

Earl Harold was deprived of Sutherland, which was given to Hugo Freskin, father of the 1st Earl of Sutherland and a member of the great Pictish family of Moray,[1] who were already established in Sutherland as well as owning vast possessions in Moray and elsewhere. Harold was deprived of half Caithness, which was granted to Jarl St. Ragnvald's grandson, Harald Ungi, and to this was added half the Jarldom of Orkney by the King of Norway. St. Ragnvald of Orkney was the founder of the Cathedral at Kirkwall which he had dedicated to his uncle Jarl St. Magnus. Ungi did not, however, live long to enjoy the possessions, as Harold Maddadson returned the same year and slew him in battle.

After this Harold tried to make his peace with the King of Scots, but was unsuccessful, not because he had liquidated Ungi but owing to the fact that he refused to comply with the monarch's demand that he should take back to his bosom his first and lawful wife Afrika; so instead of granting a pardon King William invited Harald Gudrodson, King of Man to drive out the truculent Earl. This he did, leaving six stewards to run Caithness, Orkney and Shetland, returning himself to the Isle of Man.

But Harold was not yet through; he returned in 1201, slew one of the stewards, severely punished the Caithness folk, and when Bishop John interceded for them, blinded that cleric and removed part of his tongue. It is nice to know that in spite of this harsh treatment, the poor man partially recovered and was able to administer his diocese till 1213. The remaining stewards removed with all haste to the Scottish Court, where King William to avenge the Bishop so mutilated the hostage Thorfinn III, that he died in Roxburgh Castle. The King then marched north but Harold thinking discretion the better part of valour fled to King John in England, returning about a year later, when he was allowed to keep a part of Caithness till his death in 1206, when he was succeeded by his remaining sons David and John in Orkney and the half of Caithness.

Ross and Moray were the focal point of these northern rebellions as their population and leaders were predominantly Pictish, and they clung to the old Celtic laws of succession, especially as their *Mormaers* and Earls, so closely connected with the Crown, saw their chances of kingship slipping with the new-fangled notions of invariable succession by the eldest son or grandson of the reigning monarch, but it was not only in these provinces that the new system was unwelcome. In addition to all this, William the Lion early in his reign had not endeared himself to the country when he was caught by the English, which of course might happen to anybody, but in order to get free he had sworn allegiance to Henry of England—an allegiance which was not his to

Note 1. For Freskins of Moray and Sutherland and Earls of Sutherland see Appendix I e/.

barter, and was only cancelled for a heavy ransom later paid to King Richard Coeur de Lion of England, who was finding the customary difficulty in financing his crusades; Ross's share, collected by the clergy in 1189 being 100 marks.

In 1211 the Thanes of Ross rose under Guthred son of the late Royal claimant Donald Bane MacWilliam, with claims to the *Mormaerdom* of Ross; but a few years later he was defeated and beheaded by the most able military leader of his time, Fearchar O'Beolan *Mac an-t-Sagairt*—son of the Red Priest—Lay Abbot and Lord of Applecross. Fearchar was knighted for a victory in Galloway 1215, which province he was later to subdue for the Scottish Crown, and soon after as a reward for his many services he was to win the Earldom of Ross.[1]

Yet another rising faced the new King Alexander II not only in Moray, but in other parts of Scotland, particularly the part Brython-Pictish Province of Galloway, the rebel leaders being Donald Bane MacWilliam the Younger, and Kenneth MacHeth, son of Donald MacHeth of Moray,[2] who to increase their own resources had imported Irish mercenaries. But Sir Fearchar speedily crushed this last outbreak, which left him free to continue his successes in Galloway, the whole Province being finally subdued in 1235. Fearchar was created Earl of Ross in 1226 adding to his own patrimony the lands of his new Earldom; other estates which had been granted to him in Galloway remained in the family for two hundred years. From the obscurity of Applecross he had stepped into a position of major importance in the Nation, so that it is not surprising to find his daughters chosen as wives by two other important men of the time. The first Euphemia married Walter Freskin de Moravia of Duffus bringing as her dowry the lands of Clon in Ross; while the second daughter Christina had as husband Olave 'the Black' King of Man and the father of Leoid the ancester of the MacLeod Chiefs of Glenelg, Harris and Dunvegan in Skye and Lewis.[3]

While campaigning in the south-west Fearchar had recruited two White Canons from the Praemonstratensian Abbey of *Candida Casa* to take charge of his new Abbey of *Fearn* founded by him about 1223–1227, first at Mid-*Fearn* on the site of the old Ninian foundation but moved between the years 1238–1242 to New *Fearn* in the Parish of Tarbat. The marriage of his second daughter involved him in fighting on behalf of Olave; but in 1244 he went with a commission to Rome to inform the Pope of a Peace Treaty with England. A story is told that the Earl accompanied his King to the christening celebrations of Edward I

Note 1. For table of Earls of Ross, see Appendix I b/2.
Note 2. For table of MacHeth Earls of Moray, see Appendix I b/1.
Note 3. For table of MacLeods, see Appendix I d/.

in London, where he was challenged by the Court Champion to a duel; Fearchar made a vow to found a Religious House in far-away Ross in the event of his victory which to the great joy of King Alexander and the ill-concealed annoyance of the English Court he won. Thus, it is said, was born the idea of *Fearn* Abbey.

Early in Alexander II's reign more trouble developed in Caithness, because their Earl, John,[1] had either participated, or at least remained an interested spectator, in the roasting of Bishop Adam by his flock over a disagreement as to the amount of 'Peter's Pence' that was due to the Bishop. This, not unnaturally, caused consternation among other clerics in St. Andrews, so that they persuaded the King to go north in 1222 to deal with the matter, which he did with severity, helped by the Munros and the Sutherland Freskins. Earl John excommunicated by the Pope, died in 1231, leaving an only daughter a hostage at the Scots Court. She eventually married Magnus, son of the Earl of Angus, carrying to him the Earldom of Caithness and Orkney which passed in time to the Earls of Strathearn and thence to the St. Clairs by marriage.

The development of Ross was progressing rapidly as Scotland's prosperity increased by leaps and bounds. Tain was already venerated for its girth and shrine of St. Duthac, who had suffered martyrdom at the hands of Norwegian pirates in c. 1088; while just across the Firth Bishop Gilbert the translator of the Psalms into Gaelic, was building Dornoch Cathedral dedicated to the Blessed Virgin Mary, the site being very near to the old church dedicated to the Pictish Saint Barr (Finbar). Of Gilbert a legend tells how he saved Dornoch from destruction: soon after the completion of the cathedral a great beast, which with its fiery breath had been laying waste the forests of Sutherland, approached Dornoch threatening its destruction, but Gilbert having the additional powers of a saint went out to meet the great beast, thus with the sharpest arrow in his quiver slew the monster and saving the town. Possibly legend has represented Viking raiders as the 'great beast'.

The Bishop of Ross was established in his Cathedral church at Chanonry, at Fortrose, while south-east across the Moray Firth close to the castle of Duffus rose the Cistercian Abbey of Kinloss completed about 1150, and at Elgin was being built the beautiful cathedral, which was to become the headquarters of the See of Moray in place of the older buildings at Spynie.

In Easter Ross the small Burghs were growing, Fortrose and Rosemarkie both benefiting from their position as the ecclesiastical capital of Ross and the consequent presence of the Bishop with his numerous

Note For the connecting links of the Jarldom and Earldom of Caithness see table, Appendix I a/.

Note For growth of Religious Houses during this period in Scotland, see Appendix II.

clergy; Tain and Cromarty were increasing in importance, while Dingwall had received its first charter as a Royal Burgh in 1226, a gift which carried with it many trading privileges including the right of holding a weekly market within its bounds.

At Beauly, which until much later in history lay within the Earldom of Ross, a Cistercian Priory had been founded in 1230 by Sir John de Bisset, an adventurer of Norman extraction whose relations are famous in Irish history as the Lords of the Glens of Antrim, and several branches of this family had acquired lands in Berwick, western Inverness (*Garmoran*) and Ross; this new endowment in Ross was confirmed the following year by a Bull of Pope Gregory IX. But a few years later Sir John was deprived by the Crown of the Castle and lands of Lovat, having failed to take in a sporting manner the defeat of a member of his family during a tournament; indeed he went so far as to express his resentment by burning to death in his castle the victor of the match, the Earl of Atholl. The Bisset strain was, however, carried on by his daughter who married the next Lord of Lovat, Graham, and their heiress daughter in turn married the first Fraser Lord of Lovat whose descendants still quarter the Bisset arms.[1]

King Alexander II meanwhile was endeavouring to terminate the Norwegian domination of the Hebrides as well as subdue those parts of Argyll which were held by the Norse supporters, Somerled's descendants. To accomplish this scheme the King made full use of his general the Earl of Ross with his eldest son and heir William MacFearchar, who after his father's death c. 1250 harried the Norse subjects in Skye with such vigour, not to say cruelty, that it caused King Hakon to complain bitterly to the Scots King, with special reference to the depredations caried out by Ross and other west coast Chiefs, especially Kiarnach Maccamal; and finally to start preparations for his invasion of Scotland which terminated at Largs in 1263.

The homes of the people had not greatly altered, being simple structures of wood or turf though sometimes of stone, in which case they closely resembled the solid but primitive Black House still to be seen in the west. The majority of the Castles in Easter Ross were probably of the Motte and Bailey type: a central timber built hall of two or three storeys erected on either a natural or artificial Motte or mound, surrounded by a timber stockade which with the area it enclosed was known as the Bailey, holding other buildings such as stables and storehouses. The Castle at Dingwall was of this type, as were David's Castle near Conon House and Avoch at Pitfour on the Black Isle, owned by Walter of Avoch, Petty, etc., a member of the great Freskin de Moravia family and in 1255 one of the guardians of the boy King Alexander III and his young wife Princess Margaret of England.

Note 1. For table of Frasers, Lord of Lovat, see Appendix I f/.

The Hall served as the dwelling-place of the Scottish nobility, and the whole enclosure as a place of refuge for the neighbouring folk; to prevent fire, so often the cause of disaster to the defenders during a siege, the walls were sometimes daubed with clay.

These castles were now being reconstructed on much the same layout, but in stone, though there were already a number of all stone castles, especially in areas where timber was scarce as on parts of the west coast, while it should be remembered that the Picts already had behind them the tradition of a thousand years of building in stone. The newer castles remained simple in design: a tower of stone and in place of the timber stockade a stone wall enclosing the area about the tower, i.e. the bailey; sometimes either the whole castle, or an exposed flank, had the added protection of a dry or wet fosse. The main defensive line was the 'wall head' of the tower where the platform or walk was protected by a crenellated parapet; and this walk—in early times of wood—often projected on stone 'corbels' with spaces in between, through which all forms of unpleasantness could be dropped on the uninvited guest; these wooden platforms were not replaced by permanent stone battlements until the close of the 14th century.

The Earl of Ross had become the most powerful man in the north, owning many castles which dominated the most fertile areas in Easter Ross. His lands in Ross stretched from Evanton to the Dornoch Firth and over most of the Black Isle; while in the west lay the great Lay-Abbacy, or Barony, of Applecross with its outlying territories reaching into Torridon, *Gairloch*, Lochalsh, *Lochcarran* and part of Lochbroom. In the three latter districts the descendants of the mighty Somerled, who had met his end in battle at Renfrew 1164, had as legatees of the Norwegian powers certain rather nebulous claims and interests, eventually made good during the 15th century by the marriage of Alexander MacDonald Lord of the Isles and 10th Earl of Ross, who took as his second wife the heiress of Applecross. This lady, the last of her line, was descended from Malcolm the Green (or Red) Abbot Earl Fearchars' second son who had received Applecross as his patrimony.

The Earl's very numerous Superiorities lay over the rest of Ross which then included much of what was to be the County of Inverness; from there they spread over some fifteen Baronies in Moray, Badenoch, and Aberdeen; while in addition Fearchar had collected various estates in south western Scotland and Argyll. *Coigach* and Assynt still held by Clan MacNical, were not yet included in Ross, they formed part of the old Province of Ness but now had some connection with Sutherland though influenced by the Island Principalities of the Gall-Gael.

The Ross Earls came to rely greatly on Clan Munro[1], who under

Note 1. For table of Munros, see Appendix I g/.

their Chief the Baron of Foulis were enlarging their territories and
increasing in power, no doubt helped by their Charter from King
Alexander. From 1232 dates a friendship between George Munro of
Foulis, whose mother was a daughter of William 1st Earl of Sutherland,
and the Sutherland family which was to last through the centuries to
the present day. Fearchar's own clan, Anrias, much later to be known
as Clan Ross, previously in occupation of Mid and Wester Ross, were
becoming increasingly in evidence throughout Easter Ross, especially
round Tain, *Fearn*, on the southern bank of the Oykel river and south of
the Dornoch Firth.

In the west Clan *Mathan* (Matheson) centred on Lochalsh were
probably the most numerous and powerful, but before long were to be
superseded by their kinsmen, Clan Kenneth (Mackenzie)[1] who were to
spread from their stronghold of *Eilean Donan* in Kintail[2] north and east,
conquering or absorbing all who stood in their way, until in later
centuries their lands stretched from coast to coast. The Chief of this, as
yet, small clan in all probability shared a common ancestor with the
Earls of Ross and Clan Anrias; at any rate there is no tradition to
connect them in any way with the Gall-Gael, whereas it is probable
that Clan Matheson had come into the Norse orbit.

'Mackenzie's shirt of Mail,' the Clan Mac Rae [McRa] were not yet
located in Kintail where they were to become so famous as the loyal
followers and bodyguard of the Mackenzie Chiefs, Barons of Kintail,
providing the archers for the clan forces. They were still a very small
clan living on the south shore of the Beauly Firth with headquarters at
Clunes within the lordship of Lovat, till they moved west early in the
14th century. Another clan, which was to arrive in Kintail about the
same time eventually providing many of the hereditary standard-
bearers to Clan Kenneth, were the MacLennans (Logans) of the Black
Isle. Tradition says that early in the 14th century their chief Gilliegorm
had a row with his relative Hugh Lord Lovat, which resulted in a
battle at Kessock and the extermination of Clan Logan with the
exception of Gilliegorm's wife, Lovat's daughter, who shortly after gave
birth to a deformed son, which deformity saved his life, as it was on this
account that Lovat spared him. This boy, brought up by the Monks of
Beauly, eventually took Holy Orders, founding the churches of Kilmor
in Skye and Kilchrinnan in Glenelg, while like many another he left
progeny in spite of being a priest. One of his sons became a devotee of
St. Finnan, while his descendants in turn were known as MacGhille
Fhinnein (Maclennan) who settled beside the MacRaes in Kintail.

During the 13th and 14th centuries several smaller clans or septs of
Kintail and west Ross joined themselves to Mackenzie: MacIver, a

Note 1. For table of Mackenzies; Earls of Seaforth; Cromartie, etc. see Appendix I h/.
Note 2. For consecutive history of *Eilean Donan* Castle see Appendix IV.

sept from Argyll who had settled round Loch Broom, Leckmelm being the home of their Chieftain; Clan Tearlaich in Glenelchaig; some Farquharsons a sept of Clan Buchanan, known locally as Murchisons, in Lochalsh and Kintail; as also Finlaysons or Mac Fhionnlaigh, who are said to have come from Ireland in the 6th century; MacAulays a sept of Clan Alpin, in Kintail; and the MacBeolans, a section of Clan Anrias who dwelt in Glenshiel and on the south side of Loch Duich, their territory reaching as far as Kylerhea; lastly a small number of the name MacVanish though these may have been a later Mackenzie sept as they are not mentioned till 1600.

Turning again to Easter Ross: Sir William de Montealto [Mowat], member of a Celto-Norman family and possibly holder of the Castle Leod Barony, was appointed Sheriff of Cromarty in 1263. But by 1306 Sir William Urquhart—whose family probably sprang from the same roots as Clans Mackay and Forbes in the Province of Moray, had been for some time the hereditary constables of Urquhart Castle, a Royal stronghold on Loch Ness—had become Sheriff of Cromarty, partly due, no doubt, to his matrimonial alliance with the House of Ross, his wife being a daughter of William the IInd Earl. In 1315 the Bruce was to grant this valuable and now hereditary office to the boy Hugh son and heir of William IIIrd Earl of Ross, but soon after it was resigned officially into Urquhart hands, which probably in fact it had never left, Adam de Urquhart becoming before 1349 hereditary Sheriff of Cromarty with which post went the hereditary Vice-Admiralty of the north eastern coasts of Scotland. After the advent of Clan Urquhart to the Black Isle the Mowat family fade out in Ross to reappear further north as vassals to the Earls of Sutherland.

Ross less Cromarty was included in the Sheriffdom of Inverness; not till 1504 was a separate Royal Sheriff appointed to hold Courts at Dingwall, Tain and in Caithness, but Ross did not become a sheriffdom on its own until 1649, though there had been for a period, a sheriffdom of Tarbat in Easter Ross prior to 1480.

Clan Anrias had several septs and/or vassals of importance. The Celto-Norman family of Vass, De Vaux or De Vallibus, of Loch Slyn Castle in Easter Ross—where the name still exists—whose progenitor had come north from Lothian where previously his family had settled, building Dirleton Castle in the 13th century; MacCullochs (McLulich) of Tarrel, Plaids, etc.; and the Dingwalls, later Lords of Kildun situated below Humberston, and Ussie, who were to remain important lairds in Ross till early in the 18th century. We shall see them appearing on many occasions during the story. Much of their land was to be sold to the House of Kintail during the 16th and 17th centuries, Ussie, Kildun etc. but there still survives a direct descendant of the Dingwalls of Kildun in Mexico, where his properties are held under the name of

Kildun, Meikle Ussie, and Stadbruck, the latter being another Scottish property once belonging to the family.

Ussie was obtained by them from the last Earl of Ross in 1463, in exchange for lands held previously by the Dingwalls at Arkboll and Inchfure in the Barony of Delny. Sir John Dingwall of Kildun the Provost of Trinity College, Edinburgh, was given lands by James V in *Gairloch* in 1527, but he resided in the old Lazar House in Dingwall, and it is unlikely that he gained much profit from these western possessions where the Mackenzie and MacLeod influence was predominant. In addition to these there existed in the west the powerful MacTagart family in Applecross; and in Glenshiel the O'Beolans who, however, seem to have had a closer affinity with Clan Kenneth at an early date.

Ross was taking a full share in what has been described as a 'Golden Age for Scotland'; Dingwall, Cromarty and Inverness were becoming important sea-ports; to these places came the wines and silks of the Continent and the products of the Netherlands and Baltic countries, in exchange for salted fish of all sorts, hides, wool, grain, fresh water pearls, and the work of the Celtic jewellers. Inverness was building ships and we find during this reign a 'great ship' being built to the order of the Breton Count of St. Pol.

CHAPTER VI

THE END OF A NORWEGIAN KINGDOM—THE CLAN

Chronological Table

The Golden Age, made possible by a flourishing trade and peaceful relations with England, still had a few years to run before it was destroyed by the desperate struggle for independence against English aggression. The Church in Scotland was very vigorous, still uncorrupted by its growing wealth; Scottish students from all the Cathedral schools and Religious Houses were spreading out to other seats of learning, especially Paris, Bologna in Italy and Oxford. This is the age which produced in Scotland such great names as Thomas of Ercildonne the poet, the scholars Duns Scotus a Franciscan monk, and Michael Scot the translator of Aristotle, while another sidelight on this era of advance is given by references to the popularity of the masque, dancing and music, as well as the very high esteem in which scholars and physicians were held.

Farming, the major industry of the country, was being encouraged, and laws enacted to increase areas under the plough; from these laws the town dweller was not exempt, for in addition to the Burgh lands, each householder had to own his 'toft' of one rood for which he paid a rent of 7d. to the Crown. The land measurements of the Middle Ages are still recalled in the names of many field and place names: The *fearann peighinn*, the penny land was subdivided into the lephin ½d. and feorling ¼d. land, the last being reckoned as 'one cow' land—the amount one bullock could plough in a day. The larger units were the merkland, about 35 acres assessed at 4d. and davoch assessed at twenty pennies, covering about 416 acres, commemorated in Ross by the Four Davochs of Maluach, Cairnie, Carte and Pollo situated on the Heights of Fodderty and Brae.

An effort was being made to introduce a heavier breed of horse, for military purposes; many were imported from as far afield as Hungary and Poland as well as England, the nobles being encouraged to raise the size of their mounts 'by plenishing their studs with mares and great stallions,' while severe penalties were exacted for exporting horses. Not till after Bannockburn and the capture of the English heavy cavalry, were these horses to become noticably more plentiful. Roads as we understand them hardly existed, though the Burghs and private individuals made some effort, seldom very great, in this direction; the rest of the country depended on tracks made by the constant passage of man and his 'Kye', traversing the flanks of the Straths, as the lower levels were more often than not swamps. On both east and west coasts, great use was made of the sea routes, the western chiefs for many centuries modelled their *Birlinns* on the famous Norwegian galleys.

The practice of Heraldry, introduced by the Normans, was becoming common among noble families throughout Scotland, as this naturally appealed to a people who for long had used emblems for decoration as well as recognition in battle, and who like all Celts were genealogically-minded. Their enthusiasm together with a marked sense of independence led some families in the Highlands to create arms which did not conform altogether with the strict laws of heraldry or the authority of the Lyon King of Arms, this trait being, naturally, more marked in the isolated clan areas of the west where certain characteristics of the modified Norman feudalism were adopted but slowly. It was not till the 16th century that heraldry throughout the Highlands became regularized though at some earlier date the Lord Lyon had appointed a Ross Herald, and a Dingwall Pursuivant, with another for Ormond.

We read of an unfortunate incident in 1596 when John Gledstanes, nephew and heir to the laird of Quothquhan in Lanarkshire, 'stikit' John Purdie, Ross Herald, both having quarrelled in their cups; Gledstanes was beheaded as a result of the incident.

From the middle of the 13th century judicial records and land charters, introduced north of the Forth by King Alexander I, 1107–24, become more frequent in the Highlands; fortunately a large number of these still survive, though many have perished by fire, through deeds of violence or international theft, and far more from simple neglect. Some of these were written in Gaelic, though the majority that survive are either in Monk Latin or Scots. Despite the theory that the Celt was very averse to parchment it is nevertheless true that the majority of extant documents referring to a nearly hundred per cent Celtic Ross are drawn up, signed, sealed, and witnessed by Celts.

It is, however, surprising to find the Norman Writ known as Mort d'Ancestor by which succession by an eldest son is placed beyond dispute, being upheld in Inverness A.D. 1260 by a jury summoned by the

King to settle a succession dispute relating to Blantyre and composed almost entirely of Highlanders, MacEdolf, MacMalcolm, MacHoutre, MacKersan, etc. Although in theory, and at times, in practice the law of tanistry was applied after the 13th century to regulate the succession to the chiefship of a clan, it is noticeable in all clan genealogies that succession by the eldest son is far and away the most usual procedure, though chiefship, and celtic dignities generally, passed if need be to females with the provision in most mediaeval entails that the heiress marry a gentleman of the clan or one who would assume the clan name and designation.

In the last chapter we left King Hakon of Norway preparing a great fleet in order, not only to consolidate his island kingdom, but to invade Scotland itself. Early in 1263 having summoned Orkney pilots, he sailed from Norway making Shetland in two days, thence concentrating his fleet off Kirkwall in Scapa Flow. Having failed to induce a part of his fleet to sail south and ravage the lands of Moray, Hakon sailed on the 10th August, after an eclipse of the sun, for his western expedition, but without the Orkney contingent of ships which he had ordered from the Earl of Orkney and Caithness Magnus III, the excuse given being that the ships were not yet ready. This lack of keenness was probably due to the foresight of King Alexander III who had collected hostages from Caithness, and these were already in the custody of the Sheriff of Inverness, Laurence de Grant. The same day the fleet rounded Cape Wrath coming to anchor off Durness, the next port of call on the following day being Stornoway, Lewis.

At Kyleakin Hakon was joined by the reinforcements of Magnus King of Man and Dougall of Bute, King of the South Isles, but John of Lorn and Argyll the senior descendant of Somerled the King of all the Sudreys (Hebrides) did not appear, as he had already submitted to the Scots King. The fleet consisting of some two hundred galleys, the largest number ever seen in these waters, then sailed south to Kerrera, the place where Alexander II had died on his last campaign against the Norsemen. Now the King of Scots had no idea where the landing would take place, which made it extremely difficult to decide on the concentration area for his army, so that he was forced to rely on levies and local chiefs to watch much of the long and vulnerable coast-line, while he himself held a mobile reserve in the south west. There followed a certain amount of raiding but by means of parleys Alexander managed to hold up proceedings till far into September, thus gaining a most valuable ally, the weather, which was showing signs of becoming rough and would prove invaluable in upsetting Hakon's sea-based force.

On October 2nd the storm broke, and the attempted landing at Largs was defeated by the Royal Army, who took full advantage of the disorganization caused among the ships by the gale, defeating in detail the enemy as they attempted to land in their smaller craft. The gallant old warrior Hakon withdrew to sea, and on October 14th parted from his allies, returning to Orkney, where he died in the Bishop's Palace; his body lying in state in St. Magnus Cathedral till it was removed to Bergen for burial.

The results of the victory were great: the King of Man submitted becoming liegemen to the Scots king, the Hebrides being finally subdued by an army under Buchan and Alan the Doorward. Certain readjustments were made in the possessions of the several Kings of the Isles, Somerled's descendants: the Islands of Arran and Bute were removed from Dugall and his brother Allan the chiefs of Clan Ruari, but they were recompensed with some of the North Isles. Skye and Lewis now came under the Earl of Ross, who, however, was fined in 1266 £45 and 180 cows for his lack of enthusiasm in the recent struggle, probably due to the influence of his sister Christina, wife of the late King of Man Olave, and mother of King Magnus. This fine, taking into account the different values of the present day, was heavy but Ross, apart from some injury to his pride would not have experienced any difficulty in paying the imposition. As we saw, the lands set aside for the maintenance of the Earldom of Ross at its erection in 1226, stretched from Evanton to Tarbat Ness and the Dornoch Firth including also a large part of the Black Isle; in other words most of the best agricultural land in Ross and indeed the north of Scotland.

This area was divided up into Baronies each one being administered from its castle which was occupied by a vassal of the Earl unless he was in residence himself, such strongholds were Balcony at Evanton; Delny; Lochslin; Balloan at Tarbat Ness; Ormond—which being the same as Avoch was probably a superiority because, as previously mentioned, it belonged to the de Moray family; and Cromarty; both on the Black Isle. Dingwall, Redcastle and Dunskaith were held for the King at this period but over all other Castles in Ross the Earl would doubtless claim a superiority, not necessarily acknowledged by their owners. Further west above Strathpeffer was his hunting lodge of Kinellan, a small castle built on the ancient *Crannog* in the *Loch*.

In Wester Ross his position is more obscure, but probably depended on a number of rather doubtful superiorities, except in those areas which still remained in his family, namely, the Barony—or great Lay Abbacy—of Applecross, which original heritage had gone to Malcolm the Green Abbot Earl Fearchar's second son who, in alliance with Kermac *MacMathan*, had proved himself to be an enthusiastic warrior against the Norwegians during the recent wars, and who was to be ancestor in the female line of the MacDonalds of Lochalsh.

The main revenue producing units for the Earldom, in Easter Ross were: the five Mains or Home Farms of Kinnairdie, Balcony, Delny,

Kessock, Kinellan, and all the ferries and mills in the *Machair* (eastern lowlands) of Ross, the latter of considerable value though the Law of Thirlage passed in 1284 forbidding private milling was never rigorously enforced in the Highlands, vide the great numbers of Querns and grinding songs. Such monopoly mills were: Milnain, Tympan Mill at Kinettas and Milntoun, which eventually passed from the Earls of Ross to the Earls of Cromartie; but the chief source of wealth in the Highlands were the great herds of hill cattle, the price of a good beast being about nine shillings during the 13th century.

In addition to the 'home area' the Earl possessed estates, already referred to, in Galloway, Renfrew and Argyll; while holding Superiorities in Glen Urquhart with its castle; and Glen Morriston; in Moray the Baronies of Balmakyth, Boath, Banchre, Rate, Knowdie, Kinsteary, Kilravoch, East Geddes, Dumnaglass, and Cawdor; in Badenoch Inneurmerky; in Aberdeenshire the lands of Auchterless and King Edward. Some few of the above lands and superiorities may not have accrued to the Earls of Ross till slightly later, among them Kinnardie. This farm attached to Dingwall Castle, naturally did not come to the Earl till the family got possession of the castle.

With the marches of our own Province yet other changes and events followed the Norwegian failure to refound a western Kingdom, John of Lorne and Argyll who as King of the Hebrides had refused to fight for Hakon of Norway remained in possession of his mainland territory and southern Islands, while Somerled's other great-grandson, Angus *Mór*, Lord of Islay the ancestor of the Lords of the Isles, retained Islay and Kintyre in spite of his somewhat half-hearted support of Norway. A force was sent into Caithness to impose a fine on the people for having contributed a levy on behalf of Hakon's expedition; probably both impositions were equally unpopular, 'but needs must when the devil drives'. Among the fines shown in the national accounts for the Sheriffdom of Inverness during the 13th century, and collected by the Justiciar who made his progress twice yearly, are the following for 1263: £5 from Ross—£7 from Moray—£1 from Caithness, probably exclusive of the expenses for his compulsory entertainment, while the Earls of Caithness and Sutherland made further payments of £33.6.8. and £20 respectively which are described as part of their fines.

The Treaty of Perth signed in the summer of 1266 finally brought back the Hebrides to the Kingdom of Scotland after 400 years of Norwegian domination. Another result was the immediate increase in the number of east coast and Netherlands fishing boats exploiting the western grounds, now less troubled by the 'Broken men of no clan' about whom they had complained in 1260, but these free-lance brigands of no clan were to appear again in the future as a menace to the fishing fleets. The western waters had been famous for their herring for a long time, the Vikings naming one place in Wester Ross Sild Vik which means Herring Bay, and known to-day as Shieldaig.

The Clan histories and tradition state that the Mackenzie Chief of this period was Colin and there are two theories as to his identity, either of which may be right. Sir George Mackenzie, Viscount Tarbat who wrote a Clan History in the 17th century maintains that Colin was a younger son of the great Celto-Norman Geraldine family in Ireland and married an heiress daughter of *MacMathan* (Matheson) Chief of the Clan and its septs in the west, closely connected with Applecross and Clan Anrias, and that through this lady he came into possession of Kintail and the Chiefship of the clan or sept in that district.

The other theory is that Colin was by birth a Mackenzie, and a very attractive legend tells us about him. Colin was born during the reign of Alexander II (1214-49) and his father, the Chief of Clan Kenneth, desired to imbue his only son with supernatural powers, so in order to accomplish this gave him his first drink from the skull of a Raven, and when the boy grew up he discovered that he could understand the language of birds. One day a flock of starlings settled on the roof of the Chief's *dun* on *Eilean Donan*, and made so much noise that they annoyed the old man who told his son to go and find out what all the disturbance was about. On his return the young man reported that the conversation among the starlings was to the effect that one day the Chief would find himself in the position of servitor to his own son, while still residing in his own castle. This and perhaps the youth's uppishness rankled with the old man, so that shortly afterwards Colin took himself off to France where his powers greatly impressed the King, whose court he rid of a plague of sparrows. For this service he was presented with a fully equipped galley in which he visited many lands, including one in which he gained merit by ridding the court of a plague of rats, through the medium of a cat which always accompanied him on board.

After a lapse of ten years he returned home and moored his splendid galley between Totaig and *Eilean Donan*; his father thinking his visitor to be, if not a king, some puissant prince, entertained him royally, serving with his own hand the wine to his guest; in this manner was the prophecy of the starlings fulfilled. When Colin made known his identity, his father, at first, could not believe that this rich and ex-perienced man of the world was truly his son, but was eventually con-vinced by the sight of a birthmark on the youth's shoulder.

Now whether Colin was a Geraldine or Mackenzie born, his possible foreign experiences and the strategic position of his territory made him useful to Alexanders II and III in their struggle with the Norsemen, so that he was told to re-build and modernize *Eilean Donan* Castle as a strong point against their raids. It was while hunting with the former monarch in the Royal Forest of Mar that he was able to save the royal life which was endangered by a wounded stag, the King having been unhorsed, for which service Alexander granted him the *Cabar Feidh* (stag's head) for his coat of arms, a device borne ever afterwards by his descendants.

At the battle of Largs Colin played a distinguished part; tradition stating that he was with the Royal Army, which resulted in succeeding generations of Chiefs claiming the right to form part of the King's body-guard, a right exercised for the last time on Flodden Field. As a reward for his services Colin was granted a charter for the lands of Kintail, which lands were always held direct from the King, unlike certain later Mackenzie possessions held under charter from the Earls of Ross, a fact proved by a charter renewing the original grant, to 'Murdo filius Kennethi de Kintail' given by David II in 1362.

Possibly owing to the independent position and growing power of Clan Kenneth after Largs, a feud developed between them and the Earls of Ross, which lasted spasmodically for many years, only properly closing down during periods when both parties were fighting in the wars against the 'auld enemy' England. William, second Earl of Ross was the first who tried to settle the misunderstanding by force of arms; he attempted to take the castle of *Eilean Donan* by storm but was repulsed by Kenneth, with loss. Many similar attempts were to be made in the future and all were to meet with the same fate.

Leod, a brother of Magnus the last King of Man who died in 1265, had inherited from his father King Olave III, the Islands of *Uist*, Harris, Lewis and Glenelg on the mainland, while the lands of Dun-vegan in Skye were added to his patrimony by his marriage to the daughter of MacHarald, the Norse King's Chamberlain or Armunn, a post held by this family since the end of the 9th century. Leod died in 1280 leaving two sons, the first Norman who inherited Glenelg, Dun-vegan and Harris, the second, Torquil, whose patrimony was the Islands of Lewis, Raasay and South Rona, Waterness in Skye, and part of *Gairloch* on the mainland of Ross. Skye and Lewis were, nominally at least, held from the Earl of Ross, while Glenelg was probably held in conjunction with the Bisset family who still had interests in this part of Inverness.

The first charter to *Siol* Torquil is granted by David II 1341-71, to Torquil MacLeod for the Barony of Assynt acquired by conquest plus marriage with the MacNical heiress. His other lands were held from the Earl of Ross and the Lord of the Isles;—with Assynt went *Coigach*.

By the end of the century it was appreciated that the Royal Sheriff of Inverness could not administer the King's justice efficiently in the west, so in 1290 John Balliol created a separate sheriffdom for Skye and Wester Ross, vesting in the Chiefs the administration of justice in their own areas, a measure which shows unusual sense on the part of Balliol. In practice they had always done this, as, beside their more recent

Baron's right of 'Pit and Gallows,' they exercised the far older Brehon laws, while it was seldom that a Royal Sheriff visited the more independent areas at any rate on duty, as his reception might not have been cordial. The ties between chief and clan were very close, and they infinitely preferred the more purely Celtic forms of procedure.

Before leaving this period of the last King of the House of Dunkeld, Alexander III, and entering the troubled epoch introduced by the untimely death of the Maid of Norway, let us for a moment look at the Clan system in more detail, as carried on with varying degrees of change due to outside contacts till half way through the 18th century. The leader of the clan was the chief *ceann-cinnidh*, he and his family circle, together with a very large number of officials, lived in his castle. If he had more than one castle it was put in charge of a reliable relative or a constable. The numbers of his entourage depended on the clan's importance, but usually consisted of the *ard ghillean an tighe*, the Gentlemen of the Household; *an seanachaidh* the clan historian, keeper of the records, bard and orator for all ceremonial occasions; the harper, an hereditary office; one or more seneschals, whose duties included the seating of guests at table in correct order of precedence by touching the place with the white wand of their office; *am fear* sporain, the treasurer, who for his services held some land in the township. Next in order of importance came the standard-bearer and piper both hereditary offices; the sword bearer, who corresponded to the squire, carried the helmet and two-handed sword of his chief; and a henchman, who stood fully armed behind his master's chair at meals. In addition there was a considerable body-guard, the pick of the young gentlemen of the clan.

The internal economy of this great household was the job of *am fear fardaiche*, best described as the quartermaster, who also made all quartering and feeding arrangements when the chief was travelling, he held no lands but was recompensed from a due on the hides of all cattle killed on festive occasions, or captured during a *creach*. Then there was the cup-bearer and taster—poison not being unknown; and the cockman or warder who had the care of any prisoners.

The forester in charge of the chief's domain had the right, in ancient days, to claim the hunting dress and weapons of his chief on return from the hunt, but this custom proving rather inconvenient had been changed to a croft with free grazing for his own beasts in the forest. Lower down in the scale were grooms, the gillie in charge of sumpter ponies, the running footmen, the head piper's and harper's servant, and last but not least the Fool or Jester, allowed plenty of licence provided he was funny. Often a private chaplain acted as tutor to the children and secretary to the chief unless, like the Lords of the Isles, he kept a separate scribe for this duty. To this great household must be added the numerous female helpers controlled by the lady of the house.

The clan was divided into further divisions or septs under chieftains (*ceann-tighe*) the heads of the most important houses of the clan, all relations or kinsmen of the chief and who, if their sept was of sufficient size and influence, were known in early days as the *flath*—that is the lord or prince. In time of war these chieftains would bring out their companies and join up with the chief's forces, coming under his command, unless this was delegated to one of the chieftains as *tòiseach* or Captain of the Clan. The junior officers were drawn from the *duine-uaislean*—the smaller gentry of the clan and sept, men belonging to cadet families sprung from the chief's or chieftain's house, who acted as a useful link between the *moirear*—a word meaning lord or noble and derived from *mòr-fhear* big man—and the main body of the clan with its dependents. These chieftains lived their lives in similar surroundings to the chiefs, the most powerful among them being the senior cadet, *maor* (steward) and the *tòiseach* second in command to the chief and captain of the clan, the latter in later times combining the old office of *maor* or steward responsible for collection of the chief's revenues but still being the oldest member of the senior cadet family.

As time went on some houses and septs expanded in numbers and territory to a degree which made them into more powerful organizations than many of the smaller clans, while in some cases they tended to become independent of the parent clan. Under this system, as was only natural, the rank of chief took precedence over any other rank of nobility while in the Highlands, whether held by the chief himself, a chieftain, or anyone else.

A great part of the now denuded mountains and glens were still clothed with forest till as late as the latter part of the 15th century; on the edge of these rose the castles of chief and chieftain and the clansmen's dwellings. The lands outside the cultivated areas about the township, were known as the *fàsach*—wilderness—here the clan cattle, goats, horses and sheep grazed at large.

Extensive forest area were reserved as private hunting-grounds for the castle and were in charge of the forester. Apart from these reservations for sport and pasturage, the *fàsach* was shared in common by the community who paid for the privilege with sword, service, and certain dues mostly in kind, such as *calpa* the first fruits of cattle and produce due by every clansman even if he were living elsewhere than on clan territory; Herezeld exigible if the man occupied more than an eighth part of a davoch (416 acres) of land. Should the chief be travelling every family he visited was bound to provide one night's board and lodging for him and his retinue, including his hounds, a form of tribute termed *cuid oidhche*; while there were other levies on special occasions such as marriages and deaths.

Game and fish played an important part in the clan food supply, though the netting rights for salmon were cherished possessions from a very early date. The red deer, still predominantly a dweller in the woods, was hunted in a manner very different to the present-day method, the 'silent stalk' was practised only by the professional stalker for the larder. The great sport of the day was the *tainchel*—or great drive common to all Mediaeval Europe. These gatherings were held, usually, in the autumn, often on a huge scale: chiefs—barons—knights and the *duine-uaislean* from miles around collected at the castle. There they remained for a considerable time feasting, listening to the poetry and stories of the Bard interspersed with the music of *clarsach* (harp), and pipes which during the 13th and 14th centuries were less complicated instruments than later models, having only one drone, a development of the 9th century pipe which consisted of a small bag and blow-pipe connected to a chanter of three or four holes, but with no drone.

The consumption of food, especially meat and drink—French and Spanish wines above the salt, beer and bland, whisked whey strongly fermented, lower down the hall, was considerable while the party filled in time till the red dear and roe had been rounded up by many gillies under the forester, and moved into the area from which they were to be driven. Probably a gathering would be held in which the men and lads of the clan would compete in wrestling, swimming, running, tossing the caber, etc. much as is done to-day. There would be archery contests while expert swordsmen would vie with each other, sometimes as the result of a serious challenge, 'à outrance'.

Perhaps Mackenzie, if he were host, would wager on his falcon against Munro or Ross; though with the last he would need to be canny lest small rivalries re-open the feud never far beneath the surface between these two. At last the great day would come, and the guests mounted and on foot would move off to their places, armed with bows and arrows, spears and dirks. The deer would be driven down some pass, the massacre that followed not being without some risk to the hunters as everything took place at close quarters and a wounded stag, when cornered, can be a dangerous adversary to a man, who disdaining to use another arrow intends to finish the job with his dirk. Should a beast get away wounded but still be in sight, it would not get far before being pulled down by a couple of Scottish deer hounds. Much of the meat would be salted down; the entire community would indulge in a gargantuan feed, while each gentleman, forester and gillie would have a new story of his prowess, with which to regale, or bore, his wife and family.

Naturally, in the castle as without, the most spoken language would be Gaelic, though French was widely known among the nobles and gentry; but English or rather Scots would not be known to many of the guests at this period, though it would be among the merchants of the

Burghs. In the unlikely event of a non-French-speaking Englishman being of the party, he would have found it possible to carry on a conversation with many of the guests in Latin. At length the party would come to an end with new friendships and perhaps new enemies made; the clan would settle down to its normal routine of agriculture, fishing, military training and hunting for the pot. On the women would fall countless tasks, for beside their usual household and farm duties there was spinning, weaving, the making of linen from locally grown flax, while on top of all, there were in those days large families to control.

In spring the girls of the clan suitably chaperoned would take the cows with their calves from the glens to the high summer grazings. The ruins of the shielings in which they dwelt during this season can still be seen in many places, while this happy incident of each year is remembered in many of the Highland songs. It was a great time for the courting, and it is not difficult to imagine the young warriors of the clan making their way up to the shielings on a soft spring evening to meet their dark-eyed girls, singing the spinning songs round their wheels, or the milking songs while girl and calf together robbed the patient cows of their milk. A good deal of flirting would follow while the serious wooer and his lady might evade the watchful eye of the chaperone by going out onto the hillside, watched only by the soft eyes of the Highland cattle.

The internal affairs of the clan were administered by the Clan Council, (the Sabaid-sab = prop) while the judicial system within the clan was delegated by the chief or chieftain to one or more *breitheamh* (brieves) in exactly the same way as had been done by the old *mormaers* and *maors*. This judicial office was usually hereditary—as in the case of Lewis where for centuries and until 1613 the Morrisons were judges for the MacLeod of Lewis Chiefs—being supported by a proportion of the fines imposed and some arable land; the chief remained the final Court of Appeal and of course had the use of the residue of fines. As the story progresses the development of the system will appear, though apart from some borrowing from the modified feudal laws of Scotland and the gradual increase of money rents in lieu of service and kind, the clan system and organization remained fundamentally unchanged till 1746.

Like every other system of life it possessed shortcomings, many of which were in process of righting themselves through normal development, never completed owing to the imposition of an alien control which brought in its wake a period of gross materialism and selfishness. The clan system at its best produced a virile, healthy and honourable people who appreciated the beauty of nature, song and poetry, and who were intensely loyal and brave, knowing nothing of class hatreds and the petty snobberies of a later age. These latter traits could not exist in a community where every man, at least in theory, claimed blood relationship with his chief, while every chief was brought up to the realization that every member of the clan was a member of his own family to whom he naturally gave affection and patriarchal care. Neither was any member a serf but a free man with a greater or lesser stake in the clan territories, either in land, cattle, or both.

The 19th century historians, through ignorance and Whig bias, have presented a very false interpretation of the clan system. Unfortunately all but a few of the more up-to-date writers of history have continued to depict a society of people who occupied a very large area of the British Isles, if in a less offensive manner, still in a way which shows that they still labour under much the same cloud of ignorance as their predecessors. They still try to draw a hard and fast line between the clan and family organization of the Highlands proper and southern Lowland and eastern Scotland. This difference did not in reality exist, though there were modifications which became marked on the Scots-English border.

Apart from the fact of close blood relationship between families of importance in Highlands and Lowlands we find the Highland title of Chief and that of Baron in use by the same individual. Thus Munro of Foulis the Chief of Clan Munro is referred to in 13th century documents as Baron of Foulis, likewise Mackenzie Chief of Clan Mackenzie (Kenneth) as Baron of Kintail. Their powers were identical with those of their Lowland cousins, being modified only by the custom and tradition of their clans, in the same way as the Lowland Baron was governed by the same beneficial Scots custom and tradition of Celtic origin, which modified so fundamentally the feudalism of Scotland as a whole, and made it so very different to—as well as better than—the oppressive and sometimes savage feudalism of France and England.

Note. In addition to the names already mentioned which appear witnessing numerous Ross Charters of late 13th and early 14th century are the following:

Sir Andrew de Bosco, a member of an important Norman family owning lands round Sheffield and in Derbyshire, but the name disappears after the Earl of Ross changed his allegiance from Balliol to Bruce. Sir Andrew's widow Elizabeth Byset exchanged some land at Glastullich and Kilcoy for some at Àrd Tarbat and Byndal in Tarbat, with William Earl of Ross.

Sir William de Fentona of Baky. Held Beaufort Castle, Beauly, his descendants shared the Barony of Àird (Inverness-shire) with 'The Chisholm'. There is a deed dated at Kinrossy 25th April 1403 confirming an indenture betwixt William Fenton of Baky, on the one part, and 'Margaret de la Àrd domina de Erchless and Thomas de Chishelme her son and heir', on the other part, dividing these the lands of which they were heirs portioners, among these lands is the Barony of *Àrd*. The Lady Margaret's father Alexander de Chishelme is mentioned as comportioner of the Barony of *Àrd* with the Lord Fenton in 1368.

The Chiefs of Clan Chisholm came north from the county of Roxburgh during the 14th century; the first of the northern branch being Constable of Urquhart Castle. Probably by marriage became the Chief of the Clan in the area Comer, Strathglass, Erchless Castle, etc.

Sir William de Haya. A member of the Hay family which held land between the upper waters of the Rivers Dee and Don, (Aberdeenshire), as well as a large area located north of the River Tay mouth, and east of Perth. Members of this great Scottish family were to become the Lords of Yester, Marquises of Tweeddale, and Earls of Kinnoul. They were enthusiastic supporters of the Bruce.

A James Hay was Bishop of Ross in 1525, and the name reappears in connection with Ross in Montrose's campaign of 1650, and again during the late 18th century, when Edward Hay, a brother of the Marquis of Tweeddale married the heiress of the House of Cromartie, thus becoming de facto Earl of Cromartie by marriage.

The name Hay is equated with Mackay thus: In Gaelic: Mackay = MacAidh (in old Gaelic Mac Ed.); grandson of Aidh = O' h'Aedha hence = Hay—while Mac h'Aedha = MacHeth; all of which connected the Hays to the great Pictish families of Moray.

Note For derivation of Names, see Glossary.

The Scottish Succession in 1290

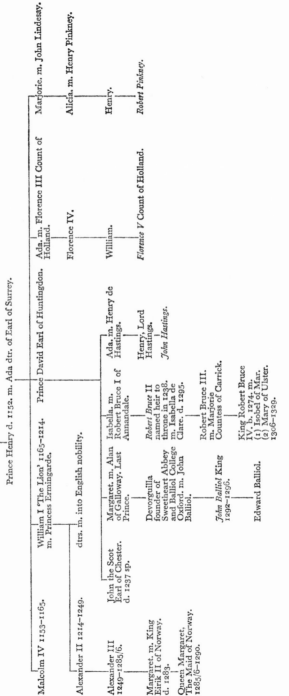

David I of Scotland, brother of Alexander I 1124–1153. m. Matilda Countess of Huntingdon in her own right.

Prince Henry d. 1152. m. Ada dtr. of Earl of Surrey.

Malcolm IV 1153–1165.

William I 'The Lion' 1165–1214. m. Princess Ermingarde.

Prince David Earl of Huntingdon.

Ada. m. Florence III Count of Holland.

Marjorie. m. John Lindesay.

dtrs. m. into English nobility.

Florence IV.

Alicia. m. Henry Pinkney.

Alexander II 1214–1249.

William.

Henry.

Florence V Count of Holland.

Robert Pinkney.

Alexander III 1249–1285/6.

John the Scot Earl of Chester. d. 1237 sp.

Margaret. m. Alan of Galloway. Last Prince.

Isabella. m. Robert Bruce I of Annandale.

Ada. m. Henry de Hastings.

Henry, Lord Hastings.

John Hastings.

Margaret. m. King Eirik II of Norway. d. 1283.

Devorguilla founder of Sweetheart Abbey and Balliol College Oxford. m. John Balliol.

Robert Bruce II named heir to throne in 1238. m. Isabella de Clare. d. 1295.

Queen Margaret, The Maid of Norway. 1285/6–1290.

John Balliol King 1292–1296.

Robert Bruce III. m. Marjorie Countess of Carrick.

Edward Balliol.

King Robert Bruce IV. b. 1274. m. (1) Isobel of Mar. (2) Mary of Ulster. 1306–1329.

See Chronological Table of Kings of Scotland.

There were thirteen competitors in all including William of Ross who claimed through Isabella, an illegitimate daughter of William I The Lion.

CHAPTER VII

AN ENGLISH OCCUPATION OF ROSS—THE WAR OF INDE-PENDENCE—DRESS AND ARMAMENT—LEARNING

Chronological Table

1296	Commencement of English aggression against Scotland.
1297	Sir William Wallace and Sir Andrew de Moray resist successfully till death of de Moray after victory of Stirling Bridge and subsequent betrayal of Wallace to Edward I.
1302	Battle of Courtrai.
1304	Petrarch born.
1306	Death of Comyn.
1307	Continuation of War of Independence by King Robert the Bruce.
1308	Reconquest by Bruce of north east and south west Highlands; Ross and far north come in for Bruce. Duns Scotus died.
1309	St. Andrews Parliament.
1310	Gaelic poem describing the fleet with which John MacSween unsuccessfully tried to recover Castle Sween for the English, from the Earl of Menteith, in that year.
1313	Edinburgh Castle recaptured from English.
1314	June 26–27. Victory of Bannockburn, eldest son of Earl of Ross, and Munro's son killed.
1315/16	Edward Bruce with 6000 Scottish veterans invades English-held Ireland.
1315/17	Irish War—Edward Bruce crowned King of Ireland.
1319	Scots victory at Chapter of Milton using a smoke screen.
1320	Manifesto of Arbroath. Birth of John Barbour, Scottish poet and chronicler. Building of Auld Brig (Bridge) O'Balgownie (Aberdeen).
1326	The Scots College at Paris founded by the Bishop of Moray, at first only for Moray students.
1327	Invasion of England.
1328	English Parliament held at York signed Treaty renouncing all pretensions to any superiority over the Kingdom of Scotland.
1329	Death of King Robert the Bruce.
1330	The 'Good' Sir James Douglas killed in Spain.

Before following the fortunes of the people of Ross who were to play such a major part in this epic struggle, we must try to get a picture of the very complicated general position. The year 1289 terminated a hundred years of virtual peace with England, and opened a period of awful enmity, which lasted between the two countries for many centuries.

One man and one alone was responsible for the legacy of hatred, Edward I, whose insensate desire for self-aggrandisement impoverished his own country and nearly ruined Scotland. Before the death of Queen Margaret in Orkney—1290—the chances of perpetual peace with England were never brighter, as despite the desire expressed by the Earl of March, James the Steward, and the Lord of the Isles, that the crown should go to Robert Bruce the elder, Margaret had been accepted and arrangements made for her wedding with the Prince of Wales. This dynastic alliance was in no way to upset Scotland's position as an independent nation, as she was to retain her own law and customs, a condition fully agreed to by Edward I, but it would have brought the countries closer together.

Alas in 1290 the young Queen of Scots died, and though the nation continued to be well governed by her six guardians or Regents, among whom were James the Steward, Black John Comyn of Badenoch, the Bishops of St. Andrews and Glasgow, the latter being the great Robert

D

Wishart, there was no certain heir to the throne but thirteen claimants. The two principal men concerned were John Balliol and Robert Bruce the elder; admittedly the latter was of a junior line but not only had his father been named heir for just such a contingency by the late King and Estates (Parliament) but the Bruces had been in Scotland for five generations, while Balliol was the son of a foreigner. Some favoured one party some the other, so to reach a fair decision it was decided to ask another King, Edward I, to arbitrate, who having posed as an honest friend to Scotland was fully trusted.

The methods of would-be world conquerors seldom vary, the majority being quite prepared to exercise every variety of mental contortion in order to give some semblance of legality to their thefts of other people's countries. Edward 'Longshanks' was no exception to the rule, and John Balliol was chosen—the choice being legally justifiable— and crowned, but as Edward's vassal, an act quickly followed by Edward's public declaration that he would treat all his former agreements and promises as a mere scrap of paper, and his theft of the Scottish Records.

At first the 'Toom Tabard' (Empty Jacket) King John complied with all Edward's humiliating orders, but the people of Scotland were becoming restless and in 1296 William 3rd Earl of Ross on King John's orders, equipped a force, £50 coming from his own pocket, to quieten the Hebrides, for which service he was promised the lands of Ferrincroscy (parish of *Cròic* in Sutherland) and the Royal Castle of Dingwall. But then came the affair of the Barns of Ayr where Wallace in 1297 burned this collection of temporary barracks erected by Edward I and with them the 500 inmates. All was now too much even for the Toom Tabard who declared war on England; a large force was assembled and moved south under the Earls of Ross, Menteith and Atholl. John, a singularly stupid man, had done his best to assure disaster by antagonizing the powerful Bruce faction having confiscated their property to provide a gift for the Black Comyn.

The Scots army captured the Castle of Dunbar but a few days later were completely defeated by Edward, William Earl of Ross becoming a prisoner-of-war, being lodged in the Tower of London, where 6d. a day was allowed for his maintenance. Edward 'moved in,' deposed John Balliol and garrisoned the principal castles of Scotland including Dingwall which was filled with English troops under Sir William de Braytoft. The conquest seemed to be complete, the country being stunned by its rapidity, while Edward improved the hour by removing most of the remaining Scottish records, and the *Lia-Fàil* from Scone.

But once again Scotland began to stir, local risings by the people led by the smaller lairds broke out here and there, which James Stewart and Bishop Wishart began uniting into a National effort. In the north the centre of the flame was young Andrew (Friskin) de Moray of Avoch in Ross, Petty etc., the heir to one of the greatest Houses in Scotland, and his uncle the Bishop of Moray, their right-hand man being Alexander Pilche a Burgess of Inverness. This gallant Bishop later founded several bursaries for poor scholars at the University of Paris thus founding the Scots College there.

The focus of resistance in the south west of Scotland was Sir William Douglas and Wallace of Elderslie, but not for another sixteen years was any signs of resistance to come from the predominantly Angle Lothians who though unhappy under the yoke, were not prepared to risk so much for freedom as their more Celtic countrymen, a fact made abundantly clear when we realize where most of the defensive fighting took place. Between the years 1296–1314 there were 16 separate invasions of Scotland, six of which came by the eastern (Lothian) route and ten by the western marches. But the time factor is more significant if a true conclusion is required by the historian; during the period of the most bitter and desperate fighting which must often have seemed hopeless to the Scots who were holding out between 1296 and 1307, no less than ten invasions came by way of the western marches and met bitter and unceasing resistance, while only four were needed to subdue the south east until the tide of battle turned in favour of the Scots.

The finest defensive battle in this area was put up by the Flemish colony in Berwick who rather than fall into English hands, immolated themselves with their families within their magnificent Hall, an action that so enraged Edward I that all the non-combatants, including women and children of Berwick were massacred.

By 1297 there was general war to restore Balliol but in the same year the south western resistance collapsed, Wallace coming north to join Andrew de Moray. The Highland army moved south under de Moray and Wallace and on the 11th September shattered the English Army at Stirling Bridge, the two leaders becoming joint Regents of Scotland, but Andrew was dying of wounds received in this battle thus depriving Scotland of its most capable general at that moment. Wallace was forced to go south into northern England and restore order, as the triumphant Scottish army was losing all sense of discipline while getting some of its own back.

Wallace was now the sole Regent of Scotland and during the five years following the Battle of Stirling Bridge the young Robert Bruce, Earl of Carrick defied his old but not admirable father, by fighting loyally for Wallace, Scotland and the restoration of the useless Balliol, only laying down his arms in 1302 when the Bruce-Balliol factions made his efforts useless.

The position in Ross was difficult, all wished to get rid of the English but their Earl was in the Tower and in Edward's power; his Countess having no illusions about that monarch's chivalry had to play her cards with care if she were to avoid the probably painful murder of her husband. Urquhart Castle in the hands of an English garrison was undergoing a siege and very short of provisions, so called upon the Countess of Ross for aid, thus putting her in a very tricky position. She raised a large force sufficient to overawe the blockading troops and delivered the necessary provisions, but did nothing further to hinder the attackers, there is little doubt that they were fully aware of the situation and the whole affair arranged.

Scotland's recovery was only transient. Wallace met Edward I at Falkirk, 1302; the Scottish Schiltroms—a double or treble circle of mail-clad men armed with long spears—broke the English knights, but in this battle the Welsh archers decimated the close packed schiltroms. The Scots army, probably numerically stronger than that which later was to win Bannockburn, ceased to exist, a crushing blow to Scotland. Guerrilla warfare continued growing ever more bitter and breeding a deep hatred against the English.

A year later a small success was gained at Roslin by Red John Comyn and Sir William Fraser but by the following February only Wallace and Sir William Oliphant were left in the field for Scotland. A form of peace was concluded and in 1303 the Earl of Ross was released being sent north under heavy guard, the journey home taking eighteen days and costing 11/- per diem. Edward decided to trust Earl William, making him Warden of the country north of Spey, and holding out the possibility of the gift of those subjects already promised by Balliol.

The eight years' struggle was to all appearances over, Scotland having been defeated more by the Bruce-Balliol feud than Edward, but the appearance was deceptive. During the year 1305 two major events occurred: the old Bruce died leaving young Robert Bruce Earl of Carrick head of the house, and a very different type of individual, and the Balliol party being out of the way, Bruce, Wallace and Bishop Lamberton were able to meet and arrange a pact of mutual support. A few weeks later Wallace was captured by treachery in Glasgow and on the 23rd of August 1305 condemned without any form of trial to a particularly vile death devised by the vindictive Edward; he was hung, drawn and quartered. Sir Simon Fraser died with him.

Events followed quickly, Comyn met Bruce to arrange an alliance, but Comyn either treacherously or by indiscretion let the cat out of the bag so was killed on February 10th, 1306, by Bruce in the Greyfriars Church at Dumfries after a violent quarrel. The sacrilege, not the killing, might easily have queered his pitch, but the Church in Scotland was loyal to Scotland, and both then and later stuck to its guns, despite fulminations, interdicts, and excommunications by certain Popes who favoured, for a consideration, the English cause of aggression.

But the Comyn connection was wide and powerful so that once again Scotland was desperately weakened by this feud.

Robert the Bruce could rely only on the Church, a large part of the Highlands, and his own Galloway, and by representatives from these areas, but few others; he was crowned at Scone King of Scots, during which ceremony he was joined by a dark visaged individual soon to become famous, James Douglas son and heir of the late Sir William. The reign started badly, Edward's general Pembroke, probably taking his ethics from his master, broke a truce thus surprising and defeating the Bruce at Methven. Meanwhile Edward was giving way to senile invective against all and sundry mentioning in particular the Princes of the Church Sir Michael de Wemyss and Sir Gilbert de Haya.

It is now time to look at the position in Ross: the Earl with memories of the Tower vividly before him was still loyal to the usurper, and this he displayed in a most unattractive way. The Bruce to ensure the safety of his wife and daughter moved them with their attendant knights and ladies from Kildrummie Castle to the sanctuary of St. Duthac at Tain, whereupon William Earl of Ross violated the sanctuary, killed the knights, handing over the ladies to Edward's none too tender care. Old Robert Munro of Foulis with his Clan, despite the policy of their overlord, remained all along staunch supporters of the Bruce, in consequence suffering severely from the Comyn party.

To the west also '*Coinnich na Sroin*' Kenneth of the Nose Chief of Clan Mackenzie, never swerved from his loyalty to the Bruce. But King Robert was once again a fugitive thanks to the feud caused by his murder of the Red Comyn, which had made the Earl of Buchan, a Comyn, together with John Lord of Lorn, another relation by marriage, his most bitter opponents. He escaped the forces of Lorn and succeeded in finding sanctuary with Angus Lord of Islay, but his enemies were hard on his tracks and were soon besieging Dunaverty Castle from which Robert only just escaped, spending a short time on Rathlin Island. From there he took refuge with Kenneth at *Eilean Donan* Castle where we may be sure he was heartily welcomed, being a proficient Gaelic speaker—as indeed he would need to be seeing that his Galloway tenants spoke nothing else—and much loved by the Highlanders. It is probable that from Kintail he went to Orkney still a possession of his kinsman the King of Norway, where he would be out of reach of both English and Comyns.

But Scotland a desperate devastated land was shaking itself for the final round. An English officer commanding at Forfar, writes on 15th May 1307 commenting on the great support the Bruce had and the general discomfiture of the English garrisons—holding every Castle of importance from Dingwall to the border. He adds: 'If Sir Robert can escape anyway thither, both beyond and on this side of the mountains, or towards the parts of Ross he will find them all ready at his will more entirely than ever, unless the King (Edward) will be pleased to send more men-at-arms to these parts'. The Church was still playing a great part, the fiery propaganda sermons of the Bishop of Moray and of the clergy all over the country was keeping alive the will to win. Then Bruce's brothers Thomas and Alexander with an Irish force suffered a defeat in Galloway by his enemy Sir Dugald Macdowall, while he himself was surrounded by a force from Lorn and an English army under De Valence; but by a miracle he escaped the net, raised fresh forces and carried on a guerrilla warfare to the great disadvantage of the English, finally capped by their defeat at Loudon Hill.

Then fate took a hand, this time on behalf of Scotland; on 7th June 1307 Edward I died ridding the world of a good general and an unmitigated pest to humanity. But Bruce before the death of his chief adversary had already gone over to the offensive; now Macdowall's lands in Galloway were laid waste after which act of justice, the King, leaving Douglas to command in the south west went north with his only surviving brother Edward, the Earl of Lennox, Sir Gilbert de Haya, and Sir Robert Boyd. Edward II marched north with a large army, but finding maintenance impossible north of the border marched back again; yet nearly every strong point in Scotland was still occupied by an English garrison, while John Comyn Earl of Buchan, and the Earl of Ross remained to be dealt with.

Between these two lay the great province of Moray, the greatest Bruce stronghold in Scotland; but north the Earl of Sutherland was temporarily under the sway of William of Ross. However, the Earl was beginning to see the light, no doubt helped by the feelings of his vassals and the Clans of Ross, so that when Bruce suggested a truce to last till 1st June 1308, he accepted, leaving the King free to deal with Buchan. In a letter to Edward II of England Ross apologises for this saying that Bruce had arrived with 3000 men all of whom were quartered at the Earl's expense on the Ross-Sutherland marches. The power of the Comyns was now systematically destroyed, little mercy being shown as their survival meant the perpetuation of a feud of sufficient magnitude to destroy the Nation. By autumn every castle in Aberdeen and the north save for Banff was in the Bruce's hands, which permitted him to turn his attention to the MacDougals of Argyll and Lorn.

John of Lorn was the chief menace in the west, so in 1308 Bruce, helped by his old friend Angus Òg MacDonald, broke the MacDougals at the Battle of Inverurie, seizing their chief stronghold Dunstaffnage. John of Lorn fled to England, Alexander of Isla submitted and was imprisoned, while his lands and position was given to his younger brother Angus Òg. Only the Earl of Ross remained, and to him in spite of his vile conduct toward the Queen and her daughter, the Bruce showed the magnanimity of a great man and statesman. Negotiations were opened with the Earl, who on 31st October 1308 made a full surrender, offering his homage to the King; this was accepted, the Earl not only being re-established in his lands but given his much coveted Dingwall Castle and lands of Ferroncoscy in Sutherland. This generous act was repaid with a life-long loyalty and the life of the Earl's son Walter de Ross at Bannockburn.

In 1309 a Parliament was held at St. Andrews and it is significant that of the twenty-eight attending eight only are Lowlanders. These twenty Barons (Chiefs) all came from north of the Forth and Clyde, including those from the recently conquered province of Argyll and Innisgall. This Parliament proposed peace to Edward II but troop movements north started in the summer; however that King's devotion to Piers Gaveston and the Scottish climate drove him south again, a truce being signed to last till 14th January 1310 which was later extended, but the English garrisons were reinforced.

In the summer of 1310 Edward prepared for a major attack which failed, putting the Scots again on the offensive, Angus Òg making a useful diversion with his galleys against the Isle of Man, now an English possession. Edward was using Perth as his northern base but getting nowhere so at length he opened peace negotiations which broke down through English treachery.

In August 1311 Bruce invaded England forcing Northumbria to sue for a separate peace, a repetition of the dose being provided during the two succeeding years, all helping to reimburse the empty Scottish exchequer. Castle after castle fell to the Scottish King and shortly after his Inverness Parliament, the vitally important and heavily fortified town of Perth fell to Highland troops after a long siege which cleared the lines of communication between Highlands and Lowlands. To make sure that this town would never again feature as an English military centre the walls were levelled and the moat filled in.

In May the Isle of Man was captured, Edward Bruce again invaded England reaching Hartlepool while the King held another Parliament at Inverness. Randolph was created Earl of Moray, but Man was recaptured by John of Lorn now Edward's Admiral of the Western Seas. At last Robert was able to turn his attention to Lothian which was soon cleared of English; Stirling Castle alone remaining to them and to relieve it Edward marched north with an army of 18,000 which included from 2000 to 2500 heavy cavalry. Against this great force the Bruce could muster 500 Light cavalry mostly from the Gordon country of Aberdeenshire and the Borders, and 6000 magnificently trained foot soldiers amongst whom Chief, Baron and Knight fought shoulder to shoulder in the schiltroms, now sufficiently well drilled to be a mobile offensive weapon as well as a stationary defensive formation.

The great battle of Bannockburn was fought on Sunday 23rd June and Monday 24th, with results known the world over. The Scottish Army was divided into four divisions, their commanders being the King, his brother Edward Bruce, Douglas and Randolph. Twenty-one clans fought for the Bruce, including Clans Ross, Mackenzie and Munro, the latter being led by their aged Chief Robert. The main body of each clan fought within the schiltroms while their numerous more lightly armed men were organized behind ready to exploit success. These are the men who the unmilitary historians so frequently refer to as the 'camp followers' who put in such a timely appearance during the battle. The victory was overwhelming and the equivalent of £3,000,000—the reparations—were collected on the spot in booty. The English gains were a valuable lesson in up-to-date tactics which they remembered at Cressy, Poitiers and Agincourt.

Old Munro lost his only son in the battle, being succeeded in 1323 by his grandson, who also was to die for Scotland at Halidon Hill in 1333. Ross' eldest son Walter, Edward Bruce's greatest friend, fell in this great fight which freed Scotland from a foreign yoke. The war continued mostly on English soil owing to Edward II's refusal to recognize the Scottish Kingdom, an army raised by Bruce from the Highlands and Islands had nearly effected his capture near Rievaulx Abbey in Yorkshire in 1322, but in 1327 Edward was deposed.

Edward III carried on the war but in 1328 was forced with his Parliament to recognize Scottish Independence and Robert Bruce as King of Scots. For some years Scotland enjoyed peace and was able to recover from her deep wounds, while people once again were able to turn to their own affairs.

Unfortunately one affair which had been in abeyance during the war, was the Ross-Mackenzie feud which this time went in favour of the Earl, who managed to trap Kenneth of the Nose, having him executed in Inverness, an action which was to cost William's descendants much blood, followed by eventual extinction within the boundaries of Ross. William died at Delny Castle in 1322 leaving two sons, Hugh his successor, and John who married Margaret Comyn, daughter and co-heiress of John Earl of Buchan. Of his two daughters Isabella was betrothed to Edward Bruce who was shortly afterwards killed in Ireland having been crowned King of that unhappy land; while Dorothea married Torquil MacLeod second Baron of the Lewis and Chief of his Clan.

Earl Hugh married twice, first Maud Bruce, the daughter of King

Note The Clans which fought for Bruce and Scotland at Bannockburn were: Cameron; Campbell; Drummond; Fraser; Grant; MacDonald; MacFarlane; MacGregor; MacKay; Mackenzie; Macintosh; MacLean; MacPherson; Macquarrie; Menzies; Munro; Robertson; Ross; Sinclair; Stewart; Sutherland.
Against King Robert the Bruce: Clans Cummin; MacDougall; MacNab and a few others.

David II and the mother of his successor, secondly Margaret, daughter of Sir David Graham of old Montrose, this lady being the mother of Hugh of Rariches, the founder of the Balnagown family and all its branches. Hugh seems to have been appointed Vice-Comes (Sheriff) of Cromarty at an early age, but transferred the post to Adam Urquhart of Cromarty, while in far Kintail the Chief must have been taking his judicial duties seriously as we read of *Eilean Donan* Castle being adorned with the heads of fifty malefactors in 1330. Edward III of England and those Scottish Lords who had lost their lands were busy preparing for another war, though they showed wisdom in waiting till the warrior King was dead, an event which occurred peacefully in June 1329.

At this point let us see how these Highlanders were dressed and armed during their great war for freedom, also how the general standard of culture in the Highlands had developed and was developing, though becoming more and more retarded by the oft repeated national struggle for existence. The use of tartan as a clan distinction comes late in history, and did not do away with localized setts within the clan area as it must be remembered that the greater clans became to some extent synthetic through absorption of areas by conquest, marriage, etc. The majority of these once numerous local setts were lost as a result of the Act prohibiting the wearing of the national dress after 1745. However, this does not mean that tartan did not exist at a very early date; for those who choose to look there is ample proof to the contrary.

The dress of the Scot, Highland and Lowland, had not changed much, at any rate since the 7th century, if then, and although a sculptured stone at Nigg of this period depicts a small figure dressed in what appears to be kilt and sporran; we know that the usual dress of the period for the nobles was a loose garment descending to the knees, belted and buckled at the waist, and a woollen or tartan plaid mantle, while the tight trews and jacket were also common. The material of the gown was linen, in colour saffron for the nobles, while arms consisted of a sword, long spear, targe and round casque, unless the Celtic hood was being worn.

The description by Magnus 'Barefoot', King of Norway during the 11th century, and the Royal seals of the 12th, show that, in principal, this dress had remained unchanged, but the early armour consisted of a shirt with circular metal rings sown on to it, worn over a padded and quilted cotún or acton of leather or linen which reached below the knees, and a round iron helmet coming up to a point; while at an early date the same cotún or gambeson was also being worn under and more or less covered by, an overcoat of true mail armour. The *breacan* (tartan) is mentioned by Turgot, Archbishop of St. Andrews in a letter, written in Latin, to King Malcolm III *Ceann Mór* during the 12th century and, again in the Chartularies of the episcopal see of Aberdeen of 1242, 1249, etc.

The effigies on the tombs of Somerled's warrior relatives of middle 12th century, at Saddell Monastery in Kintyre are shown as wearing chain mail tunics reaching to below the knee and covering the arms, and round helmets with chain tippets covering the shoulder and upper arm. The legs below the knee are protected in some way hard to interpret, but probably with leather reinforced by metal strips. Sometimes the mail coat reached to the heels, while a 13th century tomb carving of a member of this family shows a surcoat—a sleeveless *léine cròchach* (saffron shirt) worn over the mail with the MacDonald Galley depicted on the breast, as well as on the heater shaped shield.

Yet another Highland Chief c. 1306 is shown dressed in tartan trews combined with a kilt—which might well be formed by the skirts of his *léine*—a jacket and skin sporran. He holds in his right hand a spear and on his left arm a kite-shaped shield emblazoned with his arms, while in this case his round conical helmet is embellished with horns. It is recorded that Sir William Wallace while a schoolboy at Dundee (13th century) always wore a tartan plaid, and it must be remembered that for centuries there was no variation in dress between Highland and southern Lowlands, who had and still have many tartan setts of their own.

The Earldoms of Moray, Mar and Buchan provide much information on the subject of the Highland dress and it is from Aberdeen that we get some evidence that the *feile beag* (little kilt) thought by some to be a modern invention (1720), was commonly worn there up to the middle of the 16th century. There is no doubt, however, that the little kilt (as worn now) is an evolution of the *breacan-féile* or *féilleadh mór* (great kilt), which was one garment (plaid and kilt combined and worn over a less voluminous *léine*) which itself is descended from the saffron shirt or tunic of the Middle Ages and the still older and longer *léine* of c. A.D. 800, thence tracing its ancestry back to the robes of older Pagan times, brought to our Islands by the first Celts who came from more sunny lands.

Among a note of expenses, which is written out in Latin, of John Lord of the Isles in 1355 appear the following: A vest of woollen cloth; one pair of tartan trews; 3 ells of yellow cloth for a hood; one tartan plaid (which in this case replaces the mantle or cloak of wool, linen or silk, often of striking colours); 14 ells of yellow (saffron) linen for a tunic (the *léine*). The ladies of this period wore a similar garment—a tunic bound round the waist, fairly low cut in front and seldom with sleeves; over this they wore a sagum fastened with a brooch. During the next century (15th) we shall see a partial change, developing into the *breacan-féile*—the kilt and plaid combined 15–20 ft. in length and 5–6 ft.

wide—which was to last for centuries during which the tartan becomes a definite hall-mark of clan and sept.

The spoken Gaelic of the period, as for ages past, varied considerably in different localities while the scholars' Gaelic of priest, *seanchaidh* and physician—the only kind preserved to us from this date—was to all intents and purposes the same as the Erse of Ireland, due to the long dominance of the Columban (Irish) Church. This close affinity of the written languages lasted till the first decade of the 16th century when the Dean of Lismore was writing in a Gaelic which showed considerable differences to the Erse. The Irish literature had started to decline from the middle of the fifteenth century, after which the written Gaelic of Scotland began to diverge once again, assuming characteristics of its own. Both the 13th and 14th centuries have left us examples of manuscripts on a considerable variety of subjects, employing words in connection with philosophy, theology and medicine which are not now understood.

The philosophy of Aristotle is well rendered as well as the medical disquisitions of the Arab doctors—who were the most advanced medical men and scientists of their day and whose standard of civilization in Spain had far surpassed that of Christendom. The hereditary physicians to the Lords of the Isles were the family of Beaton (*MacBeatha*) some of whose medical manuscripts still exist, showing a far sounder conception of medicine than was usual in the reputedly more civilized areas of the British Isles where excessive bleeding together with much mumbo-jumbo remained the common practice till late in history. The metaphysical treatises, even judged by modern standards, give proof of an advanced culture existing among those in the Highlands who had learning.

In addition to the above the *seanchaidh* who were the clan and family historians kept written records as well as the traditional oral histories often handed down in verse from father to son. Eventually the ever increasing body of Scottish Gaelic literature, both prose and poetry was checked by the spread of English through the educated classes in the Highlands, this being brought about by the more frequent absences of the chiefs and others in the capital city, and after the reformation by political changes very inimical to the Celt, his language and his culture. Not till the late 17th and 18th centuries was another revival to come about which weathered the persecutions resulting from the 1745 Rebellion.

CHAPTER VIII

WAR AGAIN—CONDITIONS AT HOME—ROSS BECOMES A SPHERE OF MILITARY OPERATIONS

Chronological Table

1332	Beginning of a fresh war by the English.
1333	Battle of Halidon Hill, Earls of Ross, Sutherland, and the Chief of Clan Munro killed.
1336	King Edward III's march to Inverness.
1337	Start of the Hundred Years War between France and England.
1346	King David II and the Earl of Sutherland made prisoners of war after defeat of Scottish Army at Neville's Cross. Battle of Crecy.
1355	Invasion of England.
1356	Battle of Poitiers.
1359	Appearance of great French Patriot Du Guesclin.
1365	Andrew Wyntoun, Scottish poet and chronicler and a contemporary of Chaucer, writing. The great Flemish chronicler Froissart visits Scotland with letters of recommendation from his patron Queen Philippa of England. As well as being at the Court of King David Bruce, he was entertained by the Earls of Mar, of March, of Fife and of Sutherland (i.e. William the 5th Earl). He carried away such happy memories of their hospitality that in a poem written in later life he asks whether he will ever see these good friends again.
1378	Building of St. Machar Cathedral at Aberdeen.
1379	The Great Schism begins.
1384	Invasion of England.
1388	Battle of Otterburn and death of the Douglas in hour of victory.
1395	General truce with England. Death of John Barbour the Scottish poet and historian; he was born 1316. John MacDonald of *Dun Naomhaig* in Islay the 2nd son of John Lord of the Isles had been expelled by his elder brother Donald of Harlaw fame so had moved to Ulster where as the commander of a force of Scottish Galloglass mercenaries he gave his services to the O'Neill King of Ulster. When his master made submission to King Richard II of England in 1395 MacDonald as Constable of the Irish of Ulster made his submission separately to Richard in Dublin. In 1399 he married Marjory Bisset heiress of the Glens of Antrim.
1396	Combat of North Insh of Perth before King Robert III; 30 men of Clans Chattan versus 30 of Clan Dhai, (Davidson) to settle question of supremacy. Chattan won losing 19 killed, but only one Davidson survived by swimming the Tay.
1399	Henry IV of the House of Lancaster proclaimed King of England.
1400	Birth of Scottish poet, Sir David Lindsay. Died 1455. Death of Chaucer.
1402	Battle of Homildon.
1408	Treaty between Henry IV of England and Donald Lord of the Isles de Jure IXth Earl of Ross.
1409	A second drone added to the *Piob Mhor*, not until the 17th or early 18th century was the third bass drone added.
1411	Founding of St. Andrew's University. Battle of Harlaw.
1415	Battle of Agincourt.
1416	English invasion.

The same year as King David II was crowned, 1331, war clouds were again gathering in the south, the dispossessed Balliol faction blazing up on the side of England. Randolph Earl of Moray was Regent for the boy King, but died as he moved south to meet the forces of invasion; at the same time Edward Balliol, King John's son, a pretender to the Scottish throne, was attempting a 'putsch' in Fife. The Earl of Mar succeeded Randolph but was killed almost immediately at Duplin, a defeat which left central Scotland open to the enemy who seized the opportunity to crown Edward Balliol at Scone.

But once again from the north came salvation; before Edward III could exploit this success, Andrew de Moray—the son of the hero of Stirling Bridge, together with Archibald Douglass struck with such good effect that the mock King was driven over the border clad in his shirt and one boot. De Moray, usually described by historians, quite incorrectly, as 'de Bothwell,' had his home in Avoch in Ross and he belonged to the great Moray family who among countless other estates had acquired Bothwell by marriage in c. 1250, became Regent but almost at once became a prisoner of war at Roxburgh, though only for a short time, his place as Regent being taken by Douglas, who alas, was no general. His first effort to relieve Berwick was successful but by conducting a raid into England, he permitted Edward III to break a pact and re-invest that town.

Douglas returned to its relief but found himself forced to accept battle on ground of his enemy's choosing, with the English-Balliol position situated on high ground protected by a wide marsh which the Scottish Army was forced to cross in four columns under a terrible hail of arrows, arriving soaked and muddy on the far side. At the foot of the hill they formed up, then with splendid courage the Earl of Ross and his Division of Highlanders, made up from every clan in Ross and Sutherland with his division, charged up the hill smashing the wing commanded by Balliol; too late the other two schiltroms followed, led by Andrew de Moray—now back from captivity—the Stewart, and the Regent Douglas.

After a desperate fight the Scots were worsted with appalling loss which included most of their leaders. Among those who fell were the Earls of Ross, Sutherland, Lennox, Carrick, Menteith, Atholl; three brothers Fraser, William Lord Douglas, and the Regent, Archibald Douglas himself. Clan Munro suffered terrible casualties among them their Chief, George Munro VII of Foulis, the survivors being led back to Ferrindonald by his brother John, who took over the tutorship (Regency) of the clan for his young nephew, Robert Munro. Thus ended the battle of Halidon Hill fought on 19th July 1333; Berwick was lost and the English crowed loudly, fondly imagining that Scotland at last was crushed.

But the old desperate, bitter, guerrilla warfare started once again, the situation aggravated by famine and pestilence, a scene of horror lightened only by the spectacle of a people, disorganized, starving and homeless, but carrying on by sheer guts alone. Some names stand out, among them Christina Bruce, Randolph's daughter, better known as Black Agnes of Dunbar who with magnificent courage cheerfully withstood a five months' siege of Dunbar; Andrew de Moray of Petty, Avoch and Bothwell once again Regent, who somehow managed to keep alive the will to win; Douglas of Liddesdale, son of the good Lord James; Malcolm the Fleming who held Dumbarton, saving the young King and Queen who were sent for safety to France; Alan Vipont who broke the English dam at Lochleven, which swept their forces to destruction. Somehow the country held, eventually help arrived from France, and by 1340 the country north of the Forth was clear of English, young Robert Stewart, the Bruce's grandson, having taken Perth, thanks to the engineering skill of the equally young William 5th Earl of Ross.

Meanwhile, the Earls of Sutherland and March were carrying fire and sword into Northumberland, so England decided that the game was not worth the candle, their gains being negligible and losses severe; France now appeared as a more likely field for profitable aggression—thus started the Hundred Years' War.

The King came home to his own again and was received by all with great joy but he was to prove himself utterly unworthy of his great little country, being selfish, weak and quite irresponsible. In the spring of 1338 Andrew de Moray died, at the early age of forty, worn out by his gallant struggle, and knowing that death was near, he had retired for the last days of his life to his beloved Castle at Avoch on the Black Isle. This great son of Scotland was laid to rest at Chanonry, but later his body was moved, being placed beside that of the Bruce in Dunfermline Abbey.

In 1350 the Black Death had spread from England into Scotland causing further devastation, yet five years later she had answered the appeal of King Philip of France for aid and made war on England, recovering Berwick and beating the English very thoroughly at Nesbit *Muir*. Edward III invaded Lothian doing much wanton damage, but owing to Stewart's and Douglas' scorched earth policy was soon forced by starvation to retire to England. This was the last armed attack for many years, but other safer though more underhand methods were used in the effort to bring about the subjugation of Scotland.

For this Edward had a ready tool at hand, as since the Scottish defeat at Nevill's Cross in October, 1346, in which Frasers and Camerons had suffered severely, King David had been a prisoner-of-war and was proving himself to be a very pliable tool in the hands of a monarch as capable as Edward III. Scotland though utterly bankrupt and impoverished, cheerfully found the 10,000 merks necessary to ransom this King, little realising that their sacrifice, which included a debasement of the coinage, was to be to their own hurt.

In Ross the Chief of Kintail was now Kenneth's son Murdo, who in 1362 was granted by King David a new Charter for his lands, a none too popular move with William VIth Earl of Ross the Justiciar north of the Forth, who when his father was killed at Halidon Hill, had been travelling in Norway. Another to receive a charter from this monarch was Torquil MacLeod II of Lewis, for the Barony of Assynt and *Coigach* which had been seized by his father from Clan MacNical, the 'transfer' being regularized by his marriage to the MacNical heiress. The Island of Lewis itself was—at any rate nominally—held under superiority of his wife's family the Earls of Ross; the property including also Raasay Island, Waterness in Skye, and *Gairloch* in Wester Ross.

William Earl of Ross seems to have been a somewhat violent individual; in 1346 he had assassinated Ranald the Chief of Clan Ruari along with seventy of his followers in the Monastery of Elcho, an event which took place while the northern forces were moving south to join King David's disastrous expedition, an action that deprived the Scots Army of the help of the Islesmen, who not unnaturally returned home after the liquidation of their Chief. The cause of this murderous attack was the growing power of Clan Ruari in the west, partly brought about by the Earl himself who, sometime before, at a party given by Sir Thomas Lauder, in Urquhart Castle, had granted a charter for certain lands in Kintail to Ranald; whilst this had been followed soon after by the further acquisition by Ranald of the Islands of *Uist*, *Barra*, Eigg and *Rum* as well as the district of *Garmoran* in western Inverness. Hugh of Rariches, Earl William's brother seems also to have been possessed of a devil, if the story told of him is true. A woman suffering from some injustice threatened to complain to the King so in order, he said, to give her speed on the journey, he had horseshoes nailed to her feet.

Yet the bond between Ross and Robert Munro of Foulis must have been close, as is proved by charters granting additional lands to 'Robert de Munroo', some as gifts, others for '3d. sterling p.a. at Whitsunday and three suits yearly,' or again simply on payment of 'ane pair of Parisian gloves'; in the charters of this period the Earl is often referred to as Lord of Skye.

The last service rendered by Robert Munro to William was the greatest, as he saved his friend's life at the cost of his own during some quite unimportant fracas in 1369, for which a not ungrateful Earl grants lands to his beloved cousin Hugh de Munro 'for services rendered by him and by his father killed in the Earl's defense'; but generally speaking, William's character seems to have deteriorated from that of his forbears. He had married Mary, a daughter of Angus *Òg* of the Isles by her having a daughter Euphemia, a very important heiress, married by the King's express command to Sir Walter de Leslie; in other ways, also, the authorities were beginning to take an unwelcome interest in the affairs of this northern autocrat, but in 1371 he escaped further official interference by dying.

His only son William, who together with John, son of the Earl of Sutherland by Marjory Bruce, had been named as a hostage for the ransomed David II, had predeceased him, dying on the journey south; Euphemia therefore became Countess of Ross in her own right and, as we shall see, had a most eventful if unhappy career. Her first husband, Walter, seems to have been a somewhat colourless individual, at any rate he made no special mark either good or bad in story or legend. His family belonged to an Aberdeenshire clan, the first recorded chief, Bartholf, being of Hungarian origin, who had arrived in Scotland with Edgar Atheling as a refugee from England in 1066. Walter was second son of Sir Andrew Leslie, 6th in descent from Bartholf, who held the

Barony of Leslie in the Garioch, and by marriage with the Abernethy heiress had come into possession of the Baronies of Rothes and Ballenbreich, a previous marriage having brought lands in Fife.

Now the son of Angus *Òg*, John 1st Lord of the Isles—1300–1387—known as the 'good John of Isla', had espoused the cause of Edward Balliol, forsaking the House of Bruce so nobly served by his father, and for this he had been forfeited in 1344, so that twelve years later we find him in France fighting for the Black Prince at Poitiers where he was made a prisoner-of-war by the French, being released in 1357. In 1369 he rendered allegiance to David II at Inverness, was pardoned and confirmed in his possessions and superiorities in Islay, Gigha, Scarba, Colonsay, Mull, *Coll*, Tiree, Lewis, Morven, Lochaber, Duror and Glencoe. He married the heiress and survivor, of the Chief of Clan Ruari which added to his Island Principality, *Uist*; Eigg and *Rum*; the Lordship of *Garmoran*; Kintyre; Knapdale; Skye and Ardnamurchan which latter territory he gave to his relative Angus MacIan, from whom are descended the MacDonalds of Glencoe. From John of Isla and Amy Nic Ruari are descended the MacDonalds of Clan Ranald which included Knoydart, Glengarry, Moidart, and Morar.

Eventually he divorced his wife Amy Nic Ruari and married Princess Margaret, daughter of King Robert II, and the sister of Robert, Duke of Albany. Of this second marriage were born Donald and Alasdair *Carrach*, the former inheriting the Lordship of the Isles, and begetting two further families, the MacDonalds of Loch Alsh, and the MacDonalds Lords of Sleat in Skye, while Alasdair, for a time held Lochaber, becoming the ancestor of the MacDonalds of Keppoch. The power of this Island—almost kingdom, was now enormous, but as we shall see, when by marriage it absorbed the Earldom of Ross, the Lord of the Isles was to become doubly an 'overmighty subject'. So dangerous did this power grow that eventually it was destroyed by the Crown, largely through the agency of Clan Mackenzie, already a rising power in the land.

Turning to Easter Ross, the shrine and birthplace of St. Duthac had not at this juncture the best of neighbours in Paul Mactyre, a son or grandson of Olave King of Man and nephew of the Earl of Ross, who hearing that the lands of Strathcarron, Strath Oykel and Westray had 'fallen loose', sailed up the Firth in his galleys and seized these areas. But in 1366 he was told by his all-powerful uncle to disgorge, the pill being gilden by the marriage of his beautiful daughter to the Earl's other nephew the Laird of Balnagown who thus gained the lady of his heart and the lands in dispute, while Paul got a grant of land in *Gairloch*.

In 1371 David II died and Scotland despite his miserable intrigues with Edward was still free. The next heir, Robert Stewart, came to the throne as Robert II; he had a difficult road to follow as his predecessor had damaged seriously the prestige of the Crown, also he was an old man, the nobles had become very restless, and the Western Isles were threatening to break from Scotland, to accomplish which they were willing to assist England.

Walter de Leslie, Lord of Ross by right of his wife Euphemia 6th Earl, made no great mark in history, beyond adding his name to some charters, among them one: 'Granting and confirming, for the salvation of their souls, and those of all their ancestors, the Earls of Ross their heirs and successors also their other parents and successors, to the Blessed Virgin Mary and St. Boneface patron of the Church of Ross, the whole town of Drwme and providing for the Saint's Chapel at Cuthyl Curitir adjacent to Rosemarkie. Witnessed by William de Dyngwale Dean of Ross, John de Lyndesay, Adam de Urchard (Urquhart), William Bedow, David de Dunhowyn, Hugh de Munroo', at Dingwall Castle and confirmed by charter under great Seal 13th August 1380 at Inverness. Another interesting writ of 17th October 1381 is a discharge by Thomas de Rate acknowledging receipt on behalf of Hugh de Munro bailie of Auach (Avoch) £23 st. dues from Alan de Drumnemarge currwr (forest ranger) due to Lord Archibald Douglas for lands of Auach and Eddyrdor (Redcastle). The Douglas family had by marriage with their kinswoman of the De Moray family fallen heirs to much of the great Moray property. Walter died in 1381 leaving his widow with one son Alexander, who after many vicissitudes succeeded to the Earldom, and a daughter Margaret who married Donald 2nd Lord of the Isles.

The Isle of Skye—as we have seen, was once again under the superiority of the MacDonalds, but parts were attached to the House of Lewis; the MacLeods of Harris were in possession of Dunvegan though till 1480 they were still styled 'of Glenelg', having received a charter for that Barony from David II, the Bissets having faded out from this area at the termination of the Balliol regime. In 1380 a new war was started by England, each side in turn invading each other's country and in 1389 the 73 year old King Robert II abdicated in favour of his son, Robert III, who succeeded by the death of his father in 1390.

Meanwhile political storm-clouds were banking up in the west in part a legacy of those 400 years of separation from the kingdom during which control by Norway had been at best only spasmodic. Donald Lord of the Isles, of whom we shall hear a good deal in the next chapter, signed in 1392, 1394 and 1398 three treaties with the King of England Richard II, as an allied sovereign. In 1395 he attempted to seize the MacLeod possessions in Skye which was officially held under superiority of the Ross Earldom, sending his brother Alasdair *Carsach* Lord of Lochaber to carry out the invasion, who avoiding the vigilance of the

MacAskills the hereditary 'watchers' of the coasts for MacLeod, effected a landing and wasted Skye. But at the battle of Sligachan, Alasdair was defeated by the MacLeods so retired to Lochaber, a district which he much preferred, only to lose it a few years later after the Battle of Harlaw, and the subsequent pacification of the west by the Crown.

Though defeated at Sligachan the MacDonalds had established a footing on the Island, Sleat being occupied by Donald's elder half-brother Godfrey till 1401, which marked the beginning of the division of the Island between the MacLeods and the MacDonalds with their Mackinnon vassals, as next year the MacDonalds were to seize the important strongholds of Castles *Camus*, *Dun Sgàthach*, and Sleat.

The new King Robert III was a kindly, dignified and gentle cripple who realized his own incapacity to deal with such difficult times, for though the Scots were now enjoying friendly tournaments with the English, things at home were ugly. His brother, the Wolf of Badenoch—whose exploits we shall follow in Ross, had sacked Elgin Cathedral in 1398—later repaired—during the course of a personal quarrel with its Bishop, this action being a typical example of his violent behaviour. The King could not control his own family let alone Scotland so that in 1399 the Estates very gently and politely, but firmly, deposed the King on the grounds that 'sickness of his person' prevented him from governing and 'restraining trespassers and rebellers'. The next heir James Stewart, the son of King Robert III was a child, so that the government fell to Regents, in this instance not very successful ones.

Scotland for the first quarter of the 15th century, suffered seriously from these rulers, who were remarkable neither for their skill in the art of government, nor for their singleness of purpose, family feuds playing far too great a part in their politics. The period of their rule was lengthened by the fact that Prince James, sent by the old King for safety to France, had been captured by an English privateer and handed over to the King of England who was delighted to keep such an important individual as his prisoner.

Largely through the fault of the Regents a sporadic war broke out with England, resulting in the burning of Edinburgh though little else, as the English army were soon starved out of south Scotland. This was followed by another unofficial war in which Douglas and the Regent Albany's son were beaten at Homildon Hill in 1402. But the chief troubles were now at home, and in Ross we can find excellent examples of what these troubles were like.

In 1408 a league was renewed between Henry IV of England and Donald Lord of the Isles, who shortly afterwards was to be given ample excuse for conducting a major war against the Regent Robert Stewart Duke of Albany. Outside our own area the Lochaber and Badenoch feuds terminated for a time with the combat of the North Insh of Perth; a long drawn out feud developed between the House of Sutherland and the Mackays, then between the Mackays and the MacLeods of Lewis.

At home the Countess of Ross Euphemia had not long remained a widow, but was forced into a second marriage with no less a person than the infamous Wolf of Badenoch, the fourth son of King Robert II, and at that time the King's Lieutenant in the north. Her life with this gentleman was no bed of roses, both parties eventually deciding to live as far apart from each other as their duties would permit. Lady Ross remained at the Castle of Dingwall while Alexander 'the Wolf' took up his residence in the Castle of Delny, where apart from signing a few charters as Earl of Ross, he seems to have passed the time scandalizing a fairly tough-skinned community.

At last his goings-on became so public that Countess Euphemia was forced to take some notice, complaining to the Bishops of Moray and Ross. This resulted in an enquiry being held in the Church of the Preaching Friars at Inverness, which recorded its findings as follows: 'In the name of Christ; We, Alexander, and Alexander, by the grace of God, Bishops of Moray and Ross, diocesans and judges ordinary of the parts underwritten, sitting in the judgment seat, and having God alone before our eyes, by the advice of skilled men with which we have been in communication as to all these matters, having heard and understood what each party wished to offer against each other; and having considered the mode of procedure, pronounce, discern, and declare by this writ, that Lady Euphemia, Countess of Ross, must be restored to Lord Alexander, Seneschal, Earl of Buchan, and Lord of Ross, as her husband and spouse, together with her possessions. And we have restored her so far as the law can, to be treated honourably with matrimonial affection at bed and board, in food and raiment, and all others, according to what becomes her station, and that Mariota, daughter of Athyn, must be sent away; and we do send her away, as by law we are able; and that she shall not hereafter dismiss her (the Countess). And since the aforesaid Lady Euphemia, the Countess, alleges fear of death . . . from his men, slaves, nobles and others, the said Earl shall find and deliver to us by way of surety, and security of great and honourable persons, and that under penalty of two hundred pounds, that he shall treat the said Lady becomingly, as above said. . . . This our sentence was read, published in the Church of the Preaching Friars of Inverness, the second day of November, in the year of the Lord, 1398. Present, the great man, Robert, Earl of Sutherland, and the religious man, Adam Abbot of Kinloss, Masters William de Spynie, and William de Dingwall, Deans of the Churches of Aberdeen and Ross, etc., and many other witnesses especially called to the premises. And the said Lord Alexander, thus personally constituted, promised, and faithfully undertook to perform and fulfil the premises all and sundry enjoined upon him by us, under the penalty aforesaid; and to this end gave us as sureties the said lord Earl of Sutherland, Alexander de Moravia, Lord of Culbyn, and Thomas de Chisholm, then present, and consenting to pay to us the foresaid penalty, when and how often he, which God forbid, would come to do anything against the premises or any of them. Given and done as above, and before the above mentioned witnesses'.

But this was not sufficient. The Wolf after a short interval relapsed into his old ways which resulted in a formal separation, however, very soon afterwards he died lamented by few, with the possible exception of Mariota, who had borne him five sons, all chips off the old block, though probably the worst was Alexander Earl of Mar, which title he gained by marriage, under suspicious circumstances, to Isobel, in her own right Countess of Douglas, Mar and Garioch, having first murdered an inconvenient husband (Sir Malcolm Drummond) and seized the widow's person with her Castle of Kildrummy.

His official widow, Euphemia, having now sampled two husbands, one by official choice, the other having espoused her by cave-man methods, decided to choose the next of her own free will even if it involved some compulsion on her own part, as her eye had fallen on a certain youth, Alexander Mackenzie, who appealed to her very much indeed. He was young, more than ordinarily handsome, as well as being endowed with a good head on his shoulders, while in addition his prospects were bright, as he was the son and heir of Murdo the old Baron of Kintail, the star of whose House was quite obviously in the ascendant. The Mackenzie lands were steadily increasing and by 1427 this virile clan with its septs and dependents could put 2000 men into the field, a number, which in a few years, was to be greatly increased.

The story goes that Euphemia now in her fortieth year was immodest enough to personally propose marriage to young Kintail, while he was on a visit to Dingwall; as politely as possible he refused, some say because he was already engaged to a daughter of MacDougall of Monar, others giving the more worldly reason that the Countess was only the liferentrix of her Estates which would, of course, go to her only son Alexander Leslie. But she would not take no for an answer, continuing to press her suit while entertaining the young Mackenzie at her Castle. The result of all her efforts were disappointing and as 'hell knows no fury like a woman scorned' the obstinate youth found himself moved from the guest chamber to the Castle prison.

The tale now takes a grim turn; Euphemia, possibly by the torture of Mackenzie's page, got possession of his master's golden signet ring, the lady having found out that MacAulay, Kintail's Constable of *Eilean Donan* Castle, had orders never to quit his post or admit a stranger, in the absence of the family, unless he received this ring as a token. The ring was at once dispatched by a horseman who passed on the bogus order that MacAulay was to return with him to Dingwall, as the son of the house was now married to the Countess of Ross. Suspecting nothing, though probably surprised, MacAulay set off but seems soon to have smelt a rat before reaching Dingwall as he did not actually enter the Castle but hung around the Burgh till he had discovered where young Kintail was lodged. These two managed at last to communicate and by means of an allegory in Gaelic the prisoner was able to explain the situation, making MacAulay understand that the only way to bring about his release was the quid pro quo apprehension of Walter Ross of Balnagown, the Countess' first cousin.

Meanwhile Euphemia had placed a garrison of her own in *Eilean Donan* Castle, but despite this MacAulay quickly raised a force of Mackenzies, MacRaes, MacLeays, MacIvers and MacConnans in Kintail and Wester Ross, then by forced marches crossed to the opposite side of the county, surprised Balnagown and successfully abducted the laird Walter. Everyone now started to join in, Lord Lovat as the King's Lieutenant in the north was informed of the Balnagown kidnapping so sent off a mounted troop from Beauly who were joined by Munros of Foulis, and Dingwalls of Kildun. Somewhere between Dingwall and Fodderty this force caught up with MacAulay who wisely had sent on the captive with an escort, retaining a strong rearguard.

There followed a very stubborn action, known as *Bealach nam brog* the Pass of the Shoes, as according to Tarbat (17th century) some of the Mackenzies having no other protection since they were travelling very light, tied their brogues on their chests to afford some protection against arrows. The men from Kinlochewe put up a specially fine defence, the majority dying on their position; but MacAulay had won, the race of 'Dingwalls' was almost wiped out by the loss of 140 men, while eleven of Munro of Foulis household fell, including two of the Chief's sons, the succession falling to a child. MacAulay continued on his way unmolested making for Kintail; at Glenluing five miles from *Eilean Donan* he caught up with a gang of thirty men sent by the Countess with grain for the provisioning of her garrison in the Castle, these were promptly made prisoner while thirty Kintail men took their place. The supposed victualling party were at once admitted into the Castle and without much difficulty overpowered the surprised garrison together with the temporary governor, so that MacAulay now held all the trump cards, effecting without further trouble the desired exchange of prisoners.

Shortly after this abortive attempt at matrimony the sorely tried Countess of Ross retired to the Abbey of Elcho, the place where her father had murdered the Islesmen, she became the Abbess of this establishment dying somewhere about 1394 when she was succeeded by her son Alexander Leslie, the 7th Earl of Ross. Alexander did not long survive his mother, dying in 1402 leaving an only daughter, also named Euphemia, a cripple, who was to be the unwitting cause of a serious war. This poor girl's mother was Isobel the eldest daughter of Robert Stewart Earl of Fife, Duke of Albany, the Regent of Scotland, who outlived her husband Alexander, but seems to have been very pliable regarding the tortuous schemes for her daughter's welfare.

Albany decided, partly for reasons of state and partly for the further aggrandisement of his own family—the latter being the greater part—that the absorption of the Earldom of Ross into his own family was practical politics. The cripple girl was persuaded to take the veil, retiring to Elcho where eventually she, too, died as its abbess but was buried at home in the Abbey of Fortrose (Chanonry). Meanwhile the Regent, ignoring the girl's Aunt Margaret, the rightful heir who had married Donald Lord of the Isles, presented the great Earldom of Ross to his own son John Earl of Buchan. This action made war inevitable as Donald could never, in those days, have passed by such an insult, even if he had been content with the Lordship of the Isles, which of course he was not. The Lord of the Isles was, as we saw, in touch with England, emissaries from both parties passing between the English Court and that of this new independent Principality.

In July 1411 Donald moved, his intention being to recover on behalf of his wife the great Earldom which stretched into Aberdeenshire. Now this war was not a revolt against the Crown, still less was it a clash between Highlands and Lowlands, a grotesque theory once popular with historians; it was in fact, a very big family quarrel revolving round the Earldom of Ross and its vast properties, which was being settled in a quite typical mediaeval way. John Earl of Buchan the 'usurper' Earl of Ross was himself on the Continent and never had much to do with Ross; but he greatly distinguished himself in the fighting by the Scots Army of 6000 men under Douglas who at that time were holding France together against the English attacks. At the victory of Baugé he helped to rout the English, personally slaying the Duke of Clarence, the brother of King Henry, but was to fall himself at the Battle of Verneuil in 1423. His father the Regent Albany had taken care to have the Castle of Dingwall in safe hands and as early as 1402 entrusted the governorship to a man called 'The Black Captain' who, however, was killed in a dual with Thomas Munro, second son of Robert of Foulis, after a quarrel at Maryburgh. Thomas was forced to remove, settling with his mother's people at Corstorphine, for greater security changing his name to Roach.

The year 1411 saw Mackay of Farr as the new governor in the Castle with a garrison of his own clansmen and a few Dingwalls of Kildun; this force was quickly augmented by a strong body of Mackays,

Munros and Mackenzies, the whole coming under command of Hugh Munro of Foulis. Donald of the Isles had divided his great army—the chroniclers say 10,000—into two columns, the southern one moving south of the River Farrer, in Inverness; the northern column, who hoped to capture Dingwall Castle, a vital strongpoint, before rejoining the southern force, were under command of Donald himself, and followed the route: Glen Ling—Glen *Fiodaic*—Strathconon and Contin. From Contin three approaches to Dingwall were possible: south of the Cat's Back between the Brahan precipices and the River Conon; or by *bealach 'n cor* east of the village of Jameston; or across the steepish north flank of the Cat's Back and Knockfarrel, an area known as Park lying to the south west of Strathpeffer (Spa), a fairly difficult way but the one Donald chose as being the safest.

The opposing forces met between Knockfarrel and Ulladale and a fierce defensive battle followed, raging from above the present railway station to the other side of the valley round Nutwood, where the strath opens out northwards to Castle Leod. By force of numbers Donald could doubtless have forced the position, but time was a factor in his plan of campaign as he wanted to join up as quickly as possible with the southern column at Inverness. He therefore disengaged, retracing his steps to the crossing of the Conon south west of the Cat's Back, and from there he marched to Inverness by way of *Muir* of Ord.

The battle of *Blar 'n Inich* (The battle of the solitude) had taken a heavy toll of the defending force so that they could not follow up his retreat, but they had done their job as Dingwall was for the time safe. The ancient Eagle stone—the origin of which was discussed in Chapter III—still standing at Nutwood was moved and set up by the Munro contingent to commemorate the battle, and as a memorial to the Munros who fell; it was named *Clach 'n Tionpain*, the Stone of the Turning.

The great battle of Harlaw followed, where Donald's Army met the forces of the Wolf's son the Earl of Mar, and the Provost of Aberdeen Robert Davidson; it ended in a draw, the casualties on both sides being very heavy. Neither side was in a position to continue next day and Donald withdrew, seemingly taking undisputed possession of Dingwall Castle where he remained for ten months. This odd proceeding may be explained by Letters of Remission of 24th August 1428 issued under the Great Seal in favour of George de Monro, John de Monro the elder, John Huchounson Monro, Hugh Munro, Lawrence Munro, Hugh de Tarrale, John Corbate, John Pluket and twenty others by name, for actions against them for killings, thefts, burnings, robberies, etc. The inference is plain and backed by a story that the Munros had joined Donald for reasons unknown, though here we may hazard a guess: The Mackenzie influence was spreading east which, not unnaturally, was resented by the powerful Munros; before long this was to lead to blood-shed until the Munros, by bitter experience, learned the futility of trying to stem this tide. After this truth was appreciated the Munros gave up fighting with Clan Kenneth but married them instead.

At length Donald was dislodged from Dingwall, returning to his western home, still undefeated though he had failed to win his objective, the Earldom of Ross. Eventually this de jure Earl of Ross made his peace with the Regent, and dying in Isla the same year that the de facto but absentee Earl of Ross John Earl of Buchan was killed at Verneuil—1423.

Donald's son Alexander succeeded to the Lordship of the Isles only, but after a hiatus of twenty-seven years divided between the field of battle and prison, he was to regain the Earldom of Ross. Alexander married twice, firstly Elizabeth Seton of Gordon and Huntly who bore him one son his eventual successor to the Lordship of the Isles and Earldom of Ross, while his second wife the last MacTaggart of Apple-cross (descended from Earl Fearchar's second son the Green Abbot) presented him with two more, the first founding the family of the MacDonalds of Lochalsh—who through this lady held parts of Loch-carron and Lochbroom—the second son becoming the 1st Lord of Sleat.

During the early part of the 15th century a certain free-booter Macneil whose principal habitat was in Sutherland caused considerable damage in the Burgh of Tain, burning the edifice which contained the shrine of St. Duthac, and with it certain important records. About twelve years later (1439) there was summoned to meet at Tain, under the Seal of Alexander Earl of Ross, a jury of the most important people in Ross, Inverness and Sutherland, to hold an inquisition into the rights and privileges of the Burgh. The jury in a document of which an ancient notarial copy exists declared that the town of 'Tayne' was under the protection of the Holy See, founded c. 1057 by King Malcolm III Canmore, the Burgh being confirmed by Kings David, Bruce and Robert II in all the rights of a 'free trading town' which rights are enumerated. The claim by the witnesses that they had lost in the fire a charter from King Malcolm can probably be dismissed as it is unlikely that charters of any kind were used so far north as early as this.

In March 1424 the great King James I returned from captivity, Fraser of Lovat being amongst the first to welcome him at Durham. At last Scotland had a real King again, and one who intended to carry out a much needed clean up in the Kingdom of *Alba*. His ambition is well summed up by the words: 'Let God but grant me life, and there shall not be a place in all my kingdom where the key shall not keep the Castle, the bracken-bush the cow, though I lead the life of a dog in securing it'.

Much of his work as we shall see in the next chapter lay in the north and it was there among the chiefs and clansmen that loyalty to him remained firm when the greed of certain nobles eventually brought about his death.

CHAPTER IX

THE CLEAN UP—THE INVERNESS PARLIAMENT—CIVIL WAR IN THE NORTH—THE DOUGLAS–ROSS PACT—PROGRESS

Chronological Table

1425   The Duke of Albany executed. Birth of the Scots poet Robert Henryson about this time.
1427   Scottish Parliament held at Inverness. Amongst other business was an order for the destruction of wolves, an act commemorated by a Gaelic poem. Dunois the Bastard of Orleans appears.
1428   Renewal of Auld Alliance with France after refusal of England to make a definite peace.
1429   Appearance of Jeanne d'Arc, the Maid of Orleans. Scots Army in France under Kennedy—who had saved the day for the French at Baugé—now fight for Joan of Arc (whose personal banner was painted by a Scot—Hamish Power). Soon after Charles VII of France formed the Compagnie Ecossaise, the senior Company of the Royal bodyguard, as an acknowledgment of the great services rendered by Scotland to France. They retained this position till the French Revolution 1789.
1431   Revolt in Highlands. First Battle of Inverlochy. Royal troops under Earls of Mar, son of the Wolf of Badenoch, and Caithness v Macdonalds under Donald Balloch son of John of Isla and cousin-german of the Earl of Ross. Mantegna born.
1448   English Invasion. Invasion of England.
1451   Founding of Glasgow University.
1452   Birth of Leonardo da Vinci.
1453   End of Hundred Years' War. Taking of Constantinople by Mahomet III.
1456   Start of the Wars of the Roses in England.
1459   *Mairy Do'n galar an gradh'*, great love song composed by Isabel, 1st Countess of Argyll.
1462   Treaty between Edward IV of England and John Lord of the Isles, XIth and last Earl of Ross.

The new King James I 'Rex Legifer', did not let the grass grow under his feet for he knew that time was short and thanks to the Regents, Scotland had been bled white by poverty, war, famine, pestilence, and family feuds. Within a year the laws were reformed, and Parliamentary attendance enforced, while a change was made for the benefit of the Lesser Barons. The Great Barons, Bishops and Burgh members were to attend but the smaller Lairds might now send their representatives to the 'Estates', as the burden and expense of travelling long distances to attend frequent Parliaments had been for them a real hardship. Then backed by Bishop Cameron of Glasgow and his old tutor Bishop Wardlaw, James carried reform into the Church, an action which brought him into conflict with the Pope though eventually he won his point.

There followed measures for the improvement of agriculture and the fishing industry, though many years were to pass before reafforestation was considered, though in certain areas this was becoming necessary already, as during the reign of James I Aeneas Sylvius the future Pope Pius II visited Scotland and was impressed by the scarcity of trees in Lothian; protection was given to the smallholder while ensuring that the farmer made use of all his available land.

Foreign relations were much improved but the defence of the Kingdom was not neglected, castles being rebuilt, and artillery imported from Flanders, while the training of archers and men-at-arms were improved, and last but not least the King began to build up a

Navy. The welfare of his poorer subjects was always near to his heart, a Stewart characteristic which is seldom mentioned by the average historian—and in this it is noticeable that the Estates of Scotland, right up to the Act of Union (1707), always showed the greatest sympathy to measures introduced to benefit the 'pure men inhabitaris of the grund'. Regulations were made providing relief for the sick poor, the security of travellers, stabilization of prices and wages as well as the standardisa-ation of weights and measures.

In 1425 the Duke of Albany and his two sons were executed, Alexander Lord of the Isles being a member of the jury that secured his conviction; but the King having in mind the past record of the family did not recognize Alexander as Earl of Ross. This omission did nothing to improve the temper of the Lord of the Isles or that of his ambitious mother the Lady Margaret, who used all her great influence with her son to force him into drastic action. Two years later King James came north opening his Parliament in the Royal Castle of Inverness, sum-moning every Highland Chief of consequence to attend, among them 'his lovit cusins' Lord Alexander and the Lady Margaret. Forty chiefs responded to the summons in all good faith, but then King James pro-ceeded to make his first bad mistake which was to cause much blood-shed, till by a reversal of these methods the King was able, partially, to make good the damage caused.

The chiefs were separated from their followers and suspecting no harm entered the Royal Audience Chamber, where a large number were instantly seized and imprisoned, some being executed on the spot among the latter being MacGorrie of *Garmoran*; John MacArthur; and John Campbell. Fordun relates: 'The King caused to be arrested Alexander of the Isles and his mother, each of whom he invited singly to the Castle and caused them to be placed in strict confinement apart'. Margaret passed most of her remaining days imprisoned in Inchcolm as a hostage for her son's good conduct after his release which probably took place within a year. Our old friend Angus *Dubh* Mackay of Farr was given a lecture on the inadvisability of being a partizan of such people as the late Regent Albany while his son Neil went to the Bass Rock as a hostage. Others were given a straight talk, among them *MacMathan* (Matheson) from Wester Ross, still a powerful Chief with a following of 2000 men, though this is the last mention of a chief of that name for two hundred years, as after his death the Clan *Mathan* rapidly decreased probably attaching themselves to Clan Mackenzie and the House of Kintail, who by then held nearly all of Wester Ross. The only Chief received with marks of favour was old Murdoch Mackenzie of Kintail and Alexander 'The Upright' his son, who had accompanied his father to Inverness.

King James was one of the most cultured men of his day, a great scholar, a talented musician and poet; and a fluent Gaelic speaker, as indeed were all the Kings of Scotland till James VI and I, several of them being gifted bards in that language. In Alexander he saw a young man out of the ordinary who would more than repay any help which would enable him to receive a more advanced education than was customary among the Barons and Chiefs of that day. The result of this was that young Kintail said farewell to his father who returned to *Eilean Donan*, and went south with the King who found a place for him in the famous school at Perth.

But the chance of swinging Alexander Lord of the Isles, to loyal service was lost; even though he was soon released his haughty spirit cried for revenge. Within two years the Lord of the Isles had summoned his vassals and with an army of 10,000 men—a favourite figure with the chroniclers—captured and burnt Inverness including the Castle, following this by wasting all the Crown lands within reach, which would have included a large section of the Black Isle. The Highland capital would have burnt easily for as yet the majority of buildings in the northern burghs were of wood, while those of stone would normally be thatched.

The King marched north again with a strong force, accompanied by the Earl of Douglas, an interested party because as heir of the de Moray family he had inherited lands in Banff, Aberdeen, Moray and in Ross Edderdar (Redcastle), and Avoch, as well as Bothwell in south west Scotland. Battle was joined in Lochaber. Clans Chattan and Cameron deserting Alexander and joining the King, so that the complete defeat of the Islesmen followed. The Lord of the Isles made an abject surrender at Holyrood which coupled with the intercession of Queen Joan and the attendant nobles saved his life, but he spent the next two years in Tantallon Castle.

Yet in 1431 the Clan was out again under his relations Donald Balloch the younger of Islay and Alasdair *Carrach* of Lochaber. The Royal Army under the Earls of Caithness and Mar who was killed, was completely defeated; the King came north but there was little more fighting and this time he succeeded in quietening the Highlands, but as a result of this last rising Alasdair lost Lochaber which went to the Chief of Clans Chattan—the Mackintosh.

The Earl of Mar, despite his roguery, which was almost inevitable seeing that by the natural chances of inheritance he must have got at least some of the characteristics of his disreputable father the Wolf of Badenoch, was yet a brilliant character. As Ambassador Plenipotentiary to England he concluded peace between the two countries in 1406. He never moved without a retinue of sixty well mounted and armed gentlemen and his magnificence set the fashion even for the Court of France, where he was well-known, becoming the Lord of Dufflé in Brabant after successful fighting in Flanders. Neither was he a mere flashy soldier as is shown by his care in importing Hungarian stallions and mares into Mar in order to improve the stock of horses; at sea he was equally successful though often quite illegally.

As High Admiral of Scotland he had done well, but when the necessity for this was over he concocted a private venture with his old friend Robert Davidson—Lord Provost and Inn Keeper of Aberdeen; together they formed a 'limited liability company' to seize merchant ships from Danzig and Rostock on the Baltic. This developed into a private war against the Prussians which one is delighted to know went in favour of the men of Mar and Aberdeen, so that a large number of Prussians found themselves employed quarrying and carrying stone for building operations either at Kindrochit or Kildrummy Castle.

At the end of his two years' imprisonment Alexander Lord of the Isles was granted a free pardon by the Estates, it being realized that he had no part in Donald Balloch's insurrection. The MacDonalds were now firmly established in Skye and as they were the de jure Earls of Ross the MacLeods of Glenelg, Harris and Dunvegan had given their support, during all these troubles, both to Alexander and his father Donald; the Lewis MacLeods may have done the same, though during the early years of the century they had their hands full with the Mackay feuds.

Throughout the course of this century the Sanctuary of Saint Duthac at Tain was becoming ever more famous and venerated as a place of pilgrimage for the Nation; in 1420 Sir James Douglas of Dalkeith had died of 'the Quhew' (flu) leaving great possessions including the robes of cloth of gold and silk which he bequeathed as vestments to the churches of St. Duthac Tain and St. Nicholas at Dalkeith. Some years later another interesting endowment came from Alexander Sutherland of Dunbeath on 15th November 1456; it is dated at Roslin Castle the home of Alexander's son-in-law William Earl of Orkney—later Caithness. Among other bequests intended to ensure the welfare of his soul, are sums of money to the Canons of Ross (Chanonry), *Fearn*, Tain, Dornoch, Kinloss and Orkney (Kirkwell), while the Abbot of *Fearn* received £100 for the repair of the Church and to buy himself a flat tombstone. In addition to this certain annual sums derived from the lands of Easter Kindace were put aside for the employment of a priest to sing masses for Alexander and his wife, in the 'Chanonrie of Ross'.

His son Alexander of Sutherland, Archdeacon of Caithness got £200 to cover the expenses of a pilgrimage to Rome for the benefit of his father's soul, an arrangement already made at his father's last confession. The executors for this will were: Finlay Abbot of *Fearn*; Master Thomas Lochmalony Chancellor of Ross; Alexander junior, the Archdeacon of Caithness; and his sister's son Alexander of Strattone Lord of Loranton. He left also a chalice to the Church of Roslin, another 'guilt' to St. Magnus' altar in Kirkwall Cathedral, while yet another is mentioned as being in the testator's Kist in Tain.

By 1436 the King appeared to be master of all Scotland, he had succeeded in his purpose of ruling a peaceful well-run kingdom, where justice was available to all, while the arts and other outward signs of increased prosperity were everywhere in evidence; but certain turbulent nobles in league with England were to retard this progress. The King spent Christmas day 1436 at Perth, during this period the virtual capital of Scotland, and while here received several warnings regarding a new plot, but they were ignored or miscarried.

On the 20th February King James was brutally murdered and though his devoted English Queen, Joan, took a terrible vengeance on the perpetrators of the crime, Scotland had lost her King. The heir to the throne Prince James was only six years old, and to make matters worse the House of Douglas were next in the running for the Crown, and from being the mainstay of that Crown this great family were becoming a standing menace to the kingdom by their arrogance and ambition.

With the assassination of the King the Earldom of Ross was restored to Alexander Lord of the Isles, who thus after a gap of twenty-seven years became the 10th Earl, as well as Justiciar north of the Forth, a post he owed to his friend the Earl of Douglas now the Lieutenant of the kingdom. Douglas died and for the next seventeen years civil war flickered over Scotland while the shadow of the Black Douglases lay over the land. The power of this family was immense, being in no way lessened by their proximity to the throne; their well-earned glory gave them a name second to none while both in Scotland and France they enjoyed vast possessions. Then both Crichton and Livingstone proclaimed themselves Regent while the boy King James II spent much of his time being kidnapped by one or other of the contending parties. Alarmed at the growing power of the young Douglas, Crichton and Livingstone combined forces and the former by murdering Douglas before the eyes of the small but protesting King, for a time curbed this power.

Alexander MacDonald Earl of Ross left no great mark in Ross, though he chased the Chief of Clan Cameron out of Scotland in revenge for his old desertion; but we find on the 2nd February 1441 Thomas Fraser Lord of Lovat signing a Bond of Manrent to become the 'lele man' of Sir Alexander of Ila, Earl of Ross and Lord of the Isles, the bond being signed in the house of Andrew Rede, Alderman, Inverness and witnessed by John de Ross the Laird of Balnagown, George de Munro Laird of Foulis, Alex. Makcowlach of Pladdis, Neil McLoyde and Neil Flemyng. The absence of signature by any representative of

Note 1. For explanation of Manrent, see Glossary.

Clan Kenneth is significant, they loved neither the old house of Ross nor the MacDonalds while the fusion of both was a disaster, for not only would this great combine tend to restrict further Mackenzie expansion, but the past experience of the secessionist efforts by the Lord of the Isles and equally rebellious behaviour by the Earls of Ross did not appeal in the least to the House of Kintail, who right through their history followed an unwavering policy of loyalty to the Royal House.

The Earl died 1449 in his Castle of Dingwall and was buried at Fortrose; the following year this Royal Burgh was to combine with the adjoining Royal Burgh of Rosemarkie, thus becoming one municipal entity. Alexander was succeeded by his sixteen-year-old son John, who inherited the Lordship of the Isles and the Earldom of Ross, being the 11th and last Earl of this House and a Ward of King James II. By his second wife, Alexander had left two sons, Celestine of Lochalsh and Hugh the first Lord of Sleat, who was to establish himself in the old MacLeod Castles of *Dun Sgatáich* and *Camus*.

Some trouble had developed on the Border, Dunbar and Dumfries having been burned by the English in 1448, but they were countered by the Douglases, who returning to their old tradition, had invaded England, eventually smashing their army at Sark with bloody losses.

Next year James II married Mary of Gueldres; at the celebration a great tournament was held and among the Scottish knights who entered the lists against the Burgundian visitors was Sir John Ross of Hawkhead, no relative of the Earls of Ross, but of whose descendants we shall hear during the early 18th century, when by a very odd manoeuvre they inherited Balnagown.

King James II had to face much the same problems as his father and although his reign only lasted ten years he succeeded in pulling Scotland together once again. Young James was a true son of his father and though not so great a scholar had the compensating virtue of being able to win the deep love and loyalty of men; by the people he was adored and soon proved himself a friend to all honest folk. Just in time he broke Livingstone, but the 8th Earl of Douglas who had recently returned from Rome found the new order not to his liking. Intrigue with England followed, while a highly treasonable pact was concluded with that country involving also his three brothers the Earl of Moray, the Earl of Ormond (Avoch), and Lord Balvany, as well as 'Tiger' Earl of Crawford and the young Earl of Ross, with the result that our old friend Donald Balloch appeared in the Clyde with a flotilla of galleys, sacking Inverkip in Renfrew, and razing Brodick Castle in Arran—all of which was due to the Douglas promptings.

Meanwhile Earl John seized the Royal Castles of Inverness and Urquhart, giving the governorship of the latter to his father-in-law Sir James Livingstone, this coup being followed up by the destruction of the fortalice of Ruthven in Badenoch. Then the Douglas, without waiting for English help, defied the King by almost setting up as an independent sovereign murdering the King's envoys and generally behaving very badly indeed.

The King hesitated to start a civil war which was misconstrued by the Douglas as a sign of weakness resulting in further outrages, yet in spite of every provocation James still sought a peaceful way out, inviting Douglas to meet him under safe conduct in order to talk over the points of difference. At the subsequent meeting the visitor became more and more arrogant, refusing point blank to break his pact with Ross. But Douglas had gone too far, the young King had reached the breaking point and reaching across the table he dirked the Douglas, while the rest of his entourage, which included the uncle of the murdered envoy MacLellan of Bombie, only too willingly joined in, liquidating the entire Douglas party present.

Civil war broke out but the Gordons broke Crawford at Brechin *Muir*, Angus head of the Red Douglas' joined the King while behind him stood four square the Church and Estates of Scotland. John Earl of Ross and Lord of the Isles sued for peace, being pardoned on condition of his good conduct which seems to have been satisfactory as in 1457 John was appointed one of the Wardens of the Marches, a post demanding absolute loyalty and trustworthiness. By 1453 things were quiet once more, the power of the Black Douglases being, for the time, broken.

John Earl of Ross was now living in semi-Royal state at Dingwall Castle while John Monro of Foulis on 4th August 1453 was served as heir to his father George, who had been killed, a short time before. John Monro was, however, a minor so that his uncle John Monro the 1st Baron of Milntown (New Tarbat) and later Chamberlain of Ross, was appointed tutor of Foulis and Captain of Clan Munro.

As often happened national upsets presented opportunities for the settlement of private quarrels and in the year 1454 John the Tutor fought a quite private battle with part of Clan Mackintosh, at Clachnaharry, a spot just north of Inverness, marked by a monument. It seems that the Tutor was insulted by the people of Strathardale, the insult being the removal of the tails from his horses, while he and his retinue were asleep expecting no evil as they were peacably travelling home from the south. The Tutor very angry indeed hurried home, collected two hundred men from Foulis and within a day or two had returned to Strathardale lifting a good herd of cattle as compensation for the tails of his horses.

Now by immemorial custom, if the spoils of a raid were driven through another Chief's territory that Chief could claim a small rake off, normally a perfectly amicable transaction, but on this occasion

E

while passing Moy the Mackintosh or his steward appeared and asked for too large a share of the beasts, at least this was the opinion of Monro, who after a heated argument marched on paying nothing. A force of Mackintosh's followed catching up with the Monro party at Clachnaharry where the road passes below a bluff, where the Tutor had wisely posted a rearguard consisting mostly of archers well hidden. Some casualties were suffered by both sides, the Tutor himself being wounded, but the main body were soon well into Ross and the battle ceased, though Monro by the time he reached Beauly was suffering severely from his wound which might have got worse had not Lovat succoured him.

Scotland as a whole was at peace when England with many ill-mannered insults declared war on King James; but this war never started as King Henry VI, who for some time had been insane, re-covered his wits and climbed down. Within a short space of time that King was asking for Scots aid against the House of York, so that in 1459 James crossed the Border taking seventeen English fortresses on his way.

Alas on the 3rd August 1460 King James was killed by the bursting of one of his cannon at the siege of Roxburgh; he was only thirty years of age. At this action the Earl of Ross was present with the Royal Army having contributed a force of 3000 well-armed Highlanders, who helped the Queen to bring the siege to a successful conclusion, Roxburgh being levelled to the ground as it proved too convenient a base for the invading English.

The new King was once again a boy of nine so that Queen Marie supported by the great Bishop Kennedy carried on the government, but the Yorkish faction had won in England. Soon after the King's death, Earl John relapsed into his bad old ways, vacating his seat in the Estates to assemble his principal vassals in the Castle of Ardtornish, where on 19th October 1461 he granted in the manner of an independ-ent Prince to his trusty and well-beloved cousins, Ranald of the Isles and Duncan Arch-Dean of the Isles, a commission to proceed to London there to confer with a similar body for Edward IV. This assembly met at Westminster and then concocted a quite extraordinary treaty which envisaged nothing less than the dismemberment of the Kingdom of Scotland. The Army of Conquest was to consist of Earl John's forces, the Douglas vassals, and the English Army, while John Earl of Ross, Donald Balloch and another John, Donald's son and heir, were to become the sworn vassals of Edward IV, promising to assist him in all wars in England or Ireland. In consideration of this the Earl of Ross was to get £300 a year during war, Donald Balloch £40, and his son £20, the sums to be halved in time of peace.

But the main provision was the subjugation of Scotland, the whole kingdom north of the Forth to be divided between the two Earls and Donald Balloch; the young Earl of Douglas receiving in addition his former possessions, what was over to go to the King of England. This masterpiece is dated London 13th February 1462. As a first step to accomplish this scheme Earl John raised the standard of rebellion giving the command nominally to his bastard son Angus *Óg* then a boy, but in reality to the old veteran Donald Balloch. Angus seized Inverness from which town he issued orders and proclamations for the whole north, meantime the MacDonald galleys swept the western coasts causing some loss of revenue. The whole scheme then collapsed under the weight of its own absurdity for as soon as the average Highlander realized the intention of the scheme they went home having no sympathy with it.

Clan Mackenzie was fortunate in having Alexander of Kintail as its chief during this tricky period. He had fully justified the hopes of his benefactor King James I; surely and steadily he was building up the strength of Clan Mackenzie who now dwelt in peace, strong enough to keep clear of all these entanglements. His policy was to remain consistently loyal to the House of Stewart, to remain at peace with his neighbours but to build up such strength that he could be sure of maintaining that peace, even if Ross himself should think otherwise; and regarding that great House there is little doubt that he saw the writing on the wall and intended that his family and clan should participate in and benefit from its inevitable downfall. Earl John once again submitted to the Queen and Bishop Kennedy who not knowing of the secret treaty, pardoned him with the full sanction of the Estates so that John remained a free man for another fifteen years.

In 1469 James III at the age of eighteen took over control of his kingdom, a true Renaissance Prince of great artistic gifts but lacking the strength of character possessed by his father and grandfather.

Before following the final act in the drama of the Ross Earldom and Lordship of the Isles, let us take a look at certain changes that were coming to pass during the whole of this pregnant century. The 15th century was a period of great building activity both secular and ecclesiastical; in the year 1426 a Parliament of James I had passed a special act for the northern part of Scotland, laying down certain regulations for the Chiefs, Chieftains and Barons in that area. That the castles, fortalices and manor places were to be repaired and brought up to date by their owners, moreover the said owners were expected to dwell in them looking after the good governance of their lordship while expending their revenues on the improvement of their lands.

Certain castles may be said to have been almost purely military in their object, among this type being the 1412 Castle of Inverness, and to a lesser degree Dingwall and Redcastle, but by the 15th century the

normal castle stood for more than this. They were an integral part of the
national life intended to benefit all in that they not only provided the
proper residence for the nobility and landed gentry, but were the
centres for the local government of that day, giving protection from
piratical or other raids, and keeping a check on minor disturbance.

During this century alterations were taking place within the castles
changing the somewhat primitive living conditions of the past. With
the exception of Dingwall Castle—in construction an original 'great'
tower, with several smaller ones added to the encircling stone wall
which protected the bailey with its various buildings—the castles of
Ross and Cormarty conformed to the more usual Highland patterns.
These remained simple in design, consisting of a single tower, great or
small; the lesser chieftains and small lairds might have a tower with
one room only on each floor, reached by a narrow turnpike stair, this
type being exemplified by the Tower of Fairburn, Kinkell, Castle Craig
belonging to the Bishop of Ross, and Davochmaluach.

But whatever the size the principle remained the same: the vaulted
ground floor held the kitchen, usually a fine big room, the pit, though
this might be below ground-level, store rooms, still-room and the like,
and the 1st floor, the great hall, mighty fireplace and the Lady's
bower. Succeeding floors were reached by one or more spiral stone
stairways, quite undecorated till a later period in history, built within
the thickness of the wall, or in a rounded projection inside, or in an
outside turret. Sometimes the stair started from the first floor in which
case the ground floor might have its own entrance door or was reached
from above by a separate stair. By the late 14th century the stairways
sometimes ran from bottom to top though as a rule this is a later
development, again both systems often exist together.

The windows were still in the main narrow slits though glazing was
becoming more common for the principal rooms upstairs; as far back as
1329 a considerable amount of glass was in use, being mentioned in an
account of the Bruce's residence at Cardross near Dumbarton. All
flooring above the Hall was of wood resting on beams, both, frequently,
of well-seasoned Scots pine. The number of floors varied but in the
moderate sized castle five or six would be the usual number forming a
series of large rooms. Additional smaller rooms were provided by
hollowing out the wall, or a short wing or jamb from the French
jambe, was thrown out which really amounted to another tower in
which the rooms were rather smaller and having lower ceilings thus
providing more accommodation than the main block. Drainage was
not; a well usually existed within the castle, while the privies were small
closets usually situated at the corners of the building, with a shoot
leading to the outside world.

The entrance was protected by an iron yett hung on hinges, which fastened behind and reinforced the stout iron-studded wood door, thus forming a second line of defence if the door was burnt. If the castle entrance was on the first floor and therefore well above ground level, it was reached by a movable external stair or ladder, later replaced by a permanent stone or internal stair and new entrance stairway. Grouped with the tower were several humble outhouses such as stables and byre, usually surrounded by a barnekin, a not very formidable enclosing wall.

Within the castle the floors were strewn with rushes or aromatic herbs while coloured hangings covered the bare stone walls, unless these were painted. The furniture consisted of large heavily draped beds, cushioned settles, carved or metal-bound chests and metal holders for the rush lights, and wax or tallow candles, the former being reserved for special occasions, the hall and Lady's bower.

The comments of Pedro de Ayala, Spanish Ambassador to the court of James IV 1488–1513 are of interest, giving as they do an indication of the 'Castle' standard of living. He writes: 'All the furniture that is used in Italy, Spain and France is to be found in their dwellings. It has not been bought in modern times only, but inherited from preceding ages'.

Gardens were by no means unknown but were chiefly confined to the growing of herbs and quite simple plants; we have evidence of Robert the Bruce's appreciation of his garden at the new Castle of Tarbert Kintyre during the last quiet years of his gallant life which ended in 1329. At the end of the 15th, but more often during the 16th century some further changes were to appear on existing castles as well as new ones: the parapet grows smaller, sometimes disappearing altogether or from one or more sides, while its corbell became a continuous cornice. At the same time the flat roof disappears making way for a gabled roof, adorned with great chimney stacks, thus adding another storey to the tower.

Inside, furniture increased while wood panelling of oak or pine, begins to take the place of wall hangings, giving a warmer appearance to the room and providing a better background for family portraits. The appearance of the Policies also, were improved by a greater measure of ornamental tree planting. This evolutionary process can be seen in the castles of *Eilean Donan*, Castle Leod, Balloan, Balcony, Brahan, Kilcoy and Redcastle.

The number of small castles in Ross must have been very great as in addition to those we have mentioned there were many others which have left no trace. There are 14th century references to: The Tower of Badgavie in Kiltearn; Tower of Ardoch; Tower of Strathskiach; and others later.

CHAPTER X

THE END OF THE HOUSE OF ROSS—THE POWER OF CLAN DONALD CURBED BY CLAN MACKENZIE—THE HOUSE OF KINTAIL SPREADS TO EASTER ROSS—DRESS OF THE PERIOD—INTERNAL TRADE

Chronological Table

1465 Birth of Scottish poet, William Dunbar (d. c. 1520) the father of Literature in Britain. Birth of Scottish historian Hector Boetius, Principal of Aberdeen University 1505, d. 1536.
1470 Birth of Henry the Minstrel the Scots poet (Blind Harry). Birth of Scottish historian John Major (or Mair). His history was written in Latin and published in 1521.
1471 Durer born.
1472 King James III regains Orkney and Shetland from Norway, in lieu of endowment promised in his marriage contract. He married Princess Margaret of Denmark and Norway in 1467.
1475 Birth of the Scots poet Gavin Douglas, translator of Virgil.
1477 Forfeiture of Earldom of Ross by the Crown.
1480 Great sea battle of Bloody Bay off Mull. John Lord of the Isles defeated by his son Angus *Og*. Eldest son of MacLeod of Lewis killed fighting for John.
1482 Invasion of Scotland.
1487 Battle of Aldicharrish in Sutherland in which Alexander Ross of Balnagown was defeated by forces of Earls of Sutherland and Mackays, many gentlemen of name of Vass and McCulloch lost their lives.
1488 Battle of Sauchieburn, southern nobles defeat James III, who was afterwards murdered.
1490 Poem by Gioffa Coluim *Mac an Ollamh*—a lament for Angus *Og*—son of John Lord of the Isles.
1491 Henry VII attempts to kidnap James IV. Fresh war in Highlands. Battle of *Blar na Pàirc*, complete defeat of MacDonalds of the Isles by Clan Mackenzie.
1492 Columbus discovers America.
1493 Forfeiture of Lordship of the Isles by the Crown.
1494 Founding of Aberdeen University and Buildings of King's College by William Elphinstone, Bishop of Ross till 1481.

William '*Dubh*' (Black William) MacLeod of Dunvegan had combined with the Lord of Sleat for a raid on Orkney, the cause being certain derogatory remarks made by the northern Earl concerning Hugh of Sleat whom he had recently met in Edinburgh.

The secret Treaty between the Earl of Ross and England was still unsuspected by James III, leaving Earl John free to live in magnificent state, unperturbed by any fears for the future, signing many charters and a licence to his vassal the Laird of Kilravock to build a castle. But in 1476 the bomb-shell exploded, the terms of the secret Treaty of 1461 becoming known; needless to say the reaction of the Estates was powerful and immediate.

Unicorn Pursuivant arrived in Dingwall and at the barbican of the Castle which had been barred against him, summoned the traitor John Earl of Ross and Lord of the Isles to appear before the Estates at Edinburgh in December to answer the charges to be brought against him. As these summonses were not always effective a commission was given to the Earl of Argyll to formulate a decree of forfeiture while a strong Royal force was assembled under the Earls of Crawford and Atholl. John realized that he was up against something very big and although he might count on his own great Clan Donald and their Island vassals there were others within his Earldom such as Clan Mackenzie who would most certainly remain loyal to the Crown. For some days he pondered then taking the advice of the Earl of Huntly, sent in his submission, appearing soon after at the Court, in person; yet once again his luck was in, and he was granted a pardon, though this time there were formidable conditions.

The Earldom of Ross was to be resigned for ever to the Crown, together with his possessions and superiorities in Kintyre, Knapdale, Urquhart, Glenmoriston etc., but he was permitted to retain the Lordship of the Isles, while further to gild the pill the late Earl was made a Lord of Parliament. John, being no fool, realized and appreciated the generosity of the terms, and gladly bowed to the inevitable, retiring to his western Lordship apparently quite willing to pass the remainder of his life on his still vast estates.

But this was not to be, his bastard son Angus *Òg* and still more his ambitious nephew Alexander of Lochalsh together with a large section of Clan Donald turned on their Chief, who in their opinion had dragged the honour of both clan and family in the dust by his acceptance of the inevitable; this at least was the propaganda reason, though ambition and the chance of great personal gain, probably, lay at the root of their decision. It was not long before the fruits of this inter-family and clan split appeared, but meanwhile the Crown placed the Province of Ross under the nominal Chamberlainship of the Earl of Sutherland; Ross south and west of the River Peffrey coming under control of Alexander 'The Upright' VIIth Baron of Kintail and Chief of Clan Mackenzie, while Ross north and east of this area fell to John XIth Baron of Foulis and Chief of Clan Munro.

The vast properties in these areas which had fallen to the Crown by the forfeiture were in the main redistributed, especially by James IV the succeeding monarch, to other landowners who had rendered acceptable service. The Houses of Kintail and Foulis were the chief beneficiaries, which added enormously to their already wide acres. Dingwall once more became a Royal Castle, and 100 years later James VI and I was to try and regain some of the Earldom lands, so that a proportion did become Crown property.

It gives an indication of the wealth of the original Earldom to know that the much attenuated acres regained by the above 'Slobbering Jaimie' included: 140 separate farms and smaller holdings in Ross which in addition to the rents of money, oats, barley, meal and sheep produced some 100 head of cattle and 1,000 head of poultry. Other revenues which were not relinquished by the Crown consisted of: four lasts of salmon 'Red and Sweet' and 2,000 cod which were ordered to be sent to the Port of Leith. The Royal Governors of the Castle had the responsibility of collecting the rents, mostly in kind, for the King, at the Castle of Dingwall and shipping them from a pier situated north east of the Castle at the old Peffrey mouth.

But in the Western Isles war clouds were gathering, whether John Lord of the Isles willed it or not; and in 1481 Angus *Òg* raided Ross with a powerful force, his object being to retrieve the lost possessions in this Province, and among his allies was Donald Gallach, later the 2nd Lord of Sleat. At Laguidh Bhride (Logiebride) near where Conan House now stands he was opposed by a Mackenzie force which he defeated; but what had seemed a formidable insurrection collapsed when a Royal force—largely from the Inverness–Moray area—surprised the MacDonalds at Drumderfit, killing many and driving the remainder out of Ross.

In 1484 Angus fought the indecisive but bitter naval action of Bloody Bay against an expedition commanded by the Earls of Argyll, Atholl, and incidentally his own father who was supporting the Government forces. The MacLeods of Dunvegan who had supported John Lord of the Isles suffered in consequence as Angus seized from them the strong Castle of Duntulum at the northern end of Skye, which went a few years later to Hugh of Sleat and his son Donald Gallach. It was to remain the principal residence of that family for the next two hundred years.

In 1488 the southern nobles rose against James III who was defeated at Sauchieburn and afterwards murdered. At this battle Hector Roy Mackenzie 1st of *Gairloch* had commanded a force of 500 Mackenzies on the side of the luckless James, but the battle was a pretty half-hearted affair all round and Hector returned north with his contingent soon after, seizing Redcastle en route as it was being held for the rebels. This matter being settled in a satisfactory manner, as incidentally it gave the House of Kintail their first firm footing in the fertile Black Isle, Red Hector reported to the Earl of Huntly, the King's Lieutenant in the north, who was raising a Highland Army to avenge the King's death. Orders arrived from the young King James IV to disband, an order which was reluctantly carried out by the Highlanders, but avoiding a fruitless war of revenge, as despite the tragedy of James III, Scotland was flourishing and James IV was just the King she needed, having all the Stewart virtues and but few of their defects.

In 1490 Angus *Òg* was assassinated in Inverness by an Irish harper *Diarmed Cairbreach* and though this ambitious son of the Isles was reputed both brave and generous he was no loss to either Scotland or Ross. Of Donald *Dubh* the son of Angus *Òg* MacDonald we shall hear later, but the greatest menace from the west was now the capable Sir Alexander MacDonald of Lochalsh who had for some time ignored his chief, John, by openly assuming the title of Lord of the Isles.

The Chief of Clan Kenneth was still the now venerable Alexander, but much of the work fell to his son and heir Kenneth a great warrior but short in the temper, who for mundane reasons had married the

Lady Margaret only daughter of John Lord of the Isles, who at the time of the wedding had still been the Earl of Ross. Alexander and his son and daughter-in-law were now in residence in one of the new acquisitions, the Ross hunting lodge Castle of Kinellan, and about this time an incident occurred which served to add a personal bitterness to the political animosity already existing between the Clans MacDonald and Mackenzie.

A year or two before his death Angus *Òg,* who had been allowed to retain the not very formidable Castle of Balconie at Evanton, decided to give a Christmas party inviting a number of Chiefs among them Kenneth the Master of Kintail together with his wife Lady Margaret, Angus's half sister, Sir Alexander of Lochalsh by now the de facto Lord of the Isles despite the existence of John, acting as joint host with his cousin. Kenneth duly arrived with the customary following of forty men but without his wife Margaret, an omission which gave considerable offence.

But worse was to follow; Angus had given to MacLean of Duart the task of allotting accommodation, no easy job, as the number of guests far exceeded the space available. Now MacLean had recently quarrelled with Kenneth so perhaps with malice aforethought offered to him very indifferent quarters outside the Castle; Kenneth took umbrage, words followed to be succeeded by blows which ended in MacLean being knocked down. The house party took the side of their hosts and Kenneth realizing that things were getting out of control, left, with his tail of men behind him, making for the Cromarty Firth where boats had been collected for the transportation of guests. He took sufficient of them to embark his troop stoving-in the bottom of the others in order to prevent possible pursuit, and crossed to the Black Isle, possibly lodging in Castle Craig as a guest of the Bishop.

The following day Kenneth returned to Kinellan when he gave an account of the proceedings to his father that greatly distressed the old Chief who considered that his son should have shown more forebearance and control, realizing that bloodshed might well follow this childish quarrel. Small beginnings may have big endings and four days after Christmas an ultimatum arrived from Alexander MacDonald with a notice to quit Kinellan within 24 hours or expect the direst consequences, the only exception being the Lady Margaret, Alexander's cousin, who could remain at her leisure.

Kenneth in a fury sent back a suitable reply and despite remonstrances from his father added further insult by a very ungallant action. Margaret, his wife, was no beauty, and among other things being short of one eye, Kenneth probably only too glad to get rid of her, and fuming with rage, committed the cruel and inhuman act of sending the poor lady back to her family, mounted on a one-eyed horse, led by a one-eyed servant accompanied by a one-eyed dog. This final deed had nothing to recommend it especially as the wretched lady was in bad health and died very soon after; but war was now inevitable, Alexander MacDonald returning to the west in order to start preparations for a major onslaught. Kenneth now improved the occasion by investing Beaufort Castle, demanding Lovat's daughter Agnes Fraser as a wife; as neither Agnes nor Lord Lovat were at all averse to the alliance despite the violence of the wooing, both agreed willingly, the marriage taking the form of hand-fasting[1], being at a later date regularized by the Church.

In 1491 the storm broke, Alexander MacDonald with a force of some thousand MacDonalds advanced from the west while his allies Clans Cameron and MacKintosh mustering between them about another thousand, moved north to effect a junction with him, seizing en route the Royal Castle of Inverness which they garrisoned. Here they were joined by Young Rose of Kilravock who took the opportunity of crossing at Kessock, wasting the Urquhart lands in the Black Isle and lifting '600 Ky and oxen, price of the piece 13/4; four score horse, price of the piece 26/8; 200 swine, price of the piece 3/– with insicht (inside) plenshing to the avail (value) of £300; and also 25 score bolls of victual, and £300 of the mailis of the said Sheriffs (Urquhart) lands'.

On a Sunday the combined forces joined together at Contin, the MacDonalds having already left their mark on Strathconon. Here Alexander of Lochalsh assumed supreme command and then occurred the prelude to one of the bloodiest fights of clan history. The women, children and old people only were left in the hamlet of Contin, who, warned of the close proximity of the enemy by the skirling of the Pipes, left their houses and crowded into the little church, but this was not to save them, and a scene of horror followed, as the MacDonalds fired the thatched roof of the church, first of all making sure that the exit was blocked. Many non-combatants perished in the flames, the act being witnessed by the Mackenzie scouting parties and outposts on the high ground further east.

This quite unexpected and callous massacre was to cost the MacDonald's dear, especially as all the young men of Contin were with the Mackenzie forces, and in those distant times the Highlands were unaccustomed, perhaps not sufficiently civilized, to regard the murdering of women and children as a natural concomitant to warfare. This occurred late on Sunday; old Alexander and Kenneth of Kintail knowing that the attack would come next morning, had not been idle, but were busy keeping the anger of their men at white heat, knowing full well that the great disparity of numbers would be more than compensated for by the bitter hatred engendered by the outrage.

Note 1. For Hand-fasting see Glossary.

The Mackenzie forces had been increased by retainers and friends, from Brahan, Strathconon, Strathgarve and the Glens to the west— all new acquisitions—as well as by men from the Burgh of Dingwall, the Dingwalls of Kildun and Innes's men from Tulloch, a chieftain whose family will appear again in the story of Ross, in origin a Moray family and clan occupying the lands of Innes in Moray given by King Malcolm IV (1160–65) to one Berowald a Fleming who taking his name from the territory, founded the family of Innes. Walter Innes is referred to as a baron in the time of King Alexander II inferring that he was a landowner holding his fief direct from the Crown. An additional reinforcement was provided by Brodie of Brodie who with the usual following had just arrived from Moray on a visit to Kinellan and insisted on standing by his host.

But the force was still very small as Kenneth had been obliged to leave a strong garrison in Kintail under his constable at *Eilean Donan* Castle having in view the possibility of another MacDonald invasion in the west. His total strength, made up of Mackenzies, their 'shirt of mail' MacRaes, MacLennans and Easter Ross contingents, amounted to less than eight hundred men, while the MacDonald army mustered not less than two thousand. But victory does not always go to the big battalions, especially when the larger force is lacking in discipline and not too well led.

Alexander MacDonald's chief lieutenants were, his kinsman Gillespie, Farquhar MacKintosh Chief of Clan Chattan, Rose of Kilravock and the redoubtable MacLean of Duart. Opposed to them were Kenneth Master of Kintail, his brother Duncan and his half-brother the veteran soldier Hector '*Eachin Ruagh*' the 1st of *Gairloch*.

Before noon on Monday, MacDonald moved east, forming up in the area east of the thick woods where Coul House now stands, and north of Jameston. Less than five hundred yards away were the Mackenzies, most of them in full view, but what MacDonald's scouts had failed to discover was the presence of a quagmire—since drained—covered with deceptive moss and grass, which lay between the opposing forces.

Kenneth at this point realizing the great numbers against him, decided to send his father, now nearing his ninetieth year, for safety to a cave on the Raven's Rock. Before leaving, the grand old chief besought Heaven's protection for his son and his men, pointing out to them that the MacDonald's though numerous, by their sacrilege and inhumanity had brought upon themselves the vengeance of God.

Through the bog were certain safe paths known only to the defenders and across them Kenneth led a decoy force having previously posted strong formations of MacRae archers in the woods that flanked the bog, with orders to stay out of sight till required. Kenneth's advance was the signal for a mass attack by the over confident enemy who already thought the battle won on seeing Kenneth start a slow retreat back to his own lines. Their disillusionment followed very quickly when the whole force, many of them encumbered with armour, found themselves floundering knee deep and more in soggy peat, the sign for Duncan and his archers to pour in flight after murderous flight of arrows.

The Mackenzie line now advanced taking care to stick to firm ground and the slaughter of the MacDonalds and their allies started. Gillespie who had found a footing forced his way through the struggling mass to get at Kenneth who already was heavily engaged, but he was seen in time and a deadly duel followed, Gillespie falling under a stroke of Kenneth's great two-handed sword which not only severed his arm, but, shearing through his mail, nearly cut him in half.

Many stories of individual feats of arms in this battle have come down to us, among them of how the Mackenzie standard-bearer—probably a MacLennan gentleman—when reproached by Kenneth for relinquishing his hold on the banner, replied that in order to free both arms for the work afoot he had first killed the MacDonald standard-bearer and then allowed him the privilege of bearing the *Caber Feidh* standard (the Stag's Head in gold on a blue background), by sticking the pole through his body. How the great MacLean of Lochbuie fell under the murderous axe of one Duncan MacRae, a somewhat 'simple' clansman who had arrived late for the battle and caused some amusement by demanding a proper man's esteem and respect before he would set to. Having killed one man he sat on the body and demanded the esteem of two men before he would continue, a performance he repeated with a third till told by Red Hector to get on with the good work, when he could have all the esteem that was his due. This provided the necessary spur and the gillie rushed into the fight proving himself a holy terror with his rusty but nevertheless deadly axe. Brodie greatly distinguished himself and was seriously wounded, but his actions on that day laid the foundations of generations of friendship between the two Houses who shortly afterwards entered into a Bond of Manrent.

What was left of the invaders broke and fled westward toward the River Conon. When a party enquired of an old woman the whereabouts of the ford, the river being in spate, the old lady purposely misdirected the fugitives, many of whom were drowned, though some who managed to cling to the bank had their hands removed by the sickles of the *cailleach* and her girl friends. Glaishean Gow, a blacksmith with whom Agnes Fraser of Lovat had been fostered gathered his friends to aid his beloved foster child, now the Lady of Kintail. He arrived too late for the fight but intercepted the flight of the remnants of Clan Chattan and Clan Cameron, killing the lot. Yet another helper is said to have been a wee man with a red night cap who suddenly appeared early in the battle, but as soon as it was over returned to his home beneath the waters of Loch Kinellan.

The remaining MacDonalds fled west into the hills followed by bands of Mackenzies who spared none they caught excepting the leader Sir Alexander MacDonald of Lochalsh who was spared by Kenneth 'to prove his victory and his honour', and brought back to Kinellan before being handed on to Lovat for six months imprisonment, after which he was released on swearing never again to molest a Mackenzie or Fraser, or claim any rights to the forfeited Earldom of Ross. Less than two hundred of the invaders ever reached their homes, and never again could Clan Donald threaten the existence of Clan 'Kenzie', though there were to be a few further minor clashes. Shortly after these events Kenneth, now known as *Coinnich 'a Bhlar* (Kenneth of the Battle) was knighted by James IV for his stand against the ambitious MacDonalds, a stand which suited so admirably both the policy of the King and Estates.

Sir William Munro of Foulis had failed to help the Mackenzies in their hour of need, probably having a soft spot for the old family they had served so long and so faithfully, and this omission resulted in the ravaging of his lands, the same treatment being meted out to the Baron of Kilravock. In their reprisals against the latter the customary bounds may have been exceeded so that eventually Huntly as Lieutenant of the North was forced to call a halt.

To what extent the forfeited Earl of Ross John Lord of the Isles was involved in Alexander's invasion is not known, but in 1493 he was deprived of all his remaining estates while the Lordship of the Isles was forfeited to the Crown, the formal surrender taking place in January of the next year; John of the Isles retired to the Monastery of Paisley, so often in the past enriched by his bounty. The story goes that some years later he took to wandering among the scenes of his past grandeur, finally dying in a cheap lodging house in Dundee in 1498, a sad end for the last descendant of Fearchar *Mac an t'Sagart* and Somerled King of the Isles who was to hold the mighty Earldom of Ross and the Lordship of the Isles. He was survived by his grandson—the son of Angus *Òg*— Donald *Dubh* of whom we shall hear.

Soon after the Battle of the Park (*Blar na Pàirc*) the fine old chief Alexander Mackenzie died, being buried in Beauly Priory or with his forebears on Iona. Kenneth did not long survive his father, dying on 14th February 1492, and was possibly the first chief of Clan Mackenzie to be buried in Beauly Priory where his effigy as a Knight in full armour can still be seen. The change from Iona to Beauly was caused by the fact that the Prior at this date was an illegitimate son of Kenneth—born of 'ane gentlewoman' who he had met at Dunrobin while aiding the Earl of Sutherland against MacKay. The boy was educated by Sutherland. By his first wife Margaret he left one son Kenneth Òg, and by his second Agnes Fraser of Lovat, John, for a time to be known as of Killin.

King James IV, a great Gaelic scholar whose connections with Ross were to be very close, had by his charm and good sense won over to himself the men of the Hebrides, visiting them as a friend, hunting and yachting both as host and guest with the chiefs, though through a temporary reversal of policy, he was yet to find trouble from this quarter of his now peaceful kingdom.

Before continuing with the march of events, and before we imagine that all this period was one long fight in Ross, let us look at certain developments in dress and in the normal work of the Province during this century. Little change had appeared in the dress of the upper class, which as we saw had been for ages the mantle or plaid-pleated saffron-coloured tunic (*léine chròchach*) made of varying lengths of linen, even reaching 20–30 ells (approximately yards), while in war a complete covering of mail was worn. The clansmen wore a linen shirt of similar make, which in the absence of armour, they daubed with pitch, sometimes adding a leather jerkin. Below and over this they wore the tartan kilt combined with the plaid *breacan an fhéilidh* or *fhéilidh mór* (great kilt) made up of 12 ells of cloth and fastened round the body with a belt, the lower half forming the kilt, covering that part of the body which with the advent of the shorter *léine* would have otherwise been over-exposed, while the upper part formed the plaid, fixed to the shoulder by a brooch and looped down behind.

In war they used a metal helmet, usually conical in shape, but on normal occasions went bare-headed though getting some protection from their long hair. In very stormy weather the plaid could be worn over the head and pinned at the breast. The bonnet did not appear in Scotland till the 16th century and came via south Scotland from France or Flanders. The arms consisted of the short bow of yew with iron-tipped and barbed arrows of ash, the great double-edged two-handed sword *claidheamh mór*, worn slung over the back with the hilt coming above the left shoulder, the spear or Lochaber axe, and dirk sharpened on one side only. The best blades were made by Andrea Ferrara, an Italian, who had been brought over by James III during the last half of this century. As armour became lighter or went out the two-handed swords were replaced or cut down, becoming the famous Highland broadswords with the double edge and basket hilt. Fire-arms appeared very early in the Highlands, the types used always being the most up to date of their period, the silver inlaid steel Highland pistol of 17th- and 18th-centuries being of exquisite workmanship.

The cloth from which the *breacan an fhéilidh* was woven, consisted of two qualities: the *cath-dath* or battle-dress of coarse wool, and the *breacan* of fine quality used for dress tartans and the women's plaids. The plaid of fine soft tartan cloth about 6 yards long and 1½ to 2 yards broad and trews appear to have been the earliest tartan garments worn by the 'quality'; the *breacan fhéilidh* gradually replacing altogether the mantle and old type of *léine chròchach*. The chiefs and those who could afford it sometimes wore on special occasions, plaids made of silk that was specially woven for the purpose in Spain. The normal foot gear for all was the Highland brogue of untanned leather or the *cuaran*, a knee-high boot of the same material laced up to below the knee, but many clansfolk went barefooted for choice.

From now on, with the general adoption of the *fhéilidh mór* (great kilt) an evolution, of course, of the older dress, only small alterations appeared in the general dress; a French writer in 1548 mentions the linen shirts and *breacan fhéilidh* of wool, large bows, the two-handed sword and targe. John Lesley Bishop of Ross in 1578 writes: 'They made also of linen very large shirts with numerous folds and wide sleeves which flowed abroad loosely to their knees. These the rich coloured with saffron, and others smeared with grease to preserve them longer clean (more likely to waterproof them), among the toils and exercises of a camp, which they held it of the highest consequence to practise continually. In the manufacture of them, ornament and a certain attention to taste were not altogether neglected, and they joined the different parts of their shirts very neatly with silk threads chiefly of a green or red colour'.

The kilt being quite unsuitable for riding, gentlemen had taken to the skin-tight tartan trews, a garment, as we saw, of immense antiquity, and sometimes worn later with the untanned leather riding boots. Despite remarks to the contrary by certain English writers the feather bonnet *A 'bhoineid mhar iteach* has a long history, maybe going back to Pictish times, but it was used only on ceremonial occasions, the type used at the time of Mary Queen of Scots being very similar to that used by our Highland Regiments in full dress.

The Bishop referring to the ladies' dress describes it as very becoming: 'over a gown reaching to the ankles and generally embroidered, they wore large mantles woven of different colours. The chief ornaments being bracelets and necklaces'. We shall see certain developments taking place in female dress during the 17th century, but the clothing of the people remained the same till 1746, except among the gentry who adopted the European style of dress when out of the Highlands and to some extent combined it with their national costume.

This account would not be complete without adding that there was, and is, a special tartan sett for ministers of religion, though now it is seldom seen. Within the clan the following setts were usual, though one or two may have been slightly later developments: 1. Chief's Dress sett

A Clansman

Sir Rorie Mackenzie of Coigeach
1574-1626

George, 1st Earl of Cromartie
1630-1714

Eilean Donan Castle

for himself and family; 2. The Clan Tartan; 3. A Hunting sett if number 2 was over bright; 4. Family setts; 5. Mourning setts; 6. District setts; 7. Earassaid setts for the women nearly always on a white background. Besides the clan setts there was the Royal sett as worn by Prince Charlie.

The Lord High Treasurer's Accounts of materials for a Highland dress made for King James V in 1538 (abbreviated) show the following:

		£.	s.	d.
2¼ ells of 'variant cullorit velvet' to be 'ane schort Heland Coit' at £6. the ell		13.	10.	0.
3¼ ells of 'green taffatys to line the said coit with' at 10/- the ell		1.	12.	6.
3 ells of 'Heland tartans to be hoiss' at 4/4 the ell ..			13.	0.
15 ells of 'Holland claith to be syde (long or hanging low) Heland Sarkis' at 8/- the ell		6.	0.	0.
2 'unce of silk to sew the same'			10.	0.
4 ells of 'rubaris to the hands of thame'			2.	0.
'For sowing and making the said sarkis'			9.	0.

Explanation: the suit consisted of a short jacket, vari-coloured, possibly tartan, velvet lined with green; a pair of tartan trews (stockings woul be 'short hoiss'.); two or more long shirts sewn with silk and ornamented with ribbons at the wrists. These shirts could hardly have been pleated as only 15 ells (yards) of 'claith' is used.

First the exchange, then the buying and selling of goods mark two forward steps on the road of civilization so that it is time to take a brief glance at the growth of commercial life within the Province of Ross. The internal trade of the country was organized and canalized by the Burghs and through the numerous *féills* (fairs and markets) a system which lasted through the middle ages and continued with little change in Ross till well into the 19th century. Before the 18th century and in the north till much later, shops as we know them did not exist. The Burgh craftsmen had their workshops down narrow closes and either exposed their goods for sale in the market place, protected from the weather by a temporary booth, or sent them out into the country through the agency of pedlars or chapmen, the commercial travellers of olden times.

Among the privileges conferred on the Burghs by their various charters was the right to hold periodical markets to which the people of the surrounding district could bring the fruits of their toil for sale. Then markets were of great importance to the Burghs as they brought in a considerable revenue to the town exchequer from the tolls levied on stall holders selling their agricultural and home industry products, as well as providing opportunities for the Burgh merchants themselves to do business. The scene of activity was always in the vicinity of the Tolbooth (originally the booth where tolls and taxes were collected), and around the Mercat Cross, seldom an actual cross in shape, the origins of which are lost in the mists of time, but the place, from time immemorial, where proclamations were read, offenders punished, and goods bought and sold.

Dingwall, Tain, Cromarty, Fortrose, Rosemarkie and Beauly were the chief centres for the markets controlled and protected by charter. But after the break up of the Ross Earldom in 1477 it was not long before the individual Barons, now independent of the Earl's control, started to grant special facilities to their own '*féills*' for the trade and barter of commodities raised on their lands or turned out by the local craftsmen. This 'free trade' proved to a greater or lesser degree, damaging to the Burghs, and Dingwall seems to have been the chief sufferer. Important *féills* sprang up or increased in scope, at *Muir* of Ord, and at *Milntown* (Kilmuir Easter) where a small Mercat Cross still stands at the west end of the village just outside the Tarbat House policies.

A Laird of Balnagown set up a market at Ardgay which seems to have necessitated the somewhat shady transference of the 'Fair of St. Eitachan' from western Sutherland. The original home of this *féill* was *Alltnacealgach* (the burn of deceit) its symbol and authority being, not in this case a cross, but the *clach éiteag*, a largish white stone; and where this boulder rested there the market had to be. The men of Oykel deciding that the *féille* should, in the future, be held nearer home, secretly made off with the *clach éiteag*, but their triumph was short-lived as the folk of *Port na Lic* (Invershin), having similar ideas and ambitions, soon took possession of the stone for themselves.

Balnagown now decided to step in, the problem of transportation from the west having been solved very conveniently by the men of Sutherland, so the stone was once more removed, but this time its resting place was secured from the attentions of would-be traders and dealers, by the incorporation of the *chlach eiteag* into the solid stone wall of the Balnagown Arms at Ardgay, where it may still be seen and where the *Féill Éiteagan* is, or was till very recently, held.

The Mackenzie Barony of Coul during the 17th and 18th centuries, by its three *féills*, Janet's Market, Colin's Fair, and the great *fhéill-Maree* (St. *Maol* Rubha's Market), all held at Contin, were to short-circuit a great deal of the business which might otherwise have gone eastward to Dingwall. Certain places of barter such as Contin had probably existed for centuries before 1477, but it was after that date that their competition began to interfere seriously with the Burghs in Ross.

Yet another trouble for Dingwall and Tain after 1477 was the constant efforts made by their big sister Inverness to stifle what trade they had, on the grounds of monopoly trading rights over the Sheriffdom granted by their charter from William the Lion in 1180. Inverness did not succeed, though Dingwall through all these causes was at times very near financial extinction. Later on in 1685 the Scottish Parliament was to pass an Act authorizing the Burgh of Dingwall to hold 'ane free fair (yearly) and a weekly Mercat' a copy of this being sent from Edinburgh to the Burgh by Tarbat, at that time Lord Clerk Register to his Majesty's Councils, Registrar and Records.

In 1777 the city fathers decided to hold a weekly market in Dingwall for all kinds of victuals, but it was not till 1837 that a big 'come back' was made by the inception of seven new markets, three of which were transferred by arrangement with Sir George Mackenzie of Coul from Contin. These *féilles* were:

1. New Year Market held on the 3rd Wednesday of January.
2. Candlemas Fair (*an fhéill-Bride*) held on the 3rd Wednesday of February.
3. Janet's Market held on the 1st Wednesday of June.
4. Colin's Fair held on the 1st Tuesday of July.
5. *fhéill-Maree* held on the 1st Wednesday of September.
6. Martha's Fair held on the 1st Wednesday of November, where as was the custom at the Martinmas Fairs (*an fhéill-Màrtainn*) 11th November, the men from the hills sold plough 'graiths', which they made at home, to the farmers for 1/- or 1/6.
7. Pepper Market held on the Tuesday before Old Christmas.

The *féills*, whether held in the burghs or country districts, were outstanding events in the year, providing not only opportunities for trade but also a holiday for old and young, and attended by all and sundry from a very wide area. As well as the usual sales of livestock and agricultural produce the booths contained all the necessities of a simple life with a few additional luxuries. A glance at the typical merchandise of a *féill* shows how completely self-supporting a Highland community was during the Middle Ages and indeed well into the 19th century. The industries had remained the same for centuries, largely pastoral with the rearing of cattle, horses, goats, sheep, some pigs, geese, poultry and the making of dairy produce, but with a slowly increasing area under arable cultivation.

The market booths displayed the products of a great variety of trades such as brewing, weaving, the dressing of furs and skins, the barking of hides, the making of linen, dyeing, all the dyes being natural ones made from berries, roots and plants such as crottle-stone and heath parmelia which yielded dark brown; Corcar Lichen yielding bright crimsons; bog myrtle yellows; heather greens; blackberry, with copperas, or elder with alum, blues; oak bark with acorns, or root of common dock, or iris root, black; etc. etc.; brogue and in the 17th century rough leather bootmaking, the home of the latter industry being the Black Isle, tailoring, blanket making, and pottery, while in addition the purchaser could see the work of other skilled craftsmen such as the blacksmith, wheelwright, carpenter, cooper and mason, who were responsible, among other things, for the manufacture of all agricultural instruments. The wild life of mountain, forest and *loch* also provided its quota of food for sale, while from Lochbroom and Lochcarron on the west came fishermen laden with creels of partially salted cod, and herrings salted and smoked, the famous Scatten Shiamaun.

The Easter Ross fishermen from Inver, or Inchbreckie (changed to Invergordon after 1760 in honour of Sir Alexander Gordon of that Burgh), Saltburn, Balintore, Shandwick and Cromarty with their creels of fresh and smoked haddocks and cod, were also very much in evidence, when in Dingwall bringing their boats some distance up the Peffrey and sometimes 'pulling a fast one' by selling their fish from the boats moored behind the castle, instead of taking their wares to the official market stance. One man would stay with each boat in order to sell quantities of very smelly fish oil, used in the crusie lamps which provided the only artificial illumination in all but the castle or Big House, where rushlights and candles, wax for the best rooms but tallow for general purposes, were used. The crusie consisted of a metal bowl filled with this oil on which a wick, made from the bullrush fibre, floated.

Perhaps the oddest industry of all, peculiar to Ross, was reported by a Cromwellian officer, Richard Franck, in 1656; in his own words: 'The earth in Ross hath an antipathy against rats. . . . in parts of the country more remote, the people, as ignorant as themselves, transport the earth of Ross into most parts of Scotland for sprinkling on fields, moors, gardens, so that the very scent on't shall force that enormous vermin, the rat, to become an exile. . . . and I never saw a rat in Ross'. In spite of his reference to the ignorance of others, this Roundhead seems half way to believing in the product of what must have been a lucrative trade, at any rate he must have been a singularly unobservant individual if he never saw a rat on the banks of the Peffrey!

Beside all these useful articles, there were numerous pedlars, chapmen, and cheap-jacks selling ribbons and toys with all kinds of odds and ends no more rubbish and probably better made than much of what is turned out by modern cheap emporiums. The ballad sellers advertised their wares vocally, competing with itinerant pipers, fiddlers, tumblers, the general uproar of bargaining, and periodical fights usually starting in the very numerous drinking booths, and other dens of unsophisticated iniquity.

The *fhéill-Maree* lingered on till 1880, but slowly the old leisurely bargaining with all its picturesque and pleasant adjuncts gave way to methods which though more efficient in no way added to the general happiness of mankind. One by one the *féills* faded out or remained in a much attenuated form their place being taken by the Auction Mart.

CHAPTER XI

GENERAL CHARACTER OF THE REIGN OF JAMES IV— THE KINTAIL SUCCESSION—A MACKENZIE EMBROGLIO —CENSUS TROUBLE WITH MUNROS WHO RECEIVE A HAMMERING AND MAKE FRIENDS—THE MACDONALDS AGAIN—FLODDEN—RECOVERY—A BAD MAN—FEUDS IN THE WEST

Chronological Table

1496 Scottish Education Act to ensure training of those in responsible positions, i.e. the Chiefs, Chieftains and Barons. Birth of the Scots poet Sir Richard Maitland, died 1586.
1497 Hans Holbein born.
1498 Louis XII ascends throne of France; as a compliment to his allies the Scots to whom France owed much he granted Letters of General Naturalization for the whole Scottish Nation. This Act has never been removed from the French Statutes.
1501 Rising in the Isles.
1505 Founding of College of Surgeons in Edinburgh.
1506 Birth of George Buchanan, the greatest Latin scholar and Latin poet of his day. Became tutor to Mary Queen of Scots but latterly turned against her producing a lot of very biased and inaccurate propaganda. Died 1582.
1507 First Scots printing.
1509 Birth of Reformation in England. John Calvin born at Noyon near Paris.
1511 Encomium Moriae by Erasmus.
1513 Flodden.
1515 John Knox born.
1516 Utopia by Sir Thomas More. Dingwall Castle and Redcastle fortified and garrisoned against men of the Isles and other evil disposed persons.
1517 Publication of Luther's Theses.
1519 Death of Leonardo da Vinci probably the world's most versatile genius of Art and Science.
c. 1520 Death of the great Scots poet William Dunbar.
1522 War with England. Conquest of Mexico. Death of Gavin Douglas, Scottish poet and translator of Virgil.
1524 The Regent Albany leaves Scotland for the last time, returning to France.
c. 1525 Birth of Scots poet Alexander Scott. Died c. 1584.
1529 Reformation Parliament in England till 1536.
1531 Henry VIII supreme head of Church in England.
1532 Founding of College of Justice (Court of Session) in Edinburgh.
1533 Flight of John Calvin from Paris.
1536 Calvin at Geneva.
1539 Hugh O'Neill's rebellion in Ireland supported by the MacDonalds of Antrim and Western Isles.
1540 First coastal survey of Scotland by James V.
1543 Barbarossa in western Mediterranean.
1545 Scots under Earl of Angus rout English at Ancrum *Muir*. Birth of Alexander Montgomerie the Scots poet. Died c. 1611.
1546 Death of Martin Luther.
1547 Scots defeated at Pinkie, 7 sons of Sir Thomas Urquhart of Cromarty fell in this battle; he had, it is said, 25 sons and 11 daughters. He was the great-great-grandfather of the famous 17th century Sir Thomas Urquhart. The Chief of Clan Munro also was killed. Cervantes born.
1549 Sir Donald Monro, High Dean of the Isles writes in Gaelic his description of the Hebrides and Western Coasts.
1550 England forced to make peace.
1551 Death of James MacGregor Dean of Lismore a great Gaelic scholar. The Book of the Dean of Lismore contains a vast store of Gaelic literature; the Heroic Poetry alone is a manuscript which contains 11,000 lines of Gaelic Verse by Scottish and Irish poets written between A.D. 1310 and 1500.
1556 Queen Elizabeth's general the Earl of Sussex fails to defeat the MacDonalds in Ireland who during the early years of the century had reinforced themselves in Antrim after the forfeiture of the Lordship of the Isles, their centre being Dunluce Castle—next year they defeated Shane O'Neill the Lord Deputy. The earlier settlement of the MacDonalds had come to pass in 1399 when John of *Dun Naomhaig* the 2nd son of John Lord of Isles had married the Heiress of the Glens of Antrim Marjory Bisset. In 1586 the MacDonalds of Dunluce became 1st Earl of Antrim, while Hugh O'Neill (Red Hugh) became Earl of Tyronne after his submission in 1603 which followed his defeat by Blunt Earl of Mountjoy with whom he established a firm friendship.
1557 Beginnings of Reformation in Scotland.
1558 Marriage of Mary Stewart and the Dauphin Francis.
1559 John Knox in Scotland.
1560 Last Mass in St. Giles, Edinburgh.
1561 Birth of Francis Bacon, Lord Verulam.
1562 Mary Queen of Scots makes a Progress through the Highlands.
1563 Birth of Scots poet Mark Alexander Boyd. Died 1601.
1564 Birth of Shakespeare. Death of Calvin. Birth of Galileo.

Under James IV the Kingdom of Scotland reached a state of prosperity such as had not existed since the far off days of the Alexanders.

His reign was the climax of a brilliant century the like of which was not to appear—so far as Scotland was concerned, for many a long year—if indeed it ever has reappeared.

Abroad, Scotland was buttressed by treaties and alliances with France, Spain, England, Scandinavia, the King of the Romans, Naples, Burgundy, Milan, Gueldres, Cleves, Holstadt, and Brandenburg (Prussia to be). The only war was a short but successful naval one with Portugal, the Scottish Navy being small but good, while her armed forces, because of centuries of war for existence, were second to none.

Scholarship was going ahead, encouraged by King and Estates, who introduced the first Education Act '1496' to ensure that those whose responsibility was to lead the nation should be fitted to do so; all Barons, Chiefs and Chieftains were ordered to see that their heirs took full advantage of the opportunities provided. Scottish literature was the liveliest in northern Europe having forged ahead of anything yet produced in England, who had still a few years to wait for More's Utopia and the great Elizabethan School. In the north, Aberdeen University had been founded by a Bishop of Ross, the great Elphinstone, and Scotland was showing its characteristic keenness in the science of medicine.

But at the root of the great Renaissance lay a worm, common to all Europe at that age. The Church was becoming corrupt, orders were in decay and Prelates too often placemen; though in Scotland the decadence was as yet less prominent than elsewhere. This age was to end with the defeat at Flodden in a fair fight gloriously lost, the only man dishonoured by it being Henry VIII, but of this tragic but magnificent termination we shall hear later.

The usual encouragement was being given to the vital agriculture of the land, which for the first time we find in horse breeding, considerations of speed overriding weight, and to accomplish this two Royal Stud grooms were sent by James IV to France and Spain in order to bring back the best Jennets and Arab Barbs; but for pack, and saddle the Garron still remained the usual general purposes horse.

Sir Kenneth Mackenzie of Kintail was succeeded by the son of his first marriage Kenneth *Òg* of whom very little is known, as he was killed at Torwood by the Laird of Buchanan only a few weeks after his father's death, so that John of Killin, Kenneth's oldest son by Agnes Fraser, became Baron of Kintail and Chief of Clan Mackenzie. John being still a boy the Tutorship of the Clan fell to his uncle Red Hector of *Gairloch* now in possession of a charter for his lands in the west. When he dwelt in the old MacLeod *Tigh Dìge* (Moat House) now known as Flowerdale he had obtained in the east the Baronies of Wester Fairburn and Big and Little Scatwell and possibly Castle Leod though the latter probably formed part of the Chief's personal property as it was given up to John of Kintail on his coming of age. Of *Tigh Dìge* a tragic story tells how in 1480 Allan MacLeod of *Gairloch* was living in this house with his wife, a daughter of Kintail and sister to Hector Roy: they had two little boys, who were brutally murdered by Allan's two brothers in an effort to exterminate the Mackenzie influence in the district. They also killed their brother Allan while he slept by the River Ewe on *Cnoc na Miochomhairlich*, the Mound of Evil Council. The frantic mother fled with the two bloodstained shirts to Brahan, the affair was reported to Edinburgh and Hector Roy receiving a commission of fire and sword against the MacLeods of *Gairloch*.

There now arose a temporary split in Clan Mackenzie, some maintaining that owing to the irregularity of the Agnes Fraser marriage, Hector should not only act as Tutor (Regent) but should assume the actual chiefship of the Clan. Hugh Lord Lovat took the side of his nephew John, as did the Justiciar within the Sheriffdom of Inverness, Sir William Munro of Foulis. These two procured from James Stewart Duke of Ross, second son of James III, Archbishop of St. Andrews, a Precept of Clare Constat dated 30th April 1500 in favour of John as heir to his father, followed by a sasine thereon dated 16th May of the same year signed by Sir John Barchaw and Sir William Munro of Foulis as Baile to the Duke. Hector who at no time showed any animosity toward John, resented the outside interference and was besides attempting to get possession of the Castle of Dingwall, an action which was bound to antagonize the representatives of Government in that area.

Munro decided on a show of force, so accompanied by his Sheriff Alexander Vass (Lochslyn) and a small force, went to Kinellan where Hector was living and removed a corichen from one of the barns on the shore of the *loch*—the castle being situated on the small island in the middle of the *lochan*—as a warning to Hector who was absent at the time. Now Hector was a man of spirit, so followed up with a message to Sir William, saying that if he, William, were a man of courage it was up to him to return and take the other corichen when the owner was at home. The challenge was accepted and Foulis returned with some 900 followers including Dingwalls and MacCullochs.

Hector Roy had not expected such a speedy reply to his challenge only having had time to muster 140 men, and realizing that foolhardy gallantry would be out of place resorted to strategy. Giving his small force provisions for two days, mainly dry oatmeal, he led them by night to the top of Knockfarrel, the site of the old vitrified fort, from where he had under observation the only two possible lines of retreat from Kinellan: the tracks running through Strathpeffer, or south of the Cat's Back and Knockfarrel.

Sir William duly arrived and finding Kinellan deserted caused some destruction, rounded up all available cattle and retired by the southern route, posting a strong rearguard, imagining that Hector had retired west, little realizing that his enemy was now between him and his base. The Munro main body, hindered by the spoils and oblivious of danger had reached a point near the farm of *Bealach 'n Cor* between Loch Ussie and the Cat's Back *Druim a Chait* when they were violently attacked in the flank by the Mackenzies, who gave no quarter realizing that any respite might show up the disparity of numbers. *Tobar nan Ceann*—the Well of the Heads—is still pointed out as a place where many Munros heads found a resting place.

The Munros were routed with heavy loss, so that 'there could not be ane secure friendship made up twixt them and the Mackenzies till by frequent allyances and mutual benefits at last the animosities were settled'; the first reconciliation being the marriage of Catherine, John of Kintail's sister, to Sir William's heir, Hector Munro. Shortly after the fight Red Hector became reconciled with his nephew John IX of Kintail handing over to him the Chiefship and all the great properties which John had inherited from his father, which besides most of western Ross included Brahan and Strathconon now confirmed by charter from King James IV and Castle Leod where of the two mighty Spanish chestnuts probably planted by John about this time, one still stands.

Sir William Munro was killed in 1505 at Achnashellach in Lochaber by the Camerons when assisting the MacKays in a raid—probably instigated by the Earl of Huntly. He left two sons, Hector Munro who succeeded him at Foulis; and William for long the vicar of Dingwall till presented by Queen Mary to the Chaplaincy of St. Monan (Balconie) on the death of John, the eldest son of Munro of Coul (near Balconie) in 1551; and a daughter Margaret who married Alexander Mackenzie the first Laird of Davochmaluah.

In the east a new castle was rising very close to the Ross stronghold of Balnagown, a fact that was causing some perturbation to that House. The cause of the trouble was Andrew *Mór* Monro, second Baron of Milntown—later New Tarbat—who in order that his masons might work unmolested was forced to borrow a garrison from John Earl of Sutherland who himself stayed as his guest till the near completion of the castle. Andrew died in 1501 being succeeded by his son Andrew *Beg* Monro 'The Black Baron' a very bad man indeed as cruel and bloodthirsty as any wicked Baron of the Fairy Stories, of whom we shall hear later.

In 1503 trouble came again from the west when Donald *Dubh* MacDonald, Angus *Óg*'s son, entered the picture by burning Inverness, having as his ally Torquil MacLeod of Lewis, who as a result suffered forfeiture for a time; but after some hard fighting the rising was quelled. Seven years later we find Torquil MacLeod IX Chief of the MacLeods of Lewis granting to his second son Calum Garbh the islands of Raasay and South Rona, and on the mainland the territories of *Coigach*; and *Gairloch* where MacLeods were already in conflict with Hector of *Gairloch* over territorial rights.

When the Royal Duke of Ross James Stewart was made a Bishop in 1488, he relinquished to the Crown his Ross properties, but maintained his right to the titles which went with them by retaining the Mote of Dingwall to warrant the title of Duke of Ross; the Mote of Ormond (Avoch near Rosehaugh) on the Black Isle for Marquis of Ormond; and Redcastle for the dignity of Earl of Ross; this being necessary as prior to 1587 'Honours' in Scotland were territorial and not personal, all lands being created into either an Earldom or a Barony.

King James IV knew his country like few other monarchs before or since, making it a habit to travel incognito and mix with all degrees of his subjects. The violent death of his father James III weighed heavily on his conscience, because as a boy he had backed the coup d'etat for the sake of his country, though without any intention of hurting his father. The story is well known how for a pennance he always wore an iron chain round his body adding a fresh link each year. The fact that his favourite place of pilgrimage was the shrine of St. Duthac at Tain brought him much among us, sometimes in the role of a private individual travelling quite alone, at other times coming north with his full court.

In the year 1503 he twice stayed at his Castle of Dingwall entertaining the Chiefs and being entertained by them in return; thus he forged links in the chain of devotion to the Stewarts which was to last for centuries to come and prove the eventual destruction of so many Scottish loyalists. This King loved the northern parts of his Kingdom, often speaking of the Brahan slopes, for which he had given the charter to his friend Kintail, and the attractions of the Tulloch Hill, while sometimes he would mention that he had in his dominions a city with twice seventy bridges, referring to the Boggan Burn and the Peffrey, which was then and had been for centuries crossed by planks and tree trunks, at intervals of only a few yards, though an early Monro of Foulis had constructed a proper bridge during the 15th century.

Of James's second official visit to Dingwall we know quite a lot; the first day was supposed to be spent in a stag hunt the scene being the top of Tulloch Hill into which area the deer were to be driven, but so great was the concourse of the Chieftains of Ross and their followers that the arrangements went somewhat wrong so far as the hunt was concerned, in spite of which the great feast that followed seems to have been an unqualified success.

On the second day the forenoon was given up to music and dancing, the best harp players that Ross could supply giving a performance on their beautiful instruments, the 30 stringed *clarsach*, at that time still considered the aristocrat of all instruments even above the pipes. The bards sang and recited their poetry, but good as they were it is doubtful whether they would have excelled their *Ard Righ*, the King himself, who a master of Gaelic was also a great lover and performer of music.

This of course all took place within the castle where every Chief and Chieftain of Ross was being entertained; neither were his more humble subjects forgotten, they never were by the Stewarts whose enemies were always to be found among the great vested interests. At the magnificent feast that followed preparations had been made for every man, woman and child who could come, trestle tables laden with food covering the muster ground outside the castle walls, more than one ox would be roasting whole over the glowing wood fires, while from the castle brew-house came a plentiful supply of beer, which in those days was beer.

The four lairds of the Four Davochs: Cairn, Carte, Pollo and Maluach all of which lay between Fodderty and Tulloch, the first three being Munros and the last Alexander Mackenzie, the first of Davochmaluach, a son of Sir Kenneth, were all blessed with daughters whose beauty and accomplishments were the talk of the north, each being named Mary, and on this occasion the four young girls danced and sang both in Gaelic and English for the King—to his great delight. They were dressed in tartan plaids, plaited and tied round the waist with a silver studded leather belt, their arms loosely covered with the scarlet sleeves of their gowns and ornamented with gold lace, their long hair was partly plaited and set with curiously wrought silver ornaments. The scene was brilliant, the tartans and safroons of the Highlanders mixing in with the bright colours of the courtiers, while the harpers, trumpeters and attendants of the Chieftains all had their distinctive dress and colours, and among all these would be another brightly dressed gentle-man, the Dingwall Pursuivant in his brilliantly coloured tabard worn as a cape in accordance with the rules of his heraldic office.

Eventually the time arrived for the King to continue north to Tain where he could now worship in the great new collegiate Church of St. Duthac completed and consecrated on 12th September 1481 by Bishop Thomas of Ross. In this venerated Borough his entertainment would be more in keeping with the religious purpose of his visit and he would meet many churchmen among them the saintly Patrick Hamilton Abbot of *Fearn*, a near kinsman of the King, who alas was to be one of the very few in Scotland to suffer martyrdom for his religious ideals during the next reign.

As the King passed out of the castle gate the four Davoch Marys sang in unison a farewell song accompanying themselves on their harps. They were followed by twenty harpers, brought by as many chiefs and chieftains, who played a set of 'merry chords', soon lost in the fanfare of the trumpeters lining the castle wall. So pleased was James with his visit that he gave orders that a covered hall was to be built in the castle court-yard, to be used for festive gatherings and entertainments, giving £20 towards the cost of the hall which was completed four years later.

The Mackenzies' influence was now firmly established in Easter Ross, Garbat, Castle Leod, Kinellan, Strathconon, Brahan, Fairburn, the two Scatwells, Davochmaluach, Ord, Redcastle, now in possession of the House of Kintail, soon to reach yet further toward the fertile Black Isle and Easter Ross. The Royal Burgh of Dingwall already had Mackenzies among its citizens as is shown by a charter of 4th December 1490 in which Alexander Garreachson grants lands in the Borough of Dingwall to John 'MacKenedye', the document being witnessed by Sir—the mediaeval equivalent of the Rev.—Ranalde Vicar of Fodderty and others; up to the Reformation the Church held a certain amount of land in Strathpeffer including Fodderty.

The Dingwall family were still extensive landowners but from now on we see considerable activity in the real estate market between Dingwall and Kintail resulting in a decrease of land for the former family and an increase to the latter, as exemplified by the following:— William Dingwall of Kildun received a grant from James V 1527 of Davochpollo and the Forest of Strathvaich which had previously been possessed by the 'MacKanedye' and 16 years later sold to John, Chief of Kintail, the lands and fishings of Lochbyne in exchange for lands of 'Fotherty' with the mill to be held of the Queen as Earl of Ross for payment of six pennies as blanche-ferme at Whitsunday; Queen Mary gave crown charters of the respective lands exchanged in 1543 and 1544. These lands of Fodderty had previously been given in heritage to John of Kintail by James V in 1532, but in 1583 John Dingwall of Kildun 'alienated' to James VI the lands of 'Kirktown of Fodderty and Mulnain' which the King granted in heritage to 'Colin McKeinze of Kintail.' Again in 1527 William Dingwall of Kildun had received a Royal grant of the lands of Western 'Ferburn and Middil Ferburn' with other lands and the fishings of the 'Erche of Balbrait', which came into the hands of Colin of Kintail in 1619.

Despite all James's strenuous and patient efforts to keep the peace, Henry VIII launched a war of aggression against France, who attacked by Spain from the south called on Scotland for aid. Neither James nor Scotland wanted war, a statement fully substantiated by the continual forbearance shown by James and his Estates in taking no forceful action against either Henry's many provocative and underhand actions or military raids on Scotland. But the King felt in honour bound to help France, and Scotland stood behind him.

On the 22nd August 1513 one of the finest Scottish armies ever seen crossed the Tweed—among them being two old enemies now united against the common foe, Red Hector of *Gairloch* and Alexander MacDonald of Lochalsh, the latter to be knighted on the field of battle. John of Kintail was commanding the Clan Mackenzie and here for the last time in history claimed the old Mackenzie right of forming part of the King's bodyguard. For eighteen days the Scottish army was successful, but on the 9th September was forced into action by Surrey near Flodden Edge.

The order of battle was as follows:— on the right the Clans, the King's bodyguard and others in the centre, on the left the Border Lords. James who had perfected his Navy and his Artillery train had somehow neglected one thing—to bring up to date his infantry weapons. The Scots were still using the 18 ft. spear, and the cutting sword for close work, a perfect combination till then and still winning victories in Europe for Swiss and Germans, but the English had a new weapon the 'Bill', or halberd combining the spear and battle-axe, which was better.

The course of the battle is well known, a great victory for the English and a glorious defeat for the Scots who died where they stood. The King was killed, twelve earls, fourteen Lords, the splendid young Archbishop of St. Andrews, the Bishop of Caithness, and the Bishop of the Isles; there were four grown men only left in the Scottish Peerage. The rank and file died in like proportion; there being no officers left to tell them to retire, they just fought on and died, taking as many Englishmen as possible with them. After night fell the enemy drew off and the remnants of the Scots army left the field among them the badly wounded John of Kintail who was carried off by the few survivors among his clansmen who had taken part in the battle. No-one knows where the gallant James was laid as Henry to whom his body was sent refused his sister's husband a proper burial.

The Provost of Edinburgh on hearing of the disaster issued one of the finest 'back to the wall' orders known to history, comparable to the Declaration of Arbroath in 1320, but it was not needed. The English army had suffered such casualties that any exploitation of the victory was out of the question, and they retired south.

For years the Scots would not believe that they had lost their beloved King and all sorts of legends grew up around him much as they had around King Arthur of the Round Table. Somehow, again by sheer guts, the Scots successfully repulsed three major attempts at invasion, but during the minority of James V the usual troubles connected with Scottish minorities arose. From Flodden to 1707 and after, a new element appears which was to prove the undoing of Scotland—the division not only of nobles which was an old story, but something far worse, the division of Scotland, which by the end of this century was to produce in the name of Religion a pro-English and anti-Royal party.

In 1514 Hector Munro of Foulis and John Mackenzie of Kintail were given the appointments of Lieutenants of Wester Ross as signs of trouble from the quarter were not lacking, Sir Alexander MacDonald of Lochalsh this time with the Dunvegan MacLeods in alliance, was on the war path. Sir Alexander, still quite openly styling himself the Lord of the Isles, was taking up such a threatening attitude that the Castles of Dingwall and Redcastle were put into a state of defence, their garrisons being increased; at the same time we find a charter under Great Seal dated 10th December 1516 being issued to Foulis, granting him the Oykel Salmon Fishings, which had been in the possession of Lochalsh.

But next year Sir Alexander was killed, leaving an only daughter as his heiress; she had married Alister MacDonald of Glengarry bringing to him half the district of Lochalsh, half Lochcarron, and part of Lochbroom, areas not to be wrested from the MacDonalds by the Mackenzies till about 1590. However this lady was in financial straits so that by 1540 part of this territory had been disposed of to Foulis, though an earlier sale of the lands may have taken place to Duncan Bayne 1st of Tullach the son of Alexander Bayne who had settled in Dingwall at the end of the 15th century, acquiring Tulloch c. 1513 from Walter Innes of Tulchis and becoming a Burgess of the Royal Burgh. Duncan, probably the builder of Tulloch Castle, was to receive a charter for the lands of Oulch (Tulloch) from King James V in 1541, soon adding the lands of Docharty purchased from Munro; this family were to remain in possession of Tulloch till 1762 when the property passed, with the marriage of Jean Bayne, cousin to the last Bayne of Tulloch, to the descendant of the Chiefs of Clan Dhai, Davidson. In 1515 the MacLeod of Dunvegan, Alasdair (Alexander) *Crotach* the VII chief, had been pardoned by the Regent Albany for his participation in the late Sir Alexander's rebellion, with the result that from now on a state of bloody feud existed between these two clans of Skye.

The period of Royal minority was marked by turbulence in other spheres beside the Isles and in Easter Ross Andrew *Beg* Monro the 'Black Baron' of Milntown was establishing a minor reign of terror. As we saw he had succeeded his father in 1501, being, it seems, wise enough to keep the peace during the reign of James IV; had he not James would have known of it, and taken the requisite steps, instead of which he had added to his Barony in 1512. The croft called the Markland of Tullich for 1 lb. of wax payable at midsummer within the chapel of Delny; Milntown of Meath with the Mill, and the office of Chief *Maor* of the Earldom of Ross, granted by letter under privy seal. This office gave Black Andrew many perquisites, such as a share of every sack of corn brought to the shore to be shipped, 'ane gopin of corn'. By purchase and other grants he had increased his possessions to such an extent that among his more polite nicknames was Andrew of the Seven Castles, namely Delny, Newmore (Roskeen), Contullich and Kildermorie (Alness), Docharty (Dingwall), Allan (*Fearn*), Culnauld or Culnaha (Nigg).

The following incidents in his career shed some light on this abnormal gentleman's character. While residing at Contullich he treated his vassals with a quite unnecessary and unusual severity demanding from them an outward show of respect beyond all reason, the people of Boath, who had to pass Contullich, being forced not only to uncover when Andrew appeared but to throw themselves flat on the ground, the penalty for non-observance being death. For some reason or perhaps none, he bore a strong dislike to the tenants of a place called Garvary, so, characteristically decided to remove them, whether dead or alive was immaterial, there were no half measures about Andrew. There were eight families concerned, who realising the danger in which they stood, kept a constant look out for the Rothach *Dubh* (The Black Baron), but one very stormy night, thinking that no-one would be out in such weather the heads of the families were assembled in one of the houses, without their usual watch.

The Black Baron however had decided on a midnight ride with a troop of his followers; they set off through the storm their goal unknown until they happened to see a light in one Garvary house. Black Andrew drew near to one of the slits which served for a window, and listened to the conversation within, probably hearing some unwelcome truths. At length one of the men came to the door, looked out at the storm and remarked that Black Andrew, were he the devil himself, would not be riding on such a night, but hardly were the words out of the man's mouth when in rushed the furious Baron and slaughtered the assembled company.

On another occasion an old woman gave evidence against him in a march dispute with Balnagown, and lived to regret it, as he caused a deep pit to be dug in which the lady was buried upside down; the spot is still known as *Uaigh na Callich*, the old woman's grave. His final effort was an order that all the female harvesters working in the fields below the Castle of Milntown—and the present Tarbat House—should work in the nude.

Both the 'drowning pool', used for witches and female criminals, and the Gallows Hill of the Barony, situated by the Church at Logie Easter, were scenes of great activity during this man's regime. It is interesting that this pool was last used for its proscribed purpose late in the 17th or early 18th century, a man living in 1750 having witnessed the drowning of a woman convicted of child murder. At length Andrew's evil course was run and it is said that he was murdered by his own servants about 1522, being buried at the east end of St. Mary's Church of Kilmuir Easter.

That the stories of his atrocities are fundamentally true is borne out by the fact that during the lifetime of my great-grandfather a whole cart load of human bones were unearthed from beneath the old castle dungeon—some few hundred yards east of Tarbat House—and given Christian burial in the Churchyard of Kilmuir Easter. Black Andrew's wife was Euphemia, a daughter of James Dunbar 1st of Tarbat, a son of Sir James Dunbar of Westfield in Moray, who had purchased c. 1520 the lands of Portmahomack, Tarbatness and the old Ross Castle of Ballone which he brought up to date.

Andrew as might be expected left his affairs in some confusion to his eldest son George IV of Milntown, two other sons inheriting Allan and Culnauld. Much of the land round about still belonged to the Church, Shandwick being attached to *Fearn* Abbey, while the Chapel of Delny was served by a priest who had his land and house north of the Chapel on Priest Hill, but as we shall see a change was on the way.

The coming Reformation was already in the air and Patrick Hamilton the Duke of Albany's nephew and the Abbot of *Fearn* like so many of the best Churchmen realized that reform was urgently needed; his sermons however were judged heretical being influenced by the teachings of Martin Luther whom he had met, and this very charming and gallant man died at the stake before the gate of his old school St. Salvator's College, St. Andrews.

The Bishop of Ross at the time was Robert Cockburn who in 1516 had been sent by the Estates to France to arrange for a marriage between Francois I's daughter Louise and James V, but he failed as the lady was already promised to Charles of Spain. Eventually (1537) James after a romantic personal wooing married another daughter Madeleine but she died at Holyrood within the year, his next wife being a woman having great courage beauty and brains, who also loved Scotland, Marie of the Great Houses of Guise-Lorraine, and the mother of Mary Queen of Scots.

In the year 1528 James V took over the reins of government and things began to improve despite the animosity of Henry Tudor who was expending much gold in order to sow dissension among the nobles of Scotland, including our old friend Donald *Dubh* of the Isles already sufficiently disturbed by their own feuds, Donald '*Gruamach*' 5th Lord of Sleat now an aspirant to the Lordship of the Isles having driven the MacLeods of Dunvegan from Troternish in Skye with the help of the MacLeods of Lewis.

James V came north in 1532 and with the assistance of John of Kintail, who had the honour of entertaining his King at *Eilean Donan* Castle, pacified the Islands once again, partly by force but more by tact, charm and an appreciation of their difficulties and point of view. James like his fathers before him never forgot his Highland ancestry and the fundamental loyalty of the Clans to their *Ard Righ*; but he was the last reigning monarch to speak fluently the language of the Stewarts' best friends, though it is probable that Mary Queen of Scots had a little Gaelic.

Five years later Donald *Gorm* who had married Margaret NicLeod of Lewis, succeeded to Sleat, claiming by descent and the wish of his clan the Lordship of the Isles, but this was strenuously opposed by John the Chief of Kintail, and Alasdair MacLeod of Dunvegan. For the second time Dunvegan lost Trotternish and Donald of Sleat made Duntulum Castle the principal family seat, which it remained till 1717–20 when it was changed to Armadale in Sleat, the southern part of Skye. Donald then beseiged *Eilean Donan* Castle, at the time very lightly garrisoned, but was killed by a lucky shot from an archer who hit him in the leg, which proved fatal as the enraged chief severed an artery when attempting to extract the arrow.

The King again visited the Isles—with a strong fleet—staying at Duntulum with the young chief Donald 'Gormson' VII and his brother, Tutor and Captain of the Clan, Archibald the 'Clerk', trained for the Church. After this things quietened down for a while; Archibald, on the 22nd March 1541 being granted a remission for their treasonable fire raising, and burning of boats at *Eilean Donan* and for plundering Kinlochewe and Troutterness.

The Royal visit over, the King embarked and sailed back to loyal Kintail, thence to Edinburgh having taken the precaution of carrying with him as captives and hostages certain firebrands such as Donald *Dubh*, many other MacDonalds and MacLeod of Lewis. Among those who may have attended the King was Donald Munro the Dean of the Isles who in 1449 had made a tour of his diocese and written an account of the Hebrides during this period.

In 1542 James, the one stable factor in the Scotland of that day, died of a broken heart, betrayed and let down by his nobles; leaving a new born daughter as Queen of Scots and his gallant Queen Marie as Regent of poor old Scotland, threatened from outside by a greedy Tudor and inside by selfish factions, aggravated by deep religious perplexity. Still the country held together sufficiently to fight the hated enemy England to a standstill and defeat the last attempted subjugation of Scotland by force of arms, but alas other methods proved more effective.

At Pinkie the Scots suffered a defeat and here John of Kintail had fought at the head of his Clan as had Robert Munro XIV of Foulis who died for his country in this battle, having only succeeded his father Hector in 1541; he left several sons, his heir being Robert *Mòr* Munro. No less than seven sons of Sir Thomas Urquhart of Cromarty fell at Pinkie, which still however left another eighteen.

John of Kintail was made a prisoner of war and having been recognized by Protector Somerset whom he had met during a hunting party was held to ransom; money in the Highlands has never been very plentiful yet every one of his many dependents gladly contributed toward this, which throws some light on John as a man and chief, while his sturdy refusal to ravage the estates of MacDonald of Moidart for the private gratification of the Earl of Huntly's revenge, does him honour. Donald *Dubh*, who had soon been released from Edinburgh, despite all his promises to the King had decided to rebel, making a treaty with Henry VIII of England, and in 1545 had gone to Ireland with 4,000 men, selling his services to the Tudor, but that same year Donald died, leaving no successor.

Ever since 1539 the *Gairloch* lands had been causing trouble between the MacLeods of Lewis and Raasay and the Mackenzies. One night a small force of MacLeods hid up on the little island in Shieldaig Bay, *Fraoch Eilean*, but were discovered in the morning by a Mackenzie patrol. Two MacRae archers Donald and Ian Odhar took station on 'the Slab of the Arrow' *Leac nan Saighead* a flat rock, and did such execution that it is said only two MacLeods got away to Raasay in their *birlinn*.

The situation got worse as the result of a matrimonial mix-up: Janet Mackenzie a daughter of Kintail had married Roderick, '*Ruaridh*' X of Lewis, but eloped with his nephew John of the Axe, tutor to another nephew Malcolm IIIrd Chief of the MacLeods of Raasay. The fact that the sons of the union were eventually massacred c. 1568 was to still further increase the tension between MacLeods and Mackenzies ending some thirty years after that date in the absorption of the Lewis MacLeod territories by the House of Kintail and Cromartie.

Donald Gormson of Sleat in 1553 was declared an outlaw for his constant raids into Mackenzie territory in Wester Ross, but the feud went on intermittently till 1566 when the heir of Lewis was drowned and Donald of Sleat claimed this Chiefship through his mother; the semi-final government settlement in 1569 had considerable repercussions in Ross as will appear in due course.

The Queen Regent had done her best to quieten the Isles but her generals Huntly and Argyll had failed with the result that Huntly was deprived of some of his honours, and Argyll of the wardship of Mary NicLeod 'The Heiress of the Isles' only daughter and heiress of William VIIIth Chief of Dunvegan etc. and Agnes Fraser daughter of Lord Lovat. This valuable girl Mary was warded in turn by Argyll, MacDonald of Islay, and John of Kintail, but in 1562 she became a Maid of Honour to Mary Queen of Scots, eventually marrying Duncan Campbell of Auchinbreck.

F

In spite of all these violent highlights the normal life of the country was still going on, a glimpse of which can be got from the very numerous charters and land transfers of this 16th century. Here are some examples: 15th June 1530 Precept by James Bishop of Ross directed to Sir Donald Reid Dean of Christianity of Dingwall, telling of 'perpetual' Vicarage pension of 20 Marks of Parish Churches of 'Kynnettis' (Strathpeffer); and 'Contane', laid on the kirklands of the town of Kynnettis with teinds thereof 7 Marks, and 3 Marks from fruits of the Chancery of Ross and 10 Marks from fruits of Rectory of Contane, Henry Ford, (Rector of Contin), said pension to Sir Patrick Johnstoune priest to Bishop (the prefix Sir being accorded to priests where we should write Rev.). Witness by Sir James Bordewy Prior of Beauly—John Hephorn, Rector of Kyltern, John Munro Canon of Ross—at Chanonry of Ross.

8th July 1540. An Instrument under hand of William Munro—priest witnessing that Robert Munro—heir of Foulis is tenant for his father of half the lands of Lochbroom with his wife Katherine MacLeod, but not accepted by tenants who unanimously said they were unwilling to accept their lands in occupation or tenandry from Robert—(so Robert asked for 'Instruments' i.e. legal aid.)

10th January 1547. Retour of Inquest before Sheriff of Inverness by John Mackenzie of Kintail, Alexander of Fairburn, Thos Urquhart of 'Cromarte' etc. swearing to the deceased of Robert Munro of Foulis.

1552. Letters of Remission under Great Seal in favour of Munro of Findown brother-german to Foulis for absence from Queen Mary's Army ordered to convene at Gladmuir in August 1548 to beseige and recover Hadington from English and for part played in slaughter of one John Donaldsoun.

4th November 1554. Letters of Presentation by John Mackenzie of Killin (Kintail) Hector Roy Mackenzie etc. to David Bishop of Ross, for presentation of Patrick Johnnestone, younger, to Parish Church on Kinettes his father being dead—Dated—done acted granted, Sir John Robertson priest witness, bestowal by parishoners of sprinkling vessel and keys of said Church.

By 1560 the religious upheaval brought about by the Reformation was causing considerable activity in the Real Estate market, the church selling out lands or transferring them to lay relations before the inevitable confiscations, the Munro Papers being particularly full of such transactions.

On the 14th January 1560 Foulis obtained from Quinton Monypenny Vicar-General and Dean of Ross the lands of Kiltearn, the Salmon fishings from John Cockburn, and from Henry Sinclair Bishop of Ross: Limlair, Pellaig, Wester Glens and Boath.

John of Kintail died in 1561, a good chief, an honest man and holding the office of a Privy Councillor to the Queen Regent and the tragic and beautiful young Queen who was just starting her reign full of hope and good intentions, so soon to be brought to nothing by fanaticism among her lowland subjects and the selfishness and greed of many of her nobles. John was laid beside his father Sir Kenneth in Beauly Priory and was succeeded by his middle aged eldest son Kenneth whose first public duty as chief, was to go to the assistance of the Young Queen of Scots in 1562, together with Foulis.

The Queen on her Progress north had arrived in Inverness where she found the gates of her own Royal Castle shut in her face by the governor Alexander Gordon, but the Castle soon fell and the Governor's head was set up over the gate. Followed the defeat of Huntly and his Gordons, who though a Roman Catholic, had resented Mary's non-partisan politics and in an endeavour to challenge the power of the Crown had come out in open rebellion; but it is doubtful whether the Queen would have followed up the defeat by such stern measures against Huntly had not her half brother been so keen to have for himself the title and lands of the Earldom of Moray forfeited by the Chief of the Gordons.

CHAPTER XII

GENERAL SURVEY OF THE REFORMATION—EDUCATION
AND THE STATUTES OF IONA

Till 1557, despite certain differences of dress and the slow disappearance of the Gaelic tongue from the southern lowlands, Scotland was still one nation able and willing to sink local differences in order to combine against any outside aggression. Though the Court, to a large degree made up of southern nobles was only too often either antagonistic or disinterested in the Highlands, we have seen many examples of how a good king by his personal presence and understanding, could win a truer loyalty among the Highlanders than in any other part of his dominions.

To this bond was added that of a universal church which though Roman Catholic in doctrine had always born in Scotland a peculiarly national stamp, time and time again having proved the strongest agency of Scottish unity and the most powerful force for Scottish independence. But this force was weakening, so that we now enter a period disastrous to Scotland as a nation, as the coming Reformation was to cut Scotland in half, leaving the Highlands in the main Catholic—later Episcopalian —and the southern lowlands completely dominated by Calvinism. The inevitable result of this split was to leave the Highlands as an isolated area of Royalist Nationalism, while southern Scotland formed an unnatural and often unfriendly alliance with the auld enemy England against their rightful Queen, Kings, and brother Scots.

Although in its early stages the Reformation left most of the Highlands unchanged, in order to clarify the position a very short résumé of its general progress may help. In 1557 the 'Bond' was formed, a body both religious and political, which denounced the abuses in the Roman Church and demanded the introduction of the English liturgy. Three years later John Knox the fanatical leader of the Reformed Church in Scotland introduced the 'Confession of Faith' while the first 'Book of Discipline' was approved by the first General Assembly of the Church of Scotland.

During the brief reign of Mary Queen of Scots, the Catholic and Protestant Churches fought for supremacy, the latter not being legally established as the State Church till the Regency of Moray in 1567 when the Reformed Church was set up. The new Kirk was based on the teachings of the great French humanist and reformer, Calvin, whose 'Institutes', in which he codified the theology of St. Augustine, differed only in emphasis from Catholic dogma. The corner stone of the new teaching being the Bible, though the different interpretations of this

Book as expounded by the Reformed theologians were legion, creating as time went on, ever increasing internal bickering.

More and more the intentions of the sounder elements among the many sincere founders of a much needed Reformation were forgotten; the letter of the law replacing the spirit of the law, resulting in a hard and narrow attitude, with a worship of the Old Testament, especially the more bloody passages, that almost amounted to idolatry. The fruits of this teaching were unfortunate in the extreme; joy, happiness, and beauty became a sin, cruelty to any who held different views, which of course included the majority of Highland men and women, a moral duty; while an unparalleled outbreak of religious hysteria swept parts of southern Scotland, all helping to bring about the revival of witch-craft with the consequent hunting, torture and burning of countless women alleged to be witches, a symptom that lasted through the next two hundred years.

The growing tendency to supplant Christianity by the Mosaic Law was largely due to the influence of the English Puritans who differed greatly from the early Scottish reformers, the latter tending to keep a certain catholic prelatic order in their worship, replacing the Bishops by superintendents who still were rulers over the diocesan clergy, though strictly accountable to the general assembly. During the actual reign of Mary Queen of Scots there were in existence at one and the same time the Protestant superintendents and the lawful Roman Catholic Bishops as the Queen had not confirmed the statutes of 1560, the Protestant ministers and superintendents receiving small stipends charged on ecclesiastical revenue, while Bishops and Abbots, some of whom were Protestant ministers, held seats in Parliament and kept their temporalities.

The Kirk continued to be imbued with the old mediaeval idea of a universal Church, which of course entailed the forcing of all into one fold, whether they liked it or not, so that from the modern point of view the period is one of savage intolerance, but we must remember that neither Catholic nor Protestant of that day knew the meaning of the word tolerance as applied to matters of faith. Pope Innocent III, John Knox, Andrew Melville, and the Archbishop of Canterbury, were all equally intolerant over questions of religion, and their counterparts were to remain so for another two hundred years or more. Very few people of the 16th and 17th century appreciated the possibility of religious toleration and those that did ran the risk of hanging, drawing and quartering or exile, and the abuse of posterity. Among the few were Mary Queen of Scots, those two great men, James Graham Marquis of Montrose, and Oliver Cromwell, and at a later date, strangely enough, the much abused James VII of Scotland and II of England, all of them sincerely religious people.

Yet another cause of strife was the interference and eventual usurpation by the Kirk Courts of civil jurisdiction, which produced a mixture of anarchy and quite intolerable tyranny, a state of affairs that, for a time, was rectified by the firm line adopted by Queen Mary's son James VI or I who with all his faults was less of a fool than some believed and fully realized that his position would be intolerable while there existed an opposition government of the Kirk, a power, by then, largely in the hands of lay supporters waxing fat on the proceeds of confiscated Church lands. James in 1597 backed by a powerful force made up of the loyal clans crushed the incipient rebellion and reestablished a mild form of Protestant Episcopal Church Government and the Bishops though shorn of their great temporal power, again sat in Parliament. In the Episcopal Church of Scotland the Bishops elect one of their number to hold the office of Primus, and originally this election was an annual event. Presbyterianism and Episcopacy were to all intents and purposes combined, the form of worship being very similar; common sense was the general rule, so that no objections were raised if some areas preferred to adhere to a strictly Presbyterian form of local church government.

In the Highlands, except in those areas which were still Roman Catholic, the tendency was strongly in favour of the Episcopalian form of worship, remaining so till its suppression after 1745. Episcopacy of this modified form might well have remained as the established Scottish Church for though the Tulchan Bishops had lost prestige, the people worshipped as they chose under their own ministers who were in most cases good and honourable men without being fanatics. The difference between moderate Presbyterian and Episcopalian was mainly one of church government, seemingly well settled; but as we shall see this peace was to be wrecked by the folly of King Charles I and the ambitions of English prelates and the Church of England, which antagonised all shades of opinion in Scotland and allowed the return of a fanatical minority who remained in power till smashed by Cromwell.

Probably this period has produced more controversial and partisan writing than any other, as by the extreme Presbyterian and the Whig historian the old Church has been described as utterly rotten and decadent, its clerics all wicked, lecherous voluptuaries, while the other side are equally emphatic in describing all the Reformers as a pack of savages inspired by a love of hooliganism, destruction and pillage. Without doubt there were many priests who were ignorant and lax in their office while on the other side much wanton destruction was caused by the undisciplined rabble who always follow at the heel of reform, but this simplification which tries to prove that either party is the possessor of all unqualified merit, destroys its own arguments by postulating an impossible situation in any country, let alone Scotland with its individualism and very marked localized characteristics.

Though the seat of religious fanaticism during this period was in the south, where indeed the need for reformation was most marked, there it was confined to certain areas in the south west during the early stages, being a Catholic stronghold; while the more humanitarian—one almost writes civilized—behaviour and attitude in the north eastern Highland areas effectively modified many of the movement's more evil aspects; but this is not to say that the Highlands were politically un-affected by the Reformation and accompanying chaos which served so well the cunning designs of the Tudors, by dividing against itself the House of Scotland. But north of the Forth and Clyde the atmosphere of un-Christian savagery, so often evinced in the words and actions of Knox, Melville and other divines, was ruled out by a sense of humour, chivalry and last but not least the good manners of the Highlander.

Another factor contributing to this difference was the greater simpli-city of the Roman Catholic Church in the Highlands, which existing in a poorer land, had not to the same degree, foundered on the rocks of sloth, luxurious living and misapplied worldly wealth, the latter proving such a tempting bait to the less religious reformers. Among this last type of reformer must be numbered the bulk of the southern Scottish nobility but not of course omitting the *Mac Cailein Mór* of Clan Campbell.

An interesting sidelight on contemporary life, and incidentally on the absence of bad feeling among people of different religious persua-sions in the north, is given in the account of an early school of physical training. This establishment was started in 1574 at Inverness by Lord Lovat, at that time Governor of the Castle overlooking the wooden bridge crossing the River Ness. There was a succession of these wooden bridges till 1685 when a stone one was built largely financed by the northern chiefs and Lairds, including Sir Donald MacDonald of Sleat and John MacLeod 16th Chief of Dunvegan, both in Skye. The school was placed in charge of a townsman Lt. Thomas Cerr a veteran of the wars in France and Flanders, to be run for the benefit of all the youth in the north—not only Frasers. The subjects taught were: weapon training, minor tactics, swimming, archery, football, throwing the bar, fencing, wrestling, and Highland dancing; a curriculum which seems to have appealed to the young men of the northern clans. It was attended in great numbers by: Frasers, MacKintoshes, Munros and Rosses, two clans which had taken to the Presbyterian form of worship, and Mackenzies, most of whom were still Roman Catholic, yet we know that they worked and played together in perfect harmony.

But this was not the only kind of school in the country. Inverness had had several schools for centuries, as had other centres in the north.

The Priory of Beauly during this epoch had been under Prior Robert

Reid, afterwards Bishop of Orkney, a great patron of learning: 'He kept noblemen's children with him for table and lodging, and which was best, his conference and advice. . . . the Lord Lovat, his brother William, Mackenzie (Kintail), Foulis (Munro), Balnagoun (Ross), Cromarty (Urquhart) and the Sheriff of Murray were with him all at once'. This good Prior was the first President of the Court of Session, he left many endowments to education in Scotland, among them, 'the sowme of aucht thousand merkis' to found 'ane college within the Burgh of Edinburgh for the exerceis of learning thairints'. This money was employed after the death of this 'learned, patriotic and generous Roman Catholic Bishop' for the first Protestant University, Edinburgh. Yet another far-sighted bequest was one for the education of gentlemen's sons and daughters whose parents were not well off. It was from Beauly that a Fraser of Lovat had gone on to Oxford during the 15th century, returning in due course to become Rector of Dingwall; while still earlier, during the 14th century it is described as 'an academy for training youth'. The Chanonry of Ross (Fortrose) was already famous for its Grammar School, the headmaster in 1597 being Mr. John McGillechallum.

From Tain in 1588 comes a not very serious sign of ecclesiastical strife, when the Kirks of Ross and the Moderator of the Presbytery of Tain complain to the Privy Council that a certain Laird, Ross—a Presbyterian—was depriving them of the use of the Chapter-house and Collegiate Kirk of Tain, pointing out that of old (1481) the Chapter-house had been used for a school. Other schools existed at Alness, Cromarty, Kiltarlity, the Abbey of *Fearn*, and rather later at Stornoway which received its charter as a Royal Burgh in 1597.

Further north were two famous schools, Dornoch and Kirkwall, the former being the place of study of the young earls of Sutherland. The chiefs and chieftains of Ross for generations had sent their sons to be educated at one or other of these schools, frequently Beauly or Chanonry, though the MacDonalds and MacLeods from the Isles usually attended the Inverness schools, but what is more significant, if they had no sons they sent their eldest daughters. Had the existence of these Highland schools been appreciated by historians in the past, less rubbish would have been written about our country, neither would these people always have misinterpreted the educational clause in the Statutes of Icolmkill (Iona) 1609 and confirmed in 1616. This lays down that the sons of chiefs and lairds will be sent to the 'lowlands' for their education, and it is at once assumed that this must mean southern Scotland; it did not, but referred to our own schools situated in the geographical lowlands of our own clan areas. To these schools a large proportion of the chiefs and others had gone since their foundation, while from them many had passed on to the universities at home and abroad, Aberdeen being a favourite for the northern clans. The subjects taught were the normal ones for the period, with perhaps a greater stress on Latin, English was sometimes taught and we know that there were establishments in the Highlands teaching languages, music and architecture.

In addition to the schools, another method was employed to bring education to the children of Highland gentlemen, which of course included that numerous and valuable section of the community the *duine-uasal*, the tenant farmers, now beginning to be known as tacksmen[1]. This consisted of the employment of a schoolmaster, or tutor, by a group of families within a district; he was lodged in the home of one or other of his employers, all the children meeting there daily for lessons.

Having touched on one clause of the Statutes of Icolmkill it may be of interest to mention and comment on the other sections, all of which were designed for the Highland area:—

1. Obedience to the Reformed Kirk. This was interpreted according to the dictates of the clan's, or chief's, conscience; the majority were moving toward Episcopalianism, others stuck to the Roman Church, while a considerable number of Munros and Rosses, as also the people of Sutherland, took their tune from their chiefs and embraced a moderate Presbyterianism. Linked with the above ordnance were: The keeping of the Sabbath and Abolition of Handfasting. With regard to the former it depended on the locality, but let us remember that even Calvin played bowls on Sunday, and John Knox quite often gave supper parties. The humane and sensible practice of handfasting continued.

2. Establishment of Inns throughout the Highlands. The Highlander was very hospitable, so that inns were few and remained primitive for a long time.

3. Limitation of household and followers of Chief. To some extent this was being carried out, more for economic reasons than any particular desire to comply with the law.

4. 'Sorning' prohibited. The custom by which beggars and other wanderers were boarded and lodged by the hospitable and charitable clansfolk, often themselves very poor. The exceptionally kind treatment made wandering with no visible means of support a popular pastime, while the abolition of the Religious houses abolished the only existing poor houses and hospitals.

5. An Act by which the trade in French wines and Aqua Vitae was made illegal in the Highlands in order that it might become a monopoly trade for the Lowland—especially Edinburgh—merchant. An iniquitous act framed to kill a thriving trade, which had existed for centuries between the Highlands and France, for the benefit of Edinburgh.

Note 1. For explanation of Tacksmen see Glossary.

This law was rightly broken on all possible occasions, but helped to impoverish the Highlands.

6. The Education Act, providing that every gentleman and yeoman possessed of sixty head of cattle, should send his eldest son, or if he had no male children, his eldest daughter to school in the lowlands. As already stated this did not mean the southern lowlands of Scotland but the numerous Highland schools situated in or near the towns, and in the lower lands of the Clan areas.

7. A clause forbidding use of firearms for any purpose was completely ignored.

8. Forbade the keeping of bards by chief, chieftain or gentry. A stupid and narrow minded act, therefore seldom obeyed. The bards were as a rule highly educated men and the mainstay of Celtic culture including Gaelic poetry, of which there was a great revival in the 17th century.

9. Some enactments for enforcing the above. Another enlightening view on the Highlands of 1613 comes from Taylor the so-called London water poet who frequently visited our 'barbaric' Highlands but seems to have found them quite civilized. He writes that at no time did he encounter any danger coming or going, but is full of praise for the hospitality and entertainment he received from a 'pleasant and friendly society'.

Note Rental of the hail Fermes, Maills, and Kanes, within the Earldom of Ross and Lordship of Ardmeanach, assignit to the Queenis Ma[tie] in compensation. (Anne of Denmark who married James VI and I on 24th November 1590.) Money values have for the purposes of this list been shown in Sterling, not as in the original, in £1 Scots. Beir is a form of barley.

Farm–Mill, etc.	Money or Produce, etc.	Quantity
Meikill Allane	beir and meal	6 chalders
Meikill Allane	poultrie	10 birds
Culrossie	beir and meal	3 chalders
Culrossie	poultrie	4 birds
Drummendiah (Drumderfit)	beir and meal	3 chalders
Drummendiah (Drumderfit)	poultrie	4 birds
Gascullie (Glastullich)	beir and meal	6 chalders
Gascullie (Glastullich)	poultrie	4 birds
Drumgillie	beir and meal	6 chalders
Drumgillie	poultrie	9 birds
Meikill Meddat	beir and meal	6 chalders
Meikill Meddat	poultrie	6 birds
Wester Pollo	poultrie	1 bird
Ruffis	poultrie	1 bird
Knock-na-pairk	poultrie	1 bird
Ballantraid	poultrie	1 bird
Faychlathie	poultrie	1 bird
Ard-na-gaag	poultrie	1 bird
Delney	beir and meal	3 chalders
Incheffer	poultrie	1 bird
Kincraig	beir and meal	3 chalders, 8 bolls, 1 peck
Kincraig	cattle	2 animals
Kincraig	sheep	2 animals
Kincraig	oats	12 bolls
Culkenny (Rosebank)	beir and meal	1 chalder, 8 bolls
Culkenny (Rosebank)	oats	12 bolls
Culkenny (Rosebank)	cattle	4 animals
Culkenny (Rosebank)	sheep	4 animals
Craigmilne (Millcraig)	beir and meal	1 chalder, 2 boll

Farm–Mill, etc.	Money or Produce, etc.	Quantity
Cullichmamah (Coilich, Easter Ardross)	beir	6 bolls
Cullichmamah (Coilich, Easter Ardross)	cattle	2 animals
Cullichmamah (Coilich, Easter Ardross))	sheep	2 animals
Tullichmoir (Novar etc.)	beir	1 chalder, 14 bolls
Tullichmoir (Novar etc.)	oats	12 bolls
Tullichmoir (Novar etc.)	cattle	4 animals
Tullichmoir (Novar etc.)	sheep	4 animals
Brechnach (part of Newton)	poultrie	1 bird
Balcony, with the brew lands of the half dail of Kilmaloch, the lands of (Teaninich), Culfluteris, Crafteraggy, the Milne of Alnes, the Yair of Balcony, and steil (cruive) of Ardtoy (Glass)	beir and meal	2 chalders, 8 bolls
Balcony, etc.	cattle	2 animals
Balcony, etc.	sheep	2 animals
Balcony, etc.	capones	12 birds
Balcony, etc.	common poultrie	5 birds
Culcarnein (Culcairn)	beir and meal	4 chalders, 8 bolls
Culcarnein (Culcairn)	oats	2 chalders, 4 bolls
Culcarnein (Culcairn)	capones	12 birds
Swerdall (Swordale)	beir and meal	1 chalder, 8 bolls
Swerdall (Swordale)	oats	12 bolls
Swerdall (Swordale)	cattle	4 animals
Swerdall (Swordale)	sheep	4 animals
Swerdall (Swordale)	poultrie	9 birds
Fyris (Fyrish)	beir and meal	1 chalder, 8 bolls
Fyris (Fyrish)	oats	12 bolls
Fyris (Fyrish)	cattle	4 animals
Fryis (Fryish)	sheep	4 animals
Fyris (Fyrish)	poultrie	13 birds
Milne of Culcraggie	beir and meal	2 chalders
Brewland of Culcraggie	capones	12 birds
Milnton of Culmalochy (Ballachraggan)	poultrie	1 bird
Croft of (Ballachraggan)	poultrie	1 bird
Milne of Cattal (Katewell)	beir and meal	1 chalder, 2 bolls
Milne of Cattal (Katewell)	capones	24 birds
Littil Scattal (Little Scatwell)	poultrie	1 bird
Rowie (Rogie)	poultrie	1 bird
Kinellan with its Mill and Coul	money	£19. 0. 3.
Wester Drynie (Heights of Fodderty)	money	23/- S.
Wester Drynie (Heights of Fodderty)	poultrie	2 birds
Ardival	money	£3. 9. 4.
Ardival	oats	6 bolls
Ardival	beir and meal	13 bolls
Ardival	cattle	2 animals
Ardival	sheep	2 animals
Ardival	poultrie	6 birds
Its Mill termed Mulin-Tuindain	beir and meal	1 chalder, 2 bolls
The Brewlands of Kinnettas	money	16/- S.
Kinhard (Kinnahaird)	money	£4
Kinhard (Kinnahaird)	beir and meal	1 chalder, 8 bolls
Kinhard (Kinnahaird)	oats	12 bolls
Kinhard (Kinnahaird)	cattle	4 animals
Kinhard (Kinnahaird)	sheep	4 animals
Kinhard (Kinnahaird)	poultrie	7 birds
Easter Achilty	money	£3
Wester Achilty	money	£3
Wester Achilty	poultrie	4 birds
The Two Brewlands	money	£10. 8. 0.
Park	money	£3
Park	poultrie	1 bird
Voladaill (Lands of Ulladale now Golf Course at Castle Leod)	money	6/- S.
Voladaill, etc.	poultrie	6 birds
Meikill Scatwell	money	£5. 4s.
Meikill Scatwell	cattle	3 animals
Meikle Scatwell	poultrie	1 bird
Urray	money	£4.
Urray	poultrie	4 birds
Kilquhillardrum (Druim)	money	£10. 8s.
Kilquhillardrum (Druim)	poultrie	1 bird
Ord	money	£10. 9. 4.
Ord	poultrie	8 birds
Mill of Druim	money	£10. 8s.
Mill of Druim	beir and meal	2 chalders
Mill of Druim	poultrie	1 bird
Balleblana (Balblair)	money	£10.
Balleblana (Balblair)	poultrie	1 bird
Balnagowne Urray	money	£3.
Balnagowne Urray	poultrie	2 birds
Balnaknock	money	£3.
Balnaknock	poultrie	4 birds
Tarradaill, with the brewland	money	£6. 16s.
Tarradaill, with the brewland	poultrie	1 bird

Farm–Mill, etc.	Money or Produce, etc.	Quantity
Milne of Tarradaill with the alehouse	money	33/4d.
The Ferry of Scatwell	money	23/- s.
Logyreich, Connon policies and Mains	money	£4.
Logyreich, Connon policies and Mains	poultrie	4 birds
Its Brewlands	money	£10. 8s.
Easter Kessock	money	£3. 10s.
Easter Kessock	sheep	2 animals
Easter Kessock	capones	12 birds
Easter Kessock	common poultrie	10 birds
Ferry of Kessock	money	£8. 4s.
Steil of Kessock	money	16/- s.
Brewland of Kessock	money	16/- s.
Easter Pollo	money	£4. 4s.
Auchnaclerach	money	£4. 8s.
Auchnaclerach	poultrie	1 bird
The Morechmore	money	£10.
Sergasown (Gargaston)	money	£10. 5s.
Sergasown (Gargaston)	beir	8 bolls, 2 firlots
Sergasown (Gargaston)	sheep	1 animal
Sergasown (Gargaston)	cattle	1 animal
Sergasown (Gargaston)	poultrie	8 birds
Newton	money	£18.
Newton	beir and meal	2 chalders, 2 bolls
Newton	cattle	2 animals
Newton	mutton	2 animals
Newton	poultrie	1 bird
Suddy Croft and brewland	money	38/-s. 8d.
Hillton	money	£9. 13. 7.
Hillton	beir	1 chalder, 1 boll
Hillton	cattle	1 animal
Hillton	sheep	1 animal
Hillton	poultrie	8 birds
Mill of Culbokie	beir and meal	15 bolls, 3 fir, 3 pecks
Drumcuddin	money	£8. 12. 4.
Drumcuddin	beir	2 chalders, 6 bolls, 1 fir
Drumcuddin	oats	4 bolls
Drumcuddin	cattle	1 animal
Drumcuddin	sheep	1 animal
Drumcuddin	poultrie	58 birds
Wester half davoch of above	money	£5. 16s. 4d.
Wester half davoch of above	beir	10 bolls, 2 fir, 2 pecks
Wester half davoch of above	oats	4 bolls
Wester half davoch of above	cattle	3½
Wester half davoch of above	sheep	3½
Wester half davoch of above	poultrie	27 birds
Easter half davoch of above	money	£3. 3s. 11d.
Easter half davoch of above	beir	5 bolls, 1 firlot, 1 peck
Easter half davoch of above	oats	1 boll
Easter half davoch of above	beef	1 quarter
Easter half davoch of above	mutton	1 quarter
Easter half davoch of above	poultrie	13 birds
Its Brewlands	money	30/-s.
Killane (Kileen)	money	£3. 10s.
Killane (Killeen)	poultrie	1 bird
Bemethfeild (Bennetsfield)	money	£7. 18s.
Bemethfeild (Bennetsfield)	poultrie	1 bird
Milne of Petfins	money	£7. 4s.
Its Brewlands	money	£3. 2s. 1d.
Its Brewlands	poultrie	1 bird
Drynie	money	£6. 14s. 5d.
Drynie	beir	2 chalders, 6 bolls, 1 peck
Drynie	oats	4 bolls
Drynie	cattle	1 animal
Drynie	sheep	1 animal
Drynie	poultrie	27 birds
Its Brewlands	money	18/-s.
Milne of Pittonochy (Rosehaugh)	beir	2 chalders, 2 bolls
Milne of Pittonochy (Rosehaugh)	capones	24 birds
Milne of Pittonochy (Rosehaugh)	poultrie	1 bird
Sir William Keith, his augmentation of his feu farm Dunglust	money	£20.
Drumdarswood (Drumderfit)	money	£10. 16s.
Drumdarswood (Drumderfit)	beir	2 chalders, 8 bolls, 2 firlots, 2½ pecks
Drumdarswood (Drumderfit)	oats	4 bolls
Drumdarswood (Drumderfit)	cattle	1 animal
Drumdarswood (Drumderfit)	sheep	1 animal
Drumdarswood (Drumderfit)	poultrie	27 birds
Milntown of Meikle Meddat with its brewlands	money	13s. 4d.
Milntown of Meikle Meddat with its brewlands	beir and meal	6 chalders, 3 bolls
Tulloch Ballafies (Milne) and brewland	money	£18. 4s.
Tulloch Ballafies (Milne) and brewland	poultrie	2 birds
Moy, Midfairbairne, Auchnasoul, and Balavaird	money	£30. 17s. 4d.
Moy, Midfairbairne, Auchnasoul, and Balavaird	beir and meal	1 chalder, 2 bolls
Moy, Midfairbairne, Auchnasoul, and Balavaird	oats	9 bolls

Farm–Mill, etc.	Money or Produce, etc.	Quantity
Moy, Midfairbairne, Auchnasoul, and Balavaird	cattle	3 animals
Moy, Midfairbairne, Auchnasoul, and Balavaird	sheep	3 animals
Moy, Midfairbairne, Auchnasoul, and Balavaird	poultrie	23 birds
Coilmore, Drumnamairg, Muren, Milne of Redcastle	beir	2 chalders, 2 bolls
	cattle	2 animals
Coilmore, etc.	sheep	2 animals
Branmore	money	18/-s.
Forrest of Rannoch	beir and meal	8 bolls
Forrest of Rannoch	cattle	3 animals
Easter Tarbat	money	£12.
Minren	beir	2 chalders, 10 bolls, 2 pecks
Minren	cattle	2 animals
Minren	sheep	2 animals
Minren	poultrie	46 birds
Milne of Redcastle	money	26s. 8d.
Augmentation of John Stewart's feu farm	money	£12. 17s. 8d.
Castleton	beir	1 chalder, 5 bolls, 1 peck
Castleton	oats	4 bolls
Castleton	cattle	1 animal
Castleton	sheep	1 animal
Castleton	poultrie	59 birds
Its Croft	beir	1 boll, 1 peck
Balmaduchtie (Balmaduthy)	beir	1 chalder, 5 bolls, 1 peck
Balmaduchtie (Balmaduthy)	oats	4 bolls
Balmaduchtie (Balmaduthy)	cattle	1 animal
Balmaduchtie (Balmaduthy)	sheep	1 animal
Balmaduchtie (Balmaduthy)	poultrie	55 birds
Suddy	beir	1 chalder, 5 bolls, 1 peck
Suddy	cattle	1 animal
Suddy	sheep	1 animal
Suddy	poultrie	57 birds
Milne of Suddie	beir	1 chalder, 3 bolls, 2 pecks
Milne of Suddie	capones	18 birds
Milne of Suddie	poultrie	2 birds
Auchtercloy (Auchterflow)	beir	2 chalders, 2 bolls
Auchtercloy (Auchterflow)	oats	8 bolls
Auchtercloy (Auchterflow)	cattle	2 animals
Auchtercloy (Auchterflow)	sheep	2 animals
Auchtercloy (Auchterflow)	poultrie	35 birds
Dacchorne, Dalpollo, Inver(gordon), Mains, Kinkell, Clarschor (Carnclarsar), Pitilarndy (Pitlundy), Culboks (Culbokie) with the brewland	cattle	2½ animals
Dacchorne, etc.	sheep	3½ animals
Dacchorne, etc.	poultrie	96 birds
Pittomochrae (Tore)	beir	1 chalder, 5 bolls, 1 peck
Pittomochrae (Tore)	oats	4 bolls
Pittomochrae (Tore)	cattle	1 animal
Pittomochrae (Tore)	sheep	1 animal
Pittomochrae (Tore)	poultrie	55 birds
Tollie, Brahan	dry multure	6 bolls
Wester Kessock	capones	48 birds
Wester Kessock	poultrie	10 birds
Wester Kessock	sheep	4 animals
Lord Dingwall's Lands	poultrie	43 birds
Lord Dingwall's Lands	sheep	8 animals

CHAPTER XIII

MARY QUEEN OF SCOTS—A LONG SIEGE—THE HOUSE OF KINTAIL SPREADS INTO THE BLACK ISLE—WITCH-CRAFT TROUBLES IN ROSS—A CLEAN-UP IN THE WEST—THE HOUSE OF CROMARTIE—AGRICULTURE

Chronological Table

1568 Earl of Moray and rebels defeat Queen Mary at Langside.
1570 Regent Moray shot.
1572 Knox died.
1579 Epoch of English literature opens: Lyly—Spencer—Sidney—Bacon—Marlowe—Shakespeare.
1582 Founding of Edinburgh University. Scots poet William Fowler writing.
1585 Birth of Scottish poet William Drummond of Hawthornden.
1587 Beheading of Mary Queen of Scots. Birth of Scottish Latin poet Arthur Johnston.
1592 Montaigne died.

In order to get a clear picture of certain changes which were taking place in Scotland, it was necessary in the last chapter to take a general survey up to and including the opening years of the 17th century. This left many important gaps which must now be filled in, so that we shall retrace our steps to the year 1561, when Mary Queen of Scots really started her brief reign. By her charm and genuine Queencraft she almost succeeded in restoring unity to her divided Kingdom, but not quite, she failed largely through her fairness of mind and a desire for religious toleration. Had she gone all out either for the Protestant or the Catholic party she would have won through as the big majority of Scots, Highland and Lowland, were loyal to Scotland and the Stewarts. As it was, the attempt to be fair to both sides angered both, the Catholics being furious that she did not forcibly re-establish the old faith, the Protestants equally annoyed that she would not forcibly suppress the Catholics, and herself worship in their own 'seal pattern' way; again her wish to recall the Estates of Scotland in place of the packed Assembly which had supplanted the legal government, caused great alarm. The reason for this alarm was not far to seek, as this body consisted largely of those Lords who were doing so well out of con-fiscated Church property, and the return of the Estates might well mean the resumption of government by patriotic, non-fanatical and less self interested men.

Behind all these difficulties English gold and promises were playing havoc with the loyalties of many of the Lowland nobility, amongst them the Queen's half brother, a cold, calculating gentleman the 'good' Earl of Moray, who had his eye on the throne from which his bastardy had kept him. By 1568 she had lost the fight, though had not the Bothwell affair occurred she might still have won through; but re-garding this affair though we must admit that Bothwell, on his father's

side a Border Hepburn and on his mother's a Highland Sinclair, was a
violent and headstrong individual, he was at least loyal, while the
propaganda tales which have their origin in Buchanan's 'Wheen o'
blathers' have no bearing on the true story, despite the fact that they
were accepted as gospel truth by the majority of historians till a very
recent date. As we have seen, the clans in the main remained loyal,
a fact which was to produce the unnatural division between the Scot
of the southern lowlands and the Scot of the Highlands, a division that
during the 17th century was to be fanned into a fanatical hatred by the
eloquence of the lowland divines.

Eventually Moray and the rebels defeated the Queen at the battle of
Langside, Colin of Kintail, nicknamed Colin *'Cam'* the one-eyed, with
Clan Mackenzie forming part of Mary's army; Colin, who had succeeded his father Kenneth the same year, was made a prisoner but
shortly afterwards released. Scotland was once again cursed with
Regents, as after the battle the Queen had fled to England where she
remained a close prisoner till her judicial murder by her cousin Queen
Elizabeth in 1587. The usual troubles that went hand in glove with
these rulers were now aggravated by religious animosities, which
though extant in some areas of the north eastern Highlands never
engendered the bitterness and hatreds so characteristic of the Reformation in southern Scotland.

The year 1569 brought to a close the *Gairloch* disputes as Donald of
Sleat, who as we saw had claimed the Lordship of a chaotic Lewis
through his mother, had been effectively bribed by the Regent Moray
with a pension and the fruits of the vacant see of Aberdeen. This not
only made of him a good Protestant but transferred his interest from
Gairloch to Aberdeen, leaving the Mackenzies unmolested in their
possession of the former area; but in the east where lay the richer
Church lands the situation became somewhat tense.

Andrew Monro V of Milntown, a keen reformer, was doing particularly well in the land stakes; by his marriage to Catherine Urquhart of
Cromarty he had acquired the lands and town of Castletown, Bel-
maduthy, Suddie with its brew-house, croft and mill; Achterglow 'with
all pendicles and pertinents' of these towns and lands lying in the
Earldom of Ross, Lordship of Ardmanoch (Black Isle) and Sheriffdom
of Inverness, belonging in heritage to David Chalmers formerly
Chancellor of Ross and forfeited to the King (Regent). In like manner
he got a considerable slice of Church lands in the Parish of Tarbat, in
addition to some inherited from his father which had been obtained
under charter of Sir Alexander Innes of Plaids and Cadboll, who had
replaced the MacCullochs in those places though this family were still
in existence and represented in Meikle Tarrell by an heiress, Mariot,
who later married Andrew's son.

The MacCullochs were still an important family, the descendants of John McCulloch of Tarrell on record in 1368, and another John bailie of the Girth of *Sanct Duthowis* who was requested in a letter from John Earl of Ross and Lord of the Isles in 1458 to protect the privileges of Inverness merchants in Tain. King James IV in 1512 gave a re-grant to William McCulloch of his lands: Scardy, Pladdis, Detnely, Pettogarty, Tain, Ballecarew, with office of Bailie. Seven generations are designated of Pladdis till John, Provost of Tain acquired Kindeace in 1612 from Munros of Culnald. Their holdings in Ross had consisted of: Piltown, Mulderg, Ballnagore, Easter Drwm, etc., Walter Ross of Ballamuckie conveying the last two estates to Provost Andrew McCulloch in 1649. In 1674 the Lord Lyon matriculated the Arms of Sir Hugh MacCulloch as being descended from the family of Cadboll in Ross. Certain other subjects in this parish of Tarbat had been forfeited by Bishop Leslie and these also had fallen to Andrew together with another Black Isle property known as the 'Bishop's Shed' in the Chanonry of Ross. Leslie as well as being Bishop of Ross was Queen Mary's secretary, banished from Scotland in 1568 and imprisoned in the Tower of London between 1571–74 for his participation in the attempt to arrange a marriage between the Duke of Norfolk and the imprisoned Queen.

A deed dated Stirling on 10th and Chanonry on 28th February 1571 gives an example of transactions typical of the time: George Munro Prebendary and Chaplain of Newmore with consent of (the boy) James VI and Regent Matthew Earl of Lennox, Kentigern Monypenny, Dean and Vicar General of Ross, Thomas Ross Abbot of *Fearn* and Provost of Church of Tain and the Prebendaries of that Church, grant to Andrew (Monro) the Church lands of Newmore, with Ale house, Inchendown with Mill and Strath of same, (etc., etc.) previously held by George; the excuse for the transaction being that George could not pay the necessary purchase price himself.

As far back as 1558 the last Prior of Beauly had disposed of the Priory properties to the VIth Lord Lovat (Fraser) though another seventy-five years were to pass before the last monk was to disappear from the ancient foundation of Sir John Bisset, and we shall see later the fate of *Fearn* Abbey. In addition to these transactions, official posts not devoid of profit were welcome and Andrew Monro for a time held both the Captaincy of the Royal Castle of Inverness and the Bishop's Castle at Chanonry on behalf of the Regent.

Now about 1567 Bishop Leslie foreseeing the fate of Church property had made over to his cousin John Leslie of Balquhain his rights and titles to the Castle, palace and lands at Chanonry in order to divest them of the character of Church property. However the Regent Moray gave the above into the permanent custody of Andrew Monro of Milntown, promising Balquhain some part of the Barony of Fintray in

Buchan as a sop, but before the arrangements were completed or Monro had obtained any titles to Chanonry the Earl of Moray was assassinated by a Hamilton. Andrew in spite of this took possession backed by the next two Regents Lennox and Mar, an action which did not suit Colin Mackenzie XIIth of Kintail who for reasons of religion and also having an eye on the Black Isle had already purchased from Leslie of Balquhain his rights. The Regent Mar further complicated matters by creating yet another interested party, granting to his Treasurer Lord Ruthven 'the hail laid quhairwith the Cathedral Kirk of Ross was theckit, alswail principal Kirk as queir and illis thairof'; an act of sacrilege excused because it 'wes nae paroch Kirk, but ane monastrie to sustane ydill bellies', without its roof the once beautiful building fell to ruin till partially restored in a later age.

Colin, together with his brother Rory I of Redcastle—that stronghold having been held by the Mackenzies since Red Hector of *Gairloch*'s day, an occupation to be regularized by Royal Charter in 1608—raised his vassals and allies, garrisoned the steeple of the Cathedral Church, and in 1571 laid siege to the Castle 'Irvines Tower' and the Palace, an investment that lasted off and on for three years. As there exists a very vivid account of part of the siege, by an eye witness, this will best describe the opening scene of a somewhat violent series of events.

We start with the Notarial Copy of a letter dated 8th May 1572: 'Letters proceeding in name of King James narrating that it is shown by Andro Mownro of Newmore that Henry Lord Methwen and William Lord Ruthwen, his tutor, testamentor for his interests and as Kings Treasurer alleging that Andro, his servants and certain of his friends being in the Castle of Chanonrie of Ross are denounced as rebels and put to the horn (outlawed) for not delivering the same to them and that the tenants of the temporality of the Bishopric of Ross are likewise put to the horn for non payment of their maills and duties to said Henry Lord Methwen, and said treasurer has obtained letters from the King to search etc., and if need be to raise our legis to concur and "forteify the officiaris" in virtue of which they have made convocation of most inhabitants of Ross specially Clan Kenzie, who has "leged and confermit ane assege" to the said house of the Chanonrie and has slain divers of said "Androwis" friends and Servants keepers thereof and "rinns athort" and oppresses the whole country under the "pretence" of our said letters of horning and said letters of searching which are called upon for production before the Lords to have them suspended, wherefore Ld Ruthwen, the Kings Treasurer and Kings Advocate for his interests, are charged to compear before the King and his council at Leith or where they may be on 31 May next to answer said Andrew in the matter, meantime letters are suspended.

Endorsed charge Lord Methwen and Clan Kenzie by Andrew Monro of Milntown 1572 concerning the Castle of Chanrie'.

A month later—8th July 1572. 'On Sat. 5 July 1572 at Fouils, the laird thereof, George Munro of Docharte delivered to me Richard Mader messinger our Sovereign Lords letters to charge Colin Mackenzie of Kintail, Rory his brother, Lawrence Bannerman and Robert Munro of Foulis, George Munro of Docharte, Andro Munro his son to subscribe an assurance to be had between Colin Mackenzie his kin and friends on one part and the said Robert Munro of Foulis, kin, and friends on the other part to the last day of August next thereafter and incontinent thereafter, I charged the said Robert Munro and George Munro to subscribe, which before was signed by the said Laird and George at Foulis the same day, then sent me to Mackenzie to the Chanonery of Ross where Mackenzie and MacIntosh when with their whole host to the number of 3000 men or thereby laying seige to the Castle and I delivered the letters to said Colin Mackenzie of Kintail, first my Lord Regents letter and two letters containing an assurance the one of them signed by Robert Munro of Foulis, George Munro of Docharte and Andro his son, the other letter to be signed by Mackenzie and Laurence Bannerman and delivered to the said Mackenzie the Kings letter charging him to signe another letter of assurance also to be sent to the Laird of Foulis, George and Andro Munro his son and also send letters with me to charge Mackenzie, Rory his brother, John Mackenzie of Gairloch, Hector Mackenzie the son of Alexander Mackenzie, Laurens Bannerman on one part and the Munros on the other, John his son Hucheon Munro, and Andrew Monro being in the Castle of Chanonery, and ordering them all to appear before the Lord Regent and Lords of Secret Council, at least the last day of July to answer to the charge of breaking of the country of Ross upon Sunday 6 day of July. Which letters Mackenzie took from me pleasantly and put them in his bosom and passed to his pavillion to his dinner and sent for me and caused me and the Earle of Sutherlands' falconer to be sat at the pavillion where we got our dinner sent from his own board and after dinner I went to Mackenzie to get him to signe the assurance, but there came upon me Laurens Bannerman, William Herring captain of the men sent by Lord Ruthven to Mackenzie with many other men, with them were Laurens Bannerman and the said Captain who laid violent hands on me and took me prisoner and robbed me of all other letters and writing I had and took my sword and all I had in my pouch and in all my clothes with part of my money to the sum of 10/- or 12/- about. They delivered me to Alexander Dingwall, Mackenzie's household man who led me as a trespasser in the Camp to the Chanonrie

Note There is no punctuation in the original. When absolutely necessary for clearness I have put it in.

accompanied by 16 men and held my a prisoner in Cuntane House from 10 o'c on Sunday forenoon to Monday 8 a.m. and sent into me the Kings letters charging them to appear and putting them to the horn, but got no other letters nor gear taken from me; and said Alexander Dingwall told me to get out of town at once, and said to me if I was found on the causway or passage to the Castle to execute any letters or read them, I should be hanged and quartered and drawn and so I passed to the Town of Cromartie; and this before witnesses I have written and signed the account and signed it with my signet of office at the Mylton in Ross 8 July 1572 R.M.'

Eventually a foraging party from the Castle was cut up by Ian *Dubh MacRuaridh* Mhic Alastair which forced the capitulation of the garrison who by that time were out of food. The Mackenzie took possession and subsequently the Baron of Kintail was confirmed in the possession of Chanonry Castle and lands by James VI.

Roderick (Rory) *Mór* Mackenzie 1st of Redcastle, already a Black Isle resident had played a leading part in this affair and seems generally to have upset the Clan Munro, so that in 1575 on 25th March a Bond was registered in Edinburgh by which Colin Earl of Argyll and Robert Munro of Foulis became sureties to the amount of £5,000 that Roderick of Redcastle shall return to the Regent a Bond of Walter Urquhart of Cromarty, John Grant of Freuchy, and Hugh Rose X of Kilravock obliging them to produce the said Roderick before the Council, if required and that in the meantime he shall keep good rule in the country.

On 31st May Colin of Kintail, who as Roderick's chief, had decided that the time had come to exercise control over his brother, took the matter into his own hands, handing in the bond at Holyrood, having first signed it in his new castle of Chanonry, thus relieving the cautioners of their difficult responsibility, a process that he repeated four years later.

The seventies of this century were a time of perplexity as it was extremely difficult for an honest man, whatever his religious persuasion to know where his duty lay, being faced by a situation in which the existing government operating in the name only of the child King were in fact rebels, while the highest in the land were mainly concerned in an unholy scramble for real estate. In 1573 the Earl of Sutherland petitioned that he might collect a jury in Aberdeen to serve him as heir to his father, being unable to assemble one to sit in Inverness, as the local Barons such as Colin of Kintail, Lachlan MacKintosh of MacKintosh and Robert of Foulis were all at loggerheads.

Ross had not escaped the extraordinary outbreak of witchcraft cases which followed the establishment of the Reformed Kirk in Scotland. But before discussing our own 'cause célèbre' it may make the phenomena more understandable if we first take a more general look at a subject which, like so many others, has suffered from a too facile explanation and over-simplification. Christianity did not stamp out completely the older religion of Europe with its fertility rights and beliefs; moreover it would not be safe to say that it has yet done so. Naturally in more remote areas the chances of survival for the old beliefs were greatly enhanced, and the early Catholic Church, Celtic or Roman, showed considerable wisdom when it Christianized certain pagan ceremonies, instead of attempting the impossible, and trying to abolish them.

The four principal Sabbaths of the cult were re-named as follows: (Beltane) May Eve became Roodmans; November Eve, All Hallows (Hallow-ene); 2nd February, Candlemas; 1st August, Lammas; the groves, wells and sites sacred to the old religion, were rededicated to some Christian saint, the classic example being Iona an island sacred to Druid and Christian alike. But everywhere something remained, as is proved by certain very odd happenings. During the second decade of the 15th century a Scottish priest was discovered to have led part of his flock in a fertility dance round the phallic figure of a god, yet he retained his living. At the end of this same century the Pope was compelled to issue a Bull denouncing witchcraft, which drove the Dianic Cult underground, where it lived on in a more degraded form.

In Scotland the overthrow of Catholicism caused a revival, at least in part, a reaction to the gloomy fear-ridden fatalism of the Calvinistic Kirk of that day, for it must be remembered that this nature religion, though only remembered imperfectly, was a joyous thing, and the conception that the participants were all old, poor, and half witted hags is very far from the truth. The elaborate organization was nation-wide, if not international, having among its members some of the highest and most powerful in the land. The Earl of Bothwell was a chief priest of this secret society, during the reign of James VI while in the 'North Berwick Case' a witch, Barbara Napier is described as 'a civil honest woman as any that dwelt within the City of Edinburgh'; others are Euphemia, a daughter of Lord Cliftonhall and Agnes Sampson 'the wise wife of Keith'; 'a woman not of the base and ignorant sort of witches, but matron-like, grave and settled in her answers'.

In 1537 a Lady Glamis had been burned as a witch, though the burnings usually fell to the smaller fry. John Fiar, a schoolmaster, was the 'minister' of the above North Berwick coven, during the time of the celebrated trial which found them guilty of storm raising in order to prevent the return of James VI and his bride from Denmark. The devotees throughout the land were organized into groups, governed by a body of 'Deacons', while a 'Minister' or his deputy conducted the services; locally the witches were organized into a coven under this male 'minister'.

The chief priest was regarded by his followers throughout the land as a supernatural being, for whom they would suffer or do anything, and in times of persecution these folk underwent every torment rather than deny their God and faith. So great was their resistance that to this day very little is known of the cult beyond the fact that each witch carried on her body some secret initiatory mark, while their ceremonies were concerned with the supernatural control of the forces of life and nature. That it provided some evidence of its power, at least sufficient to convince the best intellects of that and subsequent ages, we know, so it is not surprising to find a general and universal acceptance of witchcraft. The aims of these practices were not always malevolent as was shown by one Gelie Duncan of the Berwick coven, who had attracted the attention of a pious member of the Kirk by helping 'all such as were troubled or grieved with any kind of sickness or infirmity'.

The panic, for there is no other way of describing the reaction to the outbreak so far as the authorities were concerned, was due less to the pagan magic element as to the obvious political ramifications of a powerful 'hidden hand', doubly dangerous as its most influential members were entirely unsuspected.

The Ross affair happened during the years 1576–77, and significantly, enough took place in that part of Ross most affected by the Reformation. Both Foulis and Balnagown had embraced the new faith, a change not, perhaps, unconnected with certain good benefices, such as Newmore and the rich churchlands belonging to the Abbey of *Fearn*. Robert *Mór* Munro XVth of Foulis had taken as his second wife, the Lady Katherine Ross, daughter of the IXth Chief, of Balnagown. This lady together with her stepson Hector Munro the future XVII Baron of Foulis, was implicated in an attempt to poison or kill by sorcery and incantation Marjorie Campbell, a daughter of Sir John Campbell IXth of Cawdor in Nairn, who had married Katherine's brother George Ross X of Balnagown. By the removal of Marjorie the conspirators hoped to bring about the re-marriage of George Ross to the wife of the heir of Foulis Robert *Òg* Munro, which of course entailed his liquidation as well.

In order to accomplish this pleasant plan of murder and fratricide the help of the Tain coven was sought, the chief helpers being the witch Marion MacAllister alias Loskie Loutart (*loisg na lodar*—burn the ladle) and the 'wizard' William MacGillivray alias *Damh* (ox). Loskie prepared a clay image *corp-creadh* of Lady Marjorie, telling Lady Foulis that she must shoot at it with 'Elf arrows' (the tiny mesolithic flint arrow-heads), the victim would then pine away and die, but *Damh* provided a box of 'witch-craft' or plain straight-forward poison.

They did not quite succeed in killing the poor victim though thirteen years later she was still a chronic invalid as a result of their attentions.

The plot was discovered and the wizard MacGillivray or *Damh*, together with some accomplices, 'print for the samin', died at the stake after conviction by a Justice Court held within the Cathedral Kirk of Ross (Fortrose) 28th November 1577. The fate of the witch Loskie Loutart is not known except that she was not condemned to the stake, though probably flogged and imprisoned.

But what of the real culprits who were well and truly implicated at this trial; as so often happened the bigger fish got away with it, for although, at the instance of the King's advocate David MacGill, Lady Katherine Munro of Foulis and Hector Munro were brought to trial in 1590, she was acquitted. Hector was faced with some odd charges not directly concerned with the attempted murder charge, but indicative of his traffic with the 'Old Gentleman' namely, that he employed a witch to cure him of fever by carrying him in a blanket on a frosty night in January, laying him down in a newmade grave at the boundary between two Baronies, so transferring the fever to his stepbrother who would die in his stead. However the Tain Jury were all dependent on Ross or Munro, and belonged to one or other of these clans so that Hector's acquittal was a foregone conclusion.

To what extent that other pillar of the Kirk, a graduate of St. Andrews University, George Ross of Balnagown, was aware of the attempt to poison his young wife, is not known, but in 1581 he presented her with the life rent of certain lands, perhaps as a small compensation and atonement for the evil deed; 'of the quhilk poysonn the young lady of Balnagowan contracted deadlie sickness (1577) quhairin sche remains yet incurable'. This observation comes from the trial in 1590— 13 years after the crime was perpetrated. The old Baron of Foulis Robert *Mór* seems to have known nothing of the goings on of his scheming wife and son until the story, or part of it, came out at the trial.

Such was the outstanding case in Ross during this period, but Tain had no monopoly in witches, the *Gearrchoile*, a wood on the main road near Ardgay, was in olden times the meeting place for a witches' coven; while there were many other unchancy old ladies such as the notorious Fodderty witch Agnes *Mór* nin vic Eean Glaish (Big Agnes the daughter of the son of Grey John) in 1672 who however was treated very gently by the Dingwall Presbyters.

Hector Munro XVIIth Baron of Foulis, must have been a curious character; as a second son he had followed the customary fashion of studying for the Church, being appointed by a letter from Queen Mary to the Chaplaincy of Newmore, which he later changed for Obsdale (Dalmore). His entry into the Deanery of Ross was opposed by the recently deposed Dean Alexander Urquhart, but without effect,

Note His Infernal Majesty has many titles in Scotland: The Old Gentleman; old Nick; *Domhnull Dubh*; Hornie; The Earl of Hell; The Laird o' Yon Place.

though shortly afterwards Hector vacated his ecclesiastical office on succeeding his brother at Foulis, who had died in 1589 after only 8 months of chiefship. Within a few weeks of the new Baron's installation, we are presented with the curious spectacle of him bringing charges of witchcraft against Katherine Ross, his stepmother and late partner in crime, as well as a Margaret Sutherland spouse of Neil Munro, Margaret Ross and Margaret Mowat, the object of this volte-face being to dislodge his stepmother from certain lands held by her on Foulis.

The trial was conducted in Inverness by Colin Mackenzie of Kintail, Commissioner for the Sheriffdom of Inverness, which included Ross, with Rory his brother, John Mackenzie of *Gairloch*, Alexander Bayne of Tulloch, and others, the case being remitted for trial by jury court, the results of which we have already seen. On subsequent occasions various gentlemen in the north became cautioners in order to guarantee the life of Lady Katherine Munro, née Ross, together with certain other people, from the homicidal attentions of our Hector; the highest bond of £2,000 being held over John Campbell of Cawdor. Eventually Hector himself was forced to produce a caution of 10,000 Marks as surety of his good behaviour; seemingly this produced the desired result as in 1590 a commission was granted to him for the apprehension of George Earl of Huntly, William Earl of Angus, Francis Earl of Erroll, and others, for various acts, including participation in the assassination of the mis-named 'good' Earl of Moray, late Regent of Scotland.

On 4th February 1597 a serious row occurred at the Candlemas *fhéill* of Logie-*Riach* on the Conon which started with a quarrel between John MacGillichallum, brother to the Laird of Raasay, and Bayne of Tulloch over some land in Torridon, which was aggravated by the fact that Tulloch had obtained a decree of interdict against John. While John was inspecting a chapman's stall, Bayne, approaching from behind, struck him on the head with his two-handed sword, killing the man of Raasay on the spot. A Mackenzie who tried to interfere was run through for his trouble and at once the war cry of *Tulloch Ard* rang through the fairground, collecting the numerous Mackenzies present, who at once started a general tulzie. The Baynes and Munros combined but being on Mackenzie territory sought safety in flight, the Munros toward the Ferry of Foulis and the Baynes north to Dingwall. This division of their available force was unwise, both parties being followed by a mob of enraged Mackenzies who slaughtered all they could catch.

The Munro party was singularly unlucky as they chanced to run into two Mackenzie gentlemen with their attendants, coming from Chanonry, already cognisant of what was afoot; thirteen Munros fell between Logie and the Wood of Millechaich as a result of this meeting. The casualties amounted to nearly all the Baynes and 50 Munros, which caused a Lady of that clan, who had lost three brothers, to compose a Lament. The affair was brought up before the King and Privy Council then at Falkirk, by Lord Lovat, an advocate for the Bayne-Munro faction, and Mackenzie of Kintail who however reached the King first, which resulted in a more or less peaceful settlement between the clans concerned.

The rule of the regents which followed the successful rebellion against Mary Queen of Scots had produced violent reactions in the north, where Clan Mackenzie had remained loyal to the Queen, while Munros and Rosses were in the main antagonistic, though even among these clans feelings were very mixed. All this tended to aggravate local feuds which easily led to bloodshed in an age when the hand was never far from the sword hilt.

In 1599, Hector Munro had to take out a caution for 2,000 Mks guaranteeing that Farquhar Munro portioner of Little Kindeace would not harm William Corbett burgess of Tain, and another of 4,000 Mks that Hugh Munro of Ardullie would not injure William Innes of Calrossie. A year before his death, Hector was ordered, with other Highland chiefs, to hold a general muster and wappenshaw of his followers, to take place on 10th March, after which he was to report on numbers and armament, supplying one hundred men for service in Ireland on behalf of Elizabeth of England, at that time in considerable difficulties with the Irish rising; James VI by then was leaving no stone unturned to ensure his succession to the Crown of England. King James VI had with great difficulty taken over the rule of his distracted Kingdom in 1583, and as we saw in the last chapter, had gradually produced order out of chaos to the infinite relief of the ordinary mortal who wanted to work his farm and croft in peace.

The scramble for lands continued, Ross being no exception to the rule though Protestant Episcopacy had been accepted with relief in the Highlands for the reasons already given. Sir Andrew Keith was created Lord Dingwall, so becoming the King's governor at Dingwall Castle, while a great new Barony of Delny formed out of the old Barony and additional parts of the Earldom of Ross was acquired by William Keith of Ravenscraig; in 1599 the greater part of the Abbey lands of *Fearn* were created into the Barony of Geanies and granted to Sir Patrick Murray; most of what was over being annexed to the Bishop of Ross.

Alexander Ross, the Laird of Balnagown, seems to have made himself particularly obnoxious to the parishioners of *Fearn*, as we find the Commendator for the Abbey complaining to the King and Council about Alexander, thus 'quhat barbarous cruelties, injuries, and intollerable oppressions and bluidiched the saidis Alexander Ross committed' . . . . etc. Ross was duly put to the horn (outlawed), arrested, and confined to Tantallon Castle, a fate which he richly deserved.

There is a mistaken notion that all game in the Highlands was free for all: nothing could be further from the truth; for centuries past certain areas had always been strictly preserved for the use of the chiefs and chieftains. Especially was this so in the Royal forests, a fact made abundantly clear in the following poaching case in which John Dingwall of Kildun was concerned on the Forest of Bray (on the Black Isle:) 'Holyrood House 25th Oct. 1577. Anent the charge be virtew of our soverene Lordes Letters to Johne Dingwall of Kildun, to compeir personally befoir my Lord Regentis Grace and Lordis of Secret Consule on a certain day bypast, to answer to sic thingis as sould be inquirit of him at his coming, tending to the gude order of quietness of the Earldom of Ross as under the pain of rebellion and putting him to the horn with certification to him that if he failyt, he should be denouncet rebell and put to the horn, like as at mair length is contentit in the aforesaidis letters. Quilkis being callit, and the said Johne Dingwall compearend personalis, and John Urquhart, in name of Walter Urquhart, Sheriff of Cromartie, being also personalie present, the said Johnne, in name of the said Sheriff, accasit the said Johnne Dingwall as a contravener of the Actis of Parliament, forbidend to schute at wyld beist daar (red deer and roe) and other vennersoun, in sa far as he with his complices, to the noumer of XVI personis, in the month of September last bipast, and at divers utheris tymes preceding, come to the forest of Bray within the Earldom of Ross, pertaining heritable to the said sheriff, and then slew with hagbutties, bowis and pistolettis, XV or XVI greit deer, to his hurt and skayth, and manifest contempt of our Soverane Lordis authoritie and lawis. To the quilk accusation the said Johnne Dingwall maid answer that he committed na slaughter upoun any daar pertaining to the said Sheriff at ony time except ane deer slain by him with ane arrow about the Feist of Midsummer bipast. Quhairfoir, my Lord Regentis Grace, with advise of the Lordis of Secreit Counsele, in respect of the said Johnne Dingwallis confession maid in manner aforesaid, ordainis him to be put to the knowledge of ane assgise for contravening of the aforesaid Actis of Parliament in manner above written, and justice to be ministrat upon him as accordis.'

Although the game laws of Scotland were very mild compared with the savage penalties exacted south of the border, which included mutilation and even death, yet their enforcement had to be tightened up with the great increase of firearms which in certain areas threatened the extermination of all game. The same state of affairs existed in Wester Ross so that early in next century we find Colin XIV of Kintail 1st Earl of Seaforth meeting the Skye Chiefs in order to legislate against poaching. The result of this meeting was the issue of licences while a Forester was given additional powers including the confiscation of firearms, if necessary.

During the early years of James' reign we are presented with the now familiar picture of unrest in the Western Isles; but alas this time there is no friendly Gaelic-speaking *Ard Righ* who can understand their difficulties and point of view, to talk them out of their tantrums. The year 1585 saw the MacKinnons of Skye allied with MacLeans of Duart opposed to Clan Donald of Sleat, with the Earl of Argyll playing a not disinterested hand, though in the following year this gentleman was able to fix up a short truce. But the turmoil soon broke out again and the government in despair handed over the solution of the Island problem to Clan Mackenzie, who settled it in no uncertain fashion, Donald *Gorm* of Sleat spending the years till 1591 in prison. This did not end the troubles, but in 1596 the chiefs of Sleat, and Dunvegan, were pardoned, while for his efforts on behalf of the King—and himself—Colin of Kintail was knighted.

During this struggle in the west the Mackenzies invaded, c. 1590, the MacDonald of Glengarry possessions in Wester Ross, laying siege to Strome Castle which they captured and destroyed, young Glengarry being killed, thus removing another obstacle to their complete and eventual possession of all Wester Ross, but starting a feud which was not finally settled till a young Glengarry of a succeeding generation appeared alone at a function at *Eilean Donan*, which act of trust healed the old wound and established a firm friendship. Further north, Robert Munro of Foulis as guardian to Donald Bane MacLeod was drawn into a dispute regarding the Assynt succession between his ward and Neil MacLeod, all caused by a former fratricide and consequent forfeiture and execution in Edinburgh; however, by a division of the property, Robert settled this dispute. Shortly after this Foulis was being denounced with many other Highland chiefs for levying extortionate exactions from the lowland fishermen in northern waters. Torquil MacLeod of 'Cogoych', Johnne MacKenzie of *Gairloch*, Rory Mackenzie of Lochgarlin, Rorie Mackenzie of Lewis, being particularly mentioned in this connection; it all sounds very reprehensible, but there was probably another side to the story, as the lowlanders attachment to his 'bawbee' is well known.

Neither was the feeling between the new Lord Dingwall and Sir Colin all that might be desired, both claiming the right to the valuable Conon Estuary salmon fisheries, but Colin, regarding possession as nine points of the law maintained his 'coble fisheris and nettis fra the fiching of the watter Conan'. In 1594 Sir Colin Mackenzie of Kintail died and was laid with his fathers in Beauly Priory; though all his actions were by no means beyond reproach, he had still further advanced the prosperity of his Clan, but had remained loyal to his sovereign and his own faith. By his wife the XIIth Laird of Grant's daughter, he left three sons, his successor Kenneth XIII first Lord

Kintail, who died in 1611; and Sir Roderick Mackenzie, 'Rorie *Mór*, of Culteloid (Castle Leod), who was to become famous as the tutor of Kintail and Captain of Clan Mackenzie. Rorie was to be the founder of the House of Cromartie and an outstanding personality in the Scotland of his day. Colin's third son was to found the House of Kilcoy on the Black Isle, while by Mary, daughter of Davochmaluach, he had another son, the first of Coul (Contin).

Difficult as times had been since the inception of the Reformation the upheaval which had convulsed the lowlands had in the Highlands been paralleled by quite localized tremors, though the cumulative effect was in time to show the Highlands the disastrous breech which now divided Scotland into two antagonistic parts. Meanwhile the chiefs and Lairds of the Highlands were exploiting the natural wealth of their lands: cattle, timber, fish especially salmon, though no-one as yet, thought of replanting the rapidly shrinking forest areas, a wastage due to use of wood for domestic fuel, destruction by domestic animals such as goats, and the use of wood fuel for smelting. In Wester Ross iron smelting furnaces existed at Letterewe in 1607 while canon were cast at Poolewe as late as 1688. Throughout the Middle Ages and for many years to come the chief wealth of the Highlands lay in the great herds of native cattle of West Highland and Black poll mountain breeds, all of which were being improved prior to 1600 by the chiefs, chieftains and *duine-uasal*. Sheep were not numerous but of an indigenous, soft fleeced breed, raised for their wool, though the small mutton was excellent; goats, so destructive to the forests were plentiful.

Oats and barley were cultivated extensively on the small arable plots in the west; the potato was not to appear as a substitute for another century or more, the small fields being dug over with a spade or cultivated by the *caschrom* the small manual and foot plough. When a larger area had to be dealt with, two ploughs were used; first the *crann ruslaidh* which cut a strip to the required depth perpendicularly, then the *crann rusgaidh* which cut the ground horizontally, turning over the sod. The fields were not enclosed, which necessitated the employment of permanent guards to prevent damage by wild and domestic animals. The method of reaping the harvest consisted of uprooting the crop and beating the ears off the sheaves after which the straw was used first as thatch and then as manure.

In Easter Ross the open 'In field and outfield' system prevailed, under which the In was kept constantly under corn or bere, being dunged once every three years, after which a fourth crop was taken, if possible. Meanwhile the Outfield remained fallow, but much exhausted by thistles and other weeds during 4 or 5 years, until it was twice ploughed, sown with corn for three years in succession and then returned to the wilderness.

By 1600 the Black Cattle trade had assumed really great proportions which increased still more on the accession of James VI to the throne of England in 1603. Tens of thousands of store beasts from the Highlands and Islands were driven south by the drovers to the Trysts of Falkirk and Crieff where they were sold to English and Irish dealers to be fattened in East Anglia and Lothian for the London market. This great trade continued into the 19th century but the changeover from grazing to corn in East Anglia and the introduction of Black Face and Cheviot sheep to the Highlands killed this industry.

Not until the end of the 17th century did certain very slight improvements appear in general farming methods, confined mainly to drainage, carried out with hollowed-out tree trunks or wooden drains. Game was plentiful and still provided much food for the population, Sir Robert Gordon describing the fauna of the Highlands in 1630 as follows:—

Red deer, roe; wolves; foxes; wild cats; brocks (badgers); squirrels (red); whittrets (stoats); weasels; otters; martins; hares; fumarts (rabbits). In addition the game birds we know today were present though less protected from their natural enemies, vermin of all kinds, while the fresh and salt waters ensured a plentiful fish supply.

CHAPTER XIV

JAMES VI OF SCOTLAND SUCCEEDS TO THRONE OF ENGLAND—CALM BEFORE THE STORM—THE END OF THE MACLEOD HOUSE OF LEWIS—THE FIFE ADVENTURERS—FURTHER EXPANSION OF CLAN KENNETH

Chronological Table

1598   James VI conveys certain areas in the Western Isles to the Mercantile Company known as the Fife Adventurers.

1599   Velazquez born.

1600   Sir Charles Blunt, Earl of Mountjoy appointed by Queen Elizabeth Lord Deputy of Ireland, eventually with an army of 20,000 men he defeated the great Irish patriot and leader Red Hugh O'Neill. Becomes Lord Lieutenant of Ireland and by his sympathy and refusal to sanction religious persecution proves himself a good friend of Ireland, later made Earl of Devonshire, but died 1606.

1603   Union of Crowns. James VI of Scotland becomes James I of England.

1606   Rembrandt born. Conjunction of Presbyterian and Episcopalian government of the Kirk of Scotland.

1608   Milton born.

1609   The Statutes of Icolmkill (Iona) passed. Commencement of the Plantation of Ulster.

1611   Birth of Sir Thomas Urquhart of Cromarty, the scholarly and eccentric Royalist. Was educated at Aberdeen and Padua (Italy). He produced a pedigree for his family starting with 'Adam the Protoplast, whom God did create out of red earth'. Claimed to have held estates of Cromarty (Black Isle) 900 years before the Incarnation, other forbears shown being: Seth, Methuselah, Noah, etc. together with all the wives. The Pedigree takes us to Armenia, Gaul, and Achaia, while in 2139 B.C. the name Ourochartos—fortunate and well beloved—introduces Urquhart. During 1958 B.C. an ancestor in the House of Abraham attended the destruction of Soddom and Gomorrah while another Urquhart married the Pharaoh's daughter, who discovered Moses in the bull-rushes. The line continues and the family arrive in Scotland, during the 10th century B.C., where they married with both Pictish and Scottish Royal Houses.

      The main line of this ancient family died out with Col. James Urquhart, Political Agent for King James VIII, in 1741. Sir Thomas Urquhart's many literary works include: The Jewel, a very delightful work; The Logopandecteison, a treatise on the Universal Language—a quite impossible one, as it contained '25 consonants and 10 vowels, 4 varieties of numbers, 11 genders, 10 tenses, 7 moods, 12 parts of speech' and 'every word in it hath at least 10 several synonyms, and the more syllables than be in any one word of the language the manyer several meanings'. His translation of Rabelais in 1653 is now recognized as being the most perfect translation from any one language to any other. A terrifying mathematical treatise called The Trissotatres he dedicated to his dearly loved mother.

      The Urquhart Estates on the Black Isle consisted of the Burgh of Cromarty and the Castle; Kinbeachie; Braelangwell; Newhall; and Monteagh. After 1741 the representatives of this family were the Urquharts of Meldrum in Moray, an estate obtained through the marriage of John Urquhart of Craigfintry, Tutor of Cromarty with Elizabeth Seton heiress of Meldrum.

1612   Birth of James Graham Marquis of Montrose—poet and leader of men.

1616   Bishop Spottiswoode puts into effect Knox's Educational Scheme: or Parish Schools. Jamesone of Aberdeen painting.

1618   Start of Thirty Years War.

c. 1620   Birth of the great Gaelic poet Ian *Lom* (John MacDonald). Died c. 1716.

Queen Elizabeth of England died in 1603, just in time to save her reputation as the most successful Tudor, but leaving a country, to her successor James VI of Scotland, whose Elizabethan greatness had passed; its politics impregnated with corruption, and its poorer inhabitants in ever increasing misery, a condition not improved by the long persecution of Catholic and Dissenter by a none too firmly settled Church of England. The new Sovereign who had struggled so hard, and one may add stooped so low to gain this inheritance, though perhaps the boy, usually the virtual prisoner of Regent or opposition Noble, never learnt the true facts of his mother's tragic life, was faced with a task which might have daunted any man let alone a Stewart unblessed with the personal charm which graced the majority of his race. Yet in spite of English antagonism and resentment the reign of James brought peace to a Scotland, once again brought to desperate poverty and by the chaos that had existed, with a few gaps, since James IV had died on Flodden Field.

But Scotland was from now on to suffer from the effects of Absentee Kings, though for the first quarter of this bitter century a definite revival of civilization marched hand in hand with peace in Scotland, exemplified both in art and architecture. Serious trouble nearly developed when with good intentions James attempted in 1616 to speed up certain of the Scottish Bishop Spottiswoode's recommendations regarding the establishment of order in public worship, recommendations which were generally accepted, except by a fanatic few, as both reasonable and desirable. James' clumsy efforts to deal with a thorny subject in the way he did show how far he had drifted away from the understanding of his Scottish subjects, who differed and and still differ so fundamentally from their English neighbours.

Yet James, though anything but an attractive personality, was no fool and knew when he had blundered so that by the end of his reign in 1625 the two Kingdoms were at peace; the era of clan feuds, so rife since James V's day, were over, the subsequent battles being those of political and denominational origin. But it was only a breathing space before the real struggle was to start, a fight to the death between two systems of government, Monarchy and Oligarchy; a fight which was to end with a victory for the latter, and the sale of the monarchy by the lay and ecclesiastical aristocracy of England, to William of Orange, an event transformed by Whig propagandists into a blow for Democracy.

To return to Ross; the Island of Lewis had become a bedlam of warring claimants for the Chieftainship of *Siol* Torquil; Roderick the last of his race to die in possession of Lewis left two legitimate sons, Torquil *Conanach*, connected through his mother with the House of Kintail, and consequently a protége of Kenneth Lord Kintail now a member of the Privy Council, and Torquil *Dubh*. In addition Roderick left three bastards Torquil Dow, Niel and Murdoch, all with claims for which they were prepared to fight when not engaged in acts of piracy against any ships that ventured near the island. Lord Kintail like others before and since was obsessed with the desire to gain possession of this fascinating island which through the ages exerts a strange magnetism on its would-be exploiters. At length in 1596 the opportunity appeared, Torquil Dow the acting Chief, embarked seven or eight hundred of his followers in galleys, crossed to the mainland and raided *Coigach* the property of his uncle Torquil MacLeod of *Coigach*, something of a fight occurring round the mouth of the Garvey River between Inverpolly and Achnahaird. Not content with this Torquil continued on into the Strath of Lochbroom and in so doing played into Kintail's hands as Lochbroom now lay within the Mackenzie territories.

My Lord Kenneth seeing the Lewis nearing his grasp, seized his pen and wrote the following somewhat self-righteous letter to his King: 'May it please Your Majesty—Torquil Dow of the Lewis, not contenting himself with the avowit misknowledging of your Hienes authority wherebe he has violet the promises and compromit made before your Majesty, now lately on the 25th December last, has taken upon him, being accompanied with 700 or 800 men, not only of his bylands neist and adjacent, to prosecute with fire and sword by all kind of good order, the hail bounds of Strath-*Coigach*, pertaining to MacLeod, his elder brother (Uncle), likewise my Strath of Lochbroom, quilks Straths, to your Majesties great dishonour, but any fear of God himself, hurt and skaith that he hath wasted with fire and sword in such barbarous manner that neither man, wife, bairn, horse, cattle, corn nor bigging (building) has been spared, but all barbarously burnt and destroyit, quilk barbarity and cruelty, seeing he was not able to perform it but by the assistance and furderance of his neighbouring Ylesmen, (MacLeods of Skye) therefore beseeches your Majesty by advice of Council, to find some sure remeid wherebe sick cruel tyrannie may be resisted in the beginning. Otherway nothing to be expected for but daily increasing of this malicious forces to our utter ruin, quha possesses your Majesty's obedience, the consideration, quherof and inconveniences quhilk may theiron ensue. I remit to your Hienes guid consideration of whom taking my leif with maist humble commendations of service, I commit your Majesty to the holy protection of God Eternal. At the Canonry of Ross, the 3rd day of January, 1596.—Your most humble and obedient subject, Kenneth Mackenzie of Kintail.'

But Kenneth had to wait as others beside himself had been bitten by the alure of the mythical gold mine lying between the Minch and Atlantic Ocean.

June 1598 saw a very arbitrary Act of Parliament passed in Edinburgh which amounted to the confiscation of certain properties in the Western Isles, with the result that Lewis, Harris, Dunvegan in Skye and Glenelg on the mainland were forfeit and declared at the disposal of the Government. Behind all this lay the desire of certain people to exploit the fishings, as well as more mythical riches, of these areas, by 'planting' a mercantile company with colonists, starting with the Lewis; much as was done by James in Ulster with repercussions still giving headaches to many. The interested gentlemen concerned were the Duke of Lennox; Patrick Commendator of Lindores; William Commendator of Pittenweem; Sir James Anstruther, younger of that Ilk; Sir James Sandilands of Slamanno; James Learmont of Balconie; James Spens of Wormiston; John Forret of Fingask; David Hume, younger of Wedderburn; and Capt. William Murray.

The contract between these men and the Government, taking into

G

consideration the initial expense of the enterprise, gave the company a rent-free charter for seven years after which they were to pay annually to the Crown a grain rent of 140 Chalders of Beir. This was not the 'sure remid' that our Kenneth had in mind, but had to suffice for the time, especially as he had been ordered by the Crown to establish some kind of order in the Lewis before the advent of the colonists. This in some measure was done, Torquil Dow and many of his clique being captured with the connivance of Eochan Morrison the *Breitheamh* of the Lewis, who being the representative of law and order in the Island was not averse to seeing it re-established.

Torquil the eldest legitimate son of the late chief was the next to fall into the Kintail net, but by this time Kenneth was fully aware of the plantation plans so that instead of handing over Torquil to the Privy Council decided to entertain this gentleman at *Eilean Donan* Castle as in the event of certain eventualities he might prove very useful indeed. Mackenzie undoubtedly desired to add Lewis to the House of Kintail, but we must also give him credit, for realizing that nothing but disaster would result from this ridiculous mercantile experiment, but as a member of the Privy Council he dared not openly go counter to the wishes of that body; so instead he opened nego-tiations with the exiled MacLeods. The initial blunder of a series committed by the 'Fife Adventurers', was the time of year chosen for their first settlement—October of 1599, so that the weather shortly became a good ally to the outlawed brothers Niel and Murdoch who vigorously opposed the settlement. At sea a ship under Learmont was captured by Murdoch MacLeod who demanded a useful ransom for this gentleman's person, but never got it as his captive died in Orkney on his way to procure the necessary money.

Meanwhile the luckless colonists and their accompanying troops established at South Beach, Stornoway—now a Royal Burgh—suffered continual raids, though they gained a short respite by a desperate quarrel between Niel and Murdoch which ended with Niel siding with the adventurers and betraying his brother who was apprehended, sent to St. Andrews and in due time hanged, but not before he had exposed some of Kintail's tortuous policy. This resulted in Kenneth becoming an unwilling guest in Edinburgh Castle but his friendship with the Chancellor Lord Dunfermline soon rectified this temporary setback.

Treachery and betrayal though soon to become normal politics were qualities at which the ordinary Highlander looked askance, so that the Lewismen, who quite happily had watched the fraternal quarrel with sword and dirk, began to quit the unattractive Niel and offer their help to Torquil, still at *Eilean Donan*. Kenneth Mackenzie who had been watching events from a politically safe distance, saw that the time had come to play his trump card and released Torquil, with his blessing, to harass the Fifers. Torquil and Niel came to an understanding, the colonists were attacked and forced to capitulate, the terms being that they procure full pardon for the MacLeods, surrender all titles to Torquil, never return to Lewis and leave Spens of Wormiston and Moneypenny of Pitmilly as hostages.

By 1602 a Remission was granted to the MacLeods, but a new expedition with powers of fire and sword set out in the spring of 1605, one of the leaders being William MacWilliam Chief of Clan Gunn, who informed Tormond that if he would yield, they would transport him to London when the King would listen to his explanation of affairs and grant him favour. This indeed appeared to be the case as Torquil while in London put forward a good case, which alarmed the government in Scotland for obvious reasons, forcing them to great exertions in order to prevent Torquil's return to Lewis. Eventually the unfortunate Chief was lodged in Edinburgh Castle where he remained till 1616, when he was released on condition of exile to Holland where he joined the household of Maurice Prince of Orange for the remainder of his days.

Niel was still putting up an effective opposition, having secured valuable allies in MacNiel of Barra, MacDonald of Clan Ranald, and MacLeod of Harris, so that two years later the remnants of the colonists left Lewis utterly defeated. Kenneth with an eye to the main chance brought pressure to bear on the Lord Chancellor and obtained Lewis as a gift, but once again unkind fate took a hand, the original adventurers interfering by passing on their rights to certain gentlemen, namely James Elphinstone, Lord Balmerino, Sir James Spens, and Sir George Hay of Nethercliff, later Lord Kinnoul. Balmarino in 1609 was convicted of treason, leaving the others to embark for Lewis with a strong force only to meet with defeat by Niel MacLeod and the sinister influence of Kintail who himself kept in the background. This influence was exercised through his brother Sir Roderick Mackenzie of Castle Leod who on his brother's orders had attached himself to the adventurers' head-quarters in Stornoway.

The first definite blow, a foul one, which was to prove fatal to the expedition was delivered by Kintail; the garrison of Lewis was running short of provisions so appealed to Kenneth who immediately sent off a ship with a cargo of meal and supplies, but took care secretly to advise Niel of the fact, thus making sure of the non-arrival of the cargo, at least to its official destination. The effect was immediate, Hay and Spens threw up the sponge and retired to Fife leaving a party, with a promise of speedy succour, to guard the camp, but shortly afterwards the garrison was overrun and captured, being allowed to follow their masters to Fife on swearing on oath that they would never return. Thus ended the first of a series of schemes to 'civilize' the Island of

Lewis, though unlike a more recent effort, the Fife Adventurers were sufficiently honest to make it abundantly clear that their sole motive was personal enrichment; even if it entailed a partial extermination of the Lewismen.

The Fifers were gone for good, but Kenneth was not yet Lord of Lewis, though the goal was coming in sight, as by strictly legal means he obtained, first Balmerino's confiscated share as a gift, then bought for cash Spens' share, while by bartering certain woods in *Gairloch* required by Hay for iron smelting purposes, he got the final third, all of which was followed very soon after by a Charter under the Great Seal. Thus Lewis became Mackenzie property in theory but it remained to Rorie of Castle Leod to make it so in fact for the next 230 years. Before following the methods by which the acquisition was made a reality let us take a look at the gentleman who was to do the trick.

Rorie was already well known as an excellent organizer, a valiant fighter and successful general, but still more for a quality, unusual at this time in the Highlands, a hatred of disorder or anything resembling anarchy. His picture by Jamesone is not a good one but shows us a strong, shrewd and serious face, but unfortunately does not show his famous two handed sword which few others could wield. That he could be ruthless we shall see, but he was also to show a generosity to a conquered foe, and people in distress, for other motives than those of self interest; a characteristic sufficiently uncommon during the 17th century to be remarkable.

His first appearance in history, was due to an escapade more noisy than serious: it appears that at Chanonry in April 1602 considerable alarm was caused to Master George Munro son of the Archdeacon of Ross, and Donald Thornton who had entrusted the upbringing and education of his daughter Janet Thornton to Master George. The villains of the piece were our 'Rorie Maccanzie of Cultiloid, Kenneth Maccanzie of Killechrist' and an unknown Mackenzie lover. They and others were seen holding frequent consultations regarding the proposed abduction of Janet, which was carried out on 26th April by Killechrist and twenty-five others armed with 'Gunns, pistolettis, and uther forbidden weapons'. The lady was removed from the Chancellor House Chanonrie quite successfully, no-one suffering any bodily harm and all quite obviously with the consent and active co-operation of Janet. The case was brought before the Privy Council where an unperturbed Rorie appeared to answer the charge for himself as well as on behalf of Kenneth of Killechrist, flatly denying the charge of abduction which was forthwith dropped by the pursuers, who however reserved the right to raise another action before the Judge Criminal; but this is the last reference to the case in the Privy Council Records.

Jumping ahead once more to 16th July 1610; the government were castigating the Lewis as 'ane infamous byke of lawless and insolent lymmaris, under the command of the traytor Niel Maccloud' and to implement their dislike they presented Kintail with a commission of Fire and Sword to be used unsparingly in that distressed island. But Niel was to pull just one more trick out of the bag, by posing as a virtuous upholder of law and order; this he proceeded to demonstrate by double-crossing his ally Peter Lowe an English pirate, who had been giving trouble to the government for some time past, and presenting the pirate, complete with crew and ship to the Council as a peace offering. Proceedings were stayed while Patrick Grieve of Burntisland took delivery of the gift the human portion of which soon graced the gallows.

The delay did not last long and it is doubtful whether Rorie gave to it much heed as in 1611 Kenneth Lord Kintail died leaving a young son Colin to succeed him, which placed all responsibility on the broad shoulders of the boy's uncle Rorie, now Tutor of Kintail and Captain of Clan Mackenzie. As we shall see, never was a young Chief better served, for when he came of age the Tutor was able to hand him one of the largest and best ordered estates and Clan territories in Scotland, at peace with all its neighbours. The following year Rorie married Margaret MacLeod the heiress of *Coigach* who in a few years time was to be the sole survivor and representative of the MacLeods of Lewis, so that after the addition of *Coigach* to his own property the Tutor is usually referred to as Sir Rorie MacKenzie of *Coigach*. The headquarters of this area was the Manor and Fortalice of Ullapool, while a small house still exists at Achillibuis where Rorie and Margaret passed their honeymoon.

On 28th May 1612 it is recorded that there was no part of the Isles in rebellion but the Lewis, for which unusual peace Rorie was responsible; this was followed by a new Commission of Fire and Sword to 'Rorie Mackenzie of *Coigach* Tutor of Kintail; Colin Mackenzie of Killin; Murdo Mackenzie thair brother; Alexander Mackenzie of Coull; and Alexander Mackenzie of Davochmaluach; for reducing the said lymarris to his majesties obedience.' Rorie collected a powerful force, effecting a landing with his 'lynfaddis (long ships), gayleys, birlings, and boatis', making the old and very strong castle in Stornoway Bay his head-quarters. Niel MacLeod was up against an efficiency he had not met with among the Fifers, a powerful force quickly drove him into a corner on the strongly fortified islet of Berisay off Loch Roag, where Niel's garrison was small consisting of himself, three nephews, Torquil Blair with four sons and forty Islesmen, but the position was almost impregnable against any normal form of attack. So Rorie decided to use another method, or the threat of a method, to terminate the course of this wearysome struggle, he collected the wives and families of the besieged from their villages placing them on a rock, covered at high tide, within sight and hearing of the beleaguered garrison. We do not know whether Rorie would have let them drown or not and never shall; one can only say that judging from what we know of Rorie's character it seems very unlikely that he would have allowed these poor folk to perish—also he was a very good psychologist; the threat was enough and Niel's forces slipped away.

But although Niel himself escaped for the moment he had reached the end of his turbulent road as he and his son Donald were betrayed by their relative Rory MacLeod of Dunvegan, who presented them in person to the Council, for which inglorious feat he was knighted, but yet had to find security for his own behaviour to the tune of 10,000 Merks. Niel was hanged, his son being banished from Scotland and the House of Kintail came to Lewis, to stay for over two centuries. The Tutor immediately appointed a new *Breitheamh* MacIver, Morrison having died violently at the hand of Ian Begg MacDhomhnall MhicHuisdain, a MacLeod of Assynt, who made up for his small stature by his valour and married the widow of his victim; Rorie then arranged for the baptizing of a large number of people who had reached their fortieth year; legitimized the children of those who had not been able to get married by the Church; and legalized the union of many others who had been living together for the same reason.

The necessity for the above gives some indication of the general state of anarchy which had existed in Lewis since the days of Roderick MacLeod, the last strong Chief, and it is probable that the majority welcomed the cessation of continual internal and external strife. But till 1622 there remained an anti-Mackenzie party loyal to the MacLeod dynasty, headed by Malcolm Macrorie MacLeod exiled in Islay, but this was the last symptom to cause some trouble before Lewis became a loyal part of the Mackenzie heritage as well as the home of many Mackenzie families. The old Lewis possessions in the *Gairloch-*Torridon sector, so long disputed, belonged now indisputably to Kintail while the Raasay raids against the western coasts of Ross were effectively terminated by the complete defeat of this branch of *Siol* Torquil at the battle of *Lochan Fheidh* in Glen Torridon, the Island of Raasay being occupied by Rorie who however only intended this as a warning. Raasay was soon returned to its chief with the proviso that if and when required by the House of Kintail the island was to provide a 12 oared *Birlinn* for service.

The same year, realizing what a bone of contention it would prove the Tutor sold back to Sir Roy *Mór* of Dunvegan, Waternish in Skye which the late Lord Kintail had bought from the Fife Adventurers. The Glengarry dispute was finally settled while from the Butt of Lewis to Tiree the sword, good sense and humanity of the Tutor had imposed peace for the first time for many a long year.

The year 1611 saw the proscription of Clan MacGregor and the ruthless harrying of this unlucky Clan by Clan Campbell and the government, but in spite of the heavy penalties involved Ross to its lasting honour gave sanctuary to large numbers of Clan Gregor, a fact witnessed by the fines levied on nearly every family in Ross.

Sir Rorie Mackenzie of *Coigach* and Castle Leod heads the list at £4000 st. for his act of humanity; Rory Mackenzie of Redcastle 5000 Merks; Gillechallum Machutchioun in Logie (Cononside) £66. 13. 4.; William Bain, Lister (Dyer) in Dingwall £1.; Master John Mackenzie, minister of Dingwall £1333. 6. 8.; Robert Ross in Little Farness £100.; John Munro, Lemlair 100 Merks.; John Robertson in Dingwall 100 Merks.; Alexander Roy MacMillan, Dingwall 50 Merks.; Alasdair Bain of Logie (Conon Mains) 1000 Merks.; David Ross, heir to Balnagown £1000.; Ay MacBean, MacRob, in Knockanauld (Knockbain) Dingwall 200 Merks.; John Maclane Vic Bayne in Caldwell (Blackwells) 100 Merks.; James Innes of Innearbreakie (Invergordon) £1000.; Patrick Macinteir of Balnaspic £20.; Donald Macjamie Macgaw £20.; Angus Macjamie Macgaw £20.

These excessive sums were to be paid within fifteen days on pain of rebellion and escheat of goods so Rorie petitioned on behalf of all, for more time which was grudgingly granted even to Rorie, who by his actions had sufficiently shown his loyalty, and who indeed was the mainstay of the government in the north. Yet we read 'ane missive from his Majesty anent the continuation granted to the Tutor of Kintail—Master John (his son) and Rory Mackenzie of Redcastle, for payment of their fynes and direction given accordingly that no new continuation sal be grantit'.

By 1616 Roderick (Rorie) Mackenzie the Tutor of Kintail, knighted for his services in the west, had completed his major alterations to Castle Leod, building on the great gabled roof, in place of the flat one, at the same time quartering his wife's arms, as the representative of the MacLeod House of Lewis, with his own blazon over the entrance, where they still exist. An older Mackenzie armorial stone slab which this replaced lay for centuries outside but has now been built into the stone wall of the entrance hall. Beside *Coigach* he had added to his patrimony of Castle Leod, by purchase from James Dunbar, the lands of Tarbat, which included Portmahomach and the Castle of Ballone in Easter Ross, while in this area the Castle of Loch Slyn had also become a Mackenzie possession, which had fallen to the Mackenzies of Redcastle on the demise of the Vass (Vaux) line. This also was shortly to become part of the Cromartie heritage. In 1512 King James IV had given a re-grant of Loch Slyn to John Vaus who had resigned it to the Crown for a yearly payment of 'One pound cucumber or 3 pence at Whitsunday'; previous to 1477 it had of course been held from the Earls of Ross.

Rorie died, the greatest Highlander of his time, in 1626, at Castle Leod, being only forty-eight years old at the time of his death, and was succeeded by his eldest son John Mackenzie of Tarbat, who was to become the first Baronet of that name.[1] He left eight sons and one daughter. Colin Mackenzie of Tarvie who married *Gairloch*'s eldest daughter the relict of Mackenzie of Loch Slyn; Alexander of Balloan; Kenneth first of Scatwell; Charles and James, both of whom died unmarried; the daughter Margaret married Sir James MacDonald of Sleat; the seventh son John, who became Archdean of Ross, was born the wrong side of the blanket, as was another son Colin, who became Chamberlain to the family.

In his last will and testament he directed that his body be buried 'in the Kirk-yeard of Dinguall, at the eist gewill of the Kirk thairof. At which Jordain Jonne Maccanzie my eldest son and appeirand air, and Dame Maccloud, my spous, to caus build ane lairge fair Iyle or Chappel, weil wowit abone and theckit with hewin stone'.

Colin Lord Kintail whose handsome person was creating a favourable impression at the Court in London, where the beautiful daughter of King James VI and I Elizabeth Queen of Bohemia had christened him 'My Highlander', was soon raised another step in the peerage becoming the first Earl of Seafort—since corrupted into Seaforth—the title being taken from the great sea loch of that name in the Island of Lewis. The period of peace before the great struggle which was once again to tear Scotland apart into two separate camps, was coming to an end, so before following events let us see how the actors were clad, as dress plays an important part in human affairs often reflecting the contemporary attitude of mind.

In 1618 one John Taylor an Englishman had been a guest of the Earl of Mar for a great hunt and being unsuitably clothed was provided with a kilt; web hose of the same tartan with large garters; a plaid of much finer material than the hose; a Kerchief tied with two knots; and a flat blue bonnet. In thus adopting the raiment of his hosts he was following the normal custom of the southern Scottish Nobles and gentry who always wore the same dress as their relations and friends in the Highlands when on a hunting visit to their homes. It is also very probable that on these occasions the Lowlanders would wear their own family tartans. The party must have resembled a military review as the assembled gathering, both mounted and on foot, were armed with swords, targes, harquebusses, muskets, dirks and Lochaber axes.

The little kilt was probably worn when at home but never for

Note 1. For the Mackenzie table see Appendix I h/.

travelling or campaigning when the *breacan an fhéilidh*, which by 1600 had superseded entirely its forerunner the saffron *léine-cròchach*, was the ideal garment, while tartan trews remained very popular among the gentry, fitting tight to the leg and extending right over the feet, combining the duties of breeches and stockings. By this time too the heavy mantle of shaggy frieze had disappeared; in fact its replacement by the Tartan plaid had generally taken place at a much earlier date among all classes in Scotland, having for centuries been worn instead of the mantle over the saffron tunic. It is recorded that one method used to make the plaid wind proof and therefore warmer when sleeping out at night, was to steep it in water, though to the softer race of men today this practice might suggest rheumatism or worse.

It is of interest that the Royal Company of Archers, the Sovereign's Body-guard in Scotland, re-raised by the Earl of Cromartie in 1677 were dressed in a tartan coat and knee breeches, from 1713 to 1788, a red sett being used but replaced by Black Watch (Government Tartan) in 1788 which lasted till about 1823 when this distinctive uniform was replaced by a nondescript and denationalized dress; the head dress of this body in 1763 had consisted of a flat bonnet garnished with green and white feathers.

During the 17th and 18th centuries the gentlemen's dress as worn in the Highlands consisted of a coat or jacket (the *còta fiaraidh*) following the general fashion of the time, but often of a tartan which was different to that of the kilt and made up in smaller checks, this second tartan would of course be one to which the wearer was entitled, his mother's, some other near relation's or ancestor's; this garment was further adorned with silver buttons, embroidery, and lace, while the waistcoat was usually blue, green or black. The *breacan an fhéilidh* was most carefully arranged and pleated, the whole effect being very striking as can be seen from the numerous 18th century prints of Prince Charles Edward and in the pictures by Raeburn. The dress of the clansmen was similar though of course the materials were less rich having brass more often than silver buttons.

The ladies of quality usually wore the brocaded gowns of the period, but kept for general use the tartan plaid of silk or fine worsted, a practice equally common in the southern lowlands. The dress of the clanswomen during this period was very attractive, over their gown they wore the Arisaid, a white plaid with narrow stripes of black, blue or red, reaching from neck to ankle. This plaid, pleated all round, was fastened below the breast by a belt of interwoven leather and silver, while the end of the belt had an engraved silver or brass plate about 8 inches long by 3 inches broad and adorned with precious stones or pieces of red coral, the value of these belts might be 100 Merks or more. The dress or jacket usually worn underneath had scarlet sleeves closed at the wrist, embroidered with gold lace and jewelled buttons. On their pretty heads they wore a fine linen kerchief, hanging down the back taperwise, while two raven, or blond, locks hung down by each cheek, falling on to their breast where the ends were tied with a knot of ribbon. The unmarried girls usually went bare headed except for the snood, a ribbon tied round the head and keeping their long hair in place. Shoes and the long plaited stocking (*osan*) were kept for special occasions, as normally they went barefooted.

Martin in his tours at the end of the 17th century found that coats, waistcoats and breeches were in use on the Western Isles; as well as trews of tartan or one colour, many of which had in addition a square piece of cloth hanging down the front, which in fact was a somewhat unsightly cloth *sporan* or purse. The bonnets he describes as being of thick cloth coloured blue, black or grey. He also mentions meeting persons of distinction wearing both the garb fashionable in the south and the *breacan an fhéilidh*.

Here is a list, compiled by a French visitor, of part of a Laird's equipment in 1745.

'Composition d'l'equipment complet d'un Seigneur des Montagnes d'Ecosse.'

No. 1. A full-trimmed bonnet.
     2. A tartan jacket-vest-kilt-and cross belt.
     3. A tartan belted plaid.
     4. A pair of hose made up (cloth web) (trews).
     5. A pair of stockings—do—with yellow garters.
     6. Two pairs of brogs.
     7. A silver mounted purse and belt (sporran).
     8. A Target with spear (i.e. protruding from boss).
     9. A broad-sword.
    10. A pair of pistols and bullet mould.
    11. A dirk, knife and fork (in same sheath) and belt.

CHAPTER XV

TROUBLE AT FOULIS—THE SCOTS BRIGADE—THE KING BLUNDERS—THE NATIONAL COVENANT—THE GREAT CIVIL WAR—MILITARY DICTATORSHIP—THE RESTORATION—DWELLINGS

Chronological Table

1632   Death of Gustavus Adolphus at Lutzen.
1637   Descartes' Discours published at Leyden.
1638   National Covenant signed.
1642   Start of the Great Civil War. Birth of Sir Isaac Newton. General Munro, brother of Col. John of Obsdale arrives at Carrickfergus in Ulster with 7 Lowland Scottish Regiments sent by Scottish Estates at request of the Long Parliament in England.
1643   Signing of Solomon League and Covenant.
1645   Series of Royalist victories by Montrose.
1649   Charles I beheaded. Execution of Duke of Hamilton. Commencement by Cromwell of the conquest of Ireland attended by massacre and general brutality.
1650   Cromwell defeats Covenanters at Dunbar. Montrose hanged.
1651   Campaign of Worcester.
1653   Union Parliament and Protectorate.
1660   Restoration of Charles II.
1661   Ross constituted a County. Marquis of Argyll executed.
1665   Birth of Scots poetess Lady Grisel Baillie.

The great House of Foulis who for so long had played a leading part in the affairs of Ross, struck an unlucky patch under the XVIIIth Chief Robert Munro who by his extravagance nearly brought the family to ruin. So serious was the financial state, that during his regime and after, practically the whole of Foulis was wadsetted[1] (mortgaged) to Simon Lord Lovat, while much was sold outright, including Muckle and Little Clyne (Mountgerald) first to Davochcairn, then to Alexander Mackenzie of Davochmaluach, while Inverlael (Lochbroom) went to John Mackenzie Archdeacon of Ross. The funeral of this Lord Lovat in 1632 is described as 'Sumptuous and splendid, solemn, regular and orderly' and was attended by: 600 men of Clan Mackintosh 'well appointed', 800 Grants, 900 Mackenzies, 1000 'pretty men' Rosses of Balnagown, over 1000 Frasers, 'not under 1000' Camerons, MacDonalds and Munroes.

The Munro debts eventually became so pressing that on 10th October 1626 Robert raised a Company of his Clan and sailed from Cromarty for Denmark as a volunteer in the Regiment of Col. Sir Donald MacKay of Reay who with his MacKays was first in service under the King of Denmark, then Gustavus Adolphus the great king of Sweden. In 1631 Gustavus's 'Scots Brigade' amounted to 13,000 men, among them 3 generals, 8 colonels, 5 lieutenant-colonels, 11 majors, over 30 captains and a large number of lieutenants, all of the name of Munro, who played such a leading and honourable part in the Thirty Years War.

Robert was succeeded by his brother, Hector who came home to be

Note 1. For history and explanation of Wadset see Glossary.

created a Baronet by Charles I but returned to the continent almost at once, to die in Hamburg in 1635 only two years after the decease of his father at Ulm in Wurtemburg. Sir Hector's only son died young and was succeeded by his second cousin Col. Sir Robert Munro of Obsdale who returned home to Foulis after the death of his elder brother at the Battle of Lutzen, where Gustavus was killed at the height of his fame.

There is no doubt that King Charles desired above all the weal of his Kingdoms, but for all his love of art his mind ran to abstractions, while his deep devotion to his Religion and his family, were unsuitable weapons with which to fight the growing opposition to true monarchy among the wealthy who were using the difficult religious controversies to further their own ends of wealth and power. His hankering to return at least some of the Church lands to their original purposes did nothing to aleviate the position, alienating many who were bound more by their new possessions than by loyalty to their king.

But it was the Archbishop of Canterbury Laud, rather than the King who brought matters to a head in Scotland by antagonizing not only the fanatical and now extreme Calvinist south west but also the normal Presbyterian and Episcopalian, by forcing on them the English Liturgy; a first step it seemed to the imposition of something far less desirable, namely the usurpation of authority over Scotland by the Church of England. The order to use the English (Laud's) Liturgy was the signal for ugly scenes, not always for religious motives, but providing the necessary excuse; yet in the north, rioting and acts of violence were conspicuous by their absence, though some boys at Chanonry Grammar School did break into Fortrose Cathedral destroying copies of Laud's Liturgy. A general atmosphere of tension prevailed, the situation being best described in the words of that intelligent and moderate Presbyterian Baillie who wrote: 'The one side puts poperie, idolatrie and superstition in sundrie things which are innocent of these faults. . . the other seems wilfullie to add fewell to their flame, to command upon sole authoritie without ever craving the advyce of any.'

The opposition organized, and by November 1637 the 'Tables' were formed, a Committee which included Alexander Henderson, a church-man of great gifts, most of the peers, many of whom were inspired by selfish aims, together with numerous lairds, burgesses, and ministers. Charles might still have won the moderates but would not even sway to the storm, yet the instinctive respect for the Throne among the people had kept the blame from his person making the Scottish Bishops the butt, despite the fact that many like Maxwell of Ross had vigorously opposed Laud's innovations. In February things came to a head, the Tables recalled the Lords of the Congregation, once again forming a 'band', and on 25th February 1638 at a great open air meeting in

Greyfriars Kirkyard in Edinburgh the National Covenant was signed by many people of varying ecclesiastical ideas, among them being the Earl of Sutherland, a strict Presbyterian; Lord Lovat; the Laird of Balnagown; George 2nd Earl of Seaforth and the majority of his Catholic or Episcopalean Chieftains, including Sir John Mackenzie of Castle Leod, and *Coigach*, 1st Bart. of Tarbat.

But it must be remembered that a large proportion of the signatories of this document, especially in the north had neither wish nor intention to be disloyal to the king in person, or monarchy in general, so that the Highland names are, in the majority of cases, absent from the later Solomn League and Covenant; it is significant that loyalists and true patriots such as Montrose were signatories of the first Covenant. Moderate parties in Scotland were to suffer the fate of all people who see both sides of an argument during a Revolution, when victory goes to the single minded man or party who is completely ruthless and willing to employ all and every method to gain the desired end.

The king surrendered but too late as by then the anti-Royalist fanatical Kirk party were again in power and taking every precaution to prevent a settlement, knowing full well that in the event of a free assembly the extreme 'Covenanters' would be faced with the opposition of most of Scotland North of the Forth, particularly Aberdeen, except for Argyll and part of Fife. War was now inevitable as a Totalitarian Government had set itself up above the Crown while Charles made matters worse by attempting to settle the matter with the support of English arms. Alexander Leslie who had succeeded Gustavus Adolphus as head of the victorious Swedish Army came home and took command of the Covenanting army, who brought Charles' efforts to a speedy conclusion, but without fighting as terms were agreed upon. The position now reverted to what it had been six months before except that it left a Revolutionary government in power who had challenged and defeated constituted authority.

Four years passed with the Party hold tightening on Scotland and the moderates becoming ever more restless as they saw the new tyrants joining up with the anti-Royalist elements in England. The rich squire-archy and finance as represented by the merchant princes. Montrose at the head of the moderates tried to persuade the king to come north to satisfy the just and reasonable demands of the opposition, thus taking the wind out of the extremist sails. But Charles came too late, Montrose was in prison unable to guide his king's faltering footsteps, who to gain the support of the Covenant army virtually surrendered the government of Scotland to the Tables among whom was that crafty and despicable creature the Earl of Argyll, Illeasbuig *Gruamach*, Sour-faced Archibald, all set to become a Dictator, though one controlled by a body of fanatical ministers.

As the situation developed South of the border, so divisions multiplied in Scotland the crisis coming to a head in August 1642 when the king raised his standard at Nottingham; the fight was on, Monarchy versus the richer landed and commercial element transformed by propaganda history into the People's Champion. The moderates attempted to stay neutral seeking a rapprochement but as this was the last thing desired by the Covenanting Party all such moves were rigorously repressed. In Ross the leader of the Covenanting party was Col. Sir Robert Munro of Foulis (late Obsdale); Seaforth was swithering but started by giving a very half hearted support to the Covenanters. The signing of the Solomn League and Covenant, a frankly anti-Royalist and Revolutionary document caused further splits, driving that honest man and most brilliant general of his time James Graham Marquis of Montrose, to the side of his king. In 1644–45 Montrose, by a series of brilliant victories, won by his genius and the fighting qualities of his Highland Army, nearly broke the more powerful Covenant military strength.

Seaforth who might have been the deciding factor still swithered, partly because it was his nature to do so, but mainly through hereditary distrust of the Antrim MacDonalds who provided an important part of Montrose's army, being led by that dynamic giant of a man Colkitto Sir Alasdair MacDonald the son and heir of Colonsay, sprung from the ancient family of Dunyveg in Islay. That this policy was unpopular in the Clan is proved by the fact that several Mackenzie Chieftains especially that enthusiastic Cavalier, Seaforth's brother, Mackenzie of Pluscardine had joined up with Montrose. At Philiphaugh Montrose with a small part of his army was surprised and defeated, the consequent deliberate and planned butchery of prisoners who had been given quarter, and women, demonstrating the results of having a government controlled by fanatical ministers of the Kirk.

In England a new star was rising, one Oliver Cromwell, no lover of Presbyterians, and the Covenanters saw their scheme of the forcible conversion of England into the Kirk fading, with the result that when Charles sought to benefit by the internal bickerings among his English opponents, and approach the Scots, the Covenanters responded. Montrose was called off going into exile and refusing the post of Marshall of France so that he should be free to serve his king if called upon to do so. The Covenanters insisted on Presbyterianism for England and Charles hedged so that all came to nought, the king being handed over to the English Parliament in exchange for some of the moneys owed by them to the Covenanters.

The summer of 1647 was quiet in Scotland though the imprisonment of the king disturbed the growing moderate party, now known as Engagers among whom were Seaforth, Sir John of Tarbat, and the other Mackenzie Chieftains, with the exception of Kilcoy, some of the Munros and the staunch old Cavalier Sir Thomas Urquhart of Cromarty the translator of Rabelais (1653), co-inventor with Sir John Napier of Logarithms, and the inventor of a universal language, the forerunner of Esperanto. In 1647 Seaforth published his Remonstrance demanding the release of the king and the maintenance of monarchy, a document signed by the above as well as the Presbyterian Earl of Sutherland. Seaforth had for a while openly supported Montrose in 1646 but remained something of a weathercock though the Solemn League and Covenant had turned many like MacDonald of Sleat and MacLeod of Dunvegan into enthusiastic Royalists, but apart from some skirmishes there was little actual fighting north of Inverness.

In June Cromwell's new Model Army kidnapped the king from the English Parliament and purged itself of Presbyterian officers leaving Cromwell with his Independents, a sect anathema to the Kirk; Scotland as a whole swung toward the King and an Army of Engagers under the ineffective Hamilton crossed the Border, but left in their rear a hostile south west full of fanatical Covenanting 'Whiggamores'. Cromwell shattered this army at Preston in August, and the following month Argyll and his backers appointed themselves as the government of Scotland calling themselves the Committee of Estates. The next Estates to meet in January were carefully purged of all Royalists or Engagers but were nearly upset by the wave of popular feeling which followed the news of the king's projected trial.

On the 30th January 1649 the king was beheaded by the orders of a quite illegal court after a mock trial, and England was handed over to a Military Dictatorship which she learned to hate. The packed Estates of Scotland proclaimed Charles II as king but by its act of Classes kept out all who were in any way counter-revolutionary, intending that the new king should be their puppet. Months of bargaining and stalemate followed so that Charles fell back on Montrose. During March 1649 Clan Mackenzie, Ross of Balnagown and Munro of Lemlair the acting chief of Clan Munro, under the command of Seaforth's brother Pluscardine, together with a force under Reay and Ogilvy, had by their seizure of Inverness caused much trouble to the commander of the Covenant army David Leslie, which augured well for Montrose's next venture in which he intended to rely mainly on the northern Clans, particularly Seaforths, as that Chief and nobleman being present with the king at the Hague had personally pledged the support of his powerful force to the Marquis.

Ross was to be the stage where the last scene but one of the great tradegy was to be set and where the noble Marquis was to make his final effort on behalf of the exiled Charles II, the plans for the campaign which was to restore the monarch to his two unhappy kingdoms being made in Holland, a place, incidentally, that the Royal exile found very tedious. The small initial expedition was to assemble in Orkney and from there move south, the idea being that the loyal clans would then come out augmenting the very meagre numbers of the original expeditionary force as not only had Seaforth promised full support, but, despite Philiphaugh, the name of James Graham still carried with it the magic of his personality. Misfortune arrived early to join the expedition, the first contingent from Holland being lost at sea; a second followed under George Hay Earl of Kinnoull who died in Orkney, following the loyal Earl of Morton, the superior of Orkney and Shetland, by only a few days.

After many delays Montrose followed in March of 1650 taking with him certain cavaliers and soldiers of fortune such as the jolly old turncoat General Hurry who was to die bravely on the gallows tree with Montrose; Lord Frendraught, Sutherland's nephew and old opponent at Aberdeen; Sir Frances Hay of Dalgetty; Harry Graham, half brother of Montrose; William Hay the new Earl of Kinnoull; Sir James Douglas, a brother of Morton; the German War veterans Sir William Johnston; and Col. Thomas Gray possibly the ex-governor of Bergen; Drummond of Balloch; Ogilvy of Powrie; Menzies of Pitfoddels; and a few English Royalists, among them Major Lisle.

Eventually a force was collected consisting of some 500 regular Danish troops and 1000 keenly Royalist but untrained and unwarlike Orcadians, but further delay followed which allowed the Covenanters to concentrate their forces, while the Royalists expecting further reinforcements did not realize the King Charles II had again opened negotiations with the Covenant Party. This entailed the withdrawal of his most loyal subject, but this order arrived too late to reach Montrose who already had 'put his fate to the touch' and lost.

> He either fears his fate too much,
> Or his deserts are small,
> That dares not put it to the touch
> To gain or lose it all.
>   from the poem by James Graham Marquis of
>   Montrose.
>   1612–50.

To keep open his line of communication through Sutherland Montrose had detailed 500 from his tiny force to hold the Ord of Caithness, using the captured Castle of Dunbeath as a base. The Earl of Sutherland, a Covenanter, was given no time to complete preparations for offensive action but held on to Dunrobin, Skibo, Dornoch and Skelbo Castles. The Royalist force crossed the Oykel forming an encampment at Carbisdale near the village of Culrain, where they awaited the expected reinforcements especially Clan Mackenzie as well as the Rosses and Munros; Clan Kenneth were mobilized and standing by, but had received no orders from their Chief, Seaforth, who was cognisant of the changed political situation. General Strachan with a strong Covenanter force containing five troops of Cavalry was in Tain where he was joined by Clans Munro and Ross under their respective Chiefs, while Leslie was moving north with 4000 men at the rate of thirty miles a day.

On Saturday 27th April 1650 Strachan who had spent the previous night encamped at 'Strachan's Clump' Wester *Fearn*, concealed his force on the broom covered hills flanking the road running between Firth and mountain. The ambush was successful and the ill-trained Royalist levies were forced back by the cavalry to the trenches on Carbisdale Hill, *Creag na Caoineadh* or Rock of Lamentation. Meanwhile Sutherland had succeeded in cutting the line of retreat north of the Oykel, while the not over-keen Munros and Rosses changed from interested spectators to active participants.

Montrose with his small body of trained troops fought desperately but the situation was hopeless, ten officers and 386 of the rank and file fell, many others being drowned attempting to swim the Oykel, while 31 officers with 400 men capitulated. Montrose having cast his arms, some jewels, including his Order of the Garter, and the treasure into Loch Sprint at Culrain, made his way disguised into the Strathcarron woods; Lord Frendraught having been seriously wounded had given his horse to Montrose who had lost his own, and this he rode till it foundered. The weather was bitter cold with heavy snow falls, but eventually Montrose suffering greatly from exposure found himself far to the west with his last companion Sinclair of Brims in Caithness (Sir Edward Sinclair the Orcadian had died somewhere in the hills), and decided to seek sanctuary at Ardvreck Castle, the home of Neil Mac-Leod of Assynt and his wife a Munro of Lemlair. The story of his betrayal for £20,000 Scots. and 400 bolls of meal is too well known to warrant repetition, being the solitary case of a Gael betraying for gold a fugitive seeking sanctuary.

Montrose was handed over to a strong guard under Major General Holbourn one of Leslie's lieutenants, being lodged the first night at Skibo Castle where old Mrs. Gray, though a supporter of the Covenant treated the Marquis as a Royal guest, putting to shame his ill mannered lowland captors who did all in their power to heap insults on the helpless prisoner. Indeed it is said that she hit Holbourn over the head with a leg of mutton, an act which completely established the authority of the courageous old lady in her own house. The next night was passed at Tain in the Provost's house known as the Ark and only recently demolished, while Montrose's last night in Ross was spent in Brahan Castle, where he was received by General Leslie who had taken over and garrisoned that stronghold.

The story of his death at Edinburgh, perhaps his greatest triumph, is well known to all Scots, how his personality completely overawed the mob so that those who came to mock stayed to weep, silently and with bared heads, despite the efforts of the ministers to whip them into a frenzy, so that they should revile him and pelt him with filth. Throughout the last days of this great man the fanatic ministers of the Kirk were constantly put to shame by their flocks who refused to follow their cowardly, vindictive and most un-Christian lead, a shining example being the people of that strongly Covenanter town Dundee who had little cause to love the Marquis. These folk, to the horror of the ministers who had insisted that the prisoner be brought south through that town, not only welcomed the visitor with sympathetic respect but clothed and fed him, forcing his captors to behave with humanity instead of like beasts. But Assynt did not long survive the man he had sent to his death.

The Mackenzies had for some time past more or less protected this man beyond the marches of *Coigach* for he posed as something of a Royalist so that no forays had taken place since an unsuccessful siege of Ardvreck in May of 1646 when Domhnall *Ban* MacLeod was Laird of Assynt. The recent exploit of Neil XIth of Assynt altered all this. Mackenzies, MacDonnells of Glengarry and MacLeods of Skye descended on him and in 1654 the Mackenzies again ravaged Assynt, seizing a ship lying off Lochinver carrying a valuable cargo for Neil, consisting of wine, brandy and other stores valued at 50,000 Merks, all of which is said to have been destroyed, while 2400 cattle, 1500 horses and ponies, and about 6000 sheep and goats were lifted, the country of Assynt being left desolate. Yet the final retribution did not come about till July 1672 when Neil the last of his line was denounced a rebel, Seaforth obtaining a commission of Fire and Sword against him and his unfortunate people, who were not guilty of their chief's treachery. Indeed one very poor family had risked their lives in sheltering and hiding the fugitive not because they supported his politics but because they were chivalrous folk, abiding by the old Celtic code of hospitality even to an enemy at the risk of life. Ardvreck Castle was burnt and the Mackenzies took possession of Assynt, building Calda House, itself now a ruin, near the castle.

For one hundred years Clan Kenneth remained in possession, but in 1760, Assynt was bought by Sutherland, Calda House being burnt by a party of wild MacRaes who resented the idea of its occupancy by a Hanoverian Clan, Hugh MacLeod II of Geanies in Easter Ross heir to the Chiefship of Assynt having failed to buy it back being outbid by Sutherland. The ruins of Ardvreck stand on a peninsula running into Loch Assynt, while at Kirkton at the head of the Loch is the site of the first Church in that district built by Angus MacLeod the Laird in 1440, a man who had travelled widely in France and Italy receiving numerous favours from the Pope; the family vault remained in use by the Assynt MacLeods till the end of the 18th century.

Ross continued in a very disturbed state during the summer of 1650; General Carr with a strong force detached by Leslie as he had moved north against Montrose had besieged the Mackenzie Castle of Redcastle and Chanonry, hanging the garrison of the first and razing the second to the ground, as well as causing a lot of wanton destruction in Fortrose, while General Leslie garrisoned Brahan. Charles II having come to an understanding with the Covenanters landed in Scotland on the 23rd June being greeted with enthusiasm by the people but virtually kept a prisoner by the Assembly, who among other things, were trying to make him sign a Declaration professing that he was 'humbled and afflicted by his father's opposition to God's works and his mother's idolatry'. Charles could temporize but this was too much and he refused to sign, but within a fortnight Cromwell was in Scotland with 16,000 New Model troops, the Covenanters refusing to move unless Charles would sign the iniquitous document; with the enemy on Scottish soil the king signed but was allowed no control of subsequent proceedings. All chance of successful resistance was destroyed when the all powerful ministers insisted on a last minute purge from the Scottish Army of all who were not extreme Presbyterians; thus they lost their most efficient officers and all the Clan Regiments except for the Lawers Highlanders. The result of this fantastic order was the utter defeat of the Covenanters by Cromwell at Dunbar, a battle which could so easily have been a Scots victory.

Too late Scotland realized that the kingdom had been betrayed by a number of unbalanced ministers, the old national spirit revived, Presbyterians, Episcopalians and Catholics, now known as Resolutioners flocked to the king's standard; the Auld Enemy was over the Border so that even lowland divines forgot their theological hair splitting and joined in crowning the king at Scone. But the next year 1651 ended the war. Charles had reached Worcester with a mainly Highland Army of 16,000 men, among them a youth recently graduated from Aberdeen University, young George Mackenzie Master of Tarbat 17 years old now commanding a Regiment of Dragoons; Kenneth son and heir of the Earl of Seaforth; Thomas Mackenzie of Pluscardine; Sir Thomas Urquhart of Cromarty; David Ross of Balnagown; Munros; MacDonalds and MacLeods from Skye but without their Chiefs. On the 3rd September after forced marches Cromwell engaged the Scots Army with a force of 25,000 men and after a desperate battle won, fouling his reputation, already smirched through his bloody sack of Dundee, by the butchery or enslavement of prisoners of war who were sent to the Plantations in the West Indies.

The MacLeods lost 700 killed while the MacDonalds of Sleat also suffered heavy casualties; old Sir Thomas Urquhart, bewailing 'his seven pockmantles' filled with invaluable treatises hopelessly lost, went to the Tower till the Restoration, except for an interval when the Lord Protector allowed him to return to Cromarty on parole. The brilliant and eccentric old Royalist did not live long enough to pass his old age at Cromarty as so great was his gladness at the king's return in 1660 that he died of laughing! Ross was imprisoned at Windsor Castle till released by death in 1657. Kenneth younger of Seaforth and Young George of Tarbat escaped, the former to succeed as 3rd Earl of Seaforth on the death of his father in Holland to a forfeited Estate, he held out for a while in the Lewis but as we shall see eventually fell into Cromwell's hands after Glencairns hopeless expedition in 1653 and went to the Tower.

In Scotland the English Independents were in control, who within a few weeks had smashed the political power of the Kirk annulling the major achievements of the Scots Revolution. Then Cromwell showed his hand—annexation—substituting a military dictatorship for one of the Kirk, Monk becoming the Governor of Scotland. For three years more the Highlands held out, Seaforth making Stornoway Castle the centre of resistance. This ancient castle of uncertain age, situated in Anchor Bay had passed a turbulent life, taken by Huntly in 1506, successfully resisting the Artillery of the Earl of Argyll in 1554 and falling to Rorie of Castle Leod early in the 17th century. Cromwell feared that it might become the base for a Royalist effort from Holland, then Kenneth seized a Parliament Privateer the 'Fortune' causing Lilburne to breathe vengeance, so that eventually it was occupied by the Roundhead Col. Cobbett, who held Stornoway and Castle with 3 companies in the old stronghold and 4 companies in a new fortress under Major Crispe, until the Restoration, after which the Castle remained undisturbed till its destruction in 1852.

On the eastern side of Ross, Castle Leod, the Royalist stronghold of Davochmaluach, and Dingwall, were garrisoned in 1653 by Roundhead soldiers under command of Col. Fitch governor at the new castle of Inverness. One of the leading Royalists in Ross at this period was Sir George Munro of Newmore the third son of Colonel John Munro of Obsdale, whose previous career warrants some mention here. He had served with great distinction under Gustavus Adolphus returning home after that great king's death at the Battle of Lützen; joining up with his Covenanter Uncle, Col. Robert Munro, who was soon to be promoted general, with him he went overseas to Ireland assuming command of the Covenant Army when his uncle was recalled by the Estates to oppose the victorious Montrose. In 1645 George returned to Edinburgh in an attempt to wring supplies for the Scottish forces in Ireland who meanwhile in his absence had suffered a severe defeat, by O'Neil at Benbarb, while once again under the command of George's uncle General Sir Robert Munro.

Three years later George Munro, always a Royalist at heart, cast in his lot with the cavaliers being made a Major General by King Charles I and joining the ill-fated Hamilton in Scotland with 1200 horse and 2100 foot only to meet defeat by Cromwell at Preston where Hamilton was captured, though George, much the more efficient soldier, made his retreat to Scotland, in good order. Soon after we find Munro in Holland where he had joined King Charles II who conferred upon him the honour of knighthood sending him off, with some other Highlanders, to Ireland as commander of an Irish army with whom he participated in the siege of Derry, soon after capturing Coleraine. A Covenanting force under Majors Clotworthy and Ellis with some of Glencairn's Regiment thought of trying to stop Sir George's progress but they disliked equally English Sectaries and Scottish Royalists, so they thought again, finally deciding to return home.

Sir George next appeared at Carrickfergus held by Scottish Covenant forces; here orders came from Lord Montgomery of Ards, for the reduction of that stronghold, the Castle and town surrendering on terms to Sir George on 4th July 1649. Dalzell of the Binns then became Royalist governor at Carrickfergus while Munro as governor of Coleraine issued the very reasonable order to the Presbyterian ministers stating that if they would refrain from politics they were welcome to carry on with their ministry; however these gentry declined the offer so were sent back to Scotland. For a considerable time Sir George Munro held out against Cromwell but getting no support from outside, capitulated on very favourable terms to the Cromwellian Commander Coote, during April 1650. This left Munro free to join the Earl of Middleton in Caithness four years later, that gentleman having escaped from the Tower where he had been confined since the Battle of Worcester. Unfortunately Charles II, now in Paris, had given to this loyal but ineffective general the command of all Royalist forces in Scotland till then vested in the still more incapable hands of the ex-covenanter Earl of Glencairn. The force at his disposal was concentrated at Dornoch in Sutherland and consisted of 3500 foot and 1500 cavalry of which 300 were badly mounted and armed, yet it was an army with which a leader like Montrose could have worked wonders.

As it was the force quickly divided into Middleton, Glencairn factions, the time being spent in perpetual quarrelling which led to much duelling among the officers. It was not long before Munro, now

Middleton's Lieutenant General, was involved referring to Glencairn's own force as a pack of thieves and robbers, a remark which particularly annoyed MacDonald of Glengarry. At a ball that followed Sir George challenged the Earl of Glencairn to a duel which they fought next morning, first on horseback with pistols but that method proving ineffective, possibly as a result of the festivities of the previous night, they continued the engagement on foot with swords, Munro being the loser though not seriously hurt by a crack on the head that rendered him unconscious. This example in high places set all the juniors emulating their elders, and in spite of Middleton's orders against further private fighting, Capt. Lindsay killed Capt. Livingstone in a duel, the victor being forthwith court-martialed and shot at Dornoch Mercat Cross. Glencairn who had unsuccessfully endeavoured to get the sentence rescinded, then left the Army which then proceeded to indulge in a series of route marches through Ross and Inverness but avoided General Monk who was holding the passes south, while the Cromwellian General Morgan followed very cautiously behind Middleton till at length the Royalist general was surprised in a defile near Lochgarry and his army broken up after a mild fight. This was the last of the fighting; Kenneth Earl of Seaforth was lodged in the Tower while for a short time, Sir John Mackenzie of Tarbat was imprisoned at Inverness.

In Easter Ross an important change had occurred, the VIIIth and last Baron Monro of Milntown, after serving the king faithfully in Ireland had fallen in the Royalist cause at the Battle of Kilsyth (1645) while the home of his fathers had been seized by his maternal uncle Sir Robert Innes XXIIIrd of Innes in Moray, for payment of debts. Sir John of Tarbat died in 1654 being buried at Dingwall; by his marriage to the only daughter and heiress of Erskine Lord Innerteil he inherited lands in Fife which he passed on together with his Ross inheritance to his eldest son Sir George Mackenzie. His second son John died in London in 1662 'on his return from his travels', Rorie the third of Prestonhall becoming an Advocate in the Court of Session later Lord Justice Clerk and Lord of Session (1703); there were three others, Alexander of Ardloch and Kinellan; James, and Kenneth who married Isobel Auchinleck. His daughters made good marriages, Margaret to the Laird of Lawers, his second to Hugh Lord Lovat, while Isobel was Countess of Seaforth; there were two others, Barbara and Catherine.

Gradually the country settled down so that something of a normal life recommenced under the not unjust rule of General Monk, but ever increasing numbers of the people wanted the king back again while from a total of 900 Parish Ministers in Scotland some 750 were now Resolutioners who were Royalists in sympathy. Two years later Sir

George Mackenzie of Tarbat purchased Milntown from Sir John Innes, changing its name to New Tarbat and within a few years he was to start the reconstruction and additions to the old Monro Castle which were to make it for a brief space the finest building in the north.

In 1660 the king came home to his own again to the universal joy; but south of the Border the great struggle between monarchy and oligarchy still remained undecided, while in Scotland the old close relationship of king and people was broken. On the 1st of May a general amnesty and liberty of conscience in religious matters 'which do not disturb the peace of the kingdom' was granted, a measure of that toleration which was to help bring down the Stewart dynasty in the end. Meanwhile reconstruction proceeded while Charles II with great cleverness, patience, and ability to compromise in matters of policy as well as with his own conscience, succeeded in maintaining his throne, while still keeping in check the rising Whig Oligarchy. Peace brought a measure of prosperity as men could once again think of something else beside war and plots.

Certain changes were appearing in the secular architecture of Scotland which are of considerable interest as the style was still quite dissimilar to anything in England and of this we still have interesting examples in Ross. Ecclesiastical architecture was to all intents and purposes dead though some of the earlier Reformation Churches in Scotland had an attractive and pleasing simplicity. Unlike England, Scotland had no 'half timber' period in her architectural history, but instead had developed a style of her own, very pleasing to the eye and more suited to our climate and scenery. This style, too soon supplanted in southern Scotland by the European fashion of pure classicism, is to be found chiefly in the north where the typical country-house architecture of the 18th century appeared fairly late in its history.

The first introduction of classic architecture into the British Isles took place during the reign of the brilliant James III when his cultured, much travelled, but unpopular favourite Robert Cochrane designed the Renaissance Hall of Stirling Castle. Any further work by this unfortunate man was prevented by Archibald 'Bell the Cat' Douglas, who hanged the architect from a bridge in 1482. But the Scot was reluctant to lose his tower, neither had he the money for great buildings thus differing from the nobility of England, possessed of vast wealth amassed by their mercantile forebears who had in so many cases replaced the old aristocracy of England after the Wars of the Roses and during the autocratic rule of the Tudors. To meet these two difficulties the round or rectangular tower was kept but often incorporated into the more peaceful architecture of the 16th, and in the north late 17th and 18th centuries, by matching it with another tower, the pair being at opposite corners of one long side, the first story of which formed a long gallery; north of the Forth the towers were more often sited diagonally.

The Castle of Tarbat, destroyed after 1745, had been developed in this way from the old Munro Tower of 1500 by Sir George Mackenzie, who soon after was to become Viscount Tarbat and 1st Earl of Cromartie c. 1660; while such houses as Conon, 1758–60, and the 17th century Ord, Teaninich, and old Shandwick, show a very definite retention of the Scottish vernacular style as does the Castle of Balnagown though much defaced by 19th century additions. The transition continued, modifying still further the tower, now part of the central block standing behind outrunners which are formed by low buildings on either side. The old Manse above the red bay of Applecross is perhaps the most perfect example of this style in Ross; the existing Castle of Foulis c. 1720 is another though here we find a Dutch influence. The characteristics of Scottish architecture were: a charming outline, lofty roofs, dormers, bold corbelling, far-over-sailing towers, and huge chimney stacks, in other words an architecture utterly in tune with the surrounding landscape which was further aided by a growing enthusiasm for tree planting. Perhaps the most outstanding indoor feature of this period was the painted ceiling the motif as often as not being heraldic, but few of these remain. The new classic style, made so popular in England frequently by Scottish architects, such as Colin Campbell 1720, John Gibbs 1682–74, Sir William Chambers 1726–96, William Adam who died 1748, and his more famous sons, especially Robert 1728–92, arrived in Ross and Cromarty comparatively late in the 18th century being represented by such houses as New Hall on the Black Isle, Tarbat House 1780 and Novar 1782. Though an attractive and pleasant architecture it is too universal and well known to need description and good work based on it was done during the early part of the 19th century. Then came the architectural deluge of ostentatious vulgarity to be followed by the uninspired building of the 20th century with its bungaloid growths and general nastiness.

So much for the bigger houses of Ross, but what of the smaller homes of *duine-uasal* and clansmen? The houses of the Burghs are described in a subsequent chapter so that the following description covers the buildings outside the principal towns and situated both in the *Machair* (Plain) of Ross as well as the smaller townships on the coasts or in the numerous straths and glens. The clansman's home had altered but little through the centuries, remaining simple in the extreme till late in the 19th century when the Black House began to make way for the 'White' Croft house. The thick walls were made of dry stones, or landstones and divots in alternate layers, while the roof was of thatch, heather or straw, held in place by home-made ropes secured to heavy stones. The single room, adjoined the byre which stood at a lower level, being shut off by a thin partition. Windows were just narrow slits usually closed with a clod or bag of straw. The hearth-stone with its peat fire rested in the centre of the packed earth floor, the smoke, or at least some part of it, passing through a hole in the roof, any artificial lighting being provided by the crusie, the metal bowl containing fish oil which fed the wick made out of bullrush pith. The furniture consisted of a board and trestle table, some stools, a chest and the box bed built into the wall. The first improvement to this dwelling was the addition of a proper chimney at the gable end, the bottom opening out over the hearth stone now situated at the end of the chamber. A primitive house, yet it turned out the fittest and toughest folk in Britain, no doubt due in part to their plentiful and excellent diet, a feature which lasted much longer in the Highlands of Scotland than in the southern lowlands, continuing to be the case till the early 19th century.

By the 17th century the *duine-uasal* had become the tacksmen holding his farm and wide grazings on payment of a money and cattle premium, a rent in money and kind, and military service. His house changed little till the 19th century when alas many hundreds of his kind with thousands of clanspeople were lost to Scotland to make way for sheep. His home was of stone and lime, roughly 100 feet long, with the walls 8 feet in height above the foundation built about the roots of couples previously fixed in the ground. The wall was then raised to 10 feet by means of several layers of turf, the whole being thatched probably with heather. Inside the long house was divided into several apartments: first the guest chamber with a chimney at one end, a glazed window facing south, and a tent bed built into the solid stone partition wall which divided off the next room; the second room held tent beds for the junior members of the family, having a door leading into the master's and mistress's room, the third and principal room of the house. Next came the *cearn* servants' room or *tigh* slothait, used as a general room and kitchen by all in the farm house, being the largest and longest. Here the fire burned in the middle of the room, which was lighted by small boarded windows on either side. Then came the byre occupying about 50 feet of the total frontage only closed off by a thin partition.

As time went on these houses were improved, solid masonry replaced the wall head divots, another storey or L shaped wing might be added, while a slate or stone slab roof took the place of the old thatch. Many of these tackmen's homes have become the farm houses and lodges of today, and numerous examples exist throughout Ross and Cromarty, such as Inverpolly, Achnahaird, Langwell, etc. The original Langwell House was burnt in 1746 when an English frigate landed at Ullapool; the greatest loss was not the house but the Charter Chest that con-tained the old Charters in Gaelic of the MacLeods of Lewis.

CHAPTER XVI

THE GENERAL SITUATION—THE TWO SIR GEORGE MACKENZIES—THE COUNTY OF CROMARTY—THE END OF A MONARCHY

Chronological Table

1680 Magistrates and Council of Inverness pay monthly salary for a municipal doctor, Dr. Mackenzie.
1685 Completion of first stone bridge, which replaced a long series of wooden ones, over the Ness at Inverness, paid for by the town and many chiefs, including Sir Donald MacDonald of Sleat, and John MacLeod of Dunvegan.
1686 Allan Ramsay born. Poet and author, his greatest work being the Gentle Shepherd. His son became a famous painter.
1687 Last Clan contest, MacDonnell of Kepoch v MacKintosh. Granting of complete religious freedom by James VII and II.
1689 Usurpation of throne by William of Orange from King James VII and II. Battle of Killiecrankie
1690 Battle of the Boyne.
1692 Massacre of Glencoe.
1694 Voltaire born.
1695 Bank of Scotland established.
1698 Darien Expedition.
1701 Alasdair Mac Mhaigstir (Alasdair MacDonald) the great Gaelic poet, the successor of Ian *Lom*, died 1780. Alasdair's father was the Rev. Alexander MacDonald, an Episcopal minister who lived at Dalilea, Moidart.

Before following events in Ross it is important to get a true picture of the state of Scotland between the Restoration and the Revolution, as the history of this period for all of Britain has been distorted and falsified by the Whig propagandists of the two succeeding centuries. The population of Scotland in 1660 stood somewhere around the 1,000,000 mark; of these 14,000 were Roman Catholics domiciled for the most part in the Highlands, and though they continued to suffer some persecution they remained loyal and quiet throughout the reigns of the last two ruling Stewarts. The remainder north of the Tay were either Episcopalians or Resolutioners (moderate Presbyterians) many of the latter with a strong desire to return to the conditions which had existed in 1630.

During this period only five ministers were deposed in Ross for refusing to conform, an act which certainly entailed an oath of loyalty to the Crown, but in fact affected the conduct of their ecclesiastical duties not at all; these honest but rather stiffnecked men were the ministers of Cromarty, Tain, Fodderty, Kiltearn, and Kincardine and when eventually action was taken against them they received sympathy and assistance from many Episcopalian Highland Chieftains. Among the laymen fined, more for their previous records than their tenacity to the Solemn League and Covenant were Munro of Foulis £3600; Ross of Invercharron £1200; Andrew MacCulloch, Burgess of Tain, £1200; David Ross of Pitcalnie £720; and Mackenzie of Kilcoy £600. Much has been made of the above, but others who before and after did less 'agin the government' lost their estates and heads, moreover it is doubtful whether they lost a penny as of the 800 fines imposed in

Scotland the majority being in the south-west districts, few if any were actually uplifted.

At the other end of the scale were an intransigent minority the Protestors, violently Covenanter, which included some 150 out of a total 900 ministers, the minority supported by an isolated group of the least educated people in Scotland but few others, in other words just the material for a bonfire when ignited by self seeking men or crazy 'hot gospellers', they created a body of enthusiastic and bitter fanatics who were to play a part quite out of proportion to their numerical strength. This group were concentrated in the then most backward part of Scotland, the very thinly populated area west of Annan and the Clyde, but with a few outposts in Fife and Lothian. Perhaps the Restoration Government would have done better to ignore completely this sect, thus following the principle suggested by the much execrated Lord Advocate 'Bluidy' Mackenzie of Rosehaugh, an offshoot of the House of Lochslyn: 'It fairs with (Hereticks) as with Tops, which how long they are scourged, keep foot . . . but fall how soon they are neglected and left to themselves.' Obvious to us now but difficult when aforesaid 'Hereticks' not only concern themselves with matters ecclesiastical but try forcibly to upset the laws of the state. Toleration would have beaten them, it was the one thing perhaps that they hated more than anything else, as their confessed aim was to force the old ruthless Calvinism lock, stock and barrel down the throats of not only all Scotland, but England and Ireland as well. The great but understandable mistake made by the Crown was to give this violent party the chance of becoming martyrs for a cause, for which with wild and fierce gallantry they were prepared happily to die.

Another gentleman whose description varies between being a man 'worthily the darling of his friends and countrymen, happily endowed with those advantages of manhood and learning that fit him for doing the noblest offices to his prince and country', and Mephistopheles in person, was Sir George Mackenzie, now Lord Tarbat, a cousin of the other 'Bluidy' Sir George of Rosehaugh, and like him to become Lord Advocate and Lord Justice General of the kingdom. It will be my endeavour to strike a just balance and avoid a perhaps natural family bias, so let us admit straight away that Tarbat was a brilliant, charming, but tricky politician, with an eye to the main chance—what 17th or 18th century politicians were not?—but who remained a Scotsman who loved his country, believing in a greater Britain, though not necessarily by means of a one-sided incorporative union, serving her during the course of a very long life on many occasions honestly and well. That certain incidents during his legal and political career were highly questionable is true, among them the employment of torture—a common enough expedient of the day—to extract a confession from the

Covenanter Carstairs who was thought to be implicated in the Rye House Plot to murder the king and his heir. There was also his tendency to trim his political bark to the prevailing wind which was admittedly unromantic, but politics had long ceased to be anything other than opportunist. Yet such trimming as he did fades into oblivion when we compare it with the wholesale betrayal of James II for cash and place at the Revolution by the English Whig party, whose upholders have always been at such pains to describe this transaction as a victory for English democracy and sound common sense.

The restoration of Charles II, a monarch who quite definitely had made up his mind to be an absentee so far as Scotland was concerned, inaugurated a bad system by which his Northern Kingdom was in practice ruled by a Viceroy. The first was the weak Middleton, in reality a figurehead as the brains behind the vice-regal throne belonged to Tarbat who in 1662 framed the Rescissory Act, modelled on that passed by the Covenanters in 1639, and annulling the legislation of the 'forties. This of course restored the Episcopalian form of Church government, which in the past had been sufficiently broad minded to permit of those wishing to conduct their church affairs on a more strictly Presbyterian basis to do so. An initial error was made by the government appointment of two Archbishops, two men of anything but admirable character, Fairfoul an Episcopalian who had conformed, to Glasgow; and the political minded Sharp, a Presbyterian about to conform, to St. Andrews; but not all the appointments were of this stamp, Edinburgh, Dunblane and Aberdeen in particular being men of very high moral integrity and saintly character.

In May the Estates restored the Bishops to their Parliamentary seats and brought back lay patronage binding the patron to retain the sitting incumbent if so desired by the congregation. The lay patronage was not welcomed but the remainder was generally applauded except in Galloway and Campbell Argyll where there was trouble and a general strike of ministers. By 1663 the Restoration system was in being and working smoothly except in the south west where the position was difficult entailing not only measures to deal with Dissenters who might well have been left alone, but active enemies of both Establishment and the Monarchy, the driving force being quite as much political as religious.

Then unfortunately Lauderdale succeeded as King's Commissioner, a man given to a 'panick blend of oppression and concession' as well as being a full sized rogue; as an old Covenanter he loathed Coventicles, knowing that the propaganda value of politically incendiary sermons preached under romantic circumstances, so he clamped down on the south west, making these meetings illegal. Indeed there was some excuse even for this as in this area the Whigs were frankly in league with the Dutch with whom the king was at war, promising to capture Edinburgh,

Stirling and Dumbarton so as to cut off the Royalist Highlands, while the Hollanders made a landing. This Covenanting army of saints or traitors depending on the point of view, were dispersed at Rullion Green, their total number amounting to 1,200 men which indicates that even in the south west the revolutionaries were in a minority. Unfortunately some of the leaders were executed and tortured with the thumbscrew to extort confession and suffered with great bravery, which caused a reaction in their favour especially among those too young to remember the Act of Classes, massacre of Royalist women, and the tyranny of the Kirk Session; but in the north this spirit of bitter fanaticism was still absent and thither we will return.

Here once again life was peaceful, Mr. John Graham the school master at Chanonry petitioning that the damage and pillage which had extended even to the scholars' books and papers, perpetrated by David Leslie's army in 1646, the year Seaforth and many others had supported Montrose, might be rectified as the delay was causing the feuars to withhold payment owed to the school. In 1660 four Inverness merchants, two apprentices and one Tain surgeon had made a round trip overland to London, on their return complaining of the attentions of the numerous highwaymen in England which made travelling in that country very unsafe.

The following year on May 24th the annual Tomnahurich horse race meeting was revived, attended by the Earls of Moray and his vassals; Seaforth, 'Kenneth *Mór*'; Lord Lovat; the Lairds of Grant; Mackintosh; Foulis; Balnagown; the Barons of Moray; Lord Mac-Donald (Glengarry); and the English officers of Inverlochy. This race meeting had been founded in 1622, a time which must have seemed like a golden age as it was described by the contemporary writer as one of 'Great concord and much correspondence between Lovat and his neighbours, the Marquis of Huntly governor of Inverness Castle; the Laird of Grant with a house in Bridge Street Inverness; the Earl of Moray at Castle Stuart; and the Earl of Seaforth at Chanonry Castle.' The prize for the best horseman was a silver cup and spurs provided by Huntly, which were won during three early meetings three years in succession by the Laird of Inverlochy judged the best horseman in the north, twice by Lovat, once by Grant and the late Colin Earl of Seaforth. The party was very much enjoyed by the populace as well as the nobility of the northern counties.

Further north we have the picture of the young earl of Sutherland in 1661 a schoolboy at Dornoch, desporting himself at golf and archery, while on the 3rd August of that year Fraser a gallant schoolmaster of Inverness lost his life trying to save Donald Bain, Tulloch's son, and Hugh Fraser, Reelig's son, who had got into trouble while bathing with the other schoolboys in the Ness. Of the three Donald only was saved.

The same year Sir John Munro of Foulis XXII Chief and 4th Baronet, a keen Presbyterian whose convictions led him into some hot water entered into a Bond of Manrent with Kenneth Earl of Seaforth, a Roman Catholic.

The old castle of Cromarty still held by the family of Urquhart, as was much of the Black Isle, was the scene of the escape of a prisoner who 'made ane passadge throw the prison wall being 11 ft thick.' The castle which was to last through the next century till replaced by Cromarty House, had passed a fairly quiet existence, though early in the 17th century the great if eccentric Sir Thomas Urquhart, who had died of joy at the Restoration, had with his brother, during their youth, forcibly confined their father within the 'inner dortoir' or sleeping apartment, for a short time, and reasons unknown.

The Clans of Skye were at peace, Sir James *Mór* MacDonald 10th Chief and 2nd Baronet of Sleat who had married Margaret Mackenzie of Tarbat, was entertaining lavishly at his castles of Duntulum and Armadale, though unlike his father Sir Donald *Gorm Òg* who had died in 1643, he had not himself been outstanding in his services to his king. Roderick the 'Witty' XVth Chief who also had married a daughter of Sir John of Tarbat, ruled at Dunvegan.

Considerable differences of opinion had arisen between Lauderdale and Tarbat and for the moment the gross and elderly Commissioner defeated the young and handsome Highlander, the latter retiring home in some trouble, where he remained till 1677 when the chaos caused by Lauderdale caused his recall to office. Meanwhile by purchase and mortgage his lands increased, the rebuilding of Tarbat Castle (Milntown) was accomplished and filled with many treasures collected during his travels abroad including a fine collection of books and pictures. Beside his real estate activities he carried on a vast correspondence, engaged in literary pursuits of varying merit. Wherever he might be his active mind found interests, like his father and grandfather before him Aberdeen University claimed him as a son, there were laid the foundation of the brilliant legal and classical attainments of this Highlander who was to become one of the Founders of the Royal Society, as well as climb to the top of the political ladder and judiciary of his country.

To him we owe a short account of the island of North Rona probably visited soon after the Battle of Worcester (1651) during the period in which Cromartie (or as he then was George Mackenzie Master of Tarbat) was forced to 'take to the heather', part of the time in the western Isles:

'The Island of Rona hath for many generations been inhabited by five families, which seldom exceed thirty souls in all; they have a kind of commonwealth among them, in so far if any of them have more children than another, he that hath fewer taketh from the other what makes his number equal, and the excrescence of about thirty souls is sent with the summer boat to Lewis to the Earl of Seafort, their master, to whom they pay yearly some quantity of meal stitched up in sheep-skins, and feathers of sea fowls; they have no feuel for fire upon the island, but by the special providence of God, the sea yearly casts in so much timber as serves them. Their sheep there have wool, but of a blewish colour. There is a chappell in the midst of the isle, where they meet twice or thrice a day. One of the families is hereditary Beeddall, and the master of that stands at the altar and prayeth; the rest kneel upon their knees and join with him. Their religion is the Romish religion. There is always one who is chief, and commands the rest, and they are so well satisfied with their condition, that they exceedingly bewail the condition of those, as supernumerary, they must send out of this Island.'

The fate of the community is tragic some few years after 1703. A swarm of rats ate up all the corn supplies while some thieving seamen stole the island bull, communications between the island and Lewis ceased for a year during which this ancient race of people all died. A new colony settled there a few years later but either died or removed themselves since when the island has been left with its little church and graveyard, to the seals and sea birds, except for the brief occupation by two men of Ness in Lewis who left their families some eighty years ago and settled on Rona but were both found dead by a party who visited the island after an interval of two years.

1678 saw Tarbat Lord Justice General and a member of the Privy Council, three years later he became Lord Clerk Register an office which carried with it apartments in the Palace of Holyrood, though he soon built for himself the beautiful house of Royston, later renamed Caroline Park, situated outside Edinburgh near Granton. Charles by his efforts to introduce religious toleration was making enemies both in England and Scotland, among the very people that he intended to help namely the Dissenters, so that it was not long before the south west was up in arms only to meet defeat less through the very mild counter measures than their own violent divisions. Cameron and Cargill then appeared on the unhappy scene to stir up guerilla war and encourage murder and assassination, for which they received their just deserts, Cameron being killed in a skirmish and Cargill executed. But the Estates were scared into passing the Test Act in addition to one declaring that no difference in religion should affect the Royal suc-cession which was well enough as Prince James the Duke of York during his stay in Scotland as Viceroy had made himself very popular by his sound sympathetic and humane policy; but the Test Act stank to all noses alike, Episcopalian, Presbyterian and Roman Catholic.

There now appeared on the stage a man whose reputation has been blackened by the most unmitigated campaign of lies, lasting till modern times, that ever appeared as history. John Graham of Claverhouse, Viscount Dundee, was sent as a military officer to the south west to keep order; in character he was 'upright, fastidious, and able, a devout soldier of a rather stiff humanity'. This officer protested strongly against taking action against the little people who were merely the tools of their fanatical leaders. He put into practice his belief by fining the leaders and talking to the people, a treatment that for a time was effective, but broke down when he left the job in 1683, when all his good work of humane pacification was undone by the circuit courts who had been badly frightened by the Rye House Plot in which Argyll and Carstairs were mixed up. Then a reign of terror began, inaugurated not by the government but by the south west Covenanters, now known as Cameronians after their lately deceased leader, being accompanied by murders and executions ordered by their own tribunals, so that as a result stronger government action followed, since referred to as the 'killing' times.

In 1685 Charles II died and James VII and II came to the throne, who tried yet again to establish reason in the south west by an act of indemnity. But within a few weeks that area had again to be put under martial law against folk who far from dying for freedom were under restraint for their refusal to submit to a law which pronounced it unlawful to murder Episcopalian ministers, the king's servants, and those who disagreed with their methods. Much as it may offend some it is only fair to add that the noble army of Cameronian martyrs are greatly exaggerated, being in the main children of propagandist imaginations of later date; for any who doubt this, the evidence of official records is clear and quite indisputable. The Estates met in April making it abundantly clear that Scotland with the exception of the south west was solid behind the king, a fact further proved after two abortive risings when the traitor Argyll commenting on his failure, remarked 'In this country I see no great party that desires to be relieved.'

Tarbat on whom the king greatly relied was now raised from the position of Law Lord and Baronet to the peerage by King James, being created Viscount of Tarbat, Lord MacLeod and Castlehaven; the first Barony being connected with the MacLeod of Lewis and *Coigach* descent and lands; the second with the original Tarbat, which consisted of the Portmohomack (or Castlehaven) Ballone and Lochslyn lands. Tarbat with an eye to an Earldom started his manoeuvres for the segregation of the numerous areas of Ross, in his possession or under his superiority, into the separate county of Cromarty. By 1698 the new county was in being, the name being taken from the old

H

Sheriffdom of Cromarty on the Black Isle, now numbered among Tarbat's wide acres; the Earldom followed in 1703 and for two hundred years Cromarty existed as a separate county till re-attached to Ross for administration by the Boundary Commissioners in 1891.

In three years James VII and II had lost his throne, not through oppression but by his honest desire for toleration among all religious sects, and by his refusal to believe ill of the men around him, so vociferous in their loyalty, who were busily accepting bribes of place and money from that cold blooded pervert James's son-in-law, William of Orange. King James desired that all, both Catholic and Dissenter, might worship openly and what was worse should be able to enjoy the normal rights of citizenship without any restrictions, but in this the king was more than one hundred years in advance of his time, and it roused opposition even among his most loyal supporters the Episcopalians of Scotland who had no objection to Catholics worshipping in their own way in private but refused to go further, the ensuing crisis resulting in his supporters which included one Bishop, and the Lord Advocate Viscount Tarbat, losing their jobs.

In February 1687 James inaugurated an act for complete religious freedom in Scotland, to apply to all law-abiding subjects of all creeds, while the religious tests were rescinded, for one year from this date, thus Scotland for the first time enjoyed complete religious freedom; the next occasion was to be 1829. James Stewart was ruined but the opposition was almost wholly English as in Scotland the Indulgence was generally accepted, the Presbyterians in particular expressing their gratitude and loyalty in the warmest terms. The year 1689 ended the truly monarchical system of government in both England and Scotland as with the aid of Dutch troops and the lowest forms of treachery and falsehood, Plutocracy had won the day. Still Scotland hesitated, in that country only the south west showed any jubilation at the Revolution, a joy expressed by the rabbling of Parish ministers and the destruction of their houses. The Estates met in March and James now in France—a fatal blunder as the common people of England could and would have upheld him if given the chance—had permitted his supporters to attend. The Castle of Edinburgh was held for James but Dutch troops were on their way north, for as in England the foreign usurper could not rely on the private soldier who in nearly all cases remained loyal to his oath in spite of the fact that in many cases William had been successful in purchasing the loyalty of the more senior officers. After this session Dundee with fifty followers rode north to raise the Jacobite North, the Williamites having accepted the fait accompli.

In the Highlands Dundee found the support he needed and by May had raised the Clans; in Ross, Kenneth Earl of Seaforth who had succeeded his father in 1679 with the ardent loyalist Sir Donald Mac-Donald of Sleat brought out their respective Clans for the Jacobite cause, though John Ian *Breac* of Dunvegan made no response to appeals from Dundee, the King's Secretary of State in Dublin Castle, or James himself who wrote to him through Sir Donald of Sleat. On the 27th July Scotland was nearly won for James but at the moment of victory 'Bonny' Dundee fell at Killiecrankie, leaving no-one who could fill his place; his successor Cannon carried on guerilla warfare throughout the next winter but was defeated at Cromdale, an action that brought the war to a close. Considerable persecution of Episco-palians followed in the south but many people were heartily sick of religious bigotry so that moderate men were not absent from the new order and the Covenants were not mentioned in any way much to the annoyance of the south west.

North of the Tay not even military escorts could coerce the people into accepting their allocated Presbyterian pastors, and in the Dingwall Kirk Session Records of 8th December 1689 it is recorded that no sermons had been preached since October as the Minister Mr. John MacRae had been summoned south by the Council for refusing to read the Proclamation deposing James II, but he escaped as none would give evidence against him. A year later the Minister was kept in confinement at Brahan to prevent his communicating with the out-lawed Marquis of Seaforth, however Sir Donald Bayne of Tulloch and Colin Mackenzie of Redcastle on his behalf went bail for 1000 marks. These Session Records deal largely with various offences against the Ten Commandments and the disciplinary action taken by the Kirk but there are other entries such as one of 23rd October 1681 recording a money collection made at Dingwall for the relief of certain citizens of Inverness captured and enslaved by Algerian pirates. But by 1693 conditions had eased somewhat and some 300 Episcopalians who had accepted the new government de facto were still holding their parishes.

The Whigs were still frightened of the north, though after Cromdale a truce had been arranged by William of Orange who offered an amnesty to those Chiefs and Chieftains who would take an oath of allegiance to him on New Year's day 1692, the alternative being Fire and Sword. Yet the 'simple' chieftains who still attached some importance to an oath of allegiance, and did not regard betrayal as practical politics, hesitated till King James sent his permission to subscribe to the oath, a decision taken by the king in order to avoid civil war and the destruction of these loyal Highlanders by Dutch arms. William of Orange and his secretary Dalrymple the Master of Stair saw that the delay caused by the time taken to spread around King James's order might be used to advantage, so laid plans for a general massacre in the winter when the Highlanders could not escape and 'carry their wives, bairns and cattle to the hills'. But James's speedy action upset this plan for the introduction of the 'new freedom and civilization' to the Highlands; yet the permission to take the oath arrived almost too late, William refusing an extension of the date and giving orders that the general massacre should go forward.

Lord Carmarthen however induced this singularly unpleasant monarch to limit the killings to a single example, the unlucky people being the little Catholic Sept of MacIan MacDonald in Glencoe, the old Chief having been held up by the weather and the absence of the Sheriff, so taking the oath six days late. The story of this vile piece of treachery carried out by Campbell of Glenlyon and his cut-throats is too well known to warrant repeating, but even the Lowlands were shocked, the troops sent from that area to assist arriving too late, probably on purpose. Col. John Hill, the old Cromwellian officer, at this period Governor of the Fort at Inverlochy (Fort William) was horrified when the prospect of the outrage was mooted, as apart from being a friend of old MacIan the Chief whom he admired, he was a decent honest man, and did all in his power to help MacIan. Among Hill's correspondents was Tarbat, who being out of office and suspect was unable to influence the proceedings or prevent this treachery; these two seem to have established a friendship over many years through their correspondence though it is not known whether they ever met each other.

By 1695 King James, old and broken, had abandoned the struggle while his son was still only a child, so that things quietened down, some hundred Episcopalians taking the 'Assurance'. Tarbat who had retired into private life at the Revolution had trimmed sufficiently to keep his head and remain in Scotland, but beyond giving some very sound advice which probably saved Scotland in general and the Highlands in particular from very much worse treatment, he stayed out of office during the reign of William and Mary. Kenneth Earl of Seaforth played a more noble part, retiring into exile with his king to France where he died in 1701 leaving his heir William 5th Earl and 2nd Marquis of Seaforth, a title that had been granted by the exiled king. But although Tarbat had followed an unromantic course it should be remembered that he was without question the most able statesman Scotland at that time possessed and as such could be and was, of service to his country during a time fraught with danger; had he been in exile he might as well have gone to Timbuctoo for all the influence he could have exerted.

Since the middle 90's, religion as the prime mover in politics was at last falling into the background, but the general state of the nation had never been worse since King David II's time (1341–71). Poverty was everywhere on the increase and the national life since Flodden had gone steadily down hill, except for brief revivals under James V, Mary, James VI, and to some extent at the Restoration, though thwarted by Lauderdale's general misgovernment. Scholarship and arts had revived somewhat, foreshadowing the great 18th century revival in architecture, while both Gaelic verse and Scots literature had shown great vitality. The Lowlands were in far worse shape than the Highlands where material comfort as well as the graces of life had survived. The close touch between the Chieftains and every member of the Clan had much to do with this, all were influenced by the culture in the 'big house' which produced a real desire for learning as well as giving the undeniable polish in speech and manners that distinguishes a Highlander from persons of the same station in other parts of the British Isles. The *Ceilidh* House encouraged the poet and musician, giving also opportunities for free discussion; though the harp was going out of fashion and the fiddle was gaining in popularity, while the great Piping College of the MacCrimmons in Skye was still in existence.

But for Scotland as a whole the general picture was tragic, a once flourishing Scottish trade was all but dead having fallen into the pockets of Holland and England, the Darien scheme proving once and for all the lengths that the latter country would go to keep it there. In 1702 William of Orange died, unlamented, himself defeated by the power that had placed him on the throne, money, which despite the outward trappings of monarchy, was the ruler of England. For more than a century this power remained in the hands of the Whig Oligarchy till it passed from the landed to the commercial interest, soon controlled by the financier and big business, a combination which tended to regard the mass of humanity as mere pawns, to be exploited; there it was to remain till this juggernaut should destroy itself by its own ungainliness and inhumanity.

CHAPTER XVII

EXPLOIT OF A FOOL—QUEEN ANNE—UNION—CHANGE OF OWNERSHIP AT BALNAGOWN—18TH CENTURY PARLIAMENTARY REPRESENTATION

Chronological Table

1707   Act of Union between Scotland and England ratified by Scots Parliament.

A story of this period tells how a robber and his gang were operating south west of Loch Garve in the Tarvie district of Ross, a convenient area from which to pounce on travellers traversing the route between Inverness and the west. MacLeod of Dunvegan's Chamberlain in spite of a guard had been robbed at this spot while carrying a largish sum of money from Inverness to Skye, a similar fate befalling the Steward who had undertaken to be more successful. As the money was badly needed at Dunvegan someone else was required to run the gauntlet, so the family fool (Jester) having begged to be allowed to try his luck was eventually sent off on his old nag amidst the ribald chaff of the household. Having reached Inverness he collected the money safely but duly encountered the robber on his return trip through the woods of Tarvie, the two rode on for a few yards till they reached a steep bank, when the fool with a magnificent gesture proclaimed that never would he surrender his master's money, at the same time throwing a jingling bag down the bank. Quick as a flash the thief dismounted from his excellent horse and scrambled down the bank after the bag only to find it full of sea shells; meanwhile the fool having made a quick exchange of horses was soon moving west at high speed, the money safe on his person, nor was this all as the highwayman's saddle bags were full of the proceeds of the two previous robberies.

But Scotland was very much on edge, so much so that had she not been leaderless and helpless, war with England would have united the whole country once again; the cold blooded and deliberate squandering of Scottish lives and money at Darien largely brought about by the vindictive policy of William of Orange and the English commercial interests had shown people, even if Glencoe had not, exactly what they could expect from their sister over the border. The Scottish merchants then began to realize that the only way left to re-establish any recovery was by the transference of the government to London, for which the Whig interest would be willing to pay with money and other more equivocal concessions, at any rate on paper; this was eventually brought to pass by a mixture of chicanery and corruption which must stink in the nostrils of any honest man Scots or English.

The English Oligarchy had reason to fear the return of the crown to the rightful heir, the Prince of Wales, son of James VII and II, so worked up the old Catholic bogey by which they were enabled to cut out of the succession not only the descendants of Charles I's son and daughter, but also the elder children of his sister Elizabeth Queen of Bohemia, choosing her twelfth child Sophie the elderly Electress of Hanover who had two sons. Thus today the senior representative of the Stewart line is not Ruprecht of Bavaria because by British law one marriage in this family was of doubtful legality, but the Duc de Guise de Jure King of France descended from Elizabeth of Bohemia's second son Charles Louis Elector Palatine. In 1701 the English succession was settled on this lady and her heirs to follow after James VII's and II's daughter, King William's sister in law, Anne, who by this time had lost the last of her seventeen children. This act was passed a few months before the death of William of Orange, who was duly succeeded by Queen Anne, a Stewart who wished to be fair to others beside the Oligarchy if only to make up for her desertion of her father, but still only a puppet in Whig hands controlled through the medium of Sarah Churchill.

Tarbat in 1703 returned to office being created Earl of Cromartie. This same year saw the Assembly of the last Scottish Parliament a very stormy parliament indeed as the anti-Union party which was representative of the country as a whole had the backing of the people. There followed years of unabashed bribery, corruption and trickery, which on the 25th March 1707, accomplished its purpose of selling out Scotland to the Whig Oligarchy in England, against the will of the people of Scotland. It horrified the soundest and most honest elements as represented by Fletcher of Saltoun, who seeing the real advantages to both nations of a just union were working for some form of federal union as opposed to the one sided incorporative union which despite some two hundred years of propaganda to the contrary has not been altogether to the ultimate benefit or happiness of the people of Scotland. So great was the hatred of the sale that there appeared the extraordinary spectacle of an alliance of the south western Cameronians with the Jacobites, a move which was brought to nought by the ineptitude of their chosen leader, the Duke of Hamilton; so Queensberry, a Douglas, collected his 3000 pieces of gold a year, together with his English Dukedom and moved to London. Money had won, and the results soon became apparent with the open persecution of Catholics and the more subtle persecution against Episcopalians. But the victory was not yet complete; had the 12 year old James VIII not had measles in 1708 or had there been a Dundee, the Stewarts would have returned to Scotland in 1708, while it is more than probable that in 1711 England would have gladly accepted the change as well.

In the year 1711 David Ross of Balnagown, the XIIIth and last of his line descended from the 3rd Earl of Ross's brother Hugh Baron of Rariches and Coulleigh, died without heirs. The Chiefship of Clan Anrias (Ross) which since the passing of the Ross Earldom to the Lords of the Isles, had been held by David's family now passed to Munro-Ross of Pitcalnie a junior descendent of Hugh. But round the House of Balnagown arose a not very edifying intrigue.

Shortly before David's death a certain Lord Ross of Hawkhead was seized with the ambition not only to get the great Balnagown property, but also by some means to revive in his own favour the old Earldom of Ross; this despite the fact that he had no connection whatsoever with the northern family. Hawkhead was in fact a descendant of Godfrey de Ros who in the 12th century had migrated north from Yorkshire in the train of Richard de Moreville, eventually obtaining the lands of Stewarton in Cunninghame where he founded the families of Hawkhead, Lord Ross of Tarbert in Cunninghame, Ross of Sanquhar in Nithsdale, and others. The ambition of this 18th century descendant blinded him to two important facts, one being that the Estates were bonded up to the hilt, and the other the effect his presumption would have on the nobility and gentry of Ross and Cromarty. That he was a man somewhat lacking in principle we know having switched from the persecution of Covenanters, to that of Episcopalians, when the change seemed advantageous to himself.

His methods in this new ploy were no less questionable; as he proceeded with two allies, Mr. Stewart minister of Kiltearn, and another from Easter Ross, to work on David, already at death's door, but even more on his very stupid very vain wife, née Lady Ann Stewart, a daughter of the Earl of Moray. By holding out to this lady the possibility of becoming Countess of Ross—a gift never in his power to grant—he eventually succeeded in becoming heir to Balnagown.[1] However Francis Stewart, Lady Ann's brother, being the chief bond holder at once produced heavy claims that Hawkhead could not meet, which necessitated the conveyance of the Estates to his brother General Charles Ross, who died in 1737, when the Estates again reverted to Lord Ross of Hawkhead, but there being no male heirs his title died with him, the estate of Balnagown going to the Hon. Grissel Ross his sister's child who had married Sir James Lockhart of Carstairs; their son, Col. Sir James Lockhart-Ross, succeeding in due course; but in 1942 this family ended with the death of Sir Charles Ross the last of his line.

Returning to the efforts made in 1711 to revive the Earldom which, incidentally, since 1477, had belonged to the crown, the following

Note 1. For table of Ross of Balnagown, see Appendix I b/2.

extract from a letter by Cromartie is of interest, giving as it does, very clearly, his reactions to the suggestion.

'All the fiddling of this hot headed fool—whom I did but too much to oblige—is that having made of late a new kind of purchase in Ross of a reversion of David Ross of Bellnagoun's lands, on which he dreamed himself some fantastic great thing, he would needs have him and his elected for the representative of five shires and seven burghs in the north, and several others in the south.

One thing has turned his head round since he ever midled with Bellnagoun, that he being called Ross, and having a reversion of a piece of land in Ross, he must therefore be successor to, and will needs be, the Earl of Ross, who is indeed one of the first Earls in Scotland, and hade great superiorities; but, unluckily, my Lord, who is indeed ane old west country laird, knowing nothing of the Earldom of Ross, of their rights, of their rise and fall, and having no more relation to them, directly or indirectly, than the miller of Castares has to the Prince of Parma.

He does not know that the Earles of Ross were never above two hundred years Earles of Ross; and that in that tyme there were two of them of the name of MacDonald, two of the name of Lesly, and three before that of no sirname, but were called Gulielemus, or Hugo de Rosse, as being Earles of Ross; he might have known, hade he read any of our history, that these few were in frequent rebellion, that they were very early forfeited, that the Earledom was annexed to the Crown in perpetuitie, and that by a precise and solemn Act of Parliament it is Statute that the king shall never dispone it to any but a second son, and that it shall always be a title to the second son, and that it was always so with all the Scottish kings when they had second sons.

It was foolish in my Lord to think that the Queen's servants were ignorant in these things as himself; but to discover the further impudence of his project it is fit that Her Majesty and her servants know that very considerable families have parts of this Earldom of Ross, some of which would be so vain as to think my Lord but a little man either in Scotland, Brittain, or in himself.

Such are the Earles of Seaforth (Mackenzie, and several other considerable heritors of that name, the Earl of Cromartie (Mackenzie), Rosehaugh (Mackenzie), Scatwell (Mackenzie Baronetcy), *Gairloch* (Mackenzie Baronetcy), Coul (Mackenzie Baronetcy), Redcastle (Mackenzie), Culcoy (Mackenzie Baronetcy), Fowles (Munro Baronetcy), Culrain (Munro), Kilravock (Rose Baronetcy), Cadboll (MacLeod), Fairburn (Mackenzie), Tulloch (Bayne), MacLeod of Lewis, MacDonald of Applecross, Davochmaluach (Mackenzie) and Suddie (Mackenzie), many of which does not think my Lord Ross fit to be their superior; and it does not seem probable that her Majesty or her councillors will allow the interposition and the constituting of any, new man, or other man, to have superiority not (only) over persons but over so many clanns and considerable ones'.

Cromartie's letter mentions Parliamentary representation, so at this stage it may be of interest to describe some happenings connected with 18th century elections in Ross. Up to the Act of Union 1707 the Scottish Parliament, known as the 'Estates' consisted of the Great Barons; the Lesser Barons who represented the more localized districts; since 1326 the Burghs; and till the Reformation the Bishops, the latter being restored during the Episcopalian period. In 1424 the great lawgiving King James I had allowed the lesser barons to send representatives, as frequently these smaller Lairds found the expense and difficulty of attending frequent Parliaments a severe strain.

Universal suffrage was a long way off but it might surprise some people if they realized how continually and honestly both Stewart Kings and Estates were concerned for the 'pure men inhabitaris of the grund' and how insistent they were that full justice be rendered to the 'pure pepil'. The 18th century was to see a steady retrograde process in the above excellent policy, accelerated after 1746 till late in the 19th century. The Act of 1707 still debarred from voting Roman Catholics, or any who attended an Episcopal service under a non-juring minister within one year of the election. The franchise was not extended till 1832 and then only to a minor degree bringing in a few others beside free-holders, who in Scotland, it must be remembered, were not constituted by property. A man might be a free holder without owning a single acre, while a large property owner might not be a freeholder; immediate vassals of the crown alone were freeholders, Superiorities and Property being entirely separate things; the right to freehold is annexed to Superiority.

In 1721 Sir Robert Munro of Foulis was aware that in accordance with the Septennial Act there would be an election in 1722, so decided to take drastic steps to ensure his political supremacy by obtaining a majority in the Dingwall Burgh Council municipal elections. He well knew that as things stood he could only count on a minority, Dingwall being far more a Mackenzie than Munro town. His plan was no less than to abduct several members of consequence who were to be kept in durance till next Michaelmas, his right hand man throughout was the Sheriff Depute of Ross, Capt. George Munro of Culcairn. The night before the municipal election Sir Robert with sixty armed men surrounded the Tolbooth, the opposition party with Kenneth Bayne of Tulloch at their head, being assembled within preparatory to next day's elections. At daybreak Robert rushed the building, catching the inmates entirely unawares, which enabled him to remove them to Foulis Castle for a few hours before putting them below hatches on board a ship lying off Foulis Beach for transportation to Orkney. However a storm arose which drove the vessel ashore, giving the stout hearted councillors the chance to escape back to Dingwall where they arrived in time for the election.

But Sir Robert followed with a force of 200 armed men, a force further increased by another detachment from Inverness; it is said that this army entered the Royal Burgh disguised as road repairers! A certain amount of violence followed to the scaith of some townsfolk who had joined in the 'free for all'; unfortunately one woman, the wife of Bailie Mackenzie was accidently shot and later died. Tulloch and his friends were again removed but this time to a Munro stronghold Tain, where they remained till after the elections were over. Not bad for an elder of Kiltearn; but warrants were taken out against the aggressors, both Sir Robert and Capt. Munro being fined £200. at Inverness, while the poor lady's death cost this enthusiastic Whig politician another large sum of money, spent by the Burgh Council on the erection of a house in Dingwall known as the 'Pavilion'.

The Royal Burgh of Fortrose a year later is the scene of the next 'Tammany Hall' election, that venerable town having been chosen as the 'returning Burgh' for the election of the member for Ross to the Union Parliament; this time the party was to be graced by the rank and fashion of the north. The county electorate, seventy persons in all, were summoned to attend though only thirty-one turned up to return a 'Knight of the Shire'. As in the case of Dingwall, the preceding night saw the arrival of a very interested party, no less a person than the powerful Hanoverian partisan Earl of Sutherland, accompanied by a small army of both horse and foot. A parade was held through the streets, while an English sloop of war came close in firing salvos as a salute, and together with Sutherland's Highlanders doing all possible to forward the chances of his Whig protégé during this 'free' election. The necessity for this show of force was the practical certainty of a Whig defeat; yet all this parade not unmixed with intimidation, availed nothing; of the 31 Barons present 18 voted for General Charles Ross of Balnagown while the remaining votes went to Alexander Urquhart of Newhall, the Whig candidate. Sutherland's friend and relative Sir William Gordon of Invergordon, Sheriff of the County, retired with the minority who went through a form of electing their own man despite protests.

A further effort was made to cook the vote by Colin Graham of Drynie, a deputy-lieutenant of the County, who sword in hand, accompanied by Robert Gordon of Haughs, and Major John MacKintosh, having first posted armed Highlanders at the doors, entered the Court house. Colin then ordered the majority, in the name of the Earl of Sutherland, to clear out, unless they wanted a rough house, to which another Major MacKintosh, not a Whig, replied that they would all be dragged by the heels before they would budge; this stubborn attitude called the Earl's bluff, so that with his government he suffered a defeat.

The next and rather later 'Hogarthian' spectacle chiefly concerns Sir Hector Munro of Novar, a descendant on, the wrong side of the blanket, of George Monro IV of Milntown, who had died in 1576. Sir Hector as a soldier of 'John Company' had served with distinction in India, having been instrumental in breaking the power of the Nabob of Oude as well as Surajah Dowlah. In 1766 he returned to Novar, considerably more wealthy than when he left it, and a baronet withal, while in accordance with East India Company policy which kept as many tame M.P.s as possible on its books, Sir Hector was chosen by them as a suitable candidate, though neither Ross nor the northern Burghs were in the market, however the Inverness Burghs were. Through an 'arrangement' Novar found himself the owner of Muirton and Findhorn etc. near Nairn, which fulfilled the necessary residential qualification, at the same time making sure of two out of four Burghs. For reasons unknown Fortrose though in Ross, was selected as the election centre instead of Forres; once again the steps taken to insure a Town Council majority were more remarkable for their vigour than legality, subsequently becoming the subject of judicial investigation.

This time instead of a display of force, the more civilized practice of wholesale bribery was resorted to, together with a procession of oriental magnificence, which, with trumpets blowing, paraded the Burgh on the night preceding the election. Sir Hector was accompanied by Sir Harry Munro of Foulis, George MacKay of Skibo, David Ross of Invercasley, Duncan Ross of Kindeace and others. The ten opposing councillors, then within the town, were retained at the tavern with such good effect, much money as well as good liqueur greatly assisting the political arguments, that when morning dawned the night long conversion was complete. This resulted in a victory for Novar followed the next year—1768—by his return to Parliament for the Inverness Burghs, whose member he remained till 1802 despite an interval of several years in India. Proceedings in the Fortrose election case were started by Sir Alexander Grant in the Court of Session, on the very evident grounds of bribery and corruption, but failed to secure a conviction.

At the close of the 18th century, out of the total number of 74 votes, representing the number of Freeholders of Ross and Cromarty, the majority were controlled by Seaforth (Humberston Mackenzie) who then represented the County and had 24 votes in his pocket; the Hon. Capt. Mackenzie of Cromartie who had succeeded John Mackenzie,

Lord MacLeod de jure IVth Earl of Cromartie; David Ross Lord Ankerville in the Court of Session; these gentlemen controlling the remainder, while Thomas Mackenzie of Applecross was another political 'Boss' at this time.

CHAPTER XVIII

RESULTS OF THE SALE—THE GERMAN SUCCESSION— THE '15—SOME CORRESPONDENCE—THE '19 AND GLENSHIEL

Chronological Table

1713 Birth of great Scottish painter Allan Ramsay, the son of Allan Ramsay the famous author. Jonathan Swift, the great Irish patriot, becomes Dean of St. Patrick's Dublin which despite all efforts to have him imprisoned, he held till 1745. He employed his brilliant and sardonic genius to expose the appalling state of affairs in Ireland created by the Restrictive Acts, and the corruption, graft and tyranny of the English Whig despotism in that country.
1715 Jacobite Rising. Battle of Sheriffmuir.
1716 Disarming Act. Birth of Gaelic poet Dugald Buchanan, died 1768.
1719 Jacobite Rising. Battle of Glenshiel.
1721 Birth of the famous novelist Smollett in Dumbartonshire; 1736 at Glasgow University; served in the War of Jenkins Ear 1740 after which he wrote in London; obtained degree of M.D. at Aberdeen University 1750, but continued writing, residing for some time in France and Italy; died 1771.

By 1713 even the backers of the Union were regretting their enthusiasm, among them two of the chief perpetrators, Seafield and Argyll, both of whom proposed its abolition, a bill which was defeated by only four votes. The English promises were one by one being regarded by the cynical Whig politicians at Westminster, as 'scraps of paper', English vested interests having replaced monarchy on the throne. The merchants of Scotland saw to their horror heavy duties placed on Scottish linen, a major commodity, a new salt tax designed to destroy the great Scottish fish trade, a malt tax, and the English market closed to Scottish timber.

In 1714 Queen Anne died being succeeded by the Whig nominee George I whose boorish race, till Queen Victoria ascended the throne, was to bring the reputation of British monarchy to such a level that by the end of the 18th century many Scots would gladly have changed to a Republican system of government. But when all is said and done they were but unattractive puppets dressed up as kings dancing to the tune of their Whig masters, who now freed from all control by the crown were the sole arbitrators of the nation's destiny, leaving the people bereft of their one true representative the king, and more voiceless than ever in the past, thus making possible the horrors which accompanied the industrial revolution, as well as in Scotland forcible eviction of families from their homes. The last stand against this new system was to come from the Highlands where men were still free and where a simple but working aristocracy and democracy existed as a co-operative whole, yet to be divided into two separate classes which too often was to become a community of exploiters and exploited.

To both Whig and Tory Aristocracy of 18th century Great Britain much credit must be given for the great revival in all the arts to which they gave their enthusiastic patronage in a manner that showed not only the possession of well-filled purses but a very real knowledge and love of the arts concerned. The greatest fault of the Whig aristocracy was their withdrawal from and loss of touch with the common folk other than their personal servants, a characteristic accentuated by their successors in power—the mercantile magnates of the next century who, lacking any tradition of service, tended to accumulate a set of very false values which justified the most appalling treatment of their fellow creatures in order to amass gold, always provided that a strict code of surface respectability was maintained.

At the accession of George I both countries accepted the fait accompli, and with the permission of King James, the Highland Chiefs sent an address of acceptance to the new sovereign, which with typically Teutonic gaucherie, he refused to accept. Quite openly he was a party monarch, a fact made clear by his cold shouldering of all Tories and his entire reliance on his Whig supporters. Feeling in Scotland swung hard over to the Stewarts and war followed, a brief unsuccessful one thanks to the absence of any real leader, James VIII and III though a man of many virtues lacked the gift of leadership or the ability to inspire; had his son of the '45 been in his place a very different conclusion might well have followed, for not only were Jacobite troops available during this first rising but the Jacobite party in England was very numerous, while still having the spirit to do something more effective than drinking to the king over the water. In Ross the MacDonalds of Skye under Sir Donald MacDonald the 12th chief joined William 5th Earl of Seaforth at Brahan with 800 men.

Cromartie had died in 1714 at Tarbat Castle where he had spent the last four years of his life, laying out the beautiful gardens, planting trees, draining farm land and recovering the land below Meddat from the sea, in Nigg Bay, and writing. He was buried under the monolith at Dingwall, which some few years ago had to be reconstructed on a smaller scale by my mother and father, owing to its imitation of the Leaning Tower of Pisa, a condition brought about by an earth tremor during the 19th century. His son John succeeded as second Earl and was active in the Jacobite cause though he played no great part, but seems to have been in control for Seaforth during the earlier stages of the affair in Ross.

The Mackenzie rally of between three and four thousand men including some 200 from Lewis, took place at Inchrory (Milnain) from where a detachment was sent under Sir John Mackenzie of Coul, a loyal and very capable Jacobite, to take over the Castle of Inverness in the name of the Chevalier, (King James), Sir John becoming his governor. While this was going on Sir Robert Munro, leader of the Hanoverian interest was politely requested to hand over his arms, but replied by garrisoning Foulis and sending his second son Capt. George

Munro of Culcairn to join the pro-Hanoverian Earl of Sutherland at his strongly entrenched Camp at Alness which had been further strengthened by artillery borrowed from a warship in Cromarty Roads. Sutherland had been appointed supreme commander in the north for the Hanoverian party, the forces at his disposal in the Alness camp consisting of some 300 of his own men, the remainder were blocking the passes north of the Oykel as an invasion of some 2000 fighting men from Ross was expected, the MacKays under Lord Reay and MacKay of Scourie, Munros under Lemlair, and Newmore, some Rosses under Braelangwell making a total in the camp of some 1200. Here a council of war was held attended by the above leaders as well as some new arrivals, Ross of Pitcalnie, Ross of Easter *Fearn* and Ross of Tolly, who all agreed that their supporters from the six Eastern Parishes of Ross should rendezvous at Muldearg and march on Inverness while those from Strathoykel and Strathcarron were to concentrate at Braelangwell and Kindeace. The total strength of the Ross supporters of the House of Hanover amounted only to some 700 men as the Munro-Ross areas were confined to the north eastern part of the county while even here there were large Mackenzie of Cromartie zones, nor were Munros or Rosses out for Hanover in anything like full force—either in fact or spirit.

On 8th October Seaforth moved but not south to join the Royal Army under the Earl of Mar as obviously something had first to be done to deal with the enemy strongpoint at Alness, which otherwise would have been a standing menace in his rear. Accordingly the Mackenzies and allied forces ascended the heights of Fodderty and Brae, descended into Strath-Skiach, crossed the Burn, spending the night of the 9th in the township of Clare at that time part of Foulis. Next day they traversed Swordale, crossed the Aultgraad above the abyss, ascended Glenglass going through the defile between *Cnock Gille Bhroenach* and Chaslan down to the township of Boath where by fording the Alness and marching some five miles via Strathrusdale and Ardross, Seaforth was in a position not only to attack the enemy position from a quite unexpected quarter but also to cut off Sutherland's retreat to Bonar Bridge.

On the 13th Sutherland evacuated his fortified camp and beat a hasty retreat while the road remained open, having decided that to face an attack from flank and rear with a not over-keen force would be very unwise. Foulis capitulated on terms handing over 200 stands of arms, and a heavy levy for the Jacobite war chest, having already lost some cattle; while Sir William Gordon of Invergordon, whose daughter 'Bonny Belle Gordon' was one day to marry the unlucky John II, Earl of Cromartie—suffered some depredations. Meanwhile Tain was occupied by a mixed force of Mackenzies, Chisholms and MacDonalds, to the number of some 400 or 500, under command of the Jacobite Lord Duffus[1] of the Sutherland family, the son in law of Kenneth 3rd Earl of Seaforth, who proclaimed King James VIII at the Mercat Cross.

In 1686 Duffus had got into some trouble by liquidating William Ross of Kindeace at Invergordon, the defence being that the act was justified by being in self defence and after great provocation, David Ross, of Balnagown maintaining the contrary; however the enquiry that followed rightly or wrongly gave the decision in favour of the accused. Kenneth (Sutherland) 3rd Baron Duffus who as a young man served in the Royal Navy, in which he rose to the rank of a Captain, being wounded five times and made prisoner of war by the French after a gallant action in 1711. He joined the Jacobite cause in 1715 and was attainted the following year. Later he rose to the rank of Admiral in the Russian Navy, being married in 1708 to Charlotte, daughter of Eric de Sioblade, governor of Gothenburg, Sweden. He died in 1734.

The incompetent Earl of Mar, 'Bobbing John', Commander in Chief of the Jacobite forces, then summoned Seaforth to come south with all speed to join the army at Perth; some delays followed, for which Seaforth has been blamed, but it should be remembered that a large Hanoverian force still existed intact, north of the Oykel. Eventually the Mackenzies moved south arriving in time to take an honourable part in the drawn Battle of Sheriffmuir, which owing to lack of any inspired leadership, virtually ended the rising.

The Chevalier landed in Scotland at Christmas, but was not the man to rally a force which had lost all faith in its high command, while the Whigs had obtained reinforcements of Dutch troops. It is not without its humorous side that this party while always the first to raise its hands in sanctimonious horror at any suggestion of the use of Irish or French troops by the Stewarts, never failed to employ great numbers of Dutch and German mercenaries against their own countrymen.

In January of the following year, Perth was evacuated by the Jacobites, James disbanding his army and returning to France, accompanied or followed by many of the chiefs, including in due course, Seaforth who was forfeited till 1740, when his estates were restored, an action which had far reaching results. On this occasion, so insecure was the foreign dynasty in England as well as Scotland, that the government reactions showed an unusual moderation, General Cadogan being stationed at Inverness as the Military Governor. The 1715 Rising was defeated neither by the inadequacy of French assistance, nor the armed forces of the Hanoverian party, but by the lack of any co-ordination or drive by Mar, so that a great opportunity was lost for all time.

Ross settled down slowly but not completely over the next four years,

Note 1. For table of Duffus family see Appendix 1 e/.

while a new tune was heard in her Glens *Moladh Cabar Feidh* written by Matheson, Seaforth's Bard, in celebration of the rout of Sutherland's force in Ross. Having already changed his coat on so many different occasions, it is not surprising to find the arch ruffian Simon Lord Lovat posing as an enthusiastic Hanoverian during the last months of the Rising, and threatening Seaforth's mother the Dowager Countess Frances, with a Fraser invasion into Mackenzie territory unless she would persuade her son to submit. But the lady not only had plenty spirit but had an ally in Sutherland and the appearance of this gentleman coupled with Lady Seaforth's 'contemptuous laugh' reduced Lovat to an unusual silence. The area commander for Ross, who came under Cadogan at Inverness, was General Wightman, who together with a garrison was sharing Brahan with the Lady Frances, at least during those periods when he was not being led a dance over the hills by Clan Kenneth.

For the first few months of 1716 strong detachments of the Mackenzie forces remained embodied despite the somewhat haughty submission made by Seaforth on 30th December: 'Wee, William, Marquis of Seafort, doe promise upon honour to Simon Lord Lovat, commanding His Majesty's forces near Inverness, to disperse and dissipate my men immediately, and to set at liberty the gentleman of the name of Munro detained by my orders, and not to take arms, or appear against His Majesty King George, or his government, till the return of the Earl of Sutherland's express from Court; providing that neither I nor my friends, country, or people be molested or troubled till the said return come from Court. Given at Brahan this 30th of December. (Signed) Seaforth.'

On 20th March a brisk skirmish took place on the summit of Tor Achilty between General Wightman with his dubious ally Lovat and a small force under the Earl of Cromartie and Fraser the Laird of Inchoulter (Balconie) both of whom were taken prisoner.

Wightman on moving in to Brahan had thought fit to confiscate the horses and vehicles so that the Dowager—so she said—was unable to proceed to London to interview the king on behalf of her son, and this give rise to an animated correspondence between her ladyship, General Cadogan, and Simon Lord Lovat now in the capacity of intercessor. Those being of more than passing interest are included here.

Lovat to Countess of Seaforth.

'Madam, I just spoke now to General Cadogan, who told me plainly that he could not, nor would not, promise anything for my lord, your son, further than to receive him on mercy and send his prisoner south, and if the Bill of Attainder be past, as they say it is, it is not in the king's power to save him. This is all I can say on that melancholy head. The general, being informed that my Lord Seaforth's people have not as yet taken in their arms, was going to order a thousand men tomorrow to put all the country in flames, but I begged of his Ex. to give some days to acquaint the people, and that I was sure they would come in, so his Ex. was so good as delay the march of the troops till Saturday next. A thousand men will that day march to Brahan and Coul, and if the arms of all my Lord Seaforth's country do not come in to Brahan and Coul before Saturday night they may expect that the next day the troops will begin to destroy all, and march through all my Lord Seaforth's country to the Isle of Skye, and ships will be sent to the Lewis to destroy it. So your Ladyship should send off expresses immediately to all the highlands that the people may come and give up their arms to save themselves from being burnt. It's a very great favour that the troops do not march tomorrow; so your ladyship should profit of it to save the people and the estate, which your ladyship says is your own. I shall always be proud for an occasion in which I can have power myself to let your ladyship know how much I am, with true friendship and a great respect, madam, your ladyship's most obedient and most humble servant. Inverness, 8th of April 1716. (Signed) Lovat' 'I send you this express at Kincraig, and the E. of Cromartie who was present when I spoke to the general, is to go to Brahan to advise your ladyship. The General likewise bids me give his service to your ladyship, and to tell you that if my lady, your daughter, designs to go south it must be very soon. The General desires me to have your ladyship's answer to all this once this night. I give my duty to my lady Seafort, and my service to good Mr. Douglas, that is so good to your ladyship. If I can I will wait on your ladyship before I go for London, which will be this week.'

Lady Seaforth to Lord Lovat.

9th April 1716.
'My Lord. I'm infinitely obliged to your Lordship for the concern youre pleased to have in saving my people and lands. I have now ordered expresses to all the parishes, that the people may with all speed deliver their arms, and those in the neighbourhood are given up already. If I had a conveyance my daughter would surely go off this week. I entreat, therefore, your Lordship to speak again to General Cadogan, whose civility I shall never be able sufficiently to acknowledge. I am with a true sense of your friendship my Lord, Your Lordship's most obliged humble servant.'
'The Earl of Cromartie was at Coul at night, but is expected here

this forenoon, and then your Lordship shall be further informed if needful.'

General Cadogan to the Countess of Seaforth.

Inverness, the 10th April, 1716.

'Madam, I received the honour of your Ladyship's letter of the 9th instant, and am very sorry it was not in my power to get your ladyship's coach and horses restored. As for the two gentlemen that I left out of the passport, there are so many informations given against them by all the well-affected people in the country, that so far from granting them a pass, were it not in consideration and regard to your Ladyship, I should immediately order them to be made prisoners. But if your Ladyship pleases to name any two gentlemen who have not been in arms, I shall be ready to consent to their waiting on my Lady Seaforth on her journey to Edinburgh. I hope all your ladyship's tenants will be so much friends to themselves as to forthwith bring in their arms, and thereby prevent their being forced to do it by military execution. I beg your Ladyship to believe I shall always be very glad to show the profound respect with which I have the honour to be, Madam, your Ladyship's most obedient and most humble servant, William Cadogan.'

'I send here enclose to your Ladyship a protection for Your house and estate of Brahan.'

William Cadogan, Esq., Lieut-General and Commander-in-Chief of His Majesty's forces in North Britain. All officers and soldiers of His Majesty's Army in North Britain are hereby required not to commit any disorder, nor to take any goods, cattle, or corn in the house or on the estate of Brahan, or any other belonging to the Right Honourable the Countess Dowager of Seafort.

William Cadogan.

Given at Inverness, 10th April, 1716.

Lady Seaforth to General Cadogan.

'Sir, That I should be still troubling a gentleman of so much honour and known civility is to myself very mortifying, but the dayly distress I meet with, norwithstanding the protection your Excellency was pleased to send me, makes me the most uneasy person in the world.

Yesterday Colonel Brooks came hither with I think, 400 men, besides the garrison, and Colonel Munro's Independent Company, who I hear, are to quarter at Brahan till all the Highlanders give up their arms. It's surely hard that I, who have been so long a widow, should, without any offence given to King or Government, be the only woman in Britain so much harassed. The arms might be delivered up at

Inverness as well as here; for my diligence in sending to my tenants reiterated positive orders has appeared to the officers of this house by the delivering up of all the arms within a dozen miles of this, and by letters promising the rest at a further distance to be delivered up with all speed possible.

I got not last year £50 of £1000, which is my joynture; and the tenants and country are now so impoverished that I can expect nothing from them. Nay, I can scarce get bread to my family and the few officers that are with me.

This being my condition, I must beg of your Excellency with all earnestness speedily to compassionate the same, which will be a true act of generosity, and the greatest favour you can honour one who is with the highest esteem of your goodness and with the utmost respect, sir, your Excellency's ever obliged but most afflicted servant, F. Seafort. Brahan, 14th of April 1716.'

General Cadogan to Countess Seaforth.

Inverness, 20th April 1716.

'Madam, I received last night the honour of your Ladyship's letter of the 14th inst., and am very sorry to find by the accounts sent me by Coll. Brooke that not the tenth part of the arms of my Lord Seafort's people are yet brought in. The great desire I have to do your Ladyship all the service I can, obliges me to acquaint you that this trifling and amusing the Government will be more resented at London than open resistance, and will not leave it in my power to serve your country any longer. I shall, however, in your Ladyship's consideration, order the detachment to halt till Tuesday next, and if by that time all the arms are not delivered up, I shall be under the necessity of ordering the troops to proceed with the utmost severity against your son's people, and employ fire and sword to reduce them, of which I would have your Ladyship to give them forthwith notice in the most public manner. If they continue obstinate after this warning, it will be their own fault, and not mine if they are destroyed. I thought if further necessary to acquaint your Ladyship that Coll. Clayton is with a detachment of a thousand men towards Eilandonald, on the extremity of my Lord Seafort's country, so that his people are now surrounded on all sides. I have the honour to be, with the greatest respect and venetration, Madam, your Ladyship's most obedient and most obliged humble servant, William Cadogan.'

Seaforth at this juncture, getting no help from outside, might have given up the struggle, had not others, the chief of whom was Huntly, persuaded him otherwise, with the result that the Chief assembled a new force in the Island of Lewis, which was however dispersed by a government force under Col. Cholmondely. Campbell of Ormundel who had been with Seaforth was captured but the Earl managed to make good his escape to France. Things quietened down but the gentlemanly Cadogan got but few of the arms, for apart from his reluctance to cause bloodshed he knew only too well that the still organized Highlanders would certainly knock spots off the heavy footed yokels in red coats if they got embroiled in the mountains of Ross and Cromarty.

The Highland soldier, before he conformed to the stereotyped military pattern, was the most mobile fighting machine in the world, sensibly clad, no transport train except for a few pack ponies, always in perfect fighting condition, and able to live for days while covering great distances and fighting on a very small quantity of oatmeal; neither was he tied to any base. Much rubbish has been written about his indiscipline, possibly because his spirit and natural intelligence precluded the possibility of inculcating the wooden and brutal methods of control favoured by the 18th century, which left little room for initiative or indeed anything but a blind unthinking obedience. A system not without the excuse of necessity when a Regular Army was made up to so great an extent from the sweepings of the cities and jails, teutonic mercenaries, and those English yokels whose wits had proved insufficiently active to keep them from the clutches of the recruiting sergeant. It would be truer to say that seldom were the supreme leaders of Highland troops, in any major campaign, worthy of the men they commanded, while to revert once more to this question of discipline, let us for a moment recall some facts.

The Bruce had an army which it is now acknowledged, was the best disciplined of its day, this army, as we saw was to a very large extent a Highland one, especially during the toughest part of the struggle. Montrose, who had vision, and the gift of leadership, knew that in his Highlanders he had the best infantry of the 17th century, a fact which had already been recognized by the military genius of the Thirty Years War, Gustavus Adolphus of Sweden. Yet another of the noble House of Graham, Dundee, knew how to use this dynamic weapon against whose charge no infantry could stand, provided the co-ordination and sympathetic control was there to keep the living flame in check till the right moment.

The normal method of attack by a Highland Company or Regiment was as follows: the men drawn up in lines two or more deep depending on the ground, discharged their muskets which were then left on the ground for collection later; then with one yell the lines charged in complete silence, their targes held before them and their broadswords levelled at the throats of the enemy over the edge of the targe. That the Highland soldier found his element in the attack, rather than the more passive and wearing defence, is true; the Celt with his active imaginative mind finds it very difficult to assume that invaluable, if cowlike stoicism; he may sometimes get depressed and unhappy, often for no very obvious cause, but even this could be overcome by the right man.

As a result of a treaty the Chevalier's Court had been obliged to move from St. Germains to Spain and from here in 1719 another futile attempt to restore the king to his throne was made with the aid of Cardinal Alberoni the virtual ruler of Spain then at war with England. The Duke of Ormond attended the conference which planned to land a force of 6000 Spanish troops on the English coast while as a secondary stroke some six companies of Infantry under Don Alonso al Santarem, 5000 pistoles in money and 2000 stand of arms were to be landed in the Highlands. Both the expeditions started but the first and main force were driven back to Spain by the usual storms, the second which had on board the Earl Marischal, Seaforth, Tullibardine, Mackenzie of Coul, Campbell of Glendarale, set out from San Sebastian on 19th March 1719, and slipping past the blockading fleet succeeded in reaching the Lewis. An unfortunate quarrel broke out over the question of command between Keith the Earl Marischal, and Tullibardine, the former returning to Spain, so that once again we see any chance of success being frittered away by incompetent command, while delay destroys the only Jacobite advantage of surprise.

Not till the middle of May did the force cross to the mainland, disembarking at Lochalsh and concentrating at *Eilean Donan*, the castle being used for a depot and powder magazine. At this time the old fortalice had a flat roof, on which an old contemporary picture shows some of the Highlanders dancing, the night before the Battle of Glenshiel. From here the Jacobite force, Spaniards and Clansmen from Lewis and Kintail moved into a camp of temporary huts in the Pass of Glenshiel, where they heard for the first time of the failure of the main expedition and of the presence of three enemy men of war in Lochalsh.

Capt. George Munro I of Culcairn was in government service when General Wightman received orders to move west and repel the Spanish invasion; but to do this the general had to reach Glenshiel, and although he had now been in the country since 1715 could rely on none of his own troops to get him there safely without the aid of guides, but these he failed to get. Finally Culcairn, in the absence of his elder brother Robert, employed 1716–24 in a civil capacity as Commissioner of Inquiry into the forfeited estates, assembled the Clan and marched west with the Regular forces, some 1600 strong.

The Hanoverians arrived at the foot of the Pass of Glenshiel on

14th June and found the Highlanders well posted and reinforced by a few Murrays and one company of MacGregors under Rob Roy, an addition that made the numbers of the two opposing forces equal. The route through the Pass followed the line of the burn which was commanded by the hills on both flanks, the Spaniards being posted fairly high up in order to give them a clear field of fire while below them were the Mackenzies, MacRaes and Murrays; Rob Roy's Company being placed to form the spearhead of a counter-attack. Neither side showed any desire to move till eventually Wightman attacked at 1700 hours, being met with an effective fire from the Spaniards and an attack by the MacGregors which lost some of its impetus due to well directed enemy fire from their flank. Meanwhile some of Wightman's force, probably the Munros, had succeeded in getting above the Spaniards, who having little stomach for a real fight so far from home, gave up the struggle. For three hours the Highlanders launched attack after attack which stopped any further advance of the enemy, but numbers were now very unequal, owing to the elimination of the Spaniards, and casualties mounting up. By nightfall except for the withdrawal of the Spaniards the position was unchanged and the pass still sealed; Seaforth, Tullibardine, and Lord George Murray were badly wounded and their troops because of casualties few on the ground, so that it was decided to disperse.

During the night the Highlanders melted into the hills, taking their wounded with them, while the Spaniards capitulated the next morning. On the opposite side, Culcairn had been badly wounded in the thigh and while lying out under a heavy fire had been saved from death by his very gallant *gille*, who placed himself between his master and the bullets. Thus ended another rising, with the death of some very brave men in a cause made hopeless by lack of leadership at the top.

The grand old castle of *Eilean Donan* some six hundred years old, but a great deal older if we take into account the ancient *Dun* from which it grew, had laughed at the bombardment by the men of war, but was blown up by Wightman with the great store of powder placed there by the Jacobites. Even this did not totally destroy the building, so that two hundred years later a MacRae was able to utilise what remained as the basis of its reconstruction.

Seaforth returned into exile, the country settled down, and we find Cromartie once more leading a quiet life at Tarbat and Castle Leod, appearing as Provost of Dingwall, a town since long a Mackenzie stronghold. Munro of Culcairn got command of one of the Independent Companies in 1729, ten years later to be known as the Black Watch commanded by his brother, Lt. Col. Sir Robert Munro, both of whom we shall meet again after their service in Flanders which lasted till 1744.

CHAPTER XIX

A RENT COLLECTION IN 1720—WADE ROADS—A SURRENDER OF ARMS—THE YORK BUILDING COMPANY—THE BURGHS—RESTORATION OF A FORFEITED ESTATE—SIR ROBERT OF FOULIS—THE LAST FLING—DEFEAT—THE BLESSINGS OF CIVILIZATION ARRIVE

Chronological Table

1723	Agricultural Society formed.
1724	Duncan Ban MacIntyre, great Gaelic poet born.
1725	Disarming Act.
1726	Potatoes introduced to Scotland. Wade's Roads begun.
1727	Birth of Jean Elliot, authoress of The Flowers of the Forest. The Whigs introduce Penal Laws and a tyrannical subjugation of Ireland of which there was to be only brief alleviation under the anti-Whig George III, till repeal of the Penal Laws in 1829, but the Irish peasantry were to remain in a state of serfdom thus created for yet another sixty years.
1728	Birth of Robert Adam, the architect, in Aberdeen.
1735	Birth of Scottish poet Robert Graham of Gartmore. Died 1797.
1743	Dettingen.
1745	Jacobite Rising. James VIII and III proclaimed king in Edinburgh. Victory of Prestonpans. March to Derby.
1746	Victory of Falkirk. Defeat of Rising at Culloden. Systematic destruction of Highlands. Disarming Act. Act forbidding the Highland Dress. Penal laws against Episcopalians. English government offer £30,000 for head of Prince of Wales (Charles Edward Stewart), but find no takers. Simon Lord Lovat, Lords Balmerino and Kilmarnock executed. Earl of Cromartie forfeited and exiled.
1747	Birth of John Paul Jones in the County of Kirkcudbright. He settled in Virginia, in 1775 became a famous American sailor, successfully attacking British shipping, especially on our own coasts. After the Wars became Admiral of Russian Navy which he led against the Turks. Died in Paris 1792.
1748	Abolition of Heritable Jurisdictions.
1753	Founding of Glasgow Academy of Arts.
1754	Pitt Prime Minister.

The great Seaforth Estates were forfeit, so that the rents thereof belonged, in theory to the crown, though in fact a very large proportion of them went to the exiled Chief, thanks to the loyalty and affection of the clansfolk, as well as Seaforth's courageous model Commissioner, or Factor, Donald Murchison, whose family for many centuries had served so faithfully the House of Kintail. Donald and his brother John, the great-grandfather of the celebrated Sir Roderick Murchison of a later age, were both out with their chief during the '15, but remained in the country after Glenshiel where they might still serve both chief and clan.

Two attempts were made by the Commissioners of the forfeited estates, to extract the Kintail rents and in 1720 William Ross of Easterfearn ex-Provost of Tain and Bailie Robert Ross of that Burgh, had the temerity to undertake the duty of Stewards of the forfeited Seaforth, Glengarry (MacDonald) and Strathglass (Chisholm) estates. On making it known that they intended to hold a rent collection in the various districts, these gentlemen received a politely worded message: that since gold and silver was remarkably scarce in those districts, the rents would have to be paid in lead and that the collectors might find the process a little dangerous to themselves. In spite of this ample warning Messrs. Ross set out for Invercannich in Strathglass and

Kintail, accompanied by some relatives and an escort of thirty redcoats, who were reinforced at Knockfin by fifty more from Bernera Barracks, under Lieutenant Brymer. Meantime rumour grew apace that the path in front was infested by desperate MacDonalds, Camerons, and Chisholms, followed by the information that the pass itself was held by Donald Murchison himself with 300 men all armed with excellent Spanish muskets. But relying on the soldiery and the Sassunach law the party moved on from Knockfin at 4 a.m. on Monday October 2nd, after a 12 mile march, coming in sight of the pass at a place known as *Àrd-na-mullach*, where the River Affric reinforced by the *Allt-na-cioch* drives through a narrow gorge into the Loch. Between this and a cliff held by Murchison, the path wound its way, being at this spot so narrow that only two men could walk abreast. Murchison was no killer or he would have exterminated the party, a procedure strongly recommended by a party of Camerons, accordingly the interlopers were brought to a halt by a volley delivered at long range, but this proving insufficient to stop their advance another volley was fired, bringing down the ex-Provost wounded by two balls, his son Walter who was mortally hit, and the Bailie's son, less seriously injured. The military fired quite ineffectively, then beat a hasty retreat, un-molested by anyone, leaving the Ross family as prisoners with Donald Murchison, who treating them with every courtesy, relieved them of their estate papers, as also a promise to withdraw from the job of government stewards. He then personally conducted them past the rather disappointed Camerons, setting them on their road for home, which they reached safely after burying poor Walter at Beauly Priory.

Some time later a further attempt was made by the government to collect these rents, this time with a party of 150 Regulars under a Captain Macneil who followed the longer but safer route via Dingwall, Contin, Comrie, and Strathconon. But of course Donald had had ample warning which enabled him to take up a strong position across the route, an attack by the redcoats was laid on only to meet utter defeat after breasting the first slope. After a few casualties they gave up, retiring back to Inverness where their own and similar failures by others were reported to General Wade, Commander-in-Chief in the north, who like most Englishmen could not understand the bond of loyalty and affection which existed between all ranks in the Highland Clan system, and naively writes: 'The tenderness the subjects in North Britain have for each other is a great encouragement for rebels and attainted persons to return home from their banishment.'

Apart from these incidents peace reigned, while considerable improvements were taking place in the world of agriculture and forestry; Wade was building his military road over the Grampians, which was to shorten the way to Edinburgh and the south, cutting

out the old route running east from Inverness through Moray and
Aberdeenshire. The roads of Ross were still in the main elementary,
though the Statute service road Act of 1720 was to bring into existence
a few improvements during this century, such as the Dingwall–
Strathpeffer road constructed by the Cromartie family. The main
north and south route was very rough, with few bridges, and not till
the end of the century was this important road to be given any great
attention; though to imagine that the chiefs, chieftains and Lairds
were averse to roads and bridges is very far from the truth, a fact made
amply clear by their contributions toward both amenities.

The arms difficulty was now brought to some sort of conclusion—
the honours going to Clan Kenneth, who of course had no intention of
really being disarmed, times were too unsettled, no man knowing what
lay ahead. The heads of Clan Mackenzie, John Earl of Cromartie,
Sir Colin Mackenzie of Coul and the redoubtable Donald Murchison
entered into an engagement that the Clan would accept the de facto
regime; this was followed by a great parade at Brahan, when 800
Highlanders handed over some arms to Wade and Regular troops,
having refused to make this gesture to any Independent Company.
Brahan before it was de-militarised by Wade, beside the battlements
and turrets was surrounded by a strong protecting wall which enclosed a
wide parade ground, facing the existing front entrance. Wade stood on
the steps leading up to this entrance and received the Chieftains and
some fifty tacksmen, while the Highlanders marshalled by Parishes
marched in fours down the Long Avenue, past Wade, the arms to be
given up being carried on garrons and deposited near the General.
As the men passed refreshments were supplied in which to drink the
health of the 'Wee wee German lairdie' (King George), after which
they passed on to their homes, probably with some jokes with reference
to the motley collection of arms handed in—swords and spears of
Bannockburn and Flodden vintage, no longer of much service value
though a sad loss from the family heirlooms. The following year
Seaforth received a pardon under the Great Seal, though no provision
for his maintenance was made for some time to come.

In complete contravention of Scots Law as well as the legal clauses of
the Act of Union, the forfeited estates were to be sold, by the government to an English speculative company known as the York Buildings
Company; but once again this ploy was brought to nought by the Clan
Mackenzie and the community in general, who by enclosing the
property with a network of debts and old family settlements produced
such a situation of chaos that the Commissioner could extract only
fractional spoils. The Scots lawyers were, needless to say, highly
delighted at the failure to sell Scottish property as if it were contraband
merchandise, and an act was passed re-adjusting the position of all

Scottish estates, in the new hands to which they passed, to the dominion of the old Scots feudal law. So the government still had the Seaforth estates on their hands, which in 1741 were restored to Lord Fortrose, Seaforth's son and heir at law for the sum of £22,909. 8. 3½d. with the burden of an annuity of £1000 to the stout hearted Frances the Countess Dowager. This act of grace by the Hanoverian government was to pay them a useful dividend in the future, as was doubtless foreseen by that astute but honourable politician Duncan Forbes of Culloden the Lord Advocate and later Lord President of the Court of Session, who had pressed so hard for this action.

John Earl of Cromartie after a somewhat disturbed life, married successively daughters of the Aboyne, Elibank, and Lovat families, died in 1731, and was succeeded by George, his eldest son, to Lord Elibank's daughter. The 3rd Earl married a very lovely lady, the daughter of and heiress of Sir William Gordon of Invergordon, who was to play a romantic part in the last Jacobite Rising.

Let us now take another look at our small but important towns. The Burghs of Ross had changed but little in appearance since their early foundation. The homes were still mainly wooden structures, or, as in the Tain of 1789, clay with the corners, windows and doors finished with hewn stone. But during the late 16th, 17th and 18th centuries there were a few good looking houses of local rubble, harled or rough cast and limewashed, with steeply pitched crow stepped gables which became lower during the 18th century. These houses were built for the richer merchants or as town houses for local lairds or chiefs.

Probably the finest belonged to the Churchmen of Pre-Reformation times, a beautiful example being the Bishop's Palace at Dornoch in Sutherland; the latter buildings are remarkable for the exceptional size of their 'crow stepping', a characteristic that died out after 1560, and it is probable that of all the Burghs in Ross the combined twin Royal Burghs of Rosemarkie and Fortrose were the richest and most cultured around 1455. All these houses were primarily functional, but the work of natural artists; sometimes stair turrets were used, always excellently proportioned, the completed building being quite unlike the architectural monstrosities of the 19th century with their baronial halls for business barons, and the highly respectable villas with applied turrets which deface so many of Scotland's Straths and Glens. Such extraneous decoration as there was consisted of: initials of husband and wife, dates, coats of arms, or trade insignia above the door or carved on every variety of pediment over the attractive dormer windows; sometimes a sun dial was added, being built into a corner of the building.

The centre of civic activity was, and still is, the Tolbooth, in early days a simple tower for defensive purposes, but changing during the 16th and 17th centuries into a tower with ornamental rather than military qualities. The tolbooth of Tain is a good example of the transitional tower being built, or rebuilt about 1600. Part of Dingwall's structure dates from the same period but has suffered considerably from recent alterations; during the latter part of the 18th century it developed a spire, a characteristic transition of this period. The tolbooth as well as being the administrative centre for the Burgh was also the jail; here were kept the standard weights and measures, sometimes the public weighing beam, or Tron, for weighing merchandise, the Jougs, an iron collar made to padlock round the offender's neck, and attached by a strong chain to the tolbooth wall.

The main street of the Burgh was the High Street, a wide thoroughfare flanked by all the buildings of importance. From the High Street sometimes opened other streets called Gate or Gait (Way or Road), and the smaller streets known as Wynds or Vennels (from the French Vennelle a very low part of the city), often very narrow and steep; the Burgh of Cromarty has both a Big and Little Vennel. Still smaller passages were the closes, usually giving access to several houses, workshops, also the communal doo'cot; they led under the buildings on the High Street into a court, on to which opened the front doors of the back houses; while beyond the court lay the gardens and Kailyards. At night the close entrance was secured by an Iron Yett or wooden door, while some form of barrier existed to block the entrances to the Burgh, known as ports.

Although the Burghs were seldom walled the big Back Dykes (dry stone walls) which surrounded the back gardens, each wall being in alignment with the next one, provided a formidable obstacle to all but organized attack. Beyond these dykes lay the town common, for grazing, and, before firearms became common, the Bow Butts. In seaboard towns such as Cromarty, Dingwall, and Stornoway, which had harbours, the street that ran by the quay was known as the shore, a name still existing at Cromarty and Stornoway. As in all towns the dirt of ages accumulated within these Burghs, very little being done to rectify the matter, though frequent fires among the old wooden houses helped to keep down infection. During the 17th and 18th centuries it became customary for all householders in Dingwall to keep a sty of pigs either in the back garden or on the High Street, a state of affairs which continued till about 70 years ago, which must have added considerably to the general mess. It is true to say that a condition of filth existed in towns which was never tolerated by the people of the country proper, and the greater the town the greater the filth, the classic example being London throughout the middle ages, and to only a slightly lesser degree until the second half of the 19th century.

The political life of the country now centred, to a very great extent, round the Burghs, as already indicated, both by the examples of election events in Dingwall and Fortrose during this century of political chicanery, and the actions of Sir Robert Munro 6th Bart. of Foulis, the 24th chief, with his brother Captain George of Culcairn during the second Parliamentary elections since the Act of Union. Both these men were to die a violent death after a full political as well as military career.

Sir Robert, born in 1684, educated at Edinburgh University, had joined the Earl of Orkney's Regiment as a Captain, transferring, by 1705, to the Royal Scots in Flanders and serving with this Regiment under Marlborough till 1712, when he returned home to represent the Wick Burghs until 1729. As a young man he appears to have acted for his father in the capacity of governor of Inverness Castle after its evacuation by Mackenzie of Coul in 1715. He fought at Fontenay where he commanded the Black Watch, with distinction, though 'His great corpulency was such that when in the trenches he had to be hauled out by the legs and arms by his own men'. In spite of presenting such a wide target, he seemed bullet proof and a spectator was heard to say that his invulnerability to enemy fire when exposed to a volley 'was almost enough to convince one of the truth of the doctrine of pre-destination'. After the defeat of Fontenoy his Regiment fought a fine rearguard action 'being the only Regiment that could be kept to their duty'.

His marriage to Mary Seymour nearly fell through on account of the unchivalrous conduct of a political opponent somewhere near Inverness, who waylaid his love letters in transit from Foulis to Dorset-shire, but luckily a meeting between the two lovers in London saved the situation by clearing up the mystery of his negligence. Sir Robert was soon to prove himself the better gentleman as in 1715 when he discovered that the letter thief's family were on the proscribed list, the man himself being in hiding, Munro went out of his way to save the house and property for this Jacobite's lady, requesting her to 'tell your husband that I have now repaid him for his interest in my correspondence with Miss Seymour'.

Culcairn also had nearly lost his future wife, but for a different reason; the lady of his choice, Christian daughter of John Munro of Tearivan, 'Heiress of the Creel', had been left an orphan at a very tender age, in 1705. The baby was reputed to have inherited a consider-able fortune so that certain Mackenzies formed the plan of kidnapping the child for marriage at a later date to one of Clan Kenneth. However this plan was defeated by the family nanny who quickly placing the, luckily, silent baby in a creel and covering her with cabbages, set off with the creel on her back, marching down the avenue under the noses of a body of Mackenzies riding up to the house, thus she delivered her charge for safe keeping to Foulis castle.

By 1740 the Whigs seemed to be securely in the saddle, while the highly misleading propaganda poured out by Wodrow, Defoe, Walker, and the Kirk who controlled education, had undermined the appeal that the Stewarts possessed for the people. Politics were now distant intrigues which happened in London so that the men who once led Scotland turned to their farms, and lands, trade, or scholarship, all of which were once again blossoming out in improvements, more advanced methods, and thought. Satisfactory so far as it went but leaving the future of the Scottish people in unsympathetic or unscrupulous hands, paving the way toward the hellish slums of Glasgow and the virtual enslavement of thousands upon thousands of future factory workers, including both women and children.

Prince Charles Edward the son of King James VIII had grown to manhood, ready in 1744 to seize on the French offer of an expeditionary force of 10,000 men commanded by Marshal Saxe, the best soldier in Europe—once again the Whig winds shattered the transports and France refused to make a second attempt. Charles decided to try alone, and with seven men landed at Eriskay in late July, raising the Royal Standard at Glenfinnan on 9th August 1745. The venture was a wild one, yet wilder ones had succeeded in the past, but guns, now more important than of yore, were missing, while the leaders—as usual— were pulling in different directions. But the crucial difficulty was the changed times, the spirit of adventure was finding new outlets, while idealistic causes were less popular, so that out of a possible 22,000 or more Highland claymores from Jacobite Clans, the Hanoverian Clans account for another 8000, Charles' total force never exceeded 9000 of which 3000 were Lowlanders, Irish, English and French.

Yet how nearly did the last blow for Britain's rightful king succeed! On the 11th September the Jacobites crossed the Forth taking Edinburgh unopposed, while at Prestonpans on the 21st the government forces under Sir John Cope were smashed in fifteen minutes losing 1200 killed and wounded on the field and 1800 prisoners, the remainder flying south headed by their commander. For six weeks the Prince occupied Edinburgh, re-equipping his army and increasing his small force with many Highland but few Lowland recruits. During this period of waiting as through the whole campaign, the behaviour of the Prince's army was exemplary, a fact admitted by the more reliable Whig historians and chroniclers of this period; while six months later a 'civilized' army under Cumberland, made up in no small measure by Dutch and German mercenaries, was to perpetrate the vilest atrocities ever to shame English arms.

The Prince had reached Derby and London was in a panic with German George II packing his bags preparatory to returning to Hanover; but few English recruits were coming in to join the Jacobite army, the squires so ready to drink the health of the king over the water,

I

loved best their security and money bags, preferring to wait on the fence for a 'fait almost accompli' before risking anything. Here was an occasion for a Montrose to decide on the adoption of desperate measures to meet an apparently desperate situation, and go on, but the Prince, not quite certain of himself was persuaded by the majority of his council, among whom was one traitor, to turn back, and that decision on 5th December sealed the fate of the House of Stewart, though the war was not yet over.

The New Year saw the Jacobite army in Glasgow, still 8000 strong with 19 guns and Aberdeen held for the Prince; while a force under General Hawley which tried to block his way north was utterly defeated at Falkirk on 17th January 1746, but this victory was followed by a retreat to the Highlands for the winter, sound enough military strategy, but of very doubtful psychological wisdom, in view of which it might have been worth while to try and hold Stirling. February and March brought some success, Inverness and Fort Augustus falling to the Jacobites, leaving only Fort William as the last Hanoverian stronghold in the north, but the army was getting desperately short of food and stores while the weather worsened, till on 16th April a gallant part of a starving army was shattered on Drumossie *Muir*, Culloden.

The Whig government had been badly frightened, and fear can breed a particularly unpleasant form of 'frightfulness', so that what followed is to some extent understandable if inexcusable. Wounded men were butchered on the field, some by burning alive, prisoners were deprived of all food, clothing and water, while there is ample evidence that the policy of murder, rape and systematic destruction which continued for months under the Duke of Cumberland's leadership was quite deliberate—though, to their honour, some officers, such as a certain Captain Wolfe, refused to carry out the butcher's orders. Neither sex nor age were any protection, nor were the atrocities confined to those Highlanders who had been active in the Jacobite cause, many of the Whig supporting clans and families suffering during the reign of terror, which it was hoped would destroy Scotland north of Forth and Clyde.

To all this was added a bitter and vindictive persecution of all holding to the Episcopal Church, still by far the largest congregation in the Highlands; yet all these savageries alone would never have succeeded in their purpose, far more damaging to a Celtic world was the gradual imposition of an alien system of government and control which followed the abolition of the Heritable Jurisdictions, with their free and human

Note Extracts from a list showing the Compensation paid by the Government in pursuance of the Act for Abolishing Heritable Jurisdiction in Scotland 1747. The Earl of Cromartie £12,000 . . . paid to Barons of Exchequer for the forfeited Estates. The Earl of Sutherland £10,000. Sir George Sinclair of Ulbster £9000. Lord MacDonald of Sleat £4000. The MacKintosh of MacKintosh £5000.

mixture of modified feudalism and truly democratic control, all slowly to be replaced by a hard capitalistic system which was to drive a 'class' wedge into the clan system. This briefly was the course of the last stand by an outworn chivalry, on behalf of monarchy, against the forces of a new practical world, governed by and for money, with eventual results to the world that are only now becoming apparent to a re-awakened humanity. We will now see what part was played in this gallant tragedy by the people of Ross and Cromartie.

A few days before the unfurling of the Royal Standard at Glenfinnan, Lord President Forbes resumed, from Culloden House, his active correspondence, on behalf of the status quo, with various heads of the clans including Lord Lovat, the Earl of Cromartie, Seaforth (Lord Fortrose), Sir Alexander MacDonald of Sleat, and Norman MacLeod of MacLeod. His earliest letters to Seaforth dated 26th August are intended to impress upon all these noblemen the necessity of at once going to the aid of Sir John Cope, then on his way north to nip rebellion in the bud.

The great lands of Kintail had recently (1741) been restored to the House of Seaforth and this with the efforts of the Rev. Colin Mackenzie of Fodderty who whisked away his chief to the west as far as possible from his staunchly Jacobite lady, decided Seaforth against joining the Prince, an action which deprived the Jacobite forces of some 3000 men.

With the chiefs of Sleat and Dunvegan the Lord President's appeal to self interest was successful though many of their clansmen joined up of their own volition. The latter chief Norman MacLeod, known as 'The Wicked Man', had some ten years previously been mixed up in a very odd Jacobite plot, being deeply implicated in the abduction of Lady Grange née Anne Chiesly, a supporter of Hanover, who had married James Erskine Lord Grange, a Jacobite and brother of the Earl of Mar. Apart from her political views, she was an irascible woman and thought to be a government spy, especially after being discovered, through a badly timed sneeze, hiding under the sofa, the better to listen in to a Jacobite meeting, being held at her husband's house in Edinburgh. As certain important plans had been discussed at this party, it was decided to remove the lady to some place out of harm's way; her death was duly reported while an empty coffin was buried in Greyfriars. Meanwhile, Anne was travelling north to Skye and the supervision of her jailer Norman MacLeod, but Skye proved too near to affairs so that her lodging was moved to north Uist, then again to far away St. Kilda, where unless she learned the Gaelic she must have remained silent for seven years; from these islands she passed to Assynt, then back to Skye where the poor thing ended a comfortless existence in 1745.

Captain George Munro of Culcairn who had retired from the army in 1744, was in the absence of Sir Robert Foulis acting chief of Clan Munro who like Clan Ross supported, at least in theory, the House of Hanover, George, therefore, with 200 Munros, joined Cope at Inverness conducting this frightened gentleman to Aberdeen, after which duty George returned to Inverness where a mixed force which included some Rosses of Balnagown, MacLeods of Skye, Sutherlands and MacKays were assembled as independent companies.

John Earl of Cromartie had received a letter from the Prince, (see between pages 254 and 255), and cast in his lot for the Jacobite cause, though impressed by Forbes's letters, as well as the warning against the enterprise given to him by John Porteous the Minister of Kilmuir Easter, a grandson of one of Cromwell's troopers, who prophesied that if Cromartie came out, there were people then living who would see the room in which they were talking in New Tarbat Castle 'the most palatial mansion in the north', roofless and abandoned to nettles—a forecast that came true. All that is left of this building—the old 'pit' with vaulted ceiling and entrance, still producing a fine crop of these weeds. Old Lovat, for once chose the losing side, coming out for the Prince, for whom he was to die, very gallantly, on the scaffold in his eightieth year.

Cromartie with his 18 year old son John Mackenzie Lord MacLeod—the courtesy title sometimes used for the heir instead of Tarbat, borrowed from the family Barony connected with *Coigach* and the MacLeod ancestry—and some 800 men from Castle Leod, *Coigach*, and Tarbat with sympathizers from Dingwall and elsewhere, rallied for the cause, but owing to the presence of the government Independent Companies could not yet join the Prince. Lord Loudoun, now the Hanoverian commander at Inverness, sent off Culcairn and Norman MacLeod of MacLeod with six hundred men to oppose a small Jacobite force under Lord Lewis Gordon, who were operating in the Gordon country; the detachment halted at Inverury near Aberdeen, thus giving time for Jacobite reinforcements to arrive from Perth in aid of Gordon.

On the evening of 23rd December 1745, MacLeod, Culcairn and Captain MacLeod of Geanies, commanding a company of 100 Munros, were surprised, having only just time to post their men, who after a very half-hearted struggle—the MacLeods in particular showing no enthusiasm for the German monarch—retired in disorder, after the loss of some forty men, most of whom were prisoners. MacLeod of MacLeod and Culcairn retired across the Spey into Elgin and Forres where they remained till the Prince had moved south from Stirling, when they rejoined Loudoun, but not with their full force, as many of the MacLeods in the interval returned to Skye as fast as their legs would carry them, being quite out of sympathy with the cause espoused by their chief.

Meanwhile Edinburgh had fallen, the march to Derby was over and at last Cromartie had succeeded in joining his Prince in time for the Battle of Falkirk on 17th January 1746, in which Cromartie's Highlanders played a leading part and young Lord MacLeod 'won his spurs', the battle being commemorated by that fine march 'Wi' a Hundred Pipers and a' and a' '. Among General Hawley's forces was our old friend Sir Robert Munro of Foulis, now commanding the 37th Regiment as for obvious reasons the Black Watch were not taking part in this war. His Regiment was on the left of the Hanoverian line, partaking in the general panic and rout caused by the Highlander's charge, leaving their gallant old Colonel surrounded but fighting heroically with a half-pike, until he was slain, together with his second brother Dr. Duncan Munro, M.D., a man of fine character who had only joined in the campaign out of love for his brother, having had sufficient adventures when he was wrecked off the Malabar coast losing all but his life.

The battle over, the Highlanders behaved as usual with chivalry as is shown by this extract from a letter in which Sir Robert's son and heir Harry Munro tells Lord President Forbes of his father's death: 'That thus my dearest father and uncle perished, I am informed, and this information I can depend on, as it comes from some who were eye-witness to it; my father's corpse was honourably interred in the Church Yard of Falkirk (Kirkmichael) by direction of the Earl of Cromartie; and the MacDonalds, and all the chiefs attended the funeral.' The letter was dated a few days after the battle, the 22nd.

Loudoun's force at Inverness consisted of some 2000 which now included 2 companies from Sir Alexander MacDonald of Sleat, but their outposts at Moy having been routed by the blacksmith of that place, they soon after evacuated Inverness without waiting to be turned out by the Prince, though the Lord President was nearly 'put in the bag' by a patrol sent to Culloden House for that purpose. Loudoun, George Munro and the President, the latter worried among other things by the fact that his nephew was a staunch Jacobite, retired north by way of the Kessock, Cromarty and Meikle Ferrys, intending to establish themselves in the Hanoverian stronghold of Sutherland till relieved by Butcher Cumberland. But the Jacobites were now spreading through Ross, Moray and Inverness, so that Loudoun removed himself from the danger area by going off to Skye.

On or about the 20th February, Cromartie was ordered to go north into Ross and take over the command from Lord Kilmarnock who had been sent in pursuit of Lord Loudoun, young Lord MacLeod with his Mackenzies at once moved off, crossed the Farrar (Beauly) where he found Kilmarnock encamped, from there he marched through Dingwall but on reaching Alness was informed that Loudoun had already passed into Sutherland, taking all the available boats with him. Cromartie now joined his son and with part of their force pushed on to New Tarbat, but were, almost at once, ordered back, leaving the Stewarts of Appin, and the MacGregors at Foulis to collect badly needed supplies for the Prince's army.

On 28th February, Cromartie was at Dingwall with some 300 men and received a letter from Secretary Murray, informing him that Ross of Pitcalnie—the chief of Clan Anrias (Ross)—had undertaken to raise a number of men for the Prince and required Cromartie's aid; a further letter of 1st March says that His Highness does not think it advisable to send any more men north against Loudoun, but that he should remain on the qui vive, as Loudoun's force had recrossed into Ross, but that if he—Cromartie—is forced to retire to remember that the Frasers are in the vicinity of Beauly in support.

On the same day, and from the same writer he had an urgent demand for meal wherewith to feed the troops at Inverness, to which the Earl gave immediate effect by publishing the following:
'Pass and Protection from the Earl of Cromartie.

By George, Earl of Cromartie, Commander-in-Chief for His Royal Highness, Charles, Prince of Wales' Army, north of the River Beauly, and all others whom it concerns, to allow all and sundry, the heritors, tenants, and possessors of the Shire of Ross that are employed in carrying their farm meal, to pass and return from Inverness to their respective homes without any molestation to themselves, servants, horses, etc., hereby certifying that such as countervent them, or give them disturbance of any kind, shall be highly culpable, and punished accordingly. Given at Dingwall this 7th March 1746. Cromartie.'

Then came a letter from Sheridan on the Prince's staff, ordering him to remain at Dingwall which was a convenient base for action north and south, as well as a good centre for foraging, quickly followed by another, this time from O'Sullivan advising the Earl that a Captain Slack was coming north for the dual purpose of paying the troops and carrying out an inspection. Soon after a warning came from Sheridan that a certain Presbyterian minister was about to cross into Ross and should be watched as he was suspected of being a spy for Loudoun, but on 15th March on orders from the Prince, Cromartie moved his forces to Tain. During the stay at Dingwall the Earl was able to reside either at Castle Leod, only four miles distant, or else in Dingwall, where as the Royal Burgh's Provost, he probably had a house of his own.

At Tain the Duke of Perth virtually took over command of this northern force but soon relinquished it again after the capture of two of Loudoun's companies who were taken to Inverness accompanied by Perth with most of the northern force, while Cromartie crossed, with the remainder, into Sutherland, his main body pushing on toward

Little Ferry while his son Lord MacLeod quartered his detachment for the first night in Lord Duffus's house of Skelbo. The enemy, however, were keeping out of the way, Sutherland having disbanded his troops except for one or two companies with whom he had crossed to Banff. MacLeod ranged through Sutherland seeking contributions and recruits, but got few of either, though in Caithness some thirty rather indifferent recruits appeared, but these he civilly allowed to return home. At Thurso, he tells us in his Journal, he was joined by the Balloan and Dundonnell men from Lochbroom who at this rather unlucky stage decided to join up.

Cromartie was ordered to remain in Sutherland, collect what supplies he could, but found little, though he requisitioned the horses from the Dunrobin stables and used some of the leather from the absent Earl's carriages to repair targes—but perhaps his quartermaster was guilty of this! Three days before Culloden orders arrived to rejoin the Prince's army at Inverness; the outlying piquets were drawn in and the small force moved off while Cromartie, his son and the senior officers remained to take a farewell glass of wine with the pro-Jacobite Lady Sutherland. But during the interval, part of an independent company despatched by the Earl of Sutherland surrounded the Castle; Lady Sutherland, thinking to save her principal guest, locked him in her room, but it was of no avail, all being made prisoner; meanwhile, the Mackenzie force, deprived of most of its officers was overwhelmed by a superior force at Little Ferry. The Earl and his men were embarked on the Sloop 'The Hound', which arrived at Inverness two days after Culloden.

Ross to some extent was spared the worst horrors of the aftermath which fell heaviest round Inverness, and in the central Highlands. The story of the Prince's wanderings have been already recorded in many books, how no Highlander, whether Jacobite or Hanoverian in sympathy, could be found to betray the royal fugitive, either for the £30,000 government reward, or to avoid death and torture. After Culloden, one Roderick Mackenzie, one of the Prince's body guards, who bore a close resemblance to Charles Edward, was surprised and surrounded by one of the Butcher's patrols near the Prince's hiding place in Glenmoriston; Roderick fell mortally wounded, calling out 'villains, you have killed your Prince', the ruse succeeded, the redcoats dreaming of the £30,000 left the district with the gallant man's head, only to be violently disillusioned by their Commander-in-Chief. Incidents of a like nature were taking place all over the Highlands, where fugitives were in hiding, and on 31st August 1746, Culcairn while on duty in Lochaber was unfortunately shot in mistake for another less honourable officer.

Tradition says that during his wanderings Prince Charlie passed through *Coigach*; certainly a party of government troops landed at Ullapool, marched through Strathcaniard, burning among other buildings the farmhouse of Langwell and with it one of the Cromartie charter chests, connected with this area. At *Feadar Mór* by Loch Druing, which lies east of *Rudha Reidh*, it is said that a keg of gold, sent from France for use of the Prince, was concealed by occult powers, which every seven years are relaxed so that the keg can be seen by anyone passing at the right moment. The man responsible for the safety of the treasure and the method of concealment was Duncan MacRae of Isle Ewe who having the gift of *sian* could make either people or things invisible. A hundred years later (1846) a woman herding cattle, happened to be passing the time by spinning while seated at the right spot at the right moment and saw the keg, sticking her distaff into the top of the key which was showing just above ground at her feet, she ran home to get help and tools to dig it out; but alas on her return, the period of visibility had again passed, both keg and distaff had faded out of sight.

Maybe the *gille dubh* a dark haired faery who lived in the birch woods round Loch Druing also took a hand in protecting the treasure intended for the Stewarts. This faery was often seen, being recognisable in his suit of green leaves and mosses, as well as his good actions, which included the befriending of a little girl lost in his woods. But ever since five armed men of note conducted a search through the wood for the *gille dubh*, he has not reappeared.

There are many old ruins in this area standing beside the ancient track, among them a cairn at *Druim Carn* Neill, erected to the memory of Neill MacLeod, with whom Black Findlay had a grudge, probably way back in the days of the old MacLeod-Mackenzie *Gairloch* disputes; Neill wounded by an arrow, was followed up with the aid of Findlay's leth chu (lurcher), killed and buried at this spot under the cairn, since when the hill has been known as the *Bac an Leth Choin* or the Lurcher's Bend.

Tarbat Castle was now occupied by Sutherland's forces, for which the Countess of Cromartie and her large family were duly grateful for apart from political differences there was no bad blood between these two families while the Highland soldiery, however keen on lifting cattle, almost invariably treated women with the greatest courtesy. Cromartie and his son were taken south, being lodged in the Tower of London, there to await a form of trial for High Treason, though as no defence was allowed and the court by virtue of the legal clauses in the Act of Union was quite illegal, the verdicts were a foregone conclusion.

However, though just about to have a baby Cromartie's wife rode south and with the help of her brother, Sir John Gordon of Invergordon, Lady Stair, and the most human and cultured of all the 18th century

Hanoverians, Frederick Prince of Wales, (Father of George III) obtained a revocation of the death sentence. The Estates of Cromartie were forfeited, the title attainted, and never again was George Earl of Cromartie to see his native land, being confined for the remainder of of his life to Devonshire. Castle Leod became the headquarters of the administrator for that area while, two other 'gauleiters' took up their abode at Tarbat in the east and Achiltibuie in *Coigach*.

Thirteen months after the trial, Lord MacLeod resolved to strike out on his own in order to do something for his impoverished family; reaching Berlin he was received with enthusiasm by his countryman, Marshal Keith, the personal friend and general of Frederick the Great. The Marshal managed to get a commission for him in the Swedish Army, but the boy being quite pennyless could not equip himself, a contingency which was met by Prince Charles Edward who sent him sufficient funds for this purpose. For twenty-seven years he served the Swedish crown, fighting in the Seven Years War, of which he wrote in his Journal, eventually rising to the rank of General and becoming a Marshal of Sweden; as we shall see he was to win back the home of his fathers.

The new baby—born in the Tower with a small birthmark in the shape of an axe on her neck, survived her mother's heart-breaking adventures, later becoming a Duchess of Buccleuch. But down in Devonshire desperate poverty made it difficult even to feed the very large family, efforts were made by the loyal and ever generous clans-men—desperately poor themselves—to send money south, though it meant a double rent, the official one going to the government; others, kinsmen and old officials, succeeded in selling off much of the furniture and pictures from Tarbat so that the money could be used for the family. Thanks to Sutherland and a Mackenzie kinsman at Meddat, the charter chests, and many heirlooms had been moved to that old farm to save them from a possible Cumberland bonfire, but luckily that 'hun' had gone south.

At Inverness reigned (1751–62) an honourable gentleman and soldier who both admired and loved the Highlander, his name was Wolfe, now a young Lieutenant-Colonel of 25 years of age, who during his spare evenings was attending a maths class, with special attention to algebra and geometry, under Barbour of Inverness Grammar School, to whose teaching Wolfe ascribed much of the credit for his subsequent military career. The subjects taught in the boarding schools of this town included in their curriculum book-keeping and navigation, while since the 17th century there had been a music and dancing school for girls.

As the years passed the neglected Castle of Tarbat, which must have suffered some damage, fell more and more into ruin, thus were Porteous's words fulfilled, and when MacLeod came home again he was to find the cost of reconstruction too great, so used the once splendid mansion as a quarry for the new Tarbat house in 1780. Castle Leod though showing scars was too solid to wilt and safely weathered the generation of neglect; but many of the old trees at both places were rather ruthlessly cut down by the government, though at Tarbat, a great oak in Castle Hill, and a beech 100 feet high, known as 'Queen Mary's Tree' supposed to have been planted by the tragic queen while on her northern progress, proved too heavy to move, the former tree remaining in situ, though prostrate, till recent times.

The 'gauleiter' of *Coigach* eventually died there, but before doing so wrote out for himself a long epitaph for the mighty slab that covers his grave at Achiltibuie; one can only suppose that either he suffered from intense boredom—he was not popular locally—or had a very exaggerated idea of his own perfections. Gradually things settled down, but a new and not so good world was dawning for the Highlands.

CHAPTER XX

THE FORTROSE INN—LIFE IN GENERAL—FORESTRY AND AGRICULTURE—MACLEOD'S HIGHLANDERS— CROMARTIE COMES BACK—MACDONALD'S HIGH-LANDERS—SEAFORTH HIGHLANDERS—SHEEP—EXILES— THE FARM HOUSE

Chronological Table

1756 Seven Years War. Birth of Sir Henry Raeburn, the greatest Scottish portrait painter. Died 1823. Birth of great Scottish road engineer, MacAdam.
1757 First exodus from Highlands to America.
1758 Death of Allan Ramsay, the famous poet and author, and father of the painter.
1759 Wolfe takes Quebec and is killed. Founding of Carron Iron Works. Birth of Robert Burns. Second wave of emigration 20,000.
1760 Raising of more Highland Regiments by Pitt pressed for previously by Wolfe. Publication of MacPherson's Ossian.
1761 Bute Prime Minister.
1762 Birth of Gaelic poet William Ross. Died 1790.
1764 James Watt makes the first practical steam engine.
1766 Death of the Chevalier. James Stewart (James VIII and III) in exile. Birth of Scottish poetess Caroline Lady Nairn.
1769 Building of the 'New' Edinburgh begun.
1770 Birth of Scots poet James Hogg 'the Ettrick shepherd'.
1771 The Man of Feeling by Henry Mackenzie. Birth of Sir Walter Scott. Died 1832.
1773 Highland famine.
1774 Robert Fergusson, the Scottish poet, died.
1775 American War.
1776 Declaration of American Independence. Death of Hume, the Scottish philosopher. Adam Smith's Wealth of Nations.
1778 France enters war. Birth of Scots landscape painter, John Thomson.
1779 Birth of Scots poet John Galt. Died 1839.
1782 American Independence acknowledged. Repeal of Act against Highland Dress. Third wave of emigration, to Canada.
1783 Birth of painter Andrew Geddes. Died 1844.
1784 First Bishop of Episcopal Church of America, Samuel Seabury, consecrated in secret by Scottish Bishops in a backroom at Aberdeen. Highland Society founded. Royal Burghs demand reform. Death of Scottish painter Allan Ramsay.
1785 Pitt's Parliamentary Reform Bill.
1788 Death in Rome of Charles Edward Stewart (de jure King Charles III). Birth of Scots poet George Gordon Byron, Lord Byron.
1789 French Revolution.
1790 Flora Macdonald died.
1792 Repeal of majority of the Acts against Episcopalians.
1793 Execution of Louis XVI of France. The Lewisman, Alexander Mackenzie, crosses Canada.
1794 Volunteers raised for defence against France.
1795 Capture of the Cape (S. Africa) and Ceylon.
1796 War with Spain. Bonaparte in Italy.
1797 Duncan's victory of Camperdown smashes Dutch fleet and mark sturning point of the war at sea.
1798 Battle of the Nile.
1800 Telford starts big programme of road, bridge and pier building in Ross.
1801 Fourth wave of emigration starts.
1802 Birth of Hugh Miller the famous working mason of Cromarty, craftsman, philosopher and scientist. Found the important fossils in the old Red Sandstone round about the Ethie Burn (Cromarty) and eventually became a world renowned geologist. His cottage, a building of the best traditional type, built in 1711 by Spanish gold won by John Feddes on buccaneering exploits in S. America, is now preserved by the National Trust for Scotland.
1803 War with France—Battle of Assaye, in which Seaforth and MacLeod's Highlanders play the leading part.
1804 Invasion threat.
1805 Trafalgar.
1807 Death of Cardinal Duke of York, brother of Prince Charles Edward Stewart.
1808 Start of Peninsular War.
1815 Waterloo.
1822 Opening of Caledonian Canal, constructed by Telford. Birth of Pasteur.
1829 Catholic Emancipation. Emigration continues.
1832 Reform Act. Michael Faraday, the great scientist and electrical experimenter, deposits a sealed letter with the Royal Society. Opened in 1938 it was found to forecast the discovery of electro-magnetic waves.
1837 Highland famine. Accession of Queen Victoria. Separation of Hanover from Britain.

In 1762 the non-jurant Episcopal minister of Leith Robert Forbes was consecrated Bishop of Ross and Caithness. He came north on a visitation of which he has left an interesting account, especially regarding the excellence of Kenneth Mathieson's inn at Fortrose, a description which goes far to modify Dr. Johnson's egotistical gruntings about Highland inns and food supplied by them. The Bishop remarks on the excellent service and plentiful dinner, despite his unexpected arrival. The claret comes in for particular praise, only 2s. per Chopin (1½ pints) while he adds 'but I found out that Mathieson imported it himself, so as to pay no duty'!! His bill together with 'vails' (tips) amounted to only £1. 15s. 4d. which covered the catering for a supper party with seven or eight dishes of the best meat, followed by fruit, good claret, white wine and punch, beside the hire of two servants and three horses from Lewis MacGillavrie at Inverness, for the journey to Caithness. He adds that the provender for both servants and horses was of the best.

While travelling through Ross and Cromarty he would have found the country, with few exceptions, still unenclosed except for the policies round the Laird's houses, in some cases occupied by the agents placed there by the Hanoverian government after the 1745 forfeitures. The kye still roamed at large attended by a herd; such fences as there were consisting of excellently built dry stone dykes which were on the increase.

The kilt and tartan would be absent from the landscapes as, although the more savage and barbaric methods of repression adopted by the Hanoverian government to crush the Highlands had by now been modified, the law prohibiting the wearing the national garb was not lifted till 1782. But southern civilization had not yet succeeded in pauperising or depopulating the Highlands, the chiefs and lairds who had not been out in the '45, and consequently liquidated or exiled, still spent most of their time in their own country attending to estate matters and playing their part in the life of a self-supporting community.

Throughout this century the Gaelic bards were still making great contributions to Scottish culture. Ian MacCodrum of North Uist followed in the footsteps of Duncan MacRury as Bard to the gifted James MacDonald of Sleat who died in Rome in 1766. His '*duais*' consisted of £2. 5s. od. a year, 5 bolls of meal, 5 stones of cheese and a croft rent free for life.

In the Laird's house nearly all the necessities of life were produced on the estate: the flocks and herds supplied a large proportion of the food, also wool for clothing, blanketing and carpets; horn spoons and cups; leather home dressed; and hair for the mason. The flax crop was turned into sheets, shirts and sacking; all beer was home brewed, the bread home baked, while the candles first quality wax, second tallow were still a home product. The excellent gardens supplied all the common vegetables, such as kail, cabbages, carrots and by this time some turnips and potatoes, as well as the usual fruits augmented by the prolific raspberry and cranberry crops. From the Mains came flour, cereals, dairy produce and poultry, while the craftsmen such as carpenter and blacksmith could turn their hands to producing a great variety of useful articles, so that from the outside world came only such things as: brandy, wine, glass, silver, china, crockery, and the more exotic furniture, much of which had come into the principal houses of Ross during this century from France, and tea, a new drink, which had come so much into favour after 1715. The whisky, a very popular tipple, of course a local product, was coming more and more into favour, as the malt taxes ousted the Scottish beer, resulting in a great increase of drunkenness, eventually reaching and then exceeding the insobriety south of the border.

The 18th century Highland gentleman was inclined to be extravagant in his dress, whether in his Highland garb of kilt or trews, or in the universal dress of the period which he wore while in the south or on the continent. His lady not infrequently followed the fashions of France which gave rise to a few complaints from the older generation about undue exposure and the unveiling of, till them, hidden charms. She retained however the silken tartan plaid, a fashion also popular in the southern lowlands, where the ladies had shown a greater loyalty to Scotland's rightful king, than their canny menfolk. Among certain old die-hard Highland Lairds in Ross and Sutherland were some who till 1794 continued to follow the long outmoded fashion of square cut ample coats with heavy broad lapels and huge pockets, wearing instead of a cravat, the old-fashioned stock, despising the voluminous folds of Indian muslin made popular by the Prince of Wales (George IV). They even stuck to the cocked hat and periwig instead of powdered curls, which at this date were also worn by women. For riding they still preferred the boot-hose of zetland fabric which covered their black silks and gold shoe and knee buckles.

Among the Clansfolk the men wore the *breacan a fhéilidh*—kilt and plaid combined, as they had done for centuries, replacing it with blue trews and jacket after the Act prohibiting the wearing of the kilt and tartan, their headgear being a rather shapeless bonnet. All their womenfolk wore a plaid, the married ones being conspicuous with their large white kerchiefs worn underneath, and high white caps. Their dress was of homespun, a home dyed linsey-woolsey gown, the girls wearing a blue flannel petticoat with a white jacket, often without shoes or stockings, but with the plaid gracefully folded, but if they could afford it their sabbath gown resembled that of the matrons except that it was in bright colours, the neck being more exposed and adorned with a necklace of amber beads. An outstanding characteristic was their beautiful hair, which in the spring they washed with a decoction made from the young buds of the birch tree that gave off a pleasant scent.

By the end of the century the Laird's girls went to Edinburgh for part of their education; here they learned the pianoforte, the harp, French, Italian, drawing, writing, ciphering, and ballroom dancing: his boys, before going on the 'grand tour', were taught chemistry, moral philosophy, and natural philosophy, besides Latin, Greek and mathematics. Thus the educational tradition of Scotland was kept alive, for as we have seen the youth of Scotland had been accustomed to seek learning from the scholastic centres of Europe during past centuries; prior to the Reformation going to France and Italy while after that date the great university of Leyden in the Low Countries became increasingly popular. The outlawed Episcopal Church could only function in secret, but even in the south where abstruse theological subtleties vexed the Puritan soul, a more humane spirit was evident, in the Presbyterian Kirk.

A great revival of culture was blossoming in southern Scotland, centred on Edinburgh; James Hogg, the Ettrick Shepherd, Henry Mackenzie, the writer, Robert Burns, Sir Walter Scott, the Allan Ramsays, father and son poet and painter, whose 'Scottish Wit and Humour' illustrations were painted at the Parish Kirk of Cromarty, Sir Henry Raeburn, the greatest Scottish portrait painter, David Allan the artist, the Adam brothers, who carried their architectural and decorating genius to England, Hume and a great school of philosophy, these and many other men and women, were all bringing light and life to an arid desert of endless theological controversy. Even the drama revived, that had lain dead since the days of Mary of Scotland, killed by bigotry and fanaticism.

In the north, despite the upheaval of 1745 and the subsequent years of oppression, a Gaelic revival produced some fine poetry and music; the Kirk in the Highlands remaining immune from the 'hardness' of the south, so that despite fiery sermons of great length, made more tolerable by an occasional dog fight, and the constant use of the snuff mull, minister and flock were a tolerant kindly people. The faery lore, legends, and clan tales told around the fire side at the *ceilidh* did much to soften the humourless and metaphysical teachings which often had replaced the original ideas of Calvin himself. Here in the north as in the rest of Scotland the education of the people was far in advance of that existing among the poorer classes in England. A typical curriculum of any village school in the Highlands of about 1770, in charge of a very well-educated dominie who seldom got a greater salary than £12. a year and grazing for a cow, was Latin, English, Writing, Arithmetic, Book-keeping, Geography, and the first four books of Euclid.

The face of the country was being changed by the introduction of new types of tree, while during this century, at long last, tree planting began to repair the ravages of ages, which had practically wiped out the once great forests of *Alba*. The preceding two centuries had seen some ornamental planting, but on a small scale, while at the end of the 17th the sycamore, lime, acacia and laburnum were added to our varieties. Up till that time there had been few importations, except for the Spanish chestnut, frequently planted by the old monks. In 1728 the Duke of Atholl had introduced the larch, while about this time the silver fir made its first appearance. The spruce, once a native of Caledonia, proved by the fact of its being found in a fossilised form in the upper beds of Tertiary formations, had been re-introduced into Britain from Europe in the early 16th century and now began to appear in Ross to a moderate extent. Brahan, Balnagown, Foulis, Tulloch, Castle Leod and Tarbat, the last two with *Coigach*, returned to their rightful owner in 1784, were the scene of great arboricultural activity which continued into the next century.

The 18th century revolutionised the farming industry: a workmanlike plough replaced the old cumbersome ox drawn machines and the thresher began to replace the flail, though the sickle and scythe remain till the 19th century the instruments of harvest. All implements used on the farm were still the products of local craftsmen, blacksmith, wheelwright, carpenter, etc. The greatest advance took place between 1780–1813. Much land was enclosed, while the law establishing lease-holding introduced by Lord Advocate Grant in 1753 was now in general use, giving much greater security of tenure; also liming and draining went ahead. The in and out field system was dead with its high backed rigs and weedy cornfields. Turnips, clover and potatoes were becoming a major crop and nowhere did the improvements gain ground faster than in eastern Scotland, due in no small measure to the Honourable Society of Improvers founded in 1723 by certain noblemen and gentlemen from every part of Scotland. Their chief service consisted in spreading the reports of their own methods and experiments, with advice on cropping, manuring, deep ploughing, turnip cultivation, drilling instead of broadcasting the corn, fattening cattle under 7 years old, flax cultivation and the making of linen. As more than half of the members were loyal to the House of Stewart, this progressive society broke up after 1745. It was followed by others less successful till 1784, when the Highland Society began its magnificent work, which covered every phase of Highland life, agricultural, industrial, and cultural.

Alas by the beginning of the 19th century the vast herds of hill cattle were giving way to the Cheviot and Blackface sheep, resulting in depopulation and eventually the destruction by bracken and certain grasses of the hill grazings themselves. North eastern Scotland then began to develop an important beef industry, which in certain respects took the place of the old Highland system, though confined to the lower lying farms. The southern shorthorn was developed by

Cruickshank, while the native breeds of black cattle, largely from Ross, Cromarty and Caithness, were developed into the much bigger black polls, by such men as Watson and MacCombie. The Mains—Home Farms—of the landowners were the centres of experiment and improvement till this function was taken over, in great measure, by experimental farms and the Rowat Research Institute of the 20th century. Since the Reformation a more selective breeding of horses had been carried out till by the end of the 18th century the Clydesdale was being sought on both sides of the border and its breeding soon developed in Easter Ross, though it has since been retarded by the prevalence of grass sickness, and since then by wholesale mechanisation.

In the west the Runrig system continued till well into the 19th century, the fields being divided into parcels or ridges corresponding to the number of crofters in the township community; these plots were frequently re-allotted, so that all should have a turn of good and bad. The turnip did not arrive in the north till fairly late in the 18th century, while before 1745, potatoes were a curiosity and a garden crop only, later they were transferred to 'lazy beds' i.e. laid on a bed of turf and covered with inverted turf dug from the trench around it, but this eventually gave way to plough husbandry. Farming was to be further advanced during the 19th century by the introduction of machinery. Fanners replaced the primitive method of winnowing which had consisted of the utilization of flails and wind power on some elevated spot. The use of steam power became common, continuing till in Easter Ross my father's Glen Skiach hydro-electric scheme started in 1902 gave birth to electrical power which, first produced by the Ross-shire Electric Company and now the nationalized board at Loch Luichart, provides power and light from Ross to England.

A new industry in Ross was forecast by a member of a medical branch of the Munro family who had settled at Bearcrofts in Stirling and who in 1772 published a 'Treatise on the Sulphureous Mineral waters of Castle Leod and Fairburn in Ross-shire and of the Salt purging waters of Pitcaithly in Perthshire'. In 1777 Colin Mackenzie, a Factor on the Cromartie estate, erected a wall round the hills to keep out the cattle; in 1819 Dr. Morrison was instrumental in getting the first Pump Room built. The development of Strathpeffer Spa did not, however, assume its maximum prosperity and development till Anne Hay Mackenzie, Countess of Cromartie and Duchess of Sutherland (1829–1888), had inherited the home of her ancestors.

To return to the year 1771, through the intercession of Gustavus Adolphus Frederick, King of Sweden, John, Lord MacLeod, was allowed to return to his native land, his father having died in 1766. He was received kindly and with distinction by George III who by no means a romantic character was yet a vast improvement on his two

Castle Leod

Borodale, Aug. ye 8th 1745

Having been well inform'd of yr Principles and Loyalty, I cannot but expect yr Assistance at this juncture, that I am come with a firm resolution to restore the King my Father or perish in ye attempt. I know the interest you have among those of yr Name, and Depend upon you to exert it to ye utmost of yr Power. I have some reasons not to make any application to ye Earl of Seaforth without yr advice, which therefore desire you to give me favorably. I intend to set up the Royal Standard at Glanfinan on monday ye 19th instant, and then I be very glad to see you on that Occasion. If time does not allow it, I still Depend upon your joyning me with all convenient speed. In ye mean time you may be assured of the particular esteem and friendship I have for you.

Charles P. R.

Letter—Prince Charles to the Earl of Cromartie
17th October 1745

The Eagle Stone

Munro of Foulis

MacDonald of the Isles

LUCEO NON URO

Mackenzies, Chiefs of Kintail and later Earls of Seaforth

Ross of Balnagown

MacRae of Inverinate

Freskyn de Moray

Rose of Kilravock

Fraser of Lovat

Earl of Ross 1370

Urquhart of Cromarty

Earls of Sutherland

Chisholm of Chisholm

MacLeod of Lewis

MacDonnell of Glengarry

Earls of Cromartie

MacLeod of Dunvegan, Skye

Matheson of Lochalsh

predecessors, inheriting the goodness of heart of his father, the anti-Whig, Frederick Prince of Wales. Though home again with his beautiful wife, Majorie Forbes, he was landless, yet the genuine affection with which he was greeted by the people of Cromartie and indeed all Ross was something which he never forgot throughout his life, knowing full well how they had suffered for their loyalty to him and his family.

Meanwhile, Pitt was pressing for more Highland Regiments and it was suggested to MacLeod that this was a service he could perform which might have far reaching consequences, so again he turned to his own folk. He had nothing to offer but a pittance of bounty money, he had no legal or Clan rights, but he could and did speak to the townships and families that might have been his own tenantry, telling them the situation. From Castle Leod, *Coigach* and Tarbat, the old estate of Cromartie, 840 men at once came forward, the pick of the youth from each family; to these were added 236 Lowlanders, 34 Irish and English from Glasgow, thus was founded MacLeod's Highlanders, the 73rd, later the 71st, and then the Highland Light Infantry, since disbanded. Could he raise more men of this stamp? He could, from what had once been his own lands 1800 men came forward to form a second Battalion, the whole Regiment mustering 2200 men, the 1st Battalion commanded by himself, the second by his brother the Hon. George Mackenzie. In 1778 they were passed fit for service anywhere, recognized as being of especially robust constitution—average height 5 ft. 10 in.—and exemplary character.

The 1st Battalion under Lord MacLeod embarked for India in January 1779, taking a year to reach Madras, while the 2nd on the same day disembarked at Gibraltar. Both Battalions gained the greatest glory and renown, during the struggle for southern India against Hyder Ali and subsequently his son Tipoo Sultan, and at Gibraltar where the 2nd Battalion formed part of the garrison during the historic siege. With the resumption of peace the Battalion at Gibraltar returned home, being disbanded in 1784, many of the officers being allowed to join MacLeods Highlanders in India the following year, among them Lt. Colonel the Hon. George Mackenzie.

By 1782 Lord MacLeod had risen to the rank of Major General, this time in the British Army, while his brother George, who later died in Madras, took over command of the Regiment. But in 1783 their Colonel, General Lord MacLeod, returned home after the battle of Conjeveram, in order to protest against the waste of life caused by the action of his superior officer General Sir Hector Munro of Novar, which incidentally had brought about the sacrifice of the two flank companies of his own MacLeod's Highlanders. Shortly afterwards Munro was superseded in chief command by the abler Sir Eyre Coote. On his return home, Lord MacLeod was received at Court with great honour, while the government inspired by Pitt and Dundas took up his pecuniary interests in earnest. By a special Act of Parliament, the Act of Forfeiture was cancelled and the Cromartie estates restored to him on payment of £19,000 to cover arrears and other burdens. The rest of his life he spent very happily among his people, busily planting trees, improving the farms at Castle Leod and Tarbat, where the new Tarbat House was rising from the ashes of the old; but having nothing whatever to do with a new fangled idea which was creeping in, the replacement of human beings by sheep.

In 1789, John Mackenzie Lord MacLeod—de jure 4th Earl of Cromartie, died, regretted by all who knew him, by none so much as his best and truest friends the clansfolk of Cromartie, and other parts of Ross, especially the Burghs of Dingwall and Tain. He was succeeded by his first cousin Captain the Hon. Kenneth Mackenzie of Cromartie who completed the building of Tarbat House but died in 1796, when the estates passed to Lord MacLeod's eldest sister, Lady Isabella Mackenzie, who had married the 6th Lord Elibank (Murray); she, dying in 1801 without male issue, was succeeded by her eldest daughter the Hon. Maria Murray Mackenzie, who married the Hon. Edward Hay of Newhall, brother of the Marquis of Tweeddale, of whom with her son and heir John Hay Mackenzie of Cromartie we shall have something to say later on.

The MacLeod Highlanders received new colours from George III in 1786, changing their number to the 71st, when they became attached to the City of Glasgow, and by a curious coincidence the Lord Provost at that time was a James Mackenzie, whose duty and pleasure it was to welcome them to that great city. In 1809 they became Light Infantry, losing the kilt and bonnet except for their pipers, but still they retained their membership of the Highland Brigade and wore the tartan of Clan Mackenzie. The kilt was later returned to the Highland Light Infantry.

Many Highland Regiments were raised for the numerous wars but the government were very apt to forget their great services during the intervals of peace, and their subsequent treatment was not remarkable for its generosity, fairness or justice. The Highlands Regiments when raised were based on the Clan Regiment; every Highland gentleman of good birth who could raise 100 men became a Captain, 20 or 30 a Subaltern, and since the raising of the Black Watch, the total number of Highland Regiments raised amounted to 50 battalions of the Line; 3 Reserve; 7 Militia; 26 Regiments of Fencibles; while as early as 1763 out of 65,000 Scots enlisted a very large proportion were Highlanders. The north had supplied many, Fraser's Highlanders, led by the son of Simon Fraser, Lord Lovat of the '45, the Regiment that led the way up the cliffs to the Heights of Abraham in Canada, for a man they loved, and who returned their love, General Wolfe, against whom they and their fathers had fought at Culloden.

MacDonald's Highlanders, raised by Alexander Lord MacDonald of Sleat, though he did not serve with them, their commander being Major John MacDonald of Lochgarry; this Regiment was, like others before and since, unlucky, being captured when Lord Cornwallis surrendered to the Americans at York-Town in 1781. During that war Norman MacLeod 20th chief of Dunvegan, while en route to America with his Regiment, accompanied by his wife, Mary Mackenzie of Sudie, was captured by an American warship, both remaining prisoners of war till 1782, during which time he and his wife established a firm friendship with George Washington. Soon after their repatriation MacLeod of Dunvegan was again serving in India, where he gained fame, rising to the rank of General.

In Ross proper, the next Regiment to be raised was the Seaforth Highlanders, the lineal descendant of those Highlanders who had fought for the House of Kintail and Scotland, since the battle of Largs in 1263, and probably long before that, so that well might they bear the *Caber Feidh* in their bonnets with the slogan *Guidich'n Righ* (Save the King). As we saw, Seaforth (Kenneth Mackenzie Lord Fortrose) had not come out in the '45, so had remained in tolerably easy conditions, in possession of his great properties; with his death and burial in the Abbey of Westminster, the titles were restored to his son, Kenneth, in 1771. As a proof of his gratitude he offered to raise a Regiment, so in 1778, 1130 men were embodied, 900 from his personal estates, the remainder coming from those of his kinsmen, the Mackenzies of Scatwell; Kilcoy; Redcastle; and Applecross; 187 Lowlanders, 43 Irish and English; but the most common name in the Battalion was that of those splendid warriors from Kintail the MacRaes.

Thanks to a breach of faith and broken promises on the part of the War Office, a well organized, orderly, yet firm mutiny took place in Edinburgh, just before the Battalion's embarkation at Leith, but through the good offices of certain senior Scottish officers, among them the Earl of Dunmore, and Sir James Grant of Grant, the 'affair of the MacRaes' passed off, the Regiment happily embarking for Guernsey and Jersey. In 1781 they re-embarked at Portsmouth for India, but within sight of St. Helena they lost their chief and colonel, who died, and by the time they reached Madras 247 had died of scurvy, while the remainder were terribly debilitated, so that the few fit men were attached temporarily to their cousins from Cromartie, MacLeod's Highlanders, until their comrades had recovered, when they reformed, moving to Mysore to reinforce the army under General Fullerton. As Seaforth had died, his heir and first cousin, Colonel Humberston Mackenzie, was transferred to take command of the Regiment, being chief of Clan Mackenzie, though without the other titles. The career of the new chief was very short, as he died on 7th April 1783, while on a passage to Bombay, from wounds received previously on board the sloop of war 'Ranger', in an action against a Mahratta fleet. Meanwhile his brother, Francis Humberston Mackenzie of Seaforth, on becoming the Chief raised a second battalion, many recruits coming from the lands of Colonel J. R. Mackenzie of Sudie, the Battalions being numbered 72nd and 78th, the Major of the latter Battalion being Alexander Mackenzie of Balmaduthy, later of Inverallochy and Castle Fraser.

The year 1794 saw yet another Battalion added to Seaforth's Regiment, 560 men coming from the home ground, the remaining 190 from other parts of Scotland, their first action taking place at the capture of the Cape of Good Hope. Both Battalions of the 78th amalgamated in 1796 and the same year the chief of Kintail had restored to him the titles of Earl of Seaforth and Baron of Kintail. Yet another Battalion was raised in 1804, the last one to be influenced by the family of Seaforth in the direct Kintail male line, but by 1817 amalgamation had again taken place within the 78th, leaving the two Seaforth Battalions. As this is not a military history, we shall not follow the long and glorious record of the Seaforth Highlanders, which gained for them the title of the 'Saviours of India'.

But with the memories of 1914–18 and 1939–45 in our minds, let us recall the words of two great men, words which apply equally to the men of Ross and Cromarty, who have served Scotland so well on the sea, on land and in the air. Pitt to the House of Commons 1766, at the commencement of the American War:

'I sought for merit wherever it was to be found, it is my boast that I was the first minister who looked for it and found it in the mountains of the north. I called it forth and drew into your service a hardy and intrepid race of men, who when left by your jealousy became a prey to the artifice of your enemies, and had gone nigh to have overturned the state in the war before the last. These men in the last war were brought to combat on your side: they served with fidelity as they fought with valour and conquered for you in every part of the world.'

Again, during the great Indian Mutiny 1857, after Cawnpore the words of General Havelock to the officers of the Seaforth Highlanders: 'Gentlemen, I am glad of this opportunity of saying a few words to you, which you may repeat to your men. I am now upward of sixty years old; I have been 40 years in the service, I have been engaged in action, almost seven and twenty times; but in the whole of my career I have never seen any Regiment behave better, nay more, I have never seen any Regiment behave so well as the 78th Highlanders this day. I am proud of you, and if ever I have the good luck to be made a Major-General the first thing I shall do will be to go to the Duke of Cambridge and request that when my turn arrives for a Colonelcy of a regiment, I may have the 78th Highlanders, and this, gentlemen, you hear from a man who is not in the habit of saying more than he means. I am not a Highlander, but I wish I was one.'

But '*Mo thruaighe ort o thir, tha 'n caoirich mhor a' teachd*' 'Woe to thee O' Land, the great sheep is coming'! Between 1760 and 1783 from its population of 1½ million, Scotland lost 30,000 to the colonies, a large proportion of whom came from the Highland areas; but worse was to follow, till finally the Highland Counties which in 1801 held 1/5th of Scotland's population, soon supported only 1/20th of her people. The glens, which had provided the finest physical specimens in the British Isles, no way inferior in mental ability to other Britons, were emptied. Let us admit straight away that the Old World was changing very rapidly, the New Countries beckoning with all their unexploited possibilities and resources. Economic re-distribution was essential, but it should, and would, have been with the consent of the Highlander, had not certain things happened during the late 18th and early 19th centuries. By the end of the 18th century the store cattle trade had begun to decline, while wool prices started to rise. It was discovered that the hill and mountain grazings, left in perfect condition by centuries of Highland cattle, would support thousands of sheep. The new century saw the Blackface sheep established as far north as Caithness, while during the 1830's came the Cheviot breed, creeping north to replace the Blackface on the lower and richer grazings, as it was found that the first comers did very well higher up in the more barren and heathery country. This invasion necessitated the formation of vast sheep-runs, providing employment for but few men, as compared to the old cattle and small farm days.

An ignorant and conscienceless government in London proceeded to support a policy of forcible eviction and emigration of crofter and small farmer—except when they wanted Highland soldiers—for the enrichment of certain landowners and sheep farmers. Among these landowners were many who quite honestly thought that they were benefiting their people and advancing 'civilization', a fact made evident by the support given to the clearance policy by that great philanthropic writer Harriet Beecher Stowe, the authoress of Uncle Tom's Cabin. However, we must remember that though, by modern standards, the methods used to bring about the clearances were too often brutal, yet they were no worse than, if as bad as, the treatment meted out to the workers by the factory owners of northern England, or the administrators of the Poor Law elsewhere in that country.

Up to this century we have seen in Scotland something unique in Europe: a system that with all its faults and the failings of individuals, had produced a feeling of mutual respect and true comradeship between Chief, Laird and Clansfolk. No-one in their senses can deny that a changed world economy has to be faced and the necessary alterations made to meet the new conditions; a reasonable introduction of an improved sheep stock was desirable, just as opportunities of free, not compulsory, emigration would have been, not only advantageous to the Empire, but also to the Highlands. It was the methods used, the frantic effort of some to 'get rich quick' and 'devil take the hindermost', which stinks in our nostrils; we may well ask how these most un-Highland characteristics had developed.

The sons of the upper class, who in days gone by had received their primary education with their own people and tenants before going to either Scottish or European Universities, now went to the fashionable English Public Schools where they were brought up in a foreign atmosphere, while learning different ideals, habits of thought, and behaviour. Then also the centre of government and society was becoming London, and London only, so that here was to be found the Scottish aristocracy who wished to keep in touch with their world—political and social. This great city was expensive, becoming more so as the English middle classes became ever more rich and powerful on the sweated labour of factory or shop.

Again many Highland estates were changing hands; the Earl of Seaforth 21st Chief of Clan Mackenzie and Baron of Kintail was in deep water financially, thanks to his friendship with the Prince of Wales (George IV), so that Kintail and other lands were sold by him and a considerable population was replaced soon after by sheep. Loch Alsh had carried a large population, whose cattle grazed the hills east of Loch Monar; Coille *Mór* of Loch Alsh now deserted was the home of 67 families and Matheson of Loch Alsh could raise 700 men from Glen Udalain.

Ross, though by no means the Highland area most depopulated, has its quota of empty glens, which once supported considerable populations. The village and crofts of Achterneed and later the Cnocfarrell and the Heights crofts, on the Castle Leod estate were formed by Cromartie i.e. John Hay Mackenzie of Cromartie, the great grandson of the 3rd Earl of Cromartie attainted and forfeited 1746, for soldiers who on their return from the Peninsular War found their homes in Strathconon blackened ruins. Not only was this policy inexcusable on humanitarian grounds, but it was thoroughly bad business, resulting in many excellent hill grazings eventually becoming deserts of bracken and coarse grass, only partially compensated for by some good hill draining.

The reason for this deterioration was as follows: among the natural fauna of *Alba* were the red deer and wild cattle, the latter as we saw being replaced by domesticated breeds thousands of years ago. The balanced combination of the two kept the grazings in perfect condition as all the grasses were evenly grazed, while if bracken appeared it was soon trodden down or cut by the then plentiful labour, a process that if repeated for three years in succession effectively weakens and checks this beautiful but pernicious plant. But sheep with their selective grazing were not able to do this, instead they further denuded the land of trees and scrub, land already suffering from erosion and lessening of fertility due to the great demand for wood fuel for smelting during the 17th century.

Dean Monro in 1549 mentions that Gruinard Island, lying south of the Summer Isle group (*Coigach*), was covered with birch trees—now there is not a shrub, and similar conditions exist in all parts of the Highlands. The high summer grazings of the cattle had made the winter grazings of the deer, but without the cattle these became jungles of useless coarse grass. This new extractive farming, existing on the capital of fertility, stored in the soil by centuries of a balanced and intensive subsistence farming by a large population, reached its peak in 1870, which was followed by a sharp drop in the price of wool due to Australian and New Zealand competition.

A slow decline set in and deer forests replaced much of the sheep ground, stalking having been popularized by the writings of two great sportsmen, Scrope and St. John, so that sporting rents rose, soon paying the landlords far better than sheep farming. But the sportsmen of late 19th and 20th centuries were apt to prefer quantity to quality, so that by various artificial means the deer population was increased, while the hill grazings steadily deteriorated, together with the standard of deer. Even this was a passing phase, with the development of the motor car, people forgot how to walk, let alone how to crawl; one can only hope that cattle will one day return to the glens, and together with a reasonable stock of both sheep and deer will help to restore their lost fertility, so bringing greater prosperity and larger families to every Highland home.

The dispossessed clansmen went to the new worlds, where they were to play such a big part in the extension and formation of the British Empire. Among 20,000 Highlanders, mostly Jacobite refugees, who had emigrated to America between the years 1763–75, were many from Ross and Cromarty who chose as their new homes the settlements at New York, Delaware, Mohawk, Connecticut Rivers, Georgia and North Carolina; Lady Mary a daughter of the 3rd Earl of Cromartie going to the latter place, where she was twice married. But on the outbreak of the American War of Independence in 1775 these 20,000 exiled Highlanders who had every reason to hate the English connection, yet remained loyal to their Mother country, raising the 84th Royal Highland Emigrant Regiment, and on the conclusion of the war moved en bloc into Canada, though every encouragement was given them to stay and become citizens of the U.S.A.

As the century progressed, ever increasing numbers left their homes forever, the ranks of the clansmen latterly being augmented by the majority of the smaller lairds, tacksmen, a section of the population that Scotland could ill afford to lose, in some cases the ruined chiefs themselves, a tragic poetic justice, the wheel having come full circle. Until the end of this century Canada was their goal and though the mass evictions were things of the past, the exodus continued, New Zealand and South Africa and to a lesser degree Australia, taking a full share of the immigrants. Many of those who had made new homes on our own sea coasts emigrated, as the kelp industry, so profitable during the Napoleonic Wars, was cut out by guano imports, and as the local fishing grounds were monopolised by the steam trawler and drifter.

The population of the Highlands still falls through emigration, drift to the cities, and the desperate toll of war, which always falls so heavily on the Highlanders. Once again he has proved his worth to the world, both in battle and at home; soon, however, he will be extinct, unless it is made possible for him to obtain the just rewards of his toil on land and sea. His children must have the same chances of a good life as others nearer the so called centres of civilization. The men and women of the Highlands must know in the future that if they pull their weight in whatever job is theirs, on the croft and farm, or in their fishing boats, they can be sure of a good and secure home which their children in turn will love.

As we have seen, a real improvement had appeared during the 18th century, both in farming methods and forestry, which continued well into the 19th century. The farm steadings and houses being enlarged or rebuilt, while separate thatched cottages and bothies were constructed for the farm labourers, whose wages were still very small, £6. to £8. a year in 1827. This money payment was augmented by each man having a milch cow grazed with the master's, a patch of land for lint or potatoes, 2 pecks of meal weekly, and free fuel, carriage paid, which might be either coal or peat. At harvest time there were special issues of beer, while a piper was always provided to hearten them at their work.

Inside their cottages, the chief article of furniture was the closed-in box bed, itself like a room, the real room being open to the rafters. The clothes chests were used as tables, around which they arranged low stools, their remaining possessions being: an armoire, cast iron pot, washing cogs, pewter or wooden dishes and horn spoons. Inside the farmhouse many changes were to be seen; instead of the oaken board had appeared a mahogany table; straight backed wooden seats had made way for leather-covered, stuff-bottomed chairs with comfortable backs; and the box bed for a four poster draped with check curtains; the bare floors were now covered with draught-board pattern carpets, while the fire irons were implemented by a coal shovel, and sometimes a fender. Glass was used in all houses, and the farmer's wife had replaced the old Dutch delft, pewter and wooden platters, with Wedgwood ware, china punch bowl and tea sets; while nearly every parlour boasted its small round tea table-cum-tray, which not only could rotate an a central pivot but was made to fold up.

The improved farming has already been mentioned, but from the 1850s on, a decline had come about in forestry. Little good planting was done owing to the importation of cheap foreign timber and high sporting rents. Not till the 20th century did a partial revival come about when the Scottish Arboricultural, Highland and Agricultural Societies, with landlords in Ross and Cromarty, such as Lord Lovat, Lord Novar (Munro Fergusson) and my father, revived the duty of sound planting and forestry, a lesson only partially learned by the government as a result of the last war.

In a book written by Alexander Mackenzie dated 1860, mention is made of one Kenneth Odhar the Brahan Seer, a native of Lewis, who was handed over to the authorities as a wizard and burnt in a tar barrel at Chanonry. This must be a mistake as in a Calendar of Writs, Munro of Foulis No. 92 dated January 23 1577/78, a Kenneth Odhar was tried one hundred years prior, and Hugh Miller of Cromarty also states that Kenneth Odhar lived to a great old age, spending his time wandering the country. Nowhere can the true identity of the Brahan Seer be confirmed, so it may well be that a vast number of prophecies have been credited to him, many of which have come true, as with the doom of the House of Kintail, but not all of which have been pronounced by one man. Whatever the truth of the Brahan Seer, his prophecies are still quoted to this day.

Note Between 1797 and 1837 the Island of Skye gave to the British Army and State: 21 Lt. Generals and Major Generals; 48 Lt. Colonels; 600 Majors, Captains and Subalterns, 10,000 other ranks. 1 Governor General of India. 4 Governors of Colonies. 1 Chief Baron of England. 1 Lord of Session.

CHAPTER XXI

CHANGE—MORE ROADS—FAMINE—THE FULFILMENT OF A PROPHECY—RESULT OF A ROMANCE—HERRING—THE END OF AN ISLAND COMMUNITY—A HOPE

Chronological Table

1843 Disruption of Church of Scotland.
1844 Andrew Lang born.
1845 The Great Famine in Ireland, in a few years population dropped by 2 millions.
1846 Repeal of Corn Laws. Famine in Highlands.
1850 Robert Louis Stevenson born.
1854 Crimean War.
1857 Indian Mutiny.
1860 Lenoir invents internal combustion engine.
1861 American Civil War.
1864 Laws against Episcopalians repealed, the last ones in 1887.
1865 Opening of Highland Railway.
1868 Reform Act (Scotland).
1870 Franco-Prussian War. Sir Ronald Ross discovers cause of Malaria. Death of the Gaelic poet William Livingston.
1874 Patronage abolished in Church of Scotland.
1878 Tay Bridge opened.
1881 Lord Fife demands Scottish Office.
1882 Crofter agitation.
1884 Reform Act.
1885 Scottish Office.
1886 Crofters' Holdings Act. Home Rule Association formed.
1887 Sir Oliver Lodge makes discoveries which make him the pioneer of wireless telegraphy.
1889 First Scottish Home Rule Debate in Parliament. County Councils. National Portrait Gallery opened Edinburgh.
1890 Completion of Forth Bridge.
1894 Local Government Act.
1896 Land Purchase Act carried through in Ireland under Tory rule.
1898 Omdurman.
1899 Start of South African War. Aluminium Age. The Age of Electricity and Aerial transport, Radio-activity and Einstein.
1900 Union of Free and United Presbyterian Churches.
1914–
1918 War with Germany.
1918 Anglo-Irish War till 1921.
1919 Peace Treaty of Versailles. League of Nations. Rowatt Institute.
1921 Signing of Anglo-Irish Treaty and creation of Irish Free State.
1922 Peace with Ireland.
1923 Hitler leader of National Socialists.
1924 Death of Lenin.
1928 National Party of Scotland founded.
1929 Re-Union of U.F. Church with Establishment. Local Government Act.
1936 Abdication of Edward VIII—IInd of Scotland.
1939 Highland Committee Report. Second German War.

In the last chapter, we covered certain events which took place over an extensive period of change, when the Empire was in the making, largely through the agency of Scots, and being held against competitors such as Napoleon, on sea and land. As the 19th century advanced the 18th century intellectual 'Risorgimento' in Scotland gave way to more material interests, which though they advanced science, making available for the world countless new commodities, failed to benefit the people as they should, those men, women and children herded together —far worse than cattle—slaves to an inhuman industry. Yet there were many struggling against this corruption of life and during this century representative government, as an abstract conception was politically a major issue.

The possession of a vote was supposed to secure this, a somewhat naive supposition when we realize that in the 20th century—the vote secured to all British adults—the body elected by that vote gave to the unhappy domestic affairs of Scotland 53 hours in the course of a single year, and this was soon reduced to 16 hours, while in July 1939 a Parliament that had just found ample leisure to discuss pensions for themselves strongly opposed the suggestion that the report of the Highlands and Islands Commission should be granted a single after-noon's debate. This report was based on 2 years study of most vital and urgent problems connected with that area, but of course these 'distant and troublesome people' were of little interest to a 'democratic' body whose main interest is vote catching for their respective parties, even when with much waving of Union Jacks and display of Bulldog pipes, it calls itself a National Government, a title that fooled many honest, patriotic, but not politically minded people. Yet another symptom of verbal activity and practical neglect are the numerous Royal Com-missions held since the 1914–18 war which have been 'filed' while the recommendations contained in their reports have faded into oblivion.

No fair minded man who has studied the retrogressive condition of Scotland as a whole, since 1900, can doubt that the time has arrived for a very great decentralization of Government from London, where, even if given the necessary good will and knowledge of Scottish affairs, pressure of work is now so great that Scotland, with conditions and problems peculiar to herself, can never expect to get her fair mete of sympathetic attention. There is no reason why some form of govern-ment—under the Crown—should not be evolved which would give to Scotland the right to deal with her own domestic affairs while still playing her part in the Great Britain she has done so much to build and defend. Neither can it be of ultimate benefit to our sister across the border to have the Highlands of Scotland depopulated of what is left of a magnificent and loyal stock, while the Lowlands and industrial sections become permanently 'distressed areas'.

Since this was written the Lowlands at least are no longer a distressed area. Belated efforts are being made by Governments to stem the tide of depopulation from the Highlands particularly the west, north west, and Orkney and Shetland. In many cases the change of heart has come too late, especially as the Highland way of life has undergone radical changes in recent years. Only the people themselves with Government aid can, if they wish, alter this trend. The very few remaining repre-sentatives of the original Chiefs, Chieftans and Lairds, with very few exceptions, are themselves financially powerless as they are being taxed out of existence and their estates broken up by death duties—the revenues from which do little to help the area from which they are extracted, being absorbed into the general revenues of Great Britain as a whole.

But to return from the general to the particular. We left Ross and Cromarty producing soldiers for the Empire, while in part of Ross sheep replaced their families, yet in all this welter of tragedy real improvements, as we saw, were coming to pass. Roads and bridges were multiplying, the first serious attempt to use the Statute labour for improving the roads being made by Sheriff MacLeod of Geanies in 1809, but the great road builder of Ross was Telford.[1] Between 1803–1821 the Parliamentary Road from Perth to Wick was constructed at a cost of £540,000, £264,000 of this sum being met out of local assessments. The upkeep of this road proving very heavy, toll-bars were established at suitable points, a system that continued till 1866; here dues were levied on all vehicles and animals using the road, though the drovers with their cattle avoided this by sticking to the centuries old drove roads.

An eye-witness description of a section of this route, between Beauly and Scuddel Ferry (Conon Village) before 1809 is of interest: 'It is in the highest degree dangerous to those who have to pass that way in a carriage. To the extent of a mile, or more, large masses of stone have been thrown up on the road, preparatory, it would appear, to be broken up for mending the road, on either side of which there is barely room left at present for a carriage to pass without the greatest danger of being upset, or knocked to pieces against the rocks projecting from the roadway. Nor is the risk less at the ferry itself at present; the new bridge over the Conon being as yet only passable for foot passengers, and the horse-boat, abandoned by the ferryman, is no longer safe for taking a carriage across . . . etc.'

But two months later all was activity, 2nd June saw an advertisement for a qualified man to make the section from Dingwall to Conon Bridge, offers to Sir George Mackenzie of Coul; while Mr. Innes from Lochalsh started work on the Lochcarran Road; the Dingwall-Alness Bridge section, followed by its continuation north to Easter *Fearn* on the Dornoch Firth progressed, while in October of 1809, the important Conon Bridge was completed. With the opening of this bridge the 'Diligence', a 4-horse coach, at once commenced its run between Inverness and Tain on Mondays, Wednesdays and Fridays, doing the return journeys Tuesdays, Thursdays and Saturdays, a distance of 44 miles per day, a vast improvement on the old performance of the Seaforth, Cromartie and Fraser coaches, which in days gone by, were forced, on a journey to Edinburgh, not only to carry spare wheels but to take with them their hereditary wheelwrights, the descendant of one of these skilled craftsmen being nowadays a leading citizen of the senior Burgh.

The road from Dingwall through Strathpeffer to the west coast

Note 1. Telford's works in Ross and Cromarty, see Glossary.

branching to the two termini of Poolewe and Ullapool was not to be completed for some years yet, the first stage being by no means the easiest, though from time immemorial a road had existed from Dingwall to Strathpeffer (Castle Leod and Kinettas), continuing from the High Street of the Royal Burgh toward Ledavarigid, along the base of Knockbain on the site of the existing Strathpeffer Railway track, but joining the present road not far from the ancient Fodderty burial ground. Telford however, probably influenced by Davidson of Tulloch and the Cromartie family, drove the new roadway through the Dingwall Bog—the old silted up basin of the tidal loch—at the same time suggesting that straightening of the course of the Peffrey River, in conjunction with the deep drains involved by the new road scheme, would reclaim the Bog. This work was carried out with the modification that the Dingwall Canal was substituted for the new river channel. The building of this road was a long job but a monument of good road building, completed in 1816.

Under date 26th June 1812 a contractor was being sought for a bridge over the Blackwater at Contin, which was constructed the following year in connection with a line of road from Achnashean to the small bay called Ruorroar on the south side of Loch Maree— 11 miles 1012 yards, a work largely contributed by Sir Hector Munro Mackenzie of *Gairloch*; this bridge required 41 arches of different sizes, while another bridge of three was constructed over the Blackwater (Garve). Eventually after many difficulties the Garve-Ullapool road was completed, but not on the old 1790 survey, which suffered from serious defects, so instead of climbing the steep face of *Craggan-an-Eachglas* it follows the course of the Blackwater, the *Clach-na-charnich* burn and the *Dirie Mór*; the *Coigach* roads were still elementary but were gradually improved, remaining Cromartie estate roads till 1861. The owners of ferries must have resented the bridges somewhat, as in the past they had done good business, but that they did not always maintain their boats in ship-shape fashion was proved by the Meikle Ferry tragedy, when 100 people travelling from Sutherland to Tain for the Communion service, were upset into the Dornoch Firth by the breaking in two of the ferry boat, the loss of life being very heavy.

To return for a space to Ross's military history: beside the Regiments already mentioned the north provided others during the 19th century, for home service, which in respect to physique and discipline were fully equal to any, and greatly superior to many Regiments of the Line. Among them was the Ross-shire 5th Regiment of British Militia, who in 1809 volunteered en masse for service in the Peninsula, an offer vetoed by the Commissioners of Supply, though in the following year they were employed to garrison the 'Tower', later spending several years in Ireland on garrison duty. Two more regiments were raised for part time service, 28 days per annum, one in south Ross, with head-quarters at Dingwall, the other in north Ross, with headquarters at Tain, and these may be said to be the forerunners of our Territorial Battalions, who have proved their worth in the two greatest wars the world has ever seen.

On 11th May of 1809 the counties of Ross and Cromarty were startled by a homicide case, committed in the smithy of Balblair on the Black Isle opposite Invergordon, the victim being a Captain Charles Munro, of the 42nd Highlanders, then on a visit to his wife and family. The unfortunate gentleman had gone to that centre of gossip to pass a pleasant half hour, but got into an altercation with one Robert Ferguson, a man of ungovernable temper, who settled the argument by plunging a large dirk into the officer's side. Medical succour was obtained but within twenty-eight hours the victim was dead. Ferguson was tried on a capital charge, hanged, and his body given for dissection, while a mournful half-Gaelic, half-English ballad commemorated the affair.

The Corn Law agitation had its repercussions, as the acreage under grain during this period, far exceeded the normal peace time area under corn during our own times; but over the whole of Ross and Cromarty the potato was becoming a standard crop and an important part of the daily diet. A series of famines followed aggravated by the fact that before the days of disease-proof tubers this new crop was subject to a devastating blight which deprived the people of what had become a too-great part of their food.

Methods of relief were still primarily in the hands of more fortunately placed individuals, and the House of Dunvegan in Skye faced bankruptcy due to the vast outlay employed in their very honourable efforts in aid of their people, spending £175 to £225 a week. Godfrey Lord MacDonald of Sleat, the son of the builder of the present Armadale House in 1815, carried out numerous relief works, as did many others on the mainland, perhaps the most curious, if least useful, being the replica of part of the Indian fort of Seringapatam erected by Sir Hector Munro of Novar on top of the hill of Fyrish. Other works were carried out by the west Highlands Committee of Relief under Captain Eliott, who co-operated in the works, which included, road-making, piers, march dykes, land drainage, spinning, knitting and netting.

The flax industry was still flourishing in the north, and regular classes were held during the early part of the 19th century in Castle Leod where the Hon. Maria Hay Mackenzie of Cromartie taught the girls from the 'heights' the mysteries of linen making—thus adding to the Castle Linen while increasing the incomes of many crofts that covered, and still cover, the Heights of Achterneed, Inchvanie, Keppoch and Fodderty. At Kildary (Tarbat Estate) a regular linen industry was developed, employing a large number of people in that area though all that remains to recall this activity is a strip of field on the north side of Meddat Farm known as the 'Lint Field'.

As we have already seen, many other changes were taking place in Ross; emigration to colonies and towns was removing, not only the clansmen, but the tacksmen and smaller lairds while the greater estates were soon themselves to change hands or shrink to a shadow of their former selves. On the Black Isle the castle and estate of Cromarty which though giving the name to the Earldom had remained in the family of Cromartie for only two generations was now further split up, and early in the century, having in the interval passed yet again through Urquhart possession, was bought by George Ross of Cromarty, a gentleman satirized in the 'Letters of Junius' as the 'Scotch Agent', the builder of the present Cromarty House that replaced the Castle. It was then inherited by Catherine Ross Munro the daughter of Colonel Duncan Munro III of Culcairn who had married the Agent's sister. Catherine married Hugh Rose of Glastullich who had made a fortune in the West Indies, returning to Scotland in 1802, when he had purchased Glastullich, Calrossie, Tarlogie and Culcairn. He did much good estate work, but engaged in 40 years of litigation, to gain the Cromarty (Black Isle) property through his wife; as well as instigating the expensive and drawn out Conon fishing rights case, which left the Burgh of Dingwall, Maria Hay Mackenzie of Cromartie and all other participants much poorer in money and no better off in fish, the only winners being the Edinburgh lawyers. But the most sudden and unexpected change came with a great family tragedy.

Francis Mackenzie Lord Seaforth 21st Chief of Kintail, was deaf, the result of an attack of scarlet fever while at Eton, yet he had gained high positions in the public service, both as a soldier and as Governor of one of our great dependencies; besides this he had several healthy sons as well as six daughters. But as his sons were attaining manhood, one by one they sickened and died, and their broken-hearted father, after ceasing for years to communicate with anyone, followed them to the tomb in 1815. As we have seen, the Earl's high play in youth with the disreputable Prince of Wales, afterwards George IV, had broken the family fortunes so that only a small part of the once great lands remained. Kintail 'of the Kine' was gone, Lewis bought by Sir James Matheson, who hoped to develop the fishings, only Brahan was left to come into the possession of 'a white coifed lassie who was to kill her sister'.

The lassie in question was his eldest sister, the Hon. Mary Mackenzie who had married the late Admiral Hood, the white coif referring to the head-dress worn by widows. She married again James Stewart of the House of Galloway; Mrs. Stewart Mackenzie was one day driving her sister Caroline in her pony carriage when the ponies taking fright upset the carriage, both ladies being seriously injured, Caroline dying. Sir Walter Scott wrote:

And thou, gentle Dame, who must bear, to thy grief,
For thy clan and thy country the cares of a Chief, . . .
To thine ear of affection, how sad is the hail,
That salutes thee the Heir of the line of Kintail!

Eventually her son, William Keith Stewart Mackenzie, succeeded followed by his son, a famous soldier, for whom the old titles were restored, but who died childless in 1923; he was followed in the estates by Francis Stewart Mackenzie, the second son of the 9th Earl of Middleton and Madeleine, daughter of Lady St. Helier, the late Earl's eldest sister; but in 1943 Francis fell in Italy some ten days after his elder brother had died on the field of honour. Brahan is now owned by Mrs. Matheson, the widow of Captain Matheson, R.N., whose family have already been mentioned in connection with the Island of Lewis.

In 1832 the MacDonald House of Sleat in Skye was to be carried on by the second son of Godfrey, 19th Chief, owing to a mix-up between Scots and English law, and a wrongful interpretation of Scots law, since admitted. In very romantic circumstances, the Lord of Sleat had eloped with Louise Maria, daughter of the Duke of Gloucester, brother of George III, her mother being the famous beauty Lady Almeria Carpenter, the Duke's morganatic wife. MacDonald had first seen his inamorata, looking over a London convent wall, at this handsome cavalier riding past, a not unnatural action for a young schoolgirl, but seldom followed by love at first sight and an elopement. The form of marriage that followed though perfectly legal by Scots law was of doubtful legality in England, so that the eldest son of this marriage did not inherit the titles of property in Skye but the Yorkshire Estates brought by his grandmother; the second son born after a more formal marriage ceremony becoming the 4th Lord MacDonald and de facto 20th Chief. However, it was soon discovered that the first marriage was perfectly legal, so that the present Yorkshire branch is really the senior, being held by Sir Alexander Bosville MacDonald 16th Bart. of Sleat, while the junior branch holds the Skye lands in the person of Sir Ronald MacDonald 6th Lord and de facto 22nd Chief of Sleat—one of his sons fell in the South African war, two in 1914, while his only married grandson James Archibald died in battle for his country in North Africa in 1942.

By 1843 the question of patronage in the Church of Scotland, last exercised in Ross-Cromarty by Maria of Cromartie, apparently to the entire satisfaction of the parishioners concerned, among whom were included those of Edderton and Dingwall, was causing, justifiably,

Note 1. This was written in the 1940's. See Appendix I c/.

K

great concern, becoming one of the major causes leading to the great disruption as well as, incidentally, to a crop of architecturally unattractive churches all over Scotland—some bad feeling resulted not at all in accordance with the teachings of Christ. Happily that breach is now repaired and everywhere a more Christian co-operation evident among all denominations, none of whom have or ever have had the monopoly of good and honest ministers or congregations.

During this period the Burgh of Cromarty—no longer a Royal Burgh, an honour obtained for it in 1661 by Sir John Urquhart but relinquished in 1672 as the consequent expenses were found over heavy—produced one of the outstanding men of Scotland. This was Hugh Miller, a working mason who was to become famous as a world authority in the subject of geology and one of the founders of that science.

John Hay Mackenzie of Cromartie who had done much to help families evicted from their homes on other estates was succeeded by his only daughter of a like mind, Anne Hay Mackenzie, who in 1849 married the 21st Earl and 3rd Duke of Sutherland, which for one generation united the still very broad lands of Cromartie with the vast possessions of the northern House. In 1861 Queen Victoria restored to Anne Mackenzie the old Cromartie titles which she held in her own right distinct from the Sutherland titles which had come to her by marriage. Thus she became Countess of Cromartie, Viscountess Tarbat, Baroness MacLeod and Baroness Castlehaven, which passed on her death in 1888 to her second son Francis, who married a daughter of the 4th Lord MacDonald of Sleat.

The Highland Clearances had continued through the forties, though during the long French wars the need for soldiers and the kelp industry had done something to mitigate them. But the eighties brought other troubles, and there was a cry for which some landlords had given good excuse, for the nationalization of land, the crofters' holdings Acts however gave security of tenure and controlled rents, while the Land Court set up in 1912 brought further security. Other attempts were made to help, and these efforts became in large measure consolidated in the Scottish Department of Agriculture, while perhaps the most successful innovation was the Highlands and Islands Medical Service Board, an institution which has served as a model in other countries, notably the U.S.A.

As early as 1786 the British Fishery Society had been founded for the development of this old and important industry; three years later in *Coigach*, Aitkin had prepared the plans for the rebuilding of Ullapool and the curing factory, which was built shortly afterwards on Isle Martin, one of the Summer Isles though detached from the main group and lying off Ardmair. It is possible that the Summer Isles got their name from being used for the summer grazing of cattle, once so plentiful; though nowadays they serve as homes for thousands of sea birds and others, which include gulls, geese, duck, Arctic terns, eiders, merganders, storm petrels, peregrine falcons, not to mention that pest the hoodie crow, as well as seals, they provide also winter grazings for the weaned lambs from October to March.

The Island of Tanera (except for Isle Martin) was the only one of the group to be inhabited by a considerable population, which at the time of the '45 amounted to 21 families who cultivated the land by the sea shore, grazing the hill ground communally, and fishing. But once the male population of an island, or for that matter, of a crofting township, depending primarily on fishing, drops below the level necessary to maintain a fishing boat, depopulation follows, a process that terminated on Tanera in 1931, while the same fate has all but overtaken the little mainland township of Reiff at *Rhu Coigach*, where a sea tragedy of the 1860's wiped out the two crews of what had up to that time been a vital and flourishing little community of MacLeods, Mackenzies and MacLennans.

The known, if sketchy, history of Tanera *Mór*, as we saw, stretched back 1000 years to Viking days when their long ships anchored in the horse-shoe bay sheltered to the north by the point Ard na Goine, to the south by *Rudha Dubh* and two little islets. This haven, known to the Norsemen as Hawraray *Mór* (the island of Haven), and since those far off days as *Garadheancal* (cabbage patch or garden), can still shelter a ship of 3000 tons. Till the 14th century the Chief of Clan Nical would have exercised jurisdiction over this island, where there is said to be a tombstone in the ancient burying ground inscribed with the date 1198; then came the MacLeods of Lewis and *Coigach*, who in their turn, through a mixture of conquest and marriage, relinquished their trust in the first decade of the 17th century to the Cromartie branch of the House of Kintail. By this time the island had become a place of much activity thanks to the Loch Broom herrings which by the end of the 15th century had established Tanera *Mór* as a base for the Dutch fishing boats. In course of time this fishing industry was exercised more by the Highlanders themselves and the Dutch boats became fewer, though the anchorage still attracted many craft from the eastern fishing ports.

Then came the Jacobite Rising of 1745 and the confiscation of the Cromartie Estates which were administered by the Government Commissioners, who quite illegally sold a small part of Tanera *Mór* to a London Company who hoped to profit from the famous Loch Broom herring fisheries. Owing to this transcation the area known as *Tigh na Quay* was not restored to the House of Cromartie when Tanera with the rest of the estates came back. A short period of activity followed under the managership of Murdoch Morrison, a merchant of Stornoway, who in 1784 replaced the existing pier and older buildings at *Tigh na Quay*, with the fine range of buildings which made up the curing factory, dwelling, and the much enlarged pier. Then came a sudden change in one of nature's cycles, which was to cause great distress in the north west Highlands, hitting particularly hard the Island community of Tanera and the people of Ullapool.

The great herring shoals, which for centuries with the utmost regularity, had entered the wide mouth of Loch Broom, passing between Tanera *Mór* and the mainland of *Coigach*, finally reaching the head of the Loch 20 miles away and then returning to the open sea along the Dundonnell side as far as *Cailleach* Head, ceased this migration. The London Company went bankrupt, many changes of ownership of this once thriving centre took place, while slow but relentless decay settled over the whole island. The next owner of the 'factory' was a tacksman from Skye called Nicolson who appeared on the scene about 1849, and by renting stretches of the *Tigh na Quay* foreshore to the island crofters for the cutting of seaweed, augmented his income as the kelp industry was still fairly profitable.

A story is told of a period preceding the Nicolson era: many burials were being conducted on this island from the mainland owing to the fear of the active 'resurrection' men of the day, but the busy herring traffic brought representatives of this unsavoury trade in boats, one party being caught red-handed by the islanders who liquidated them on the spot. The little field known as the 'Irish Park' was formed of Irish soil used as ballast by the Tanera boats on their return journey having exported part of their catch which had been cured on the island; four old apple trees, reputed 150 years old and still bearing good fruit, stand as a memorial to those old days of activity.

Nicolson was followed by a man of very different type, the story of whose life would form the plot of a truly romantic novel. This was Captain MacDonald of the Clan Ranald family, who as much for the adventure as profit took to a life of smuggling, himself running cargoes from France in his schooner the 'Rover's Bride', which he used also for legitimate trade. One day as she lay in the anchorage of Tanera with a cargo of contraband, the revenue cutter was sighted. The 'Rover's Bride' weighed anchor with all speed and a stern chase followed; rounding Cape Wrath, MacDonald made for Orkney, and with masterly seamanship, took his ship under full sail between two islands, where the revenue cutter dared not follow. In due course MacDonald returned to Tanera in ballast and to this day a story still survives of a cargo of rum hidden somewhere about *Tigh na Quay*.

The next owner of this piece of the island was the eccentric Meyrick Bankes of Letterewe, a rich Liverpool merchant, reputed the meanest of men; this man's heirs relinquished the property to Dundonnell by an exchange, the other subject being the salmon fishing of the little Gruinard River. Stories of treasure buried on this island have always been current, indeed old coins have been found. Another treasure may yet be found on Horse Island, which lies near Tanera *Mór*, as a *Coigach* story relates how while some men were gathering sheep one of them fell with a leg deep in a peat hole. Thinking nothing of so common a happening he scrambled out, continuing with his work, but that night back at Achiltibuie as he kicked off a sea-boot, two golden guineas fell out; alas subsequent careful search of the area failed to reveal the cache.

Tanera *Mór* like all the Highlands was rich in story and legend, of which the following are an example, in this particular instance reflecting the element of tragedy and doom which was descending like a pall over the once happy island community. The tacksman Nicolson as well as owning the factory had rented the whole island, but did not make himself popular by charging over-high rents for the new crofts he had parcelled out, or by bringing over Skyemen to cure the herring. Among the Skyemen was a MacCrimmon with his son, a youth of fourteen or sixteen years. One summer evening while the father was at the fishing, the lad was in the house practising on the chanter but failing to get the touch just right. Suddenly the boy knew that he was no longer alone, but that a man stood just behind him, yet he felt no surprise even when the stranger placed his own fingers on the boy's as they rested on the chanter. The boy then played as never before and forgetting all else took out the full pipes, though in the meantime the visitor had vanished. Just then, the boat, with the boy's father on board, rounded Ard na Goine, and met the full sound of the wonderful music; the father with a strange look turned to his companion in the boat saying, 'The 'prentice is above MacCrimmon' a saying in *Coigach* which now means that a lad is surpassing his father at something or other.

The boy grew up to be one of the famous MacCrimmon pipers, but there were those who envied him his gift, so that the night before a great competition some evil men took advantage of the sleeping piper by making with a needle numerous small holes in the bag of the pipes. Next day when MacCrimmon came to play before the judges he experienced great difficulty in keeping the bag inflated, but being a proud lad would not give in, but continued to the end when all went black before his eyes 'and then he spewed up the blood of his heart'.

Near to MacCrimmon's house dwelt a bachelor who had the second sight which came to him in this way; he would hear a knock at the door and on looking out would see a cortège passing in the dark to the old burial ground above the Irish Park. Amongst this ghostly procession, he would see the face of the corpse, and he would then know the identity of the next islander who was to make the journey to *Tir nan Og*.

Fiona MacLeod sets many macabre stories on Tanera *Mór* and

indeed the family that dwelt in *Tigh na Quay* from 1868 to 1923 did seem to be haunted by a spirit of misfortune. There were two brothers and their wives, industrious folk, who, among other things, dug the whole of the big Park. While the first child was being born the arches which held up part of the factory fell and although it did no physical harm to the people, the great fall of masonry must have been a terrible shock to the poor mother. Soon after the death-watch beetle began to riddle the red pine timber of the buildings, so that some of the floors and roofs collapsed and life must have been both difficult and dangerous as only very rough repairs were carried out. Meanwhile the fishing industry died till Stornoway smacks quite openly started to remove much of the masonry of the pier, leaving further evidence of ruin and decay. Next came poltergeist activities—candles blew out without draught or wind, windows and doors flew open, there were the usual raps on panelling, footsteps where none walked, while occasionally a window smashed for no obvious reason, and one of the upper rooms became filled with the disturbing atmosphere of some evil presence. Whatever the explanation, life became insupportable so that the poor family decided to call in an exorcist.

Now although they were staunch and good Presbyterians, it was recognized that something more ancient than Calvinism was needed to compete with the poltergeist trouble, and they asked the aid of a man of great goodness and experience, a Catholic ship's carpenter from South Uist. He inspected the buildings from cellar to roof, after which he stated that he could lay the ghost but strongly advised against this as worse trouble of a different kind would follow. But the people had had sufficient of the pin-pricking worry, and begged him to exorcise the place, which he did, it would appear successfully. But the price had to be paid; sickness came to a previously healthy family; two members were drowned and the cattle died. In an endeavour to avoid the last evil the poor sufferers tried building a new byre instead of repairing any of the numerous old buildings, but misfortune followed misfortune, till in 1923 the last member of the family left the place suffering from a nervous breakdown—a most uncommon complaint in the Highlands. *Tigh na Quay* fell more and more into ruin, till 1938, when the Dundonnell trustees found a purchaser in Dr. Fraser Darling, the great ornithologist and naturalist, who by hard work and enthusiasm seems to have brought back peace and a measure of prosperity to this troubled corner of the earth.[1]

As we saw, the year 1931 brought to an end one phase in the history of a little island, the few remaining families moving to the mainland,

Note 1. The account of Tigh na Quay is taken from *Island Farm* by F. Fraser Darling, D.Sc., F.R.S.E., though some of it I had heard as a boy while some more was told to me on a battlefield in France during a short respite, by a man of Achiltibuie.

though not at all willingly, as among the evacuees from Tanera *Mór* to Achiltibuie was an elderly cow who resented bitterly leaving the island, and she was never cured of plunging into the sea in an attempt to swim back home. Of the other islands of this group within the County of Cromartie, none, with the exception of Tanera *Mór*, Isle Martin and Ristol, the latter almost attached to the mainland of *Coigach*, show any signs of permanent habitation, if we except the solitary Culdee of *Eilean a' Cleireach* (Priest Island).

Beside the failure due to herring movements, there arose during the 20th century the competition of the steam trawler and drifter, which as well as destroying the spawning beds, could more readily get their catches to the most favourable markets, whereas the crofter-fishermen were faced with heavy road and rail freight charges, and the uncertainty of an unstable market controlled by the powerful fish distributing combines. These events and other causes terminated the Matheson proprietorship of the Lewis, a family who since the days of the Seaforth ownership had done much good work in that island as well as extending their fishery schemes elsewhere, having bought Ullapool from Cromartie in 1870, as a centre.

To bring the story up to date—another great scheme was set afoot for the commercialization of the Lewis during recent years—by an apostle, or perhaps deity, of Big Business, a famous soap king, but despite the showers of gold, and the glorious prospects of being well paid cogs of a smoothly running machine the people of Lewis preferred to keep their souls and freedom—a victory maybe as important as Bannockburn. The year 1865 saw the opening of sections of the Highland Railway, which speeded up communications north and south as also to south west Ross, though the gradual decline of the fishing industry in Ullapool put a stop to the projected line to that town.

Since those days a new but changing industry has steadily grown in Ross, first the shooting and fishing tenant, a not altogether reliable source of income, as it fluctuates with booms and depressions, the latter state being constant since 1929. Next came people attracted by such places as Strathpeffer Spa, where he or she could regain health amidst beautiful surroundings, to be followed by countless thousands of men and women—the tourists—who through the agency of the internal combustion engine could cover distances and visit places, before quite out of reach, all of which are to be encouraged as a valuable auxiliary industry, though God forbid that the Highlander should become just a caterer to the tourist and nothing more.

During modern times many of the great Houses of Ross have changed hands altogether, while others have decreased in size owing to changed conditions, and the scarcity of money at the northern end of the kingdom of Scotland, at least amongst its own sons. In 1848 Sir Hugh

Munro, the 26th Chief had died leaving that historic House in a sad plight, during a life spent largely in London, he had entered into an irregular marriage, according to English law, with a Jane Law, daughter of King George III's chef. They had not been married long when the beautiful Jane was accidently drowned in the year 1796, while bathing off Foulis point, leaving an only daughter Mary Seymour Munro, educated by the Countess of St. Aubin and Dr. Gordon, the Principal of the Scots College in Paris. The subsequent litigation to prove the girl's legitimacy cost a small fortune, and though finally successful availed nothing as the girl died unmarried in 1849, the year after her father who had failed to break the Foulis entail on behalf of his daughter.

The next male heir was Sir Hugh's cousin, Sir Charles Munro, the 27th Chief and eldest son of George Munro of Culcairn and Culrain, a descendant of Sir George of Newmore K.B., the latter being the 3rd son of Colonel John Munro of Obsdale (Dalmore) the next immediate brother of Sir Robert, the 21st Baron and 3rd Baronet of Foulis. Sir Hugh, shortly before his death, had taken umbrage at his failure to get the entail altered, giving way to inexcusable spite, which he displayed by destroying or disposing of all non-entailed subjects on the property of Foulis, which included a magnificent library, deliberately burnt, together with many pictures, while outside was carried out a ruthless cutting down of nearly all the timber on the estate. The heir to what was left had himself been but little at home, serving in the French wars from the Peninsular War to 1815, and winning distinction at Badajoz, later fighting in the War of Independence in South America, commanding in 1817 the 1st Regiment of British Lancers in the service of Venezuela, and serving, the following year under the famous General Simon Bolivar. He in turn was succeeded by his son, another Sir Charles who died in 1888, whose son and successor Sir Hector Munro, 29th Baron of Foulis died in 1935, after a life of distinguished service both as a soldier, and as a devoted servant to Ross and Cromarty. Sir Hector's only son fell in the 1st World War aged 23 and unmarried, the succession passing through the young man's sister to her son, Patrick Munro, the 30th Chief of his line, though the baronetcy devolved on a grandson of the 27th Baron 19th Baronet.

Not only had the senior line of the House of Kintail become extinct, its representatives holding but a small fraction of the old lands, but many of the Mackenzie Houses that had risen to prominence during the 15th, 16th and 17th centuries had faded away during the 19th century, as has also the Ross line at Balnagown, though as we saw, this family ceased in reality to represent the successors of Hugh Ross the Earl's brother of 1350, during the early part of the 18th century; but some yet remain, while, though far too many have gone, a great body of

Highland men and women still inhabit the homes of their fathers, a people rightly referred to by a Private soldier of the Seaforth High- landers, as the 'salt of the earth'.

We have now reached the end of our Saga, which has tried to tell some of the story of the ancient Province of Ross, though there remains much that can never be told, having never been recorded. Some glimpse we have had of the daily life throughout the centuries of the Clansmen and women and Ross and Cromarty, and though records of their own simple private lives and thoughts are scanty, sufficient is known of them to recognize a people endowed not only with magnificent courage, but of an unsurpassed and single minded loyalty, to their own leaders or to an ideal. We have seen how chivalrous, kindly and trusting folk were shamefully treated during the latter part of the 18th and the 19th centuries, not only by foreigners but too often by people of their own race, men who had forgotten what they themselves, Scotland and the world owed to the Highlander, as well as the Lowlander of our nation.

Unity is strength, a characteristic too often lacking among the mixed races, Iberian, Goidel and Brython Celt, Scandinavian, Angle, Fleming and Norman, who go to make up the Scot who dwells in that lovely land north of the Tweed and the Border hills, the Kingdom of *Alba*. Yet could unity of ideas and policy among the Scottish peoples be found again, much good would follow; the continuous draining away of the best elements of our population to England and overseas could be modified, if conditions of life and opportunity at home were improved; the steady flight of capital from Scotland to England, so marked since 1900, could be arrested; while a vital culture of benefit to all mankind, would survive.

Surely an aim worth a struggle, as none but the most mean spirited and bigoted can doubt that Scotland if given the chance of national survival, has still much to give, both to the great Commonwealth of Nations once known as the British Empire, as well as to a new, and we hope, better and more co-operative world.

Alba gu brath.

APPENDIX I

APPENDIX I a/.
Norwegian, and Picto-Norse, Jarls and Earls of Caithness, Orkney and Shetland. Moddan, Angus, Strathearn and St. Clair (Sinclair)

In 872 Harald Harfagr—Fairhair—and the Prince Jarl Ragnvald squashed the independent Vikings of north and west Scotland.

I Ragnvald 'Moire Jarl' of Norway 1st of Orkney and Shetland relinquished to brother.

II Sigurd I—conquered part of Caithness and Sutherland. Killed 890 by his dead adversary Malbridge, Mormaer of Ross, whose buck tooth caused blood poisoning in his leg. Buried Dornoch.

Hrolf the Ganger, 1st Duke of Normandy.

III Hallad retired to Norway.

IV Torf Einer. His mother was Pictish. 831-920.

Arnkell.
Both killed in England with King of Norway Eric 'Bloody Axe'.

Erling.

V Thorfinn I 'Skull Splitter'. m. Grelaud dtr. of Duncan, Pictish Mormaer of Caithness by Groa dtr. of Thorfinn 'the Red'.

1st son   2nd son   3rd son
All in turn married Ragnhild and were liquidated by her. She and her evil mother Gunnhild helped the sons of King Eric to seize Jarldom of Orkney.

VI Jarl Ljot also married Ragnhild but killed 963 in Caithness by a MacBeth, probably Mormaer of Ross.

Skuli. Backed by Scots' Court. Defeated and killed by Ljot.

VII Hlodvr (Lewis) m. Princess Ethne dtr. of Corball Righ of Ossory. d. 980 in bed.

VIII Sigurd 'The Stout' the 1st Christian Jarl. Claimed Caithness through his grandmother Grelaud, disputed by two Celtic Chiefs, he killed one but owing to heavy losses of retired to Orkney leaving the Chief Hundi in possession. m. dtr. of King Malcolm II. Killed at Battle of Clontarf 1014.

IX Thorfinn II 'The Mighty' Earl of Caithness, Orkney, Shetland, Overlord of Ross and drawing tribute from Hebrides. m. Princess Injibjorg 1st cousin of Thora Queen Norway. Injibjorg later became 1st wife of Malcolm III. In 1040 Moddan was created Earl of Caithness by his uncle King Duncan I but was killed. Moddan's family were Pictish Mormaers of Caithness and still held much territory. He left a son probably Jarl Moddan of Dale and a dtr. FraKark who m. Liot Nidinger a Sutherland chief. Thorfinn d. 1057.

Erland.

Herbjorg   dtr.

X Paul.
Divided territories; much went back to Pictish Mormaers. Both fought with Harold with Harold Hardrada against Harold of England but were released after Stamford Bridge 3 days before Hastings 1066. Both were removed by King Magnus 'Barelegs' to Norway where they died.

Erling, Killed in Ireland.

St. Magnus.
m. 'a high born lady and the purest maid of the noblest stock of Scotland's Chiefs'. 1105 Earl of Caithness till killed by Hakon. 1116 canonised and nephew built and dedicated Kirkwall Cathedral to him.

Sigrid (dtr.)

dtr.   dtr.   dtr.   dtr.

XI Hakon.
m. Helga a dtr. of Moddan. The three Jarls quarrelled and involved their fathers—Hakon seized Orkney and Shetland. The King of Norway took them all off to the west but at Battle of Menai Straits St. Magnus refused to fight Scots with whom he had no quarrel. He escaped to Scots' Court and stayed with a Bishop in Wales. Hakon later killed St. Magnus, repented, went to Palestine and bathed in Jordan. Returned to sole possession of Orkney and Shetland, ruled well and built Templar Church at Ophir in Orkney. d. 1123.

Herbjorg dtr.
m. Kolbein Hruga.

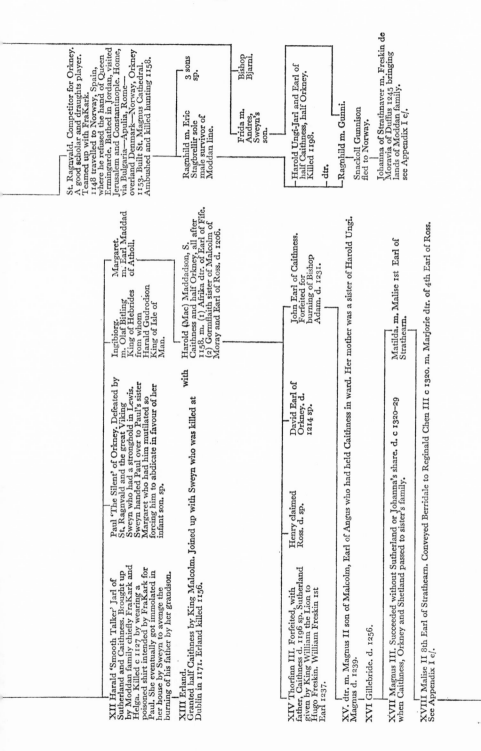

St. Ragnvald. Competitor for Orkney. A good scholar and draughts player. Teamed up with FraKark. 1148 travelled to Norway, Spain, where he refused the hand of Queen Ermingarde. Bathed in Jordan, visited Jerusalem and Constantinople. Home, via Bulgaria—Apulia, Rome—overland Denmark—Norway, Orkney 1153. Built St. Magnus Cathedral. Ambushed and killed hunting 1158.

Margaret, m. Earl Maddad of Atholl.

Ragnhild m. Eric Stagbrellir sole male survivor of Moddan line.

3 sons sp.

Bishop Bjarni.

Frida m. Andres, Sweyn's son.

Harold Ungi-Jarl and Earl of half Caithness, half Orkney. Killed 1198.

dtr.

Ragnhild m. Gunni.

Snackoll Gunnison fled to Norway.

Johanna of Strathnaver m. Freskin de Moravia of Duffus 1245 bringing lands of Moddan family. see Appendix I e/.

XII Harald 'Smooth Talker' Jarl of Sutherland and Caithness. Brought up by Moddan family chiefly FraKark and Helga. Killed c 1127 by wearing a poisoned shirt intended by FraKark for Paul. She eventually got immolated in her house by Sweyn to avenge the burning of his father by her grandson.

Paul 'The Silent' of Orkney. Defeated by St. Ragnvald and the great Viking Sweyn who had a stronghold in Lewis. Sweyn handed Paul over to Paul's sister Margaret who had him mutilated so forcing him to abdicate in favour of her infant son. sp.

Ingibiorg, m. Olaf Bitling King of Hebrides from whom Harald Gudrodson King of Isle of Man.

XIII Erland. Granted half Caithness by King Malcolm. Joined up with Sweyn who was killed at Dublin in 1171. Erland killed 1156.

with

Harold (Mac) Maddadson, S. Caithness and half Orkney, all after 1158, m. (1) Afrika dtr. of Earl of Fife. (2) Gormflaith sister of Malcolm of Moray and Earl of Ross. d. 1206.

John Earl of Caithness. Forfeited for burning of Bishop Adam. d. 1231.

XIV Thorfinn III. Forfeited, with father, Caithness d. 1196 sp. Sutherland given by King William the Lion to Hugo Freskin. William Freskin 1st Earl 1237.

Henry claimed Ross. d. sp.

David Earl of Orkney. d. 1214 sp.

XV. dtr. m. Magnus II son of Malcolm, Earl of Angus who had held Caithness in ward. Her mother was a sister of Harold Ungi. Magnus d. 1239.

XVI Gillebride. d. 1256.

XVII Magnus III. Succeeded without Sutherland or Johanna's share. d. c 1320–29 when Caithness, Orkney and Shetland passed to sister's family.

Matilda, m. Malise 1st Earl of Strathearn.

XVIII Malise II 8th Earl of Strathearn. Conveyed Berridale to Reginald Chen III c 1320. m. Marjorie dtr. of 4th Earl of Ross. See Appendix I e/.

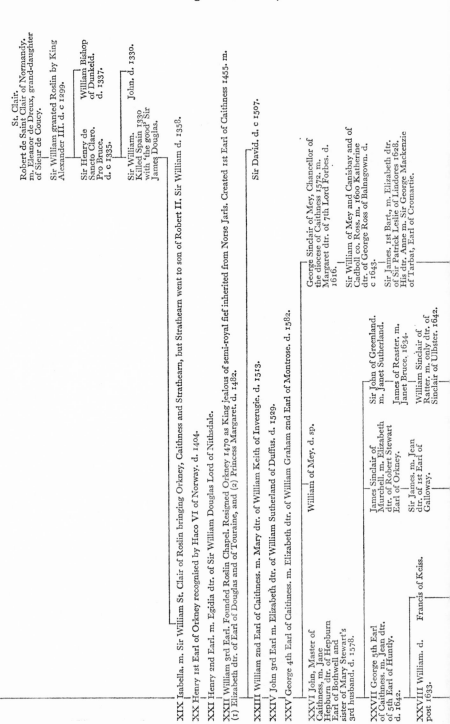

St. Clair.
Robert de Saint Clair of Normandy,
m. Eleanor de Dreux, grand-daughter
of Sieur de Coucy.

Sir William granted Roslin by King
Alexander III. d. c 1299.

Sir Henry de   William Bishop
Sancto Claro.   of Dunkeld,
Pro Bruce,   d. 1337,
d. c 1335.

Sir William.   John. d. 1330.
Killed Spain 1330
with 'the good' Sir
James Douglas.

XIX Isabella. m. Sir William St. Clair of Roslin bringing Orkney, Caithness and Strathearn, but Strathearn went to son of Robert II. Sir William d. 1358.

XX Henry 1st Earl of Orkney recognised by Haco VI of Norway. d. 1404.

XXI Henry 2nd Earl. m. Egidia dtr. of Sir William Douglas Lord of Nithsdale.

XXII William 3rd Earl. Founded Roslin Chapel. Resigned Orkney 1470 as King jealous of semi-royal fief inherited from Norse Jarls. Created 1st Earl of Caithness 1455. m.
(1) Elizabeth dtr. of Earl of Douglas and of Touraine, and (2) Princess Margaret. d. 1482.

Sir David. d. c 1507.

XXIII William 2nd Earl of Caithness. m. Mary dtr. of William Keith of Inverugie. d. 1513.

XXIV John 3rd Earl m. Elizabeth dtr. of William Sutherland of Duffus. d. 1529.

XXV George 4th Earl of Caithness. m. Elizabeth dtr. of William Graham and Earl of Montrose, d. 1582.

George Sinclair of Mey, Chancellor of
the diocese of Caithness 1572. m.
Margaret dtr. of 7th Lord Forbes. d.
1616.

Sir William of Mey and Canisbay and of
Cadboll co. Ross. m. 1600 Katherine
dtr. of George Ross of Balnagown. d.
c 1643.

Sir James, 1st Bart., m. Elizabeth dtr.
of Sir Patrick Leslie of Lindores 1628.
His dtr. Anne m. Sir George Mackenzie
of Tarbat, Earl of Cromartie.

William of Mey, d. sp.

Sir John of Greenland.
m. Janet Sutherland.

James of Reaster. m.
Janet Bruce, 1634.

William Sinclair of
Ratter. m. only dtr. of
Sinclair of Ulbster, 1642.

XXVI John, Master of
Caithness, m. Jane
Hepburn dtr. of Hepburn
Earl of Bothwell and
sister of Mary Stewart's
3rd husband. d. 1578.

James Sinclair of
Murchell. m. Elizabeth
dtr. of Robert Stewart
Earl of Orkney.

Sir James. m. Jean
dtr. of 1st Earl of
Galloway.

XXVII George 5th Earl
of Caithness. m. Jean dtr.
of 5th Earl of Huntly.
d. 1642.

Francis of Keiss.

XXVIII William. d.
post 1633.

XXIX John. d. 1639

XXX George 6th Earl of Caithness. m. Mary dtr. of Archibald Marquis of Argyll. d. 1676. sp.

XXXI George 7th Earl of Caithness. d. 1688. sp.

John, m. Elizabeth dtr. of Sir William Sinclair of Mey 2nd Bart.

John, m. dtr. of Patrick Sinclair.

XXXII John 8th Earl of Caithness. m. Jean Carmichael. d. 1705.

XXXIII Alexander 9th Earl of Caithness. m. Margaret dtr. of 1st Earl of Rosebery. d. 1765.

XXXIV William 10th Earl of Caithness. m. Barbara Sinclair of Scotscalder. d. 1779.

XXXV John 11th Earl. d. 1789. sp.

Robert of Durran. m. Anne dtr. of William Sinclair of Rattan. d. c 1709.

John, m. Elizabeth dtr. of George Sinclair of Barrock.

James. m. Elizabeth dtr. of Sir Patrick Dunbar, Bart. d. 1743.

George. m. Elizabeth dtr. of John Sutherland 13th Laird of Forse. d. 1779.

Lt. Col. John Sutherland Sinclair. m. 3rdly Euphemia dtr. of Thomas Buchan of Auchmacey. d. 1841.

Sir William 1648. m. Margaret dtr. of George Mackenzie, Earl of Seaforth.

Sir James, m. Jean dtr. of Sinclair of Keiss.

Sir James, m. Mary dtr. of James Sutherland, 2nd Lord Duffus.

Sir James, m. Margaret Sinclair of Barrock. d. 1760.

Sir John. m. Charlotte 2nd dtr. of Eric Sutherland but for the attainder 4th Lord Duffus. d. 1774.

Sir James 7th Bart. of Mey and 12th Earl of Caithness. 1793. m. Jane dtr. of General Alexander Campbell of Barcaldine. d. 1823.

Alexander, 13th Earl. m. 1813 Frances Leigh. d. 1855.

James, 14th Earl, F.R.S. m. Louisa dtr. of Sir George Richard Philips, Bart. d. 1881.

George Philips Alexander, 15th Earl of Caithness. d. unmarried 1889 when his Scottish honours passed to his kinsman.

XXXVI James Augustus, 16th Earl of Caithness, the direct descendant of Robert Sinclair of Durran, the 3rd son of Sir James Sinclair, 1st Bart. of Mey. m. Janet MacLeod. d. 1891.

XXXVII John, 17th Earl of Caithness. d. 1914. sp.

XXXVIII Norman, 18th Earl of Caithness, brother of the 17th Earl. m. Lilian Higford.

APPENDIX I b/1.
The Mormaers and Earls of Moray, and the Connection of both with the Royal House of Scotland

King Malcolm I A.D. 943–954.

King Duff 962–967.

Kenneth III 997–1005.

King Kenneth II 971–995.

Mormaers of Moray.

Mormaers of Ross.
The House of MacBeth or MaolBetha.

Malcolm II 1005–1034.

Maelbrighde a cousin or brother of

Maolbridge. c 890.

Bocdh (a dtr.).

Malcolm. d. 1029.

Findleac MacRuari m. Donada. Was murdered 1020 by Mormaer of Moray.

Royal Succession.

Gruoch who m.

(1) Gillecomgan
Mormaer of Moray. d. 1032.

and

...

(2) MacBeth or Maolbetha.
Mormaer of Ross and became by marriage Mormaer of Moray also. King of Scots 1040–1057 when he was killed in battle by his successor to the throne King Malcolm III.

See Chronological Table of Kings.

By (1)
Lulach accepted as King of Scots by a large number of his countrymen but killed in battle soon after his stepfather MacBeth.

A daughter m. Heth a member of the House of Moray.

Maelsnecte MacLulaig (Lulach) d. 1085, referred to in Irish Annals as 'Ri Muireb' (King of Moray).

Angus Earl of Moray killed and title forfeited after his defeat by Royal forces at Stracathro 1130.

The Lady Gormflaith married Harold Maddadson, Earl of Caithness.

See Appendix I a/.

Malcolm created Earl of Ross by King Malcolm IV after suffering imprisonment 1130–57 in Roxburgh Castle for his part in his brother's rebellion. He died in 1168.

Both were leaders of Northern Rebellion which was crushed by Fearchar O'Beolan Mac an-t-Sagairt of Applecross, the 1st Earl of Ross. See Appendix I b/2.

{ Donald MacHeth
{ Kenneth, d. c 1214.

APPENDIX I b/2.
The Earls of Ross, Ross of Balnagown, etc.

Gilleon na h'Airde—10th century.

Gilleon II. | Gilleon Og. m. dtr. of Rolf the Ganger c 900.

Several generations. | c 12 generations.

Anrias. | Clan Mathan = Clan Kenneth, Earls of Seaforth and Cromartie etc. (Matheson) See Appendix I h/.

Beolan—Gillianrias and Septs, i.e. Clan Anrias or Ross.

An-t-Sagairt. 'The Red Priest'. Lay possessor of and Abbot of Applecross founded 673.

I Fearchar O'Beolan Mac an-t-Sagairt. Knighted 1215. Created Earl of Ross 1226. Visited Rome on mission to Pope re Peace Treaty between Scotland and England 1244. d. at Delny Castle c 1251. Buried in Fearn Abbey, founded by him, and moved to New Fearn on removal of Abbey there.

II William MacFearchar. m. Jane dtr. of Earl of Buchan. d. at Easter Allan. b. Fearn 1274.

Malcolm 'The Green' Abbot inherited Applecross.

Euphamia. m. Freskin de Moray of Duffus. See Appendix I e/.

Christina. m. Olave III, King of Man. See Appendix I d/1.

III William. Committed to Tower by Edward I till 1303. Pro Balliol. Came over to Bruce and presented with Dingwall Castle. d. at Delny 1322.

Lilias. m. Sir William Urquhart, Sheriff of Cromarty.

IV Hugh. m. (1) Princess Maud Bruce dtr. of Robert the Bruce. (2) Margaret dtr. of Sir David Graham of Old Montrose. Killed Halidon Hill 1333.

Walter, eldest son, killed 1314 at Bannockburn. sp.

Sir John. m. Margaret Comyn co-heiress of John Earl of Buchan. d. sp.

Isabella betrothed to Edward Bruce.

Dorothea. m. Torquil I of Lewis. See Appendix I d/2.

V William, by (1). m. dtr. of Angus Og, Lord of Islay and the Isles. d. 1371. See Appendix I c/.

Euphamia, 2nd wife of King Robert II.

Marjorie. m. Malise 8th Earl of Strathearn. d. c 1357.

VI Euphemia Countess of Ross in her own right. m. (1) Sir Walter Leslie, a descendant of Barthol de Leslie 1170. Walter d. 1381. (2) Alexander Stewart, Earl of Buchan, 'The Wolf of Badenoch' who deserted her and produced only illegitimate offspring. Both Earls of Ross by right of wife. d. 1394 as Abbess of Elcho. Buried Fortrose. See Appendix I c/.

VII Alexander by (1) m. Isobel dtr. of Robert Stewart Earl of Fife and Duke of Albany, Regent of Scotland. d. 1402.

IX Margaret. m. Donald Lord of the Isles. She was de jure Countess of Ross and he through her Earl, but position and lands usurped by John Stewart Earl of Buchan, her brother in law. Hence Battle of Harlaw 1411. She died 1440. Donald died 1423 in Islay. John Stewart was killed in France at Battle of Verneuil 1423.

VIII Euphemia Countess of Ross. Resigned rights and became a nun. d. c 1415.

I Hugh by (2) of Rariches and Coulleigh. c 1330 m. Margaret de Barclay.

II William. m. Christian dtr. of Lord Livingston.

III Walter. m. Katherine dtr. of Paul McTyr who was a descendant of Christina, dtr. of 1st Earl of Ross, and Olave III King of Man.

IV Hugh. m. Janet dtr. of Earl of Sutherland as well as his heir had three other sons Hugh, William of Little Allan, and Mr. Thomas, Parson of Roskeen and Rector of Tain.

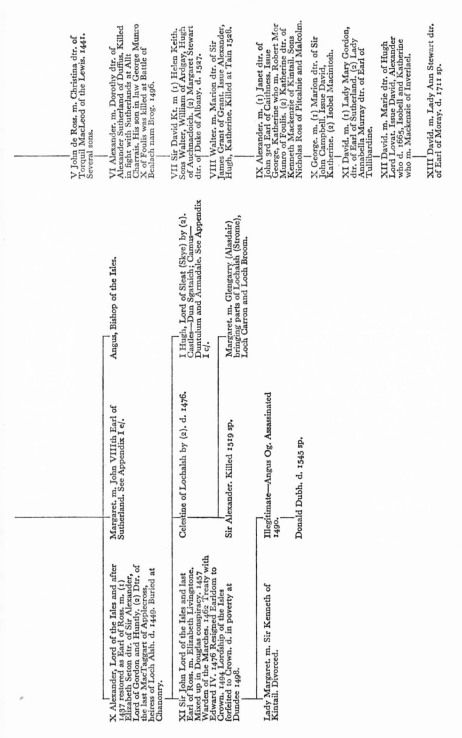

V John de Ross, m. Christina dtr. of Torquil MacLeod of the Lewis. 1441. Several sons.

VI Alexander. m. Dorothy dtr. of Alexander Sutherland as Duffus. Killed in fight with Sutherlands at Allt Charrais. His son in law George Munro X of Foulis was killed at Battle of Bealach nam Brog. 1496.

VII Sir David Kt. m (1) Helen Keith. Sons Walter, William of Ardgay, Hugh of Auchnacloich. (2) Margaret Stewart dtr. of Duke of Albany. d. 1527.

VIII Walter, m. Marion dtr. of Sir James Grant of Grant. Issue Alexander, Hugh, Katherine. Killed at Tain 1528.

IX Alexander. m. (1) Janet dtr. of John 3rd Earl of Caithness. Issue George, Katherine who m. Robert Mor Munro of Foulis. (2) Katherine dtr. of Kenneth Mackenzie of Kintail. Sons Nicholas Ross of Pitcalnie and Malcolm.

X George. m., (1) Marion dtr. of Sir John Campbell. Issue David, Katherine. (2) Isobel Macintosh.

XI David. m. (1) Lady Mary Gordon, dtr. of Earl of Sutherland. (2) Lady Annabella Murray dtr. of Earl of Tullibardine.

XII David. m. Marie dtr. of Hugh Lord Lovat. Issue David, Alexander who d. 1665, Isobell and Katherine who m. Mackenzie of Inverlael.

XIII David. m. Lady Ann Stewart dtr. of Earl of Moray. d. 1711 sp.

Angus, Bishop of the Isles.

Margaret, m. John VIIIth Earl of Sutherland. See Appendix I e/.

I Hugh, Lord of Sleat (Skye) by (2). Castles—Dun Sgataich; Camus—Duntulum and Armadale. See Appendix I c/.

Celestine of Lochalsh by (2). d. 1476.

Margaret, m. Glengarry (Alasdair) bringing parts of Lochalsh (Strome), Loch Carron and Loch Broom.

Sir Alexander. Killed 1519 sp.

Illegitimate—Angus Og. Assassinated 1490.

Donald Dubh. d. 1545 sp.

X Alexander, Lord of the Isles and after 1437 restored as Earl of Ross. m. (1) Elizabeth Seton dtr. of Sir Alexander, Lord of Gordon and Huntly. (2) Dtr. of the last MacTaggart of Applecross, heiress of Loch Alsh. d. 1449. Buried at Chanonry.

XI Sir John Lord of the Isles and last Earl of Ross. m. Elizabeth Livingstone. Mixed up in Douglas conspiracy. 1457 Warden of the Marches. 1462 Treaty with Edward IV. 1476 Resigned Earldom to Crown. 1494 Lordship of the Isles forfeited to Crown. d. in poverty at Dundee 1498.

Lady Margaret. m. Sir Kenneth of Kintail. Divorced.

Estates gifted to General Charles Ross, brother of Lord (Ros) Ross of Hawkhead—no connection with our Ross, d. 1737. Then reverted to Lord Ross, then to his sister's child the Hon. Grissel Ross who m. Sir James Lockhart 2nd Bart. of Carstairs. d. 1755.

Sir George Lockhart Ross 5th Bart. d. 1778 sp. and succeeded by his brother.

Admiral Sir John Lockhart Ross 6th Bart. d. 1790.

Major General Sir James Ross Lockhart 4th Bart. d. 1760. Succeeded by his brother.

Sir William Lockhart 3rd Bart. d. 1758. Succeeded by his brother.

Sir Charles Lockhart Ross 7th Bart. d. 1814.

Sir Charles Lockhart Ross 8th Bart. d. 1883.

Sir Charles Ross 9th Bart. of Carstairs. d. 1942 sp.

APPENDIX I c/.
The Lords of Islay and The Isles, the Later Earls of Ross, MacDonalds, Lords of Sleat

Coll Uais—grandson of Cormac MacAirt High King of Ireland d. A.D. 277, a descendant of Conn of the Hundred Battles. c A.D. 125.

Eochaidh

Niallgus

Suibhne

Morghach

Solemh

Gille Dyhamhnan (Adamnan).

Gille Bride, end of 11th century, m. a dtr. of the Norse nobility, probably of the family of Jarl Sigurd the Stout of Orkney.

Somerled of Argyll King of the Hebrides, m. Ragnhildis dtr. of Olave the Red King of Man—killed Renfrew 1164 with his son, by earlier marriage, Gillecalum whose son was defeated and killed by Alexander II of Scotland.

Dugall Lord of Lorne—Argyll—Mull—Coll—Tiree—Jura.

John King of the 'Sudreys' did not join King Hakon in 1263.

Alexander of Argyll d. 1310.

John of Lorn, Pro-Balliol and a relative of Comyn. Forfeited 1308 and lands went to Campbells and MacDugalls of Dunolly. Fled with his father to England. d. 1317.

King Robert II d. 1390.

Robert Duke of Albany Regent. d. 1420.

Earls of Ross.

Euphemia Countess of Ross d. 1395.

John Earl of Buchan killed 1423 at Vernuil. Usurped Earldom of Ross.

Ranald or Reginald Lord of Kintyre, half Arran and Islay, d. 1207. The Abbey and Convent at Iona was built by him 1203.

Donald—made the Pilgrimage to Rome. d. 1249.

Angus Mor a vassal of Hakon—not keen—d. 1296.

Alexander of Islay, Pro-Balliol and connected by marriage with Lorn died a captive 1308.

Princess Margaret dtr. of Robert II.

Sir Walter Leslie, by marriage VI Earl of Ross. m.

Isabella m. Alexander, VII Earl of Ross.

Euphemia VIII Countess of Ross. Became a nun.

Angus of Bute—half Arran. Killed Skye d. 1202. sp.

Ruarich (Roderick) of Bute.

Allan—both joined Hakon 1263 and so Arran and Bute confiscated but recompensed with some N. Isles.

Roderick (Ruaridh) 1325 forfeited for treason.

Dugall King of S. Isles d. sp. Skye and Lewis now under Ross.

Angus Og Lord of Islay. m. dtr. of Conn O' Cathan a great Ulster Baron and Lord of Limavady and Derry. Pro Bruce, fought at Bannockburn, and succeeded his brother. d. 1330.

John Lord m. (1) Amy of the Isles. m. (2). Princess Margaret, dtr. of Robert II. Made treaty with Edward Balliol 1335. Forfeited 1343, pardoned, fought for the Black Prince at Poitiers 1356, prisoner of war, released 1357. Rendered allegiance to David II at Inverness 1369. d. 1387. Founded Oronsay Priory.

Ranald MacRuary of Garmoran. Pardoned by David II. Assassinated by the Earl of Ross 1346.

Ranald.

Clans Ranald.

By (1)

Godfrey of Uist.

A son.

Alister MacGorrie. d. 1460. sp.

By (2)

Margaret m. Donald Lord of the Isles by marriage IX Earl of Ross de jure, usurped by Earl of Buchan. Fought Harlaw 1411. d. 1423 in Islay, Finlaggan Castle, which remained during 15th century the chief administrative centre for the western possessions of the Lords of the Isles.

John of Dun Naomhaig, m. Marjory Bisset, heiress of Glens of Antrim from whom Earls of Antrim. The Dun Naomhaig (Isla) family also sired the famous Alasdair Mac Colla mac-Ghille-easbuig 'Coll Ciotach'.

Alasdair Carrach of Lochaber, forfeited. Keppoch.

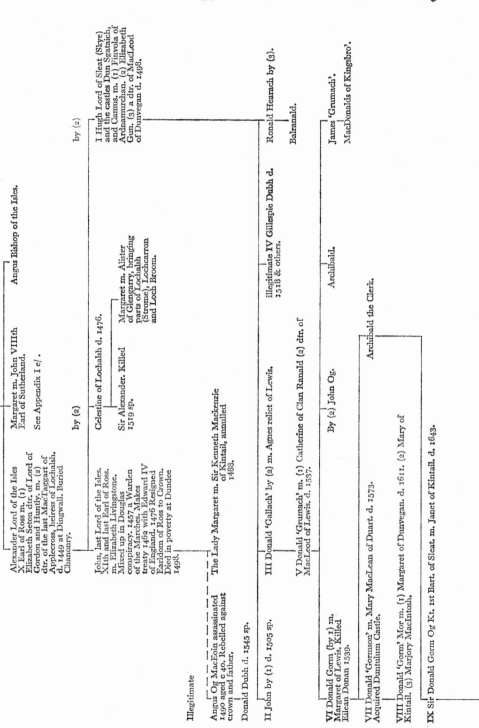

Alexander Lord of the Isles X Earl of Ross m. (1) Elizabeth Seton dtr. of Lord of Gordon and Huntly. m. (2) dtr. of the last MacTaggart of Applecross, heiress of Lochalsh. d. 1449 at Dingwall. Buried Chanonry.

Margaret m. John VIIIth Earl of Sutherland.
See Appendix I e/.

Angus Bishop of the Isles.

by (2)

I Hugh Lord of Sleat (Skye) and the castles Dun Sgataich, and Camus, m. (1) Finvola of Ardnamurchan. (2) Elizabeth Gun. (3) a dtr. of MacLeod of Dunvegan d. 1498.

by (2)

John, last Lord of the Isles, XIth and last Earl of Ross. m. Elizabeth Livingstone. Mixed up in Douglas conspiracy. 1457 a Warden of the Marches. Makes treaty 1462 with Edward IV of England. 1476 Resigned Earldom of Ross to Crown. Died in poverty at Dundee 1498.

Celestine of Lochalsh d. 1476.

Sir Alexander. Killed 1519 sp.

Margaret m. Alister of Glengarry, bringing parts of Lochalsh (Strome), Lochcarron and Loch Broom.

Illegitimate

Angus Og MacEoin assassinated 1490 aged c 40. Rebelled against crown and father.

Donald Dubh d. 1545 sp.

The Lady Margaret m. Sir Kenneth Mackenzie of Kintail, annulled 1488.

II John by (1) d. 1505 sp.

III Donald 'Gallach' by (2) m. Agnes relict of Lewis.

V Donald 'Grumach' m. (1) Catherine of Clan Ranald (2) dtr. of MacLeod of Lewis, d. 1537.

illegitimate IV Gillespie Dubh d. 1518 & others.

Ronald Hearach by (3).

Balranald.

VI Donald Gorm (by 1) m. Margaret of Lewis. Killed Eilean Donan 1539.

By (2) John Og.

Archibald.

James 'Grumach'.
MacDonalds of Kingsbro'.

VII Donald 'Gormson' m. Mary MacLean of Duart, d. 1573. Acquired Duntulum Castle.

Archibald the Clerk.

VIII Donald 'Gorm' Mor m. (1) Margaret of Dunvegan, d. 1611, (2) Mary of Kintail. (3) Marjory MacIntosh.

IX Sir Donald Gorm Og Kt, 1st Bart, of Sleat. m. Janet of Kintail. d. 1643.

X Sir James Mor 2nd Bart. d. 1678. m. (1) Margaret Mackenzie of Tarbat. (2) Dtr. of Dunvegan—issue John and Elizabeth.

By (1)
XI Sir Donald 3rd Bart. m. Margaret Douglas dtr. of Earl of Morton. d. 1695.

XII Sir Donald 4th Bart. m. Mary of Castleton. d. 1718.

XIV Sir James of Oronsay, 6th Bart. m. Janet MacLeod of Greshornish. Seat moved to Armadale (S. Skye).

William.

Janet.

XIII Sir Donald 5th Bart. d. 1720 sp.

XV Sir Alexander 7th Bart. m. (1) Ann Erskine, Issue Donald d. young. (2) Lady Margaret Montgomery dtr. of Earl of Eglinton. d. 1746.

(By 2)

XVI Sir James 8th Bart. d. 1766.

XVII Sir Alexander 9th Bart. 1st Lord MacDonald. m. Elizabeth Bosville of Gunthwaite.

XVIII Alexander Wentworth 10th Bart. 2nd Lord. d. 1824 sp.

XIX Godfrey 11th Bart. 3rd Lord. m. Louisa Maria daughter of Duke of Gloucester and Lady Almira Carpenter, dtr. of 1st Earl of Tyrconnel. Built Armadale House 1815. d. 1832.

Archibald etc.

XX Godfrey 4th Lord m. Maria dtr. of George Wyndham, Cromer Hall, Norfolk. d. 1863.

Sir Alexander, who succeeded to Yorkshire estates Thorpe and Gunthwaite. 12th Bart. m. Matilda Moffat dtr. of John Bayard. d. 1847.

XXII Sir Ronald 6th Lord m. Louisa Jane Hamilton Rose-Ross of Cromarty. d. 1947.

Lillian m. Francis Earl of Cromartie. See Appendix I h/.

XXI Somerled 5th Lord. d. 1875 sp.

Hon. Archibald. Killed in South Africa 1901 sp.

Sir Godfrey 13th Bart. m. Hon. Harriet Willoughby sister of 8th Baron Middleton. d. 1865.

Hon. Godfrey, m. Helen Bankes of Winstanley and Letterewe. Killed France 1914.

Hon. Ronald. d. France 1918.

Hon. Iona. m. Rev. MacLean.

Hon. Somerled, d. 1913 sp.

Sir Alexander Bosville MacDonald 14th Bart. m. Alice dtr. of J. Middleton of Kinfauns Castle. d. 1933.

Major Alasdair Godfrey 7th Lord MacDonald and 23rd Chief. m. 1945 Anne dtr. of Mr. Alfred Whitaker and Mrs. Andrew McLachlan.

James Archibald. Killed North Africa 1942.

Sir Godfrey Middleton Bosville MacDonald M.B.E. 15th Bart. m. Rachel dtr. of Colin Campbell.

APPENDIX I d/1.
MacLeod of Glenelg, Harris and Dunvegan

Harald, Prince of Norway, King of Man 1066.

Godred Crovan. 1079 to 1095. d. in Islay. Seized Man from Fingal Godfredsson. Probably King Orry (or Gorry) of Manx Legend.

Lagman abdicated. Died in Palestine.

Olave II, 1114–54. 'The Red'. m. Affica dtr. of Fergus Lord of Galloway. Slain by half brother.

Godred II 'The Black'. Somerled seized Man but Godred regained possession. k. 1187.

Ragnhildis m. Somerled King of Isles.

Olave III 'The Black'. m. Christina dtr. of Earl of Ross. Adopted as heir of Paul Balkeson, Norwegian Sheriff of Skye. Succeeded to Man and W. Isles 1233. d. 1237.

Ragnvald of the Isles, King of Man. Assassinated 1229.

Affica m. John de Courcy, Conqueror of Ulster.

Harald II King of Man. Drowned 1248. 1247 knighted by Henry III of England and married dtr. of King of Norway.

Reginald II King of Man. Killed 1249.

Leoid Heir to Uist, Harris, Lewis and Glenelg m. dtr. of Mac Harald of Dunvegan, Norse 'Armun' literally Warrior, the Chamberlains of Skye lands since 9th c. d. 1280.

Magnus last King of Man. d. 1265 sp.

I Torquil of Lewis. See Appendix I d/2.

Godfrey became a monk.

I Tormod or Norman m. Fingula MacCrotan dtr. of Irish chief. Built St. Clement's Cathedral, Rodil, S. Harris. d. c 1320.

Leod killed in Ireland with Edward Bruce.

II Malcolm m. dtr. of Donald 8th Earl of Mar. d. Stornoway Castle, c 1360. Charter by King David II, The Bissets forfeited Glenelg 1343.

Murdo of Gesto.

Fingula m. 6th Chief of Kintail.

III John d. c 1392.

Norman of Harris.

IV William (Cleireach) m. Niclean. d. c 1402.

Norman Clan 'ic Uillean.

George settled France.

Malcolm killed Lewis sp.

V John (Borb) m. Margaret Grant dtr. of Earl of Douglas d. 1442.

Margaret m. Roderick III of Lewis.

VI William (Dubh) d. 1480.

Norman.

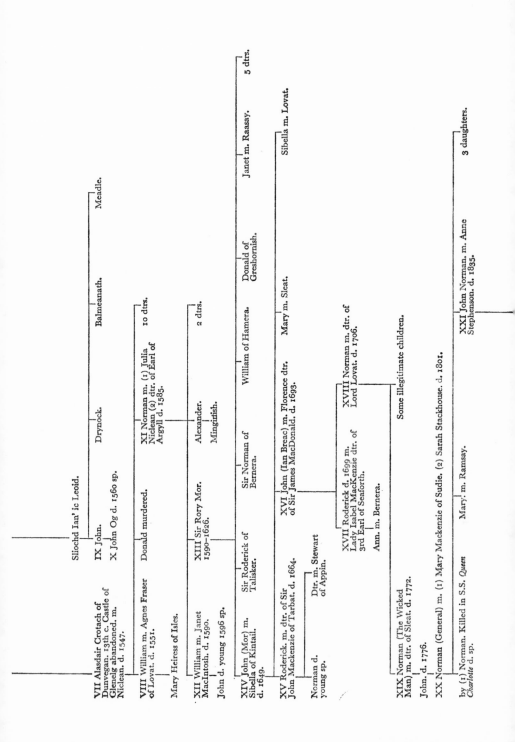

XXII Norman. m. Hon. Louisa St. John. d. 1895.

XXIII Norman Magnus d. 1905.
Daughter.

Torquil Olave.

XXIV Sir Reginald K.C.B. m. Lady Agnes dtr. of Earl of Iddesleigh. d. 1934.

Roderick Charles (Canon).
Daughter.

XXV Mrs. Flora MacLeod of MacLeod. m. Hubert Walter.

Joan. m. Major Woolridge Gordon of Hallhead.
3 sons.

Alice m. Archibald MacNab.

APPENDIX I d/2.
The MacLeods of Lewis, Assynt, Coigach and Raasay

I. Torquil of Lewis, m. Dorothea dtr. of 3rd Earl of Ross, d. during reign of King Robert the Bruce 1306–1329.

II. Norman who did not long survive his father but married with issue.

III. Torquil, m. Margaret dtr. and heiress of MacNicol of Assynt and Coigach. He died during the reign of Robert II 1371–1390.

IV. Roderick, m. Margaret dtr. of Lord of the Isles. In 1449 a charter of John of Yla is witnessed by Roderick MacLeoid of 'Leoghuis'.

V. Torquil. Prominent during reign of James II 1437–1460.

VI. Roderick. On record 1476, 1478, 1493 and 1494. m. (1) Margaret dtr. of Dunvegan. Issue a son killed at Bloody Bay. (2) Agnes dtr. of Sir Kenneth Mackenzie of Kintail ('Coineach a Bhlair') and his second wife Agnes Fraser of Lovat. d. 1498.

Tormod who succeeded to the Barony of Assynt and from whom are descended the MacLeods of Assynt, Geanies and Cadboll.
In 1508 the lands of Assynt and Coigach forfeited by Torquil of the Lews to King James IV in 1502 were bestowed on Y. Dubh Mackay for life. They were returned to Malcolm however in 1511. In 1572 James VI granted to Torquil Conanach Lewis and Assynt, but Coigach with the Lewis was made over to the Mackenzies; Tormod's descendants remaining in Assynt till taken by the Mackenzies of Seaforth c 1680 with whom it remained till its judicial sale in 1760.

Margaret 2nd wife of William of Mackintosh 7th of Mackintosh.

VII. Torquil, m. (1) Catherine Campbell dtr. of 1st Earl of Argyll; no issue, (2) dtr. of John Cathanach Macdonald of Islay and the Glynns widow of Donald Gallach Macdonald of Islay and mother of Donald Gruamach 4th of Sleat. Was pronounced a rebel and his Estates forfeit to the Crown owing to his having supported Donald Dubh in his rebellion. He held out for a long time but eventually disappears from history. Assynt and Coigach were given in life rent to Y. Mackay of Strathnaver. His son John MacTorquil was excluded from the succession and by charter under the Great Seal all the Estates passed to Torquil's brother Malcolm in 1511.

VIII. Malcolm MacLeod, m. Christian dtr. of Thomas Urquhart of Cromarty, d. c 1528 when his excluded nephew seized the Estates fully supported by the people of Lewis and he held the position during his life (d. 1534) but left no male issue, his daughter however was supported by her whole kindred and her husband's clan, Macdonalds of Sleat. An amicable arrangement was eventually arrived at.

IX. Roderick, m.. (1) Janet illeg. dtr. of John Mackenzie of Killin 9th of Kintail and widow of McKay of Reay. (2) Barbara Stewart dtr. of Andrew Lord Avandale 1541. (3) c 1585 dtr. of Hector Og MacLean 12th of Duart. In 1541 James V for the second time erected anew the various properties into the free Barony of Lewis. 1545 Roderick is among the 17 Barons and members of Council of the Isles appointed as plenipotentiaries under the Earl of Lennox for treating with the English King. Roderick's rule turned out disastrous to the Siol Torquil and terminated the supremacy of his house in the Lewis.

(by 1)

Malcolm Garbh of Raasay.

Norman of Eddrachilles.

X. Torquil Conanach, m. Margaret dtr. of Angus VII of Glengarry. This lady also married either before or after her marriage to Torquil one of the Cuthberts of Castle Hill, Inverness, by whom she became the progenitrix of Charles Colbert, Marquis of Seignelay, the famous Minister of Louis XIVth of France. There was constant and bitter strife between Roderick's sons both legitimate and otherwise. Conanach was backed by the Mackenzies against his father who wished to dispossess him. Torquil Dubh MacLeod for a time held Lewis while Conanach is designated of Coigach, but was recognised by the Lords of the Exchequer as legal heir to Lewis and mainland properties.

(By 2) Torquil Oighre drowned 1566.

(By 3) Torquil Dubh MacLeod.

John d. sp. Predeceased his father. Killed by his bastard uncle Rory Og. The fratricidal struggle continued and in July 1597 Cananach at Coigach executed his brother Torquil Dubh and many of his followers. This Torquil Dubh had been pronounced a rebel having seized and laid waste 'the Strath of Coigach pertaining to MacLeod, his eldest brother, likewise my Strath of Lochbroom.' (Kenneth of Kintail's letter).

Son who also predeceased his father.

XI. Margaret who became her father's heir to Lewis and Coigach, m. 1605 Sir Roderick Mackenzie of Castle Leod and Tarbat, and son of Colin Cam 11th of Kintail, who became the progenitor of the Earls of Cromartie. Margaret brought to him Coigach and Lewis though the latter went to Rorie's nephew Kenneth Lord Kintail. See Appendix I h/.

Elizabeth, m. Duncan Bain of Tulloch.

Catherine. m. Colin Mackenzie 3rd son of George 2nd Earl of Seaforth.

Janet, m. Roderick Mackenzie 3rd of Fairburn.

Florence, m. Neil MacLeod 9th of Assynt.

APPENDIX I e/.

The Earls (Freskins; Gordons; Leveson-Gower) of Sutherland, and Freskins of Moray—A Celtic (Pictish) family probably of the same stock as the Earls of Moray. Forfeited 1130.

I Freskin of Duffus, Strathbroch-Grant c 1130. Born c 1100, entertained David I during the building of Abbey of Kinloss 1150. Died between 1166-71. This family were probably the ancestors of the great House of Douglas.

William MacFreskin (Frisgyn) d. c 1204.

Hugo, d. sp.

Hugo Freskin of Sutherland, d. Dornoch c 1214.

William of Petty; Avoch (Black Isle, Ross); Brachalie; Borham and Artilad—'De Moravia'. d. 1226.

Sir John. Earls of Atholl.

Andrew parson of Duffus d. c 1226.

St. Gilbert, Bishop of Caithness 1204-22. Built Dornoch Cathedral. Translator of Psalms into Gaelic. d. 1245.

Richard of Culben.

William 1st Earl of Sutherland. d. 1248.

Walter de Moravia of Duffus. m. Euphemia dtr. of Fearchar Mac an-t-Sagairt Earl of Ross bringing as dowry lands of 'Clon' c 1224. d. ante 1248.

Walter de Moravia of Petty, Avoch etc. Guardian of the young King Alexander III and his Queen in 1225.

Andrew Bishop of Moray, d. 1242. Moved head-quarters of See from Spynie to Elgin.

William and Earl of Sutherland. 1248-1307.

Freskins II Lord of Duffus 1248. m. Lady Johanna of Strathnaver heiress of family of Moddan, Pictish Mormaers of Caithness and Norse Jarl Otter, FraKark and Audhild, also Harald Ungis' sister Ragnhild, Freskimus d. 1262.

Walter de Duffus, Petty, Avoch, Bothwell etc. c 1250 by m. with dtr. of John Comyn heiress of Bothwell, Drumsagard and Smailholm. d. 1294.

William 3rd Earl of Sutherland. d. 1327 sp. Was at the Parliament at St. Andrews March 1308-09, being one of the signatories to the famous letter to the Pope.

Kenneth 4th Earl. m. Mary dtr. of Donald Earl of Mar. Killed Halidon Hill 1333.

Mary of Duffus, m. Reginald Chen II.

Reginald Chen III 'Morar na Shein'. half Caithness.

Christina m. William de Federeth I.

William de Federeth II granted half Caithness to Reginald Chen III.

William of Bothwell 'Le Riche'. d. in Tower c 1300.

Sir Andrew of Avoch, Petty etc. d. Tower c 1300.

David, Bishop of Moray. Founder of 'Scots College', Paris 1325.

William 5th Earl of Sutherland. m. Princess Margaret dtr. of Robert the Bruce. d. c 1371.

Nicholas of Torboll m. Mary of Duffus. Duffus Peerage and family.

Marjory m. (1) Sir John. Douglas, (2) Sir John Keith of Invergugie.

Andrew Keith of Invergugie.

Andrew de Moray of Petty, Avoch, Duffus, Brachalie, Borham and Bothwell. d. of wounds after 'Stirling Bridge' 1297.

Sir Andrew of Petty, Avoch etc. Born after father's death. Regent of Scotland 1332. d. at Avoch Castle 1338 aged 40. Buried first Rosemarkie, moved to Dunfermline beside the Bruce. Possibly had a son Sir Thomas Moray who m. Countess of Menteith. A hostage for David II. d. c 1361 leaving dtr. Joanna who m. Sir Archibald Douglas.

John d. 1361 of the plague at Lincoln while a hostage.

Robert 6th Earl m. Margaret dtr. of Alexander Stewart Earl of Buchan. d. 1442

John 7th Earl m. Margaret, celebrated for her great beauty, dtr. or sister of Sir William Baillie of Lamington. d. 1460.

John 8th Earl. m. Margaret dtr. of the Lord of the Isles. d. 1508.

Alexander d. c 1456.

Adam de Gordon—Crusader 1270. Executed Berwick 12th century.

Sir Adam Lord Gordon. Killed Halidon Hill 1333.

Lord Gordon.

Lord Gordon.

Lord Gordon. Killed Homildon 1402.

Elizabeth Gordon d. 1439 m. Sir Alex Seton d. 1441.

Alexander Gordon 1st Earl of Huntly.

George 2nd Earl of Huntly. m. Annabella dtr. of James I, d. 1501.

Catherine who m. Perkin Warbeck, executed 1499. She d. 1537 sp.

John 9th Earl. d. 1514 sp.

Countess Elizabeth d. 1535. m. Adam Gordon (2nd son)—two other sons and dtr.

Adam, d. 1547.

Alexander, Master of Sutherland and 10th Earl—resigned to him by his mother. d. 1529.

John 11th Earl. "The good Earl John". m. Helen Stewart dtr. of John 3rd Earl of Lennox. d. 1567.

Alexander 12th Earl. m. (1) dtr. of 4th Earl of Caithness. Divorced sp. (2) Jane dtr. of 4th Earl of Huntly and divorced wife of Bothwell, husband of Mary Queen of Scots. d. 1594.

John 13th Earl. m. Agnes dtr. of Alex. 4th Lord Elphinstone. d. 1615.

John 14th Earl. m. Lady Jean Drummond. d. 1679.

George 15th Earl. m. Jean heiress dtr. of 2nd Earl of Wemyss. d. 1703.

John Kt. 16th Earl. m. Helen dtr. of William Lord Cochrane. d. 1733. Succeeded by his grandson.

William 17th Earl. m. Lady Elizabeth Wemyss dtr. of 3rd Earl of Wemyss. d. 1750.

William 18th Earl. m. Mary heiress dtr. of William Maxwell of Preston. d. 1766.

Elizabeth Countess of Sutherland and Baroness Strathnaver in her own right. m. George Granville Leveson-Gower, Viscount Trentham, 2nd Marquis of Stafford, 1st Duke of Sutherland 19th Earl of Sutherland. d. 1833. Elizabeth d. 1839.

George Granville, K.G. 20th Earl of Sutherland, 2nd Duke. m. Harriet Georgina 3rd dtr. of George 6th Earl of Carlisle. d. 1861.

George K.G. 21st Earl, 3rd Duke. m. 1849 Anne Hay Mackenzie Countess of Cromartie etc. in her own right. d. 1892.

Cromartie K.G. 22nd Earl, 4th Duke. m. Millicent dtr. of 4th Earl of Rosslyn. d. 1913.

Francis Mackenzie Earl of Cromartie etc. See Appendix I h/.

George K.T., P.C. 23rd Earl and 5th Duke of Sutherland, Marquis of Stafford, Baron Gower, Baron Strathnaver and a Baronet. m. (1) Lady Eileen Butler dtr. of 7th Earl of Lanesborough, who died 1943 sp. (2) Mrs. Clare Josephine Dunkerley dtr. of Herbert O'Brien. Born 1888, d. 1962 sp.

Lord Alastair M.C. m. Elizabeth Hélène Demarest. d. 1921.
Elizabeth heir presumptive to Earldom and Barony. m. 1946 Major Charles Jansen. 1962 became Countess of Sutherland.

Alastair Viscount Strathnaver. b. 1947.

Martin. b. 1947.   Matthew. b. 1956.   Anabel. b. 1960.

Note: The Sutherland titles together with the Dukedom were granted to the Marquis of Stafford when he married Elizabeth Countess of Sutherland. On the death of Francis 3rd Duke of Bridgewater in 1803 he became entitled to Quarter the Arms Royal of England through his mother Lady Louisa Egerton, who died in 1761, and her descent from Edward III of England, which the descent on the distaff side gave the right to Quarter the Arms Royal of Scotland. This also applies to the House of Cromartie with the additional right of the House of Kintail, allied by marriage to the Royal Houses of Bruce and Stewart, which by a different route they also connect with the Plantagenets. See Appendix I h/.

APPENDIX I f/.
The Frasers of Lovat

The family of Fraser (formerly Frisel) are of French origin and settled in E. Lothian, spreading to Tweeddale in the 12th and 13th centuries and subsequently into Inverness and Aberdeenshire. A line owned Oliver Castle, Peeblesshire in 13th and early 14th centuries, the last of whom, Sir Simon, was executed by Edward I of England in 1306. He left 2 dtrs. co-heiresses who m. Hay of Locherwart and Fleming of Wigton. Male succession continued by posterity of John Fraser a younger brother of the family in the end of the 13th century who was great-grandfather of Sir Simon Fraser. Killed Halidon Hill 1333.

Grandson.
|

Hugh Lord of Lovat portioner with Sir William Fenton, of Ard. m. heiress dtr. of Graham Lord of Lovat.
|

Hugh, High Sheriff of Inverness returned from England 1424 where he had been one of the hostages for King James I. m. 1416 Janet dtr. of William Fenton of Beaufort.
|

Thomas (or Hugh). m. dtr. of Wemyss of Wemyss. d. c 1450.
|

I. Hugh a Lord of Parliament, as Lord Fraser of Lovat, between 1458–1464. m. Margaret dtr. of Lord Glammis. One son Hugh, fell at Flodden, another founded the families of Fareline and Leedclune. dtr. Agnes m. Sir Kenneth Mackenzie of Kintail.
|

II. Thomas m. (1) Janet dtr. of Sir Alexander Gordon of Midmar. (2) Janet dtr. of Andrew 2nd Lord Gray. d. 1524.
|

III. Hugh. m. (1) dtr. of John Grant of Grant. (2) Janet dtr. of Walter Ross of Balnagown. Killed with his eldest son at Loch Lochy 1544 in an engagement with the Macdonalds.
|

IV. (by 2) Alexander. m. Janet dtr. of Sir John Campbell of Calder. d. 1557.
|

V. Hugh. m. Elizabeth dtr. of John Stewart Earl of Atholl. d. 1576.
|

VI. Simon. m. (1) Margaret dtr. of Sir Colin Mackenzie of Kintail.
|

VII. Hugh. m. Isobel dtr. of Sir John Wemyss of Wemyss. d. 1646.
|

VIII. Hugh. m. Anne dtr. of Sir John Mackenzie of Tarbat (father of 1st Earl of Cromartie. d. 1672. Grandson of Hugh 7th Lord.
|

IX. Hugh. m. Amelia dtr. of Marquis of Atholl and had 4 dtrs. d. 1696.

X. Thomas of Beaufort 3rd son of Hugh Lord Lovat and Isobel Wemyss. m. Sybilla 4th dtr. of MacLeod of MacLeod. d. 1696.

XI. Simon. m. Margaret dtr. of Ludovic Grant of Grant. 1747 executed for his part in the rising of 1745. His son General Simon was granted the forfeited estates in 1774 but died 1782 sp. Lord Lovat married secondly Primrose dtr. of Hon. John Campbell of Mamore 1733. A son of this marriage, Archibald Campbell, died 1815 predeceased by five sons when the male representation of the family passed to:

XII. Thomas Alexander Fraser descended from the second son of Alexander 4th Lord Lovat and Janet of the House of Calder. Thomas was created Baron in 1837. d. 1875.
|

XIII. Simon. m. Alice Mary. dtr. of Thomas Blundell. d. 1887.
|

XIV. Simon K.T., G.C.V.O., K.C.M.G., C.B., D.S.O., M.A. m. Hon. Laura Lister dtr. of 4th Lord Ribblesdale. d. 1933.
|

XV. Simon D.S.O. 15th Baron of Lovat, 17th but for the attainder. b. 1911. m. Rosamond dtr. of Sir Delves Broughton.
|

Simon.   Fiona.   Annabel.   Kim.   Hugh.   Andrew.

APPENDIX I g/.
Munro of Foulis

Donald Munro. d. c 1053. Desc. Siol O'Cain of N. Moray as were Macmillans and Buchanans.

Georgius de Munro. d. c 1101.

I. Hugh. 1st Baron of Foulis. d. c 1126.

II. Robert. d. 1164.

III. Donald. d. 1192.

IV. Robert. m. dtr. of Wm. 1st E. of Sutherland. d. 1239.　David progenitor of MacDhaibhidhs.　Allan progenitor of MacAllans of Ferindonald.

V. George. d. c 1269.

VI. Robert. d. 1323; his son killed at Bannockburn but grandson inherited as George 7th, by a dtr. of Earl of Sutherland.

VII. George. k. 1333. m. dtr. of Earl of Ross.　John.

VIII. Robert. k. 1369. m. (1) Jean dtr. of Hugh I of Balnagown. (2) Grace dtr. Sir Adam Forrester of Corstorphine.

IX. Hugh. c 1425.　By (2) Thomas alias Roach.　John.　John m. (1) Isabella dtr. of John Keith (2) Nicholas Sutherland (Duffus).

X. George k. 1452. m. (1) Isobel dtr. Balnagown. (2) Christine dtr. of MacCulloch of Plaids.　By (2) Janet.　Elizabeth.　By (2) John. d. 1475 of Milntown (New Tarbat).

XI George. by (1) k. 1452.　By (2) John d. 1490. m. Finvole dtr. of Earl of Cawdor.　Hugh prog. of Coul (Alness), Balcony, Carbisdale (Culrain), Linseedmore, Erribol, Colcraggie, Kiltearn, Down, Ardullie, Katewell, Teanaird, Killechoan (Mountrich), Teaninich.　William sp.

Thomas. No trace after 1499.　John of Kilmorack.　II. Andrew Mor. d. 1501.

XII. Sir William. k. 1505. Kt. m. Anne dtr. of Duart.　William Vicar of Dingwall 1561–66. etc.　Margaret m. Alex. Mackenzie I of Davochmaluach.　III. Andrew Beg, The Black Baron. d. or killed 1522.

XIII. Hector. d. 1541. m. (1) Catherine dtr. Sir Kenneth 7th of Kintail. (2) Catherine dtr. MacLeod Lewis.　IV. George. d. 1576.　Wm. I of Allan.　Andrew I of Culnauld.

XIV. Robert. (by 1) k. 1547. m. Margaret Dunbar.　Hugh sp.

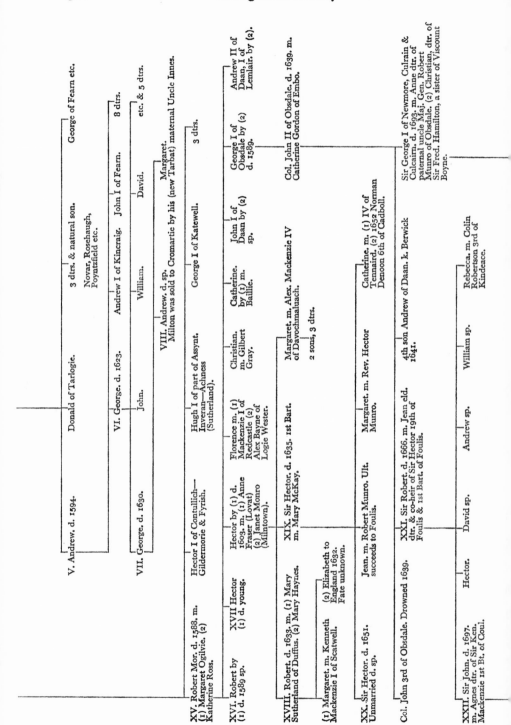

V. Andrew. d. 1594.

Donald of Tarlogie.

3 dtrs. & natural son. Novar, Rosehaugh, Poyntzfield etc.

George of Fearn etc.

VI. George. d. 1623.

Andrew I of Kincraig. John I of Fearn.

8 dtrs.

VII. George, d. 1630.

John.

William.

David.

etc. & 5 dtrs.

Margaret.

VIII. Andrew. d. sp. Milton was sold to Cromartie by his (new Tarbat) maternal Uncle Innes.

XV. Robert Mor. d. 1588. m. (1) Margaret Ogilvie. (2) Katherine Ross.

Hector I of Contullich—Gildermorie & Fyrish.

Hugh I of part of Assynt, Inveran—Achness (Sutherland).

George I of Katewell.

3 dtrs.

XVI. Robert by (1) d. 1589 sp.

XVII Hector (1) d. young.

Hector by (1) d. 1603. m. (1) Anne Fraser (Lovat) (2) Janet Monro (Milntown).

Florence m. (1) Mackenzie I of Redcastle (2) Alex Bayne of Logie Wester.

Christian, m. Gilbert Gray.

Catherine, by (1) m. Baillie.

John I of Daan by (2) sp.

George I of Obsdale by (2) d. 1589.

Andrew II of Daan, I of Lemlair, by (2).

XVIII. Robert, d. 1633. m. (1) Mary Sutherland of Duffus. (2) Mary Haynes.

Margaret, m. Alex. Mackenzie IV of Davochmaluach.

2 sons, 3 dtrs.

Col. John II of Obsdale, d. 1639. m. Catherine Gordon of Embo.

XIX. Sir Hector, d. 1635. 1st Bart. m. Mary McKay.

(1) Margaret, m. Kenneth Mackenzie I of Scatwell.

(2) Elizabeth to England 1632. Fate unknown.

XX. Sir Hector. d. 1651. Unmarried d. sp.

Jean. m. Robert Munro. Ult. succeeds to Foulis.

Margaret, m. Rev. Hector Munro.

Catherine. m. (1) IV of Tennaird. (2) 1652 Norman Denoon 6th of Cadboll.

Col. John 3rd of Obsdale. Drowned 1639.

4th son Andrew of Daan. k. Berwick 1641.

Sir George I of Newmore, Culrain & Culcairn, d. 1693, m. Anne dtr. of paternal uncle Maj. Gen. Robert Munro of Obsdale. (2) Christian, dtr. of Sir Fred. Hamilton, a sister of Viscount Boyne.

XXI. Sir Robert, d. 1666. m. Jean eld. dtr. & co-heir of Sir Hector 19th of Foulis & 1st Bart. of Foulis.

David sp.

Andrew sp.

William sp.

Rebecca, m. Colin Robertson 3rd of Kindeace.

XXII. Sir John, d. 1697. m. Agnes dtr. of Sir Ken. Mackenzie 1st Bt. of Coul.

Hector.

XXIII. Sir Robert. d. 1739. m. Jean Forbes of Culloden.
Andrew of Westertown, Kiltearn.
Christian sp.
Anne, m. her cousin Wm. Robertson of Urchany and 4th Kindeace.
Margaret, m. Capt. D. MacNeill of Kintyre.

XXIV. Sir Robert. k. 1746. m. Mary Seymour.
George of Culcairn—extinct.
Duncan M.D. sp.
Anne, m. Alex. Gordon of Ardoch (Poyntzfield).

Robert. d. inf.
XXV. Sir Harry. m. Anne Rose. d. 1781.
Elizabeth. d. inf.

Robert. d. inf.
XXVI. Sir Hugh. m. Jane Law. d. 1848.
George sp.
Jane sp.
Seymour, d. inf.
Mary Seymour sp.

By (1) Hugh II.
By (2) John sp.
By (2) George. m. (1) Catherine. (2) Anne of Culrain. d. 1724.
By (2) (2 bros. sp.) James. d. 1760. m. Anne Graham.
Charles. d. 1782. m. Mary Anne Ross of Invercassly.
George of Culcairn & Culrain. d. 1845. m. Margaret Montgomery.

XXVII. Sir Charles. d. 1886. m. (1) Amelia Brown. (2) Henrietta.
Harry.
Fredrick.
Gustavus.
Arthur.
Marion.
Amelia.

by (1)
George Fredrick d. young.
XXVIII. Sir Charles. d. 1888. m. Mary Ann Nicolson.
Charles.
George sp.
Amelia.
Maud.

XXIX. Sir Hector. d. 1935. m. Margery Stirling.
Hector. k. 1918 (France).
Eva Marion Munro. b. 1881. m. 1904 Lt. Col. Cecil Gascoigne.
Isobel.
Violet Florence. b. 1889.
Aline Margaret (Lady Wells). b. 1892.

Robert. d. inf.
Cecil Alistair Hector.
Joan Orby. m. (1) Gordon-Ingram. (2) Judge Harold William Paton, D.S.C.

XXX. Patrick Munro. b. 1912. m. 1946. Eleanor Mary French.
Robert Clifton Gascoigne.
Marion Erica. m. Brigadier George Des Champs Chamier, O.B.E.

Baronetcy to Sir George XII Bart. grandson of XXVII Baron & 9th Baronet.

This is a more likely record of the Early Chiefs and Barons of Kintail

Gilleoin na' Aird. John of the Aird.

Aonghsa (Angus) Cristin.

Coinneach (Kenneth).

Methyhamhain (Mathan) MacCoinneach.

I. Coinneach MacMethyhamhain. Distinguished himself against the Norsemen. Honoured by King Alexander II. Held Eilean Donan. m. dtr. of McIver (Crom) from Argyll. d. 1304.

II. Murchaidh MacCoinneach. m. Isabel dtr. of John MacAulay of Lochbroom. d. 1328.

III. Coinneach na Sroin. m. Morba dtr. of MacDougall Lord of the Isles. Executed by Earl of Ross 1346.

IV. Murchaidh Dubh nan Umhag. d. 1375 and was succeeded by his nephew.

V. Coinneach MacEoin (John). m. dtr. of John Lord of the Isles (MacDonald).

VI. Murchaidh (Murdoch) na Drochaid etc. vide table.

This area lay above Beauly. c early 11th century.

In 1034 after the death of King Malcolm II many foreigners were introduced into the great Province of Moray, which included much of Ross.

1040–1050 MacBeth reigned but after him there was a long period of rebellion over the Royal succession. Probably during this period the family group were mov to Kintail, later to be joined by the MacRaes and MacLennans. This was done for reasons of policy, and because this new powerful family had generations of frontier experience fighting the Norsemen, to their north, and who were now holding the Hebrides.

His brother was the founder and progenitor of Clan Matheson.

John de Comyn (Red), Lord of Badenoch. d. 1273.

Marjory Balliol m. John de Comyn, the Black. d. c 1299 at Lochwidert.

John de Comyn, the Red, killed by Bruce 1306.

Joan Comyn of Badenoch. m. David 11th Earl of Atholl. d. 1323.

King John of England.

Natural son Richard Fitzroy de Chilham. 1216. m. Rohesia de Dover and Chilham.

Countess Isabel de Dover. d. 1292. m. David de Strathbogie, 9th Earl of Atholl.

John de Strathbogie, 10th Earl of Atholl. Hanged by Edward I.

David 11th Earl of Atholl. d. 1327. Estates forfeited by Edward I.

David 12th Earl of Atholl, slain 1335.   Margaret m.

APPENDIX I h/.

The Mackenzies of Kintail: Earls of Seaforth: Earls of Cromartie: Mackenzies of Gairloch: Scatwell: Fairburn: Coul: Ord: Kilcoy: Davochmaluach: Loch Slyn: Balloan: Redcastle: Rosehaugh: Applecross, etc.

From the MacVurich Manuscript.

Ferdach

Oirbeirtaigh

Cormac

Ferchar

Loirn

Eirc

Gilleoin na' Aird

Clan Anrais		Mackenzies
Crinan		Cristin
Kenneth		Kenneth
Ewen		Murdoch
Crinan		Duncan
Kenneth		Murdoch
Paul		Gilleoin Mor
Martin	Rosses	Gilleoin Og. m. dtr. of Rolf the
Gillanrias	Paul	Ganger c A.D. 900.
	Murdoch	
Lay Abbots of Applecross and	Ewen	Kenneth
Earls of Ross.	Tire	Angus Crom.
	Paul MacTire	Kenneth, first Chief of Kintail.

See Appendix I b/2.

Colin of Kintail. Distinguished himself at the Battle of Largs and granted charter in 1266 by Alexander III for Kintail and the Castle of Eilean Donan. For saving the life of King Alexander II during a hunt in the Royal Forest of Mar he had been granted as his coat armour the Stag's Head. m. dtr. and heiress of Kenneth MacMathan (Matheson) Chief of the Wester Ross Clans in 1263. Killed by a MacMathan at Lochalsh c 1274.

II. Kenneth. m. Morna dtr. of Alexander Lord of Lorn,   Colin, eldest son, was killed at Glaic Chailean.
descendant of Donald Bane, King of Scotland 1093–97
the brother of King Malcolm III. Kenneth died 1304.

III. Ian Murdoch. m. Margaret dtr. of David de Strathbogie, Earl of Atholl. He sheltered and entertained The Bruce at Eilean Donan, the King being a fugitive from the English and Comyn faction. In 1314 he led his Clan at the Battle of Bannockburn. Died 1338 and buried with his forebears at Iona.

IV. Kenneth, Coinneach-na-Sroine. m. Fionnaghal dtr. of Torquil MacLeod 2nd of Lewis, by his wife Dorothea dtr. of William O'Beolan Earl of Ross. During the captivity of King David II he was captured by the Earl of Ross and executed at Inverness c 1350.

V. Murdoch 'dubh na h'llamha'. m. Isabel dtr. and heiress of Duncan Macaulay of Lochbroom. Granted a charter 1362 by King David Bruce. d. 1375.

VI. Murdoch, 'Murchadh na Drochaid'. m. Finguala dtr. of MacLeod of Harris and Dunvegan by his wife Martha dtr. of Donald Stewart, Earl of Mar, nephew of King Robert the Bruce. By this marriage the Royal blood of the Bruce was introduced into the family of Kintail, as also that of the ancient Kings of Man. d. 1416.

VII. Alexander, 'Ionraic' (The Upright). m. (1) Lady Agnes Campbell dtr. of Colin Earl of Argyll. (2) Margaret MacDougal of Dunolly. Alexander was one of the western Barons who attended the Parliament held at Inverness 1427 summoned by King James I of Scotland. After forfeiture of the Earldom of Ross and Lordship of the Isles Alexander was appointed by the Crown Commissioner for the South of Ross. He was established in Brahan and during his life the clan territory was vastly increased. He died at the age of 90 at Kinellan and was probably buried at Iona. d. 1491.

VIII. Kenneth, 'Coinneach a Bhlair', Kt. m. (1) Lady Margaret MacDonald dtr. of John Lord of the Isles and Earl of Ross. (2) Agnes Fraser dtr. of Hugh Lord Lovat. Defeated the MacDonalds and their allies at the Battle of the Blair 1491. Knighted by King James IV from whom he received a charter for Brahan. d. 1492 and buried at Beauly Priory.

L

King Edward III of England.
|
John of Gaunt, Duke of Lancaster. m. (1) Blanche of Lancaster, by whom a son King Henry IV of England. (2) Constance eldest dtr. and co-heir of Peter, King of Castile and Leon. Issue. (3) Katherine Swynford. Children legitimated by Act of Parliament.

(By 3) John Beaufort, Earl of Somerset. m. Margaret de Thos.
|
Lady Joan or Joanna Beaufort. m. (1) King James I of Scotland 1424. (2) Sir James Stewart, The Black Knight of Lorn, 1439.
|
(By 2) John, 1st Earl of Atholl.

John, 2nd Earl of Atholl. Killed at Flodden 1513. m. Mary dtr. of Colin, 1st Earl of Argyll.
|
John, 3rd Earl of Atholl.   Lady Elizabeth Stewart sometimes called Isabella m. ...

Lady Marjory Stewart. m. John XII. Grant of Grant.
|
Duncan XIII. Grant of Grant.   Barbara.

by (1) Duncan, ancestor of Mackenzie of Hilton and Loggie.

by (2) Hector Roy, Tutor of Kintail. Ancestor of Letterewe, Mountgerald, Lochend-Portmore, Muirton-belmaduthy, Flowerburn and Gairloch.

by (2) A dtr. m. Allan MacLeod of Gairloch.

IX. Kenneth Og the son of his father's first marriage. Did not marry. Was killed at Torwood in Stirling 1497. Succeeded by his eldest half brother.

X. John 'of Killin'. m. Elizabeth dtr. of John Grant of Grant. April 1500 obtained a precept of the clare constat including the lands of Kintail. Charter for Kintail, Eilean Donan and the other lands incorporated in the Free Barony of Eilean Donan in 1508 followed by other charters. Fought at the Battles of Flodden and Pinkie. Became a prisoner of war and was ransomed by his clan. Privy Councillor to Queen Regent Mary and Mary Queen of Scots. Probably planted the great Spanish Chestnuts at Castle Leod. Died at the age of 80 in 1561 and was buried in the family aisle at Beauly.

XI. Kenneth, 'Coinneach na Cuirc'. m. Lady Elizabeth Stewart dtr. of John 2nd Earl of Atholl. A supporter of Mary Queen of Scots and fought for her at Langside. His eldest son Murdoch predeceased him. By Kenneth's marriage the Royal Blood of the Plantagenets was introduced into the family of Kintail, further strengthened by his son's marriage. Died at Killin and buried at Beauly Priory 1568.

Agnes or Janet. m. (1) Angus MacKay ancestor of Lord Reay (2) Ruari MacLeod of Lewis by whom Torquil Conanach.

XII. Colin 'Cam' Kt. m. (1) Barbara dtr. of Sir John Grant of Grant ancestor of the Earls of Seafield. (2) Lady Marjory Stewart dtr. of 3rd Earl of Atholl. Issue (3)—but not legalized—Mary dtr. of Roderick Mackenzie of Davochmaluach. Colin also fought at Langside. He took Chanonry so adding part of the Black Isle to his vast possessions. He died 1594 at Redcastle having 'lived beloved by Princes and people' and died regretted by all on the 14th of June. Buried at Beauly.

—Murdoch predeceased his father.
—Roderick ancestor of Mackenzies of Redcastle and Kincraig.
—Mary. m. (1) Angus MacDonald of Glengarry. (2) Chisholm of Comar.
—Janet. m. Alex. Ross of Balnagown.
—Agnes. m. Lachlan MacIntosh 1567.
—Elizabeth. m. Walter Urquhart of Cromarty 1568.
—Catherine. m. Robert Munro of Foulis.
—Margaret. m. Walter Innes of Inverbreakie 19th Jan. 1556.

See page 306.

XIII. Kenneth 1st Lord Kintail. m. (1) Ann dtr. of George Ross IX of Balnagown with issue. (2) Isabel dtr. of Sir Gilbert Ogilvie of Powrie with issue. Reconstructed Brahan Castle. d. 1611. Buried at Chanonry, Fortrose Cathedral.

Sir Roderick MacKenzie of Castle Leod, Coigach and Tarbat, Kt. Tutor of Kintail; 'Rory Mor'.

XIV. Colin 'The Red Earl' 2nd Lord Mackenzie of Kintail and 1st Earl of Seaforth. m. Lady Margaret Seton dtr. of Alexander Earl of Dunfermline, Lord High Chancellor of Scotland. Colin was predeceased by his only son Alex. His dtr. Anne m. Alexander 2nd Lord Lindsay and 1st Earl of Balcarres. His second dtr. Jane m. (1) John Master of Berriedale with issue. (2) Lord Duffus with issue. Colin d. 1633, buried at Chanonry. Succeeded by

XV. George 2nd Earl of Seaforth, his brother. m. Barbara dtr. of Arthur Lord Forbes. Died in exile at Schiedam in Holland 1651.

XVI. Kenneth 'Mor' 3rd Earl of Seaforth. m. Lady Isobel dtr. of 1st Earl of Cromartie. Forfeited after the Royalist defeat at the Battle of Worcester. Died and was buried at Chanonry at 7 a.m. 16th December 1679.

XVII. Kenneth 'Og' Kt. 4th Earl and 1st Marquis of Seaforth. m. Lady Frances Herbert dtr. of William Marquis of Powis. Fought at siege of Derry. Died in exile in Paris 1701.

XVIII. William 'Dubh' 5th Earl. m. Mary dtr. and heiress of Nicholas Kennet of Coxhow in Northumberland. Out in the rising of 1715 after which his estates were forfeited and then restored.

XIX. Kenneth Lord Fortrose. m. Lady Mary Stewart eldest dtr. of Alexander 6th Earl of Galloway. Issue one son, six daughters. d. 1761.

Hon. Alexander Mackenzie. m. Elizabeth dtr. of Paterson Bishop of Ross.

XX. Kenneth Earl of Seaforth. Raised the Seaforth Highlanders (72nd). m. Lady Caroline Standhope dtr. of Earl of Harrington. No male issue, his dtr. Lady Caroline m. Count Melford. Died at sea 1781.

William Mackenzie. m. Mary dtr. of Matthew Humberston.

XXII. Francis Lord Seaforth, Baron of Kintail. Raised 2nd Bn. Seaforth Highlanders (78th). Sold Kintail etc. m. Mary Proby dtr. of Dean of Lichfield. Five sons who all predeceased their father who died 1815. End of the male line of Seaforth.

XXI. Col. Humberston Mackenzie died of wounds 1783 sp.

XXIII. Hon. Mary Mackenzie. m. (1) Admiral Samuel Hood. (2) 1817 James Stewart 3rd son of 6th Earl of Galloway. d. 1862.

XXIV. Keith William Stewart Mackenzie of Seaforth by (2) m. (1) Hannah Hope Vere of Craigiehall. (2) Alicia Bell. d. 1881.

L*

XXV. James Alexander Francis
Humberston Stewart Mackenzie,
Baron Seaforth of Brahan. d. 1923 sp.

XXVI. Susan Mary. m. (1) Col.
the Hon. J. C. Stanley, as his (2).
(2) Lord St. Helier. d. 1931.

Julia Marchioness of Tweeddale. d.
1937.

By (1) Madeline. m. 1903 9th
Viscount and 1st Earl of Middleton.
1876–1966.

By (2) Lord St. Helier.

Osma Mary Dorothy. m. 1896 Henry
Alhusen.

XXVII. Hon. Francis Stewart
Mackenzie. b. 1910. m. Margaret dtr.
of Major the Hon. Charles Henry
Lyell. Killed N. Africa 1943. sp.

Michael Stewart Mackenzie, M.C.
Killed in action Sept. 1943. sp.

(Helena) Madeline b. 1897. m. (1)
Sir Geoffrey Congreve 1922. Three
dtrs. (2) 1942 Reginald James Tyler.
d. 1950. He assumed name of
Stewart Mackenzie 1944.

from page 305

I. Sir Roderick Mackenzie of Castle Leod, Coigach and
Tarbat, Kt. Tutor of Kintail—'Rory Mor'. m. Margaret
MacLeod heiress of Coigach and Lewis dtr. of Torquil
'Conanach' of Lewis. Castle Leod was inherited by
Rorie from his father the Baron of Kintail etc. Tarbat,
Castlehaven acquired from George Munro of Meikle
Tarrell 1623 for 110,000 merks. The principal mansion
of six was the Castle of Tarbat, Ballone or Balloan in
the Tarbat Promontory, but the old name of Inverbroom
is Ballone where is Auchluanachan. Keanlochluichart in
Contin was granted in 1463 by John Lord of the Isles and
Earl of Ross, to Alexander VIII of Kintail. Prior to 1610
Easter Tarbat had been held by Dunbars who got it in
1538 from Corbet. The first of the name in these parts
Donald Corbet, had been given the property in 1463 by
the Earl of Ross for his services as the Earl's Esquire—
previously the owner had been John Tullach. In 1382 the
name of Terrell is recorded and before him Boner
Terrell was succeeded by McCulloch in 1505 the latter
being heir to his Terrell grandmother. d. September
1626.

—Alexander 1st of Kilcoy, Inverallochy, Findon,
　Kinnoch, Kernsary, Muirton and Cleanwaters.
—Colin 1st of Kinnoch and Pitlundie.
—Murdoch of Kensary.
—Margaret. m. Simon Lord Lovat. A dtr. m. MacLean
　of Duart.
—Mary. m. Donald MacDonald of Sleat. sp.
—Alexander of Assynt. Illegitimate by Mary of Davoch
　Maluach. Ancestor of Mackenzies of Applecross, Coul,
　Delvine, Auldeny, Torridon, Lentran, Kinnahaird.
—Kenneth 1st Lord Kintail. See page 305.

II. Sir John 1628 1st Bart. of Tarbat. m. Margaret
dtr. and heiress of Sir George Erskine of Innerteil in
Fife. She used the title of Lady Castlehaven in later life.
d. 1654.

—Colin. Illegitimate. Chamberlain to the family.
—John. Illegitimate. Archdeacon of Ross.
—Kenneth of Scatwell. m. (1) Margaret dtr. of Sir
　Robert Munro of Foulis. (2) Jane dtr. of Walter Ross of
　Invercarron. d. 1662. Ancestor of Mackenzies of
　Scatwell, Findon, Scotsburn.
—Colin of Tarvey. m. widow of John Mackenzie of
　Lochsline.
—Alexander of Ballone. m. widow of Kenneth Mackenzie
　of Inverlael. d. 1645.
—Charles. d. 1629. sp.
—James. d. 1647 sp.
—Margaret. m. Sir James MacDonald of Sleat.

III. Sir George Viscount Tarbat, Lord MacLeod and
Castlehaven 1685. 1st Earl of Cromartie 1703. m. (1)
Anne Sinclair dtr. of Sir James of Mey. (2) Margaret
Countess of Wemyss. 1656 acquired New Tarbat
Milntown. Lord Justice General of Scotland. Secretary
of State for Scotland. 1686 The Barony of Tarbat
erected into a regality. d. 1714.

—John. d. 1662 sp.
—Roderick of Prestonhall. Lord Justice Clerk 1702. Lord
　of Session 1703. m. (1) Mary dtr. of Archbishop
　Burnet. (2) Margaret Haliburton widow of Sir George
　Haliburton and widow of Sir George Mackenzie of
　Rosehaugh. Lord Advocate. d. 1712.
—Alexander of Ardloch and Kinellan. Issue.
—Kenneth. m. Isobel Auchinleck.
—James. sp.
—Margaret. m. (1) MacLeod of MacLeod. sp. (2) Sir
　James Campbell of Lawers. Issue.
—Anne. m. Hugh Lord Lovat. Issue.
—Isobel. m. Kenneth Earl of Seaforth. Issue.
—Barbara. m. Alexander Mackenzie of Gairloch. Issue.
—Catherine. m. Sir John Campbell of Aberuchil. Issue.

IV. John 2nd Earl. m. (1) Lady Elizabeth Gordon dtr.
of the Earl of Aboyne. (2) Hon. Mary Murray dtr. of
Patrick Lord Elibank. (3) Hon. Anne Fraser dtr. of
Hugh Lord Lovat. Out in 1715 Rising. d. 1731.

—Hon. Sir Kenneth Mackenzie of Grandvale and
　Cromarty Bart. Had six sons and several dtrs. d. 1729.
　Sir George 2nd Bart. m. Elizabeth Reid. Sold
　Cromarty to Captain Urquhart. d. 1748 sp.
—Hon. Sir James of Royston Bart. Lord of Session 1710.
　m. dtr. of Sir George Mackenzie of Rosehaugh. d. 1744.
—Lady Margaret. m. sp.
—Lady Elizabeth. m. Sir George Brown of Coalstoun.
　Issue.
—Lady Jean. m. Sir Thomas Stewart of Balcaskie. Issue.
—Lady Anne. m. John Sinclair son of Earl of Caithness.
　Issue.

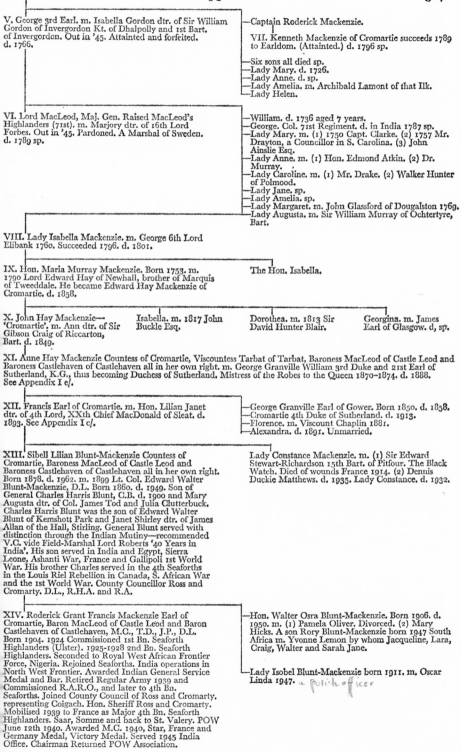

V. George 3rd Earl. m. Isabella Gordon dtr. of Sir William Gordon of Invergordon Kt. of Dhalpolly and 1st Bart. of Invergordon. Out in '45. Attainted and forfeited. d. 1766.

—Captain Roderick Mackenzie.

   VII. Kenneth Mackenzie of Cromartie succeeds 1789 to Earldom. (Attainted.) d. 1796 sp.

—Six sons all died sp.
—Lady Mary. d. 1726.
—Lady Anne. d. sp.
—Lady Amelia. m. Archibald Lamont of that Ilk.
—Lady Helen.

VI. Lord MacLeod, Maj. Gen. Raised MacLeod's Highlanders (71st). m. Marjory dtr. of 16th Lord Forbes. Out in '45. Pardoned. A Marshal of Sweden. d. 1789 sp.

—William. d. 1736 aged 7 years.
—George. Col. 71st Regiment. d. in India 1787 sp.
—Lady Mary. m. (1) 1750 Capt. Clarke. (2) 1757 Mr. Drayton, a Councillor in S. Carolina. (3) John Ainslie Esq.
—Lady Anne. m. (1) Hon. Edmond Atkin. (2) Dr. Murray.
—Lady Caroline. m. (1) Mr. Drake. (2) Walker Hunter of Polmood.
—Lady Jane. sp.
—Lady Amelia. sp.
—Lady Margaret. m. John Glassford of Dougalston 1769.
—Lady Augusta. m. Sir William Murray of Ochtertyre, Bart.

VIII. Lady Isabella Mackenzie. m. George 6th Lord Elibank 1760. Succeeded 1796. d. 1801.

IX. Hon. Maria Murray Mackenzie. Born 1753. m. 1790 Lord Edward Hay of Newhall, brother of Marquis of Tweeddale. He became Edward Hay Mackenzie of Cromartie. d. 1858.

The Hon. Isabella.

X. John Hay Mackenzie— 'Cromartie'. m. Ann dtr. of Sir Gibson Craig of Riccarton, Bart. d. 1849.

Isabella. m. 1817 John Buckle Esq.

Dorothea. m. 1813 Sir David Hunter Blair.

Georgina. m. James Earl of Glasgow. d, sp.

XI. Anne Hay Mackenzie Countess of Cromartie, Viscountess Tarbat of Tarbat, Baroness MacLeod of Castle Leod and Baroness Castlehaven of Castlehaven all in her own right. m. George Granville William 3rd Duke and 21st Earl of Sutherland, K.G., thus becoming Duchess of Sutherland. Mistress of the Robes to the Queen 1870–1874. d. 1888. See Appendix I e/.

XII. Francis Earl of Cromartie. m. Hon. Lilian Janet dtr. of 4th Lord, XXth Chief MacDonald of Sleat. d. 1893. See Appendix I c/.

—George Granville Earl of Gower. Born 1850. d. 1858.
—Cromartie 4th Duke of Sutherland. d. 1913.
—Florence. m. Viscount Chaplin 1881.
—Alexandra. d. 1891. Unmarried.

XIII. Sibell Lilian Blunt-Mackenzie Countess of Cromartie, Baroness MacLeod of Castle Leod and Baroness Castlehaven of Castlehaven all in her own right. Born 1878. d. 1962. m. 1899 Lt. Col. Edward Walter Blunt-Mackenzie, D.L. Born 1860. d. 1949. Son of General Charles Harris Blunt, C.B. d. 1900 and Mary Augusta dtr. of Col. James Tod and Julia Clutterbuck. Charles Harris Blunt was the son of Edward Walter Blunt of Kemshott Park and Janet Shirley dtr. of James Allan of the Hall, Stirling. General Blunt served with distinction through the Indian Mutiny—recommended V.C. vide Field-Marshal Lord Roberts '40 Years in India'. His son served in India and Egypt, Sierra Leone, Ashanti War, France and Gallipoli 1st World War. His brother Charles served in the 4th Seaforths in the Louis Riel Rebellion in Canada, S. African War and the 1st World War. County Councillor Ross and Cromarty. D.L., R.H.A. and R.A.

Lady Constance Mackenzie. m. (1) Sir Edward Stewart-Richardson 15th Bart. of Pitfour. The Black Watch. Died of wounds France 1914. (2) Dennis Duckie Matthews. d. 1935. Lady Constance. d. 1932.

XIV. Roderick Grant Francis Mackenzie Earl of Cromartie, Baron MacLeod of Castle Leod and Baron Castlehaven of Castlehaven, M.C., T.D., J.P., D.L. Born 1904. 1924 Commissioned 1st Bn. Seaforth Highlanders (Ulster). 1925-1928 2nd Bn. Seaforth Highlanders. Seconded to Royal West African Frontier Force, Nigeria. Rejoined Seaforths. India operations in North West Frontier. Awarded Indian General Service Medal and Bar. Retired Regular Army 1939 and Commissioned R.A.R.O., and later to 4th Bn. Seaforths. Joined County Council of Ross and Cromarty. representing Coigach. Hon. Sheriff Ross and Cromarty. Mobilised 1939 to France as Major 4th Bn. Seaforth Highlanders. Saar, Somme and back to St. Valery. POW June 12th 1940. Awarded M.C. 1940, Star, France and Germany Medal, Victory Medal. Served 1945 India Office. Chairman Returned POW Association.

—Hon. Walter Osra Blunt-Mackenzie. Born 1906. d. 1950. m. (1) Pamela Oliver. Divorced. (2) Mary Hicks. A son Rory Blunt-Mackenzie born 1947 South Africa m. Yvonne Lemon by whom Jacqueline, Lara, Craig, Walter and Sarah Jane.

—Lady Isobel Blunt-Mackenzie born 1911. m. Oscar Linda 1947. a polish officer

Secretary Scottish Peers Association House of Lords.
Returned to Local Government. Representative for
Fodderty and Strathpeffer. 1971 elected Convener Ross
and Cromarty County Council till re-organisation, then
Convener of District of Ross and Cromarty. Retired from
Local Government May 1977. Made Freeman of Ross
and Cromarty 3rd December 1977. m. (1) Dorothy
Downing Porter. (2) Olga Mendoza Stuart Laurance.
(3) Lilias Janet Garvie MacLeod.

| John Ruaridh Mackenzie Viscount Tarbat. Born 1948. By (2). m. 1973 Helen Murray. | Hon. Sibell Anne Julia. By (1) Born 1934. m. Francis Hadwen. James born 1957, Georgina born 1959. | Hon. Gilean Francis. By (1). Born 1936. m. René Welter 1959. Nadine born 1960, Michael born 1964. |

APPENDIX I i/.
The Urquharts of Cromarty (Kinbeachie, Braelangwell, Newhall, Monteagle and Cromarty: all estates on the Black Isle)

Sir Adam m. Marjorie dtr. of Griffin Prince of Wales b. 1071.

Edward m. Jane Caron Scrimjour b. 1100.

Richard Urquhart of Cromarty m. Ann b. 1123.

Sir Philip m. Magdalane dtr. of Gilchrist Earl of Angus b. 1158. Knighted by William 'The Lion' 1186.

Robert m. Girsel dtr. of Keith of Marshall b. 1187.

George m. dtr. of Crawford Lindsay b. 1215.

James m. Sophia dtr. of MacDuff Earl of Fife b. 1244.

David m. Eleanor dtr. of House of Seaton b. 1272.

Francis m. Rosalind dtr. of Gilbert Hay of Arrol (Errol) b. 1299.

William Urquhart of Cromarty, called Gulielmus de Monte Alto m. (1) Lilias dtr. of Hugh Earl of Ross. (2) Violet dtr. of John Cumming Earl of Buchan.

(Above according to Sir Thomas Urquhart 1611-1660 (Mythical). Below historical.)

Adam Urquhart hereditary Sheriff of Cromarty m. Brigida dtr. of Fleming of Cumbernauld.—Charter 1365.

John m. Agnes dtr. of Sir Alexander Ramsay of Dalhousie.

Sir William m. Susana dtr. of Forbes of that Ilk. Remission by James II 1457.

Thomas of Tarnaway (Burdsyards) Keeper of Darnaway Castle.

Helen m. Thos. Baird 1363.

Alexander m. Catherine dtr. of Sir J. Ogilvie of Deskford. Served heir 1475.

Thomas 1475-1557. m. Helen Abernethy dtr. of Lord Saltoun. (They had 25 sons and 11 daughters.) Seven sons killed at Battle of Pinkie 1547.

John in Sweden.

Alexander. m. Beatrice Innes dtr. of Innes of Auchintoul. d. before 1554.

(Monteagle branch is extinct.)

Thomas Urquhart of Davidston. m. Christina Murray, whence Kinbeachie, Newhall, Braelangwell and Monteagle. Kinudie (after 1660 Newhall) passed out of the possession of the Urquharts 1727 and passed to Gordons and a member of the family married David Urquhart of Braelangwell. In 1808 two Mackenzie brothers owned it and Dr. Shaw Mackenzie inherited it from them. The Braelangwell Estate was sold by Captain Charles Gordon Urquhart killed accidentally in June 1828.

William d. sp. m. Mariot Rose of Kilravock.

Walter served heir 1564, m. (1) Elizabeth (1579) dtr. of Kenneth Mackenzie of Kintail. (2) Elizabeth Rose of Kilravock, she married 2nd and Robert Munro of Foulis d. 1606.

John of Craigfintray (Castle Craig) The Tutor', m. (1) Elizabeth Gordon of Cairnburrow d. 1631. (2) Jean Abernethy of Saltoun. (3) Elizabeth Seton of Meldrum.

By 3rd wife. Patrick 1611–1644. Urquharts of Meldrum.

Henry 2nd son. m. Elizabeth Ogilvie of Dunlugas d. in father's lifetime.

John of Laithers. m. Isobel Irvine of Drum & Craigfintray. d. 1631.

Sir Thomas b. 1568. m. Christina Elphinstone.

John. m. Elizabeth Innes of Innes. d. 1634.

Sir Thomas d. 1660 sp.

Sir Alexander. d. 1667 sp.

Sir John. m. Lady Barbara Mackenzie dtr. of George 2nd Earl of Seaforth and became head of the Urquhart family in 1667.

Jonathan married Lady J. Graham dtr. of 2nd Marquis of Montrose. Sold Cromarty (Black Isle) with the lands of Davidstoun, Brae, Newhall, Braelangwell, etc. 1685 to Sir George Mackenzie, Viscount Tarbat, who made this property over to his 3rd son Sir Kenneth Mackenzie. In 1741 this Black Isle property was bought back by Captain John Urquhart of Craigston. His son, William Urquhart of Craigston, sold it again in 1763 to Patrick Lord Elibank, subsequently it passed again by sale in 1772 to George Ross who pulled down old Cromarty Castle and built the present Cromarty House, still occupied by his descendants.

Col. James died 3rd January 1741. Last male of the Cromarty line.

Grizel died 1761. sp.

Walter d. sp.

Note: It is supposed that W. E. Gladstone was descended from the Urquharts of Cromarty thus:—

Henry Urquhart of Cromarty.

Margaret. m. Murdoch Mackenzie of Fairburn. d. 1590.

Rev. John Mackenzie. m. Margaret Grant of Ballindalloch.

Catherine. m. Mackenzie of Kincraig.

Margaret. m. Gilbert Robertson 2nd of Kindeace.

Colin 3rd of Kindeace. m. Rebecca Munro of Foulis.

George his 2nd son. m. Agnes Barbour of Aldowrie.

Andrew Robertson Provost of Dingwall. m. 1760 Ann Mackenzie (Torridon family).

Ann. d. 1835. m. Mr. Gladstone (Sir J. of Fasque).

W. E. Gladstone.

APPENDIX II

Ecclesiastical

Parishes of the Diocese of Ross constituted 1124 as Rosemarkie, but called Ross by 13th century—these Parishes gradually replaced St. Ninian's and St. Columba's Celtic Church organization.

Parish	Patron Saint	Patrimony of	Notes
Ardersier	—	Dean of Ross	This Parish now in Moray.
Kintail	St. Duthac martyred by Vikings 1088.	Dean & Chapter	
Lochalsh	St. Congan	Dean & Chapter	Now includes Kilillan—St. Fillan.
Lochcarron	St. Maelrubha	Dean & Chapter	
Applecross	St. Maelrubha	Dean & Chapter	
Gairloch	—	Dean & Chapter	Included Inverewe and Kinlochewe.
Lochbroom	—	Dean & Chapter	Contained Kirks of *Coigach*—Meikle and Little Strath.

These Churches furnished the funds for Dean & Chapter.

Parish	Patron Saint	Patrimony of	Notes
Kincardine	St. Columba	Prebend	
Edderton	—	Subdean	
Tain	St. Duthac, probably St. Barchan previous to 1088.	Subdean	In 1481 on Sept. 12 the Collegiate Church of Tain was founded by Bishop Thomas of Ross, served by a Provost, 11 Prebendaries, 2 Deacons, a clerk as bell-ringer and Holy Water carrier and 3 singing boys, the organization being modelled on the Collegiate Church of Corstorphine. The 2nd Prebendary of Newmore, was subdean, the 3rd of Dunscaith Precentor, the others bearing the titles of Tarlogie-Morangie. Cambuscurry, the 6th of Innerathy, the old site of Tain till covered by sea near to the present mouth of the River, was Deacon, the 9th was Sacrist. The site of the shrine of St. Duthac was a favourite place of pilgrimage, and had conferred the right of a sanctuary or girth on Tain, since 11th century.
Tarbat	St. Colman	—	Belonged to *Fearn* Abbey and included till Reformation the Parish of *Fearn*.
Nigg	St. Fiacre?	—	
Kilmuir Wester	St. Mary	Dean	This and parish of Suddie now form Knockbain parish.
Kilmuir Easter	St. Mary	Prebend	
Logie Easter	—	Treasurer	

Parish	Patron Saint	Patrimony of	Notes
Rosskeen	—	Prebend	
Nonikiln	St. Ninian	—	Joined with Rosskeen Parish.
Alness	—	Subdean	
Kiltearn	St. Tighernach	Prebend	Belonged to Paisley Abbey.
Lemlair	St. Brigh (or *Bride*, Bridgit)	—	Now part of Kiltearn Parish.
Dingwall	—	—	Belonged to Priory of Pluscardine in Moray, the Parish Church having a Chaplaincy of St. Lawrence and an Aisle or Chapel of St. Clement; the Parish of Dingwall was in early times always given its Gaelic name of *Inerfueran* or *Inbherpeffer*.
Kinettas	—	Chancellor	Joined to Fodderty Parish.
Contin	St. Maelrubha	Prebend	Which has an ancient Cairn in the Coul burying ground of *Preas Mourie*.
Urray	St. Constantine?	Subchanter	
Kilchrist	St. Saviour	Precentor	13th century Tarradale now joined to the Parish of Urray.
Killearnan	St. Iturnan	Archdeacon	In 13th century Parish of Eddirdore. St. Iturnan died 668 (Annals of Tighernac.)
Suddie	St. Duthac	Chancellor	This and Kilmuir Wester now form Knockbain.
Morangie	—	Prebend	Joined Parish of Tain.
Avoch	—	—	The Chapel in the Castle of Avoch was presented to Kinloss Abbey (Moray) 1255.
Logie Wester	St. Bride	Treasurer	⎰Now form Parish of Urquhart
Urquhart	St. Maelrubha	Treasurer	⎱or Ferintosh.
Cullicudden	St. Martin	Subdean	And Kirkmichael now Parish of Resolis.
Kirkmichael	St. Michael	Prebend	
Cromarty	St. Moluag	—	One-quarter of revenues of Rosemarkie and Cromarty went to Dean, Chancellor, Treasurer and Precentor.
Locuinerherath	—not identified—		
Kynteryth	—not identified—		
Rosemarkie united with Chanonry Fortrose	St. Moluag later St. *Curadain* called Boniface who along with St. Peter came to be patrons of Cathedral Church at Chanonry, Fortrose.		
Strathmore	St. Kiran	—	Probably part of Lochbroom.
Fearn	St. Ninian	—	From part of Parish of Tarbat called Nova Farina after removal of Abbey there.
Brahan	—	—	13th century Bron, later divided between Fodderty and Urray Parishes.
Fodderty	St. Moluag & St. Mary		
Glenshiel	St. Kentigerna		Formed from part of Kintail Parish.
Kilmorack	St. Moroc		Now in Inverness.
Strathconon	—		

The Lewis formed part of the Diocese of the Isles and did not come into Ross till the Island came into possession of the House of Kintail, when the Rights of Patronage passed to Seaforth, the Parishes being largely filled by Kintail men.
Duties. The Parochial duties were performed by Vicars—the Prebendaries drew their

revenues from the Cathedral funds (Chanonry). The Archdeacon of Ross was Minister of Killearnon—the Chancellor Minister of Kinettas, who was also the judge of the Bishop's Court, Secretary of the Chapter and keeper of the Seal. The Parish of the Treasurer of Ross was Urquhart. The Precentor arranged the services and presided over choir. In cases of large Parishes like *Gairloch* and Lochbroom, there were chapels of Ease, founded for benefit of the old and infirm, conducted by Curates.

The Bishops of Ross

I.	MacBeth 1124	
II.	Simeon c. 1150	
III.	Gregory 1161	
IV.	Reinaldus (Ranald)	1195
V.	Robert I	
VI.	Duthac?	
VII.	Robert II 1260	
VIII.	Robert III 1271	
IX.	Matthaius 1272	
X.	Thomas de Fyvie 1274	
XI.	Robert IV 1284	
XII.	Thomas de Dundumore 1309	
XIII.	Roger I 1328	
XIV.	John I 1340	
XV.	Alexander 1357	
XVI.	Alexander	
XVII.	John II 1420	
XVIII.	Thomas Urquhart 1441	
XIX.	Henry 1463	
XX.	Thomas 1481	
XXI.	William Elphinstone 1482	

Founder of Aberdeen University.

XXII.	John Fraser 1485
XXIII.	Robert Cockburn 1508, in 1516 sent to France to ask for Francois 1ᵉʳ's daughter Louise as wife for James V but she was already promised to Charles of Spain.
XXIV.	James Hay 1525
XXV.	Robert Cairncross 1539
	vacant 1549
XXVI.	David Panter 1553
	vacant 1560 June
XXVII.	Henry Sinclair 1560
XXVIII.	John Lesley 1565; was also private secretary to Mary Queen of Scots, Vicar General and Dean of Cathedral Church. Mungo Monipenny acted for the Bishop.

After the Reformation—Episcopalian

1598 David Lindsay—before Presbyterian Minister of Leith. Baptized Prince Charles
—later Charles I, who had held additional title of Earl of Ross.

1633 John Maxwell—Archbishop Laud's strongest opponent.

1663 John Patterson

1679 Alexander Young

1680 Andrew Wood

1684 James Ramsay—to Revolution and dis-establishment of the Episcopal Church of Scotland.

The Destination of Church Lands

When James VI established Protestant Episcopacy the Patronage of Parishes which had belonged to the Chapter, went to the Protestant Bishop. The lands of the Monasteries and Priories were erected into Lordships or Baronies, the right of patronage passing to the lay holders of these, but some passing to the Crown. The last Prior disposed of Beauly Priory in 1558 to Lord Lovat; in 1716 its lands were forfeited by Alexander Mackenzie of Fraserdale, who had married heiress of Lovat, and became crown property. The greater portion of the lands belonging to the Abbey of *Fearn* were erected into the Barony of Geanies in 1599, going to Sir Patrick Murray.

Formation of Enlarged Barony of Delny

In addition to the Baronies founded on the ruins of the Monastic houses in Ross, the 'post' 1477 Royal Earldom of Ross became in part the Barony of Delny, itself once a smaller Barony included in the old Earldom of Ross—William Keith of the family of Ravenscraig held this swollen Barony from the Crown in 1599, and it consisted of the lands of: Allan, Calrossie, Glastullich, Meikle Meddat, Wester and Easter Pollo, Balintraid, Inchfuir, Kincraig, Balcony, Culcraggie, Miln of Alness, the Yair of Balcony, Swordale, Fyrish, Miln of Culcraggie, the Fishings of Ardmore, Morrichmore, Petnullie, Balicherry, the Superiority of Dingwall, Kinnairdie, Glack, Dochmaluog, Inchvannie, Ochterneed, Dunglust, Western Fairburn, Urray, Arcan and Inchnaclearach, all the upper waters of Conon, and Mill of Culbokie.

Within this trust went the Patronage of the Kirks of Kilmuir (Easter), Ardersier, Killearnan, Fodderty, Urquhart, Killechrist, Kilmorack, Loggie, Tain, Edderton, Kinettas, Rosemarkie, Cromarty, Urray, Roskeen, Kincardine, Alness and the Chapels of Alness, Tarbat, Nuwmore, and Tarlogie.

In 1608 this Barony and Patronage which belonged to the Keiths had been acquired by Lord Balmerino, but were conveyed to Sir Robert Innes of that Ilk in 1631. In 1606 the Bishops had been restored to their honours, Kirks, teinds etc. and in 1617 the Chapters, Deans, Archdeans etc. were restored to their manses, glebes, rents and livings. The Bishop raised an action against Innes which resulted in the Patronages being resigned to King Charles I in favour of the Bishop and his successors.

During the time of the suppression of Episcopacy, and in 1656, Sir John Innes—in spite of the resignation to the Crown—conveyed the rights of patronage to Sir George Mackenzie of Castle Leod, *Coigach* and Tarbat, 1st Earl of Cromatie, who had acquired Milntown (New Tarbat) and other parts of the Barony of Delny.

On the restoration of the Bishops in 1606 the Church lands had included:— Cullicudden, Farness, Culbo, Woodhead, Balnagiac, Rosemarkie and Chanonry, Killearnan, Raddery, Broomhill, Contin, Insch, Allangrange, Druminoir, Allanglack, Applecross, and Church lands of Lochalsh, Lochcarron, Kilmuir and Lochbroom, Little Brahan and various Mills —the latter valuable on account of dues they could levy, as well as fishings on various waters.

Many of these lands had fallen into the hands of laymen which was a great encouragement to sign the National Covenant and join the Presbyterian Party.

Religious Houses in Scotland

By 1153 a very large number were completed including Chanonry in Ross. By 1207 there were 36 Houses of Monks and Canons, including Beauly 1230, *Fearn* c.1227 in Ross, and St. Clement's Cathedral at Rodil in Harris. By the end of the 15th century this had increased to 86 Houses. From the close of the 14th century onward Collegiate Churches were founded, served by 'College' of Clergy and founded by Landowners and Trade Guilds for Canonical Services, and commemoration of founders. There were about 40 in all, including Tain in Ross founded 1481. Pre-Reformation Churches (Parish) less Argyll numbered 924—'post' 600 grouped in 53 Presbyteries.

Fearn Abbey or *Manachainn Rois*

As mentioned in the text, the original foundation, A.D. 400 of St. Ninian or St. Finbar, was situated at Midfearn near Ardgay on the flats below the junction of the Tain and the Struie Road from Alness which crosses the hills via the pass. It is possible that a Reodatius or Reodaide was an early Abbot, though the generally accepted theory is that this man was the Abb Ferna of Ferns in Ireland mentioned in the Annals of Tighernac 763 who was connected only with Tarbat. But if as is possible the original settlement at Midfearn was from the beginning connected with the parish of Tarbat, which later included New *Fearn*, he may have been the Abbot of our possible Ninian foundation, having no connection with the Irishman. There is at Tarbat Church a sculptured tombstone with the inscription in Saxon characters, unfortunately multilated and bearing the name 'Reo . . . til', and this, usually, has been accepted as referring to the Irishman.

In 1223 or 1227 Fearchar *Mac an t'Sagairt* 1st Earl of Ross re-founded the Abbey, converting it into a House for the Premonstratensian Order of Reformed Augustinians— (reformed by the Archbishop of Magdeburg 1125 at Premontre). The uniform of this order consisted of a black cassock, rochet, square cornered white cap, long white cope, with an almuce of white fur carried over the right arm. Fearchar chose as the head of this establishment a canon of Whithorn (*Candida Casa*), the ancient see of St. Ninian.

Between the years 1238–42, the Abbacy of *Fearn* was removed to New *Fearn*, (Nova Farina) in the parish of Tarbat, possibly on account of local feeling in Ardgay being still faithful to the old Celtic Church system. The new Abbey was first built in rough stone but in 1321 was rebuilt and the buildings thatched, remaining so till the Reformation. It is probable that the effigy on Earl Fearchar's tomb was sculptured at the time of rebuilding.

The year 1599 saw most of the Abbey lands erected into the Barony of Geanies and granted to Sir Patrick Murray, the remaining lands going to the Bishop of Ross. In 1617 the Abbey was united to the See of Ross and in 1628 a parish of *Fearn* was formed out of part of the parish of Tarbat, the Abbey Church becoming the Parish Church.

The next momentous event in the long history of this Abbey was a tragic accident, foretold by the appearance of a Ban-shee washing the blood-stained shrouds of the victims to be, in Loch Eye (Slyn). One Sunday in October 1742 after a heavy fall of snow the roof of the Abbey Church fell, killing 36 people, the casualties would have been higher had it not been for the conduct of the visiting preacher the 'Ministear laidir of *Gairloch*'. For about a generation the Church was not used but in 1772 a new roof was put up and the church re-opened for public worship.

The list of Abbots is interesting, showing that out of a total of 21 only six, perhaps less, were Lowlanders, people who so frequently found their way to the head of Ecclesiastical concerns; here the majority were Highlanders. Perhaps the financial inducements were insufficient in this out of the way corner to attract the Cleric from southern Scotland.

List of Abbots

1223/7–1242	Abbot Malcolm of Galloway. Abbey moved to New *Fearn*.
1242–1246	Malcolm of Nigg.
1246–1274	Matthaeus—Bishop of Ross 1272–74 (Fordun).
1274–1298	Colin—witness to a charter in 1298.
1299–1338	Abbot Martin—a Canon of *Candida Casa*.
also	John—a Canon of *Candida Casa*. 1299–1350 Abbey rebuilt.
1338–1350	Abbot Mark Ross—a Knight.
1350– ?	Abbot Donald—a nephew of the Earl of Ross.
died 1407	Adam Monilaw.
	Thomas Cattanach presented by Prior of Whithorn but rejected by *Fearn*.
1407–1440	Finlay Ferrier—grandson of William Ferrier, Vicar of Tain.
1444–1485	Abbot Finlay MacFead—whose tomb and effigy still exist.
1485	Thomas McCulloch—quarrelled with Andrew Stewart, Bishop of Caithness. Was deposed so erected a private Chapel at Mid-Geanies. Andrew Stewart was of the House of Innermeath and was also Abbot of Kelso.
1485–1527	Abbot Patrick Hamilton—nephew of the Regent Duke of Albany, his father being Sir Alexander Hamilton of Kincavel who had married Albany's half sister. John Stewart Duke of Albany was the grandson of King James II and Mary of Gueldres. Abbot Patrick was greatly influenced by the teachings of Luther, whom he had met while studying in Europe with the result that his 'reforming' sermons gave offence, being judged heretical. He was burned before the gate of his old college of St. Salvator's, St. Andrews.
1528–1540	Abbot Donald Denoon from Argyll, the Abbey lands of Cadboll became his property.
1540–1545	Abbot Robert Cairncross repaired the Abbey. He was Bishop of Ross, Provost of Corstorphine, Abbot of Holyroodhouse.
1545–1569	Abbot Nicholas Ross. Died at *Fearn*. He was also Provost of Tain Collegiate Church, a secular charge.
1569–1595	
1595–1597	Thomas Ross of Culnahar who, owing to troubles, resided at Forres but buried at *Fearn*.
1597–1599	Walter Ross of Morangy, son of the preceding and the last Commendator of the Abbey of *Fearn*.
1599	Most of the Abbey lands turned into the Barony of Geanies and granted to Sir Patrick Murray, while remaining lands were annexed to the Bishop of Ross.
1617	Abbey united to the See of Ross.
1628	Erection of Parish of *Fearn* with Abbey as Parish Church.

M

APPENDIX III

The Royal Castle of Dingwall

A stronghold of great antiquity, known to have existed prior to the Norwegian occupation (c. 1040–60), when it consisted of earthworks surrounding either a timber or stone *dun*, situated at the end of a narrow peninsula which thrust itself from the mainland into the tidal swamp formed by the western reach of the Cromarty Firth. The waters receded while more and more silt filled up this now non-existent arm of the Firth, and though there is no record of the rate of this evolutionary progress, it is probably safe to say that by the end of the 12th century, the *Dun* occupied a less obviously defined peninsula, the north and west faces now being protected by swampy ground and the winding course of the River Peffrey, though on the east the waters and mud of the Firth would still serve as a natural barrier. As time went on the *Dun* developed into a Motte and Bailey Castle with most of the internal buildings constructed with timber.

Since the days of the MacBeth *Mormaers* and Thorfinn it was held by a Royal Garrison under the command of a Governor, appointed by the King, one of whom was the Earl of Buchan, father to the Red Comyn. By early 13th century the timber buildings and bailey (stockade) were replaced by a stone tower, erected on an artificial motte (mound) at the north east corner, which threw out from each flank a bailey also of stone. In 1291 during the first Balliol interregnum, Edward I of England took over and occupied twenty Scottish Castles, appointing to Dingwall and Inverness Sir William de Braytoft as Governor. The English occupation did not last long as the 3rd Earl of Ross became the governor on his release from the Tower, while any remaining Sasunnach influence went when he transferred his allegiance from Balliol to King Robert the Bruce, who shortly after this followed a practice common in Scotland by transferring the Royal Castle to the Earl as hereditary property.

As time went on the fortress was much enlarged and improved, three additional towers being added to the surrounding bailey wall, the general effect being of a massive fort rather than a towering castle, covering an area something over an acre and enclosing a court-yard. The oldest and strongest tower was at the north east corner or the edifice directly above the river while a fosse ran round the castle joining the (old) Peffrey bed. When the Earls resided here they had their private apartments on the western side of the main block— possibly a pleasanter outlook than was provided by the mud and water vista to the east.

On the southern front was the only approach and entrance, covered by the barbican, opposite which lay the muster ground for the garrison, normally sixty men at arms, archers, and later gunners. The stables and yard being outside the bailey occupying an acre of ground where now stands the Roman Catholic Chapel. From the north east tower an underground passage ran under the muster ground southwards, the exit being where Park Street now lies.

In 1477 the Earldom of Ross was forfeited and resigned to King James III so that the Castle once again reverted to Royal ownership. Soon after that event we find a Mr. Thomas holding the office of master mason from 1504–1513, part of his dues being the grazing rights without 'grassum' on the lands around the Castle.

A list of its furnishings in charge of David Learmont, custodian of Dingwall and Red Castles for the Lord James (2nd son of King James III) in 1501, contains the following: 17 beds; 10 feather beds; one damask broad table cloth and 2 narrow; 4 prs sheets broad Flanders cloth; 8 bolsters; 12 coddis (pillows); 14 linen dusters and towels; 6 cushions; 5 spades; 2 rakes; 1 ladder; 1 creel; 14 brazen candle sticks; 2 chandeliers; 80 lbs weight of pewter vessels; 9 tables with forms and trestles; 18 vats in the fish house; 4 vats and 14 hogsheads in the cellars; 11 spits; cutlery and crockery, mashing tuns and chaldrons in the Brew House, also 4 great guns and 2 cannon of long range.

A huge girnal was built about this time to hold the grain rents which were shipped at intervals to Leith for the Royal kitchens and stables.

Governors, after forfeiture, for the Crown

(1410–19 the Regent Albany imposed a governor during his usurpation of the Earldom, called the 'Black Captain'; he was liquidated by a Munro alias *Riach*, his successor being MacKay of Farr.)

1478 Sir John Munro of Foulis who also was a Chamberlain of Ross.

1480 Sir Andrew '*Mór*' Munro (Monro) of Milntown (New Tarbat); during this period the five Mains or Granges (Home Farms) yielded a rental of 198 chalders victual, 102 merks, 98 sheep p.a.

1488 James Dunbar of Flowerburn, Chamberlain, the Castle being held for the Duke of Ross—James Stewart, second son of James III who in 1503 obtained the Abbey of Dunfermline and resigned his Dukedom to the King.

James IV visited his castle twice in 1503 and expenditure in preparation amounted to £3. 19/-, 8 bolls barley, 10 of flour and much oats. The King gave £20. for the building of a covered hall in the court for use of festive occasions, completed 4 years later.

1507–16 Andro Bishop of Caithness, also governor of Redcastle. During this period extensive repairs were made—as (1) Red Hector of *Gairloch*, Tutor of Kintail had attempted to seize the Castle; other attempts had previously been made by House of Kintail; (2) Incursions by Sir Alexander Macdonald of Lochalsh, which covered a period of 13 months. The improvements entailed the purchase of a 'perch of land' bought from some person in the town, possibly to clear a field of fire. The fighting Bishop also bought: 'engines of war—serpentines, hagbuttis, culveringis, hand-bowies, arrows, halberts, laith-axes, jeddart staves, the powder callit lezgunpulder . . . and mony utheris thingis.'

Beside the purely defensive improvements Andro seems to have tried to introduce a more home-like atmosphere and turned one of the smaller bailey towers into a 'doo'-cot'; this would also add to the food supply.

1516–22 John Earl of Atholl.

1523 John Earl of Moray, brother of James V; during his tenure of office the Castle Garrison had to deal with 'thieves and robbers' who till 1535 were causing loss on farms.

1550 Sir David Sinclair.

1561 George Munro of Docharty (Davochcarte) appointed by Mary Queen of Scots and confirmed by James VI; this included the bailiary and chamberlainship of the Queen's lands and Lordships of Ross and Ardmannach. On account of his age she exempted him for life from serving as a soldier or on any assizes or acting as witness in any court.

1584 Sir Andrew Keith, created Lord Dingwall, a relative of the Earl Marischal. This honour was given as reward for services at home and abroad; it included a seat in Parliament. In addition to the 'buildings, feufermes, dues, and services with various lands around', he got the lands of Dunglass for £6. 18. 0. in cash, 1 chalder 2 bolls oatmeal, the same of oats, six marts (cattle), six sheep, 13 hens, and 24/- of "bondage silver," receiving as keeper of the Castle 80 loads of Peats annually from the Royal property of Drumderfit. Sir Andrew left no heir.

1609 Sir John Preston, Earl of Desmond, nominated to Barony of Dingwall by James VI and I, he sat in Parliament 1624 as Lord Dingwall.

After about 1625 the Castle began to decay, the Governorship passing again to the Munros of Foulis, when some of its lands were disposed of to the Bains of Tulloch who as owners of Kinnairdie became the Castle custodians till this office passed once more, in 1762, to their successors the Davidsons of Tulloch, the 1st of Tulloch being married to Jean Bain the cousin of the last Baine proprietor, the post carrying a nominal salary of 30/- a year. By then the remaining Royal lands in Ross had gone to other owners, so that nothing being left to pay for upkeep, the great castle fell into ruin.

About 1750 the Castle and grounds came into the possession of the Rev. Colin Mackenzie, minister of Fodderty, who carted many of the stones away for the Cromartie farms of Fodderty and Millnain, while Major Forbes Mackenzie, younger son of the Rev. Colin, carried off some hundred loads of lime to use as dressing for the improvement of Fodderty and Achterneed Farms.

Much of Dingwall including the Castle residence built during the second decade of the 19th century, was built of the old castle masonry, and while all this demolition was in progress, a massive gold ring set with a large diamond was dug up from the earlier earthworks.

The year 1818 saw the virtual extinction of the once Royal castle of Dingwall.

APPENDIX IV

Eilean Donan Castle

This island fortress stands on the site of an ancient fort, showing signs of vitrification, which, very approximately, may be dated somewhere around 200 B.C. The castle was erected c. 1220, becoming the cradle of the House of Kintail—unless the previous *Dun* claims this privilege. To start with, it may have been held under a superiority, more or less, of the Earl of Ross, until the Barony became a grant direct from the Crown to the Baron of Kintail, Chief of Clan Kenneth, which had happened, certainly, by 1304.

During the 15th century, other lands and castles fell into the Mackenzie lap, so that constables were appointed by the Chiefs to take charge of the lands of Kintail and command in *Eilean Donan* Castle.

Many attempts were made to capture this stronghold, and all failed except one, when it fell by a trick only to be recaptured a few days later by a better one.

Constables

1427	Duncan MacAulay of Loch Broom.
1509	Malcolm MacIan Charrich McRa (Rae).
1511–39	Christopher McRa.
1539	Iain (John) Dhu Matheson of Fernaig, killed the same year, and replaced by a temporary constable, Duncan McRa.
1539	Sir John Murchison.
1580	Christopher MacRa.
1614–18	The Rev. Murdoch Murchison.
1618–51	The Rev. Farquhar MacRa.

After the battle of Glenshiel, 10 May 1719, the Castle was blown up by orders of General Wightman, remaining a ruin till its restoration by Lt. Col. MacRae-Gilstrap, who started this project in 1913. The first world war intervened, holding up the work, which however was completed in 1927, the owner appointing himself to the office of Constable, being the great-great-great-great-great-grandson of The Rev. Farquhar MacRa, Minister of Kintail and Constable 1618–51.

GLOSSARY

Explanation of words and phrases in the text.

'Mains' — Terrae dominicales—a farm or grange not let to a tenant but cultivated by the Laird himself, i.e. the Home Farm or Farms.

'Palace' — In Scotland this word is frequently used to describe a certain type of building and must not be confused with the English palace such as Blenheim, Buckingham Palace, etc. Palatium, or Palac, was used to describe a 'Hall' within the castle bailey to distinguish it from the great hall on the 1st floor of the castle Tower. In early times this Hall, or Palatium, was frequently the predecessor of the 'Tower'.

In construction the palace was usually a free standing hall with two storeys only, but of considerable length, but as castles became modified the palace was sometimes joined up to an existing Tower or Towers.

In Ross one of the principal buildings of Beauly Priory in 1571 was a palace, as also part of the Bishop's Castle of Chanonry, while the (*Loch*) *Luichart (Lùchairt)* means Palace or Establishment.

'Licence to build a Castle' — Except in a few cases these were not necessary in Scotland but when issued were treated more as a legal form of conveyance, frequently being given after the Castle was built. In 1346 William Earl of Sutherland and his spouse obtained a licence to build a fortalice on the *Crag* of *Dunotter*, though they did not take advantage of it.

William Urquhart the Sheriff was granted a licence to erect a tower on the mote-hill of Cromarty in 1470, probably as a replacement of the older works; at the same time this authorized the continuation of St. Norman's market held there since de Monte Alto's days.

A subject, if superior of the land could and did issue licences, for example, John Earl of Ross and Lord of the Isles in 1460, to the Laird of Kilravock.

Neither a castle, nor aqueduct, or mill-lade could pass as a pertinent of a Gift of lands; all these had to be specially conveyed.

In Scotland, as opposed to England, the Kings, probably as an economy measure, transferred nearly all the Royal Castles to their keepers as hereditary property, finally retaining only Edinburgh Castle, Holyrood, Stirling, Linlithgow Palace, Dumbarton and Falkland, though sometimes they claimed the right of free access to other fortresses, as in the case of Castle *Camus* (Knock) in Skye during the year 1617.

'Pit' — The Castle prison, often just a small cell—usually very uncomfortable.

'The Baron and Chief's Court', the 'Sabaid' — Performed identical functions, the settling of all major disputes and the trying of criminals, with the power of awarding fine, pit, or gallows. The holding of the Court could be delegated to a Bailie, the Norman term, or the *Breitheamh*, the Gaelic judge, who presided in the Church, or at some spot in the open near the Castle which had been used as a judgment place from time immemorial. The lapse of time between the judgment and carrying out of a capital sentence was usually very short, governed only by the distance to the gallows or hanging tree.

'Bond of Manrent' — The oath taken by a man to his superior in rank which bound him to leal and true service in person together with his friends, gear and heritage for peace and war against all men but the king; sometimes lasting for life, or else a term of 5 to 7 years.

The inducements were a gift of land, seldom money, and provided a precaution for the preservation of peace, the law supporting these pacts till 1555; though they lasted for another 100 years. The oath ran: 'I shall neither hear, wit, see, nor know, skaith, hurt, damage, or apparent peril to his person, goods, friends, or heritages, but I shall warn him thereof and let it at my goodly power. And if he asks at me any counsel I shall give him the best I can. And if any counsel he shows me, I shall conceal and keep it secret.'

'Fosterage' — The Celtic custom by which a chief or chieftain's son was brought up by a family of lower degree—vide, Thorfinn the Mighty and Thorkel Fostri, also Agnes Fraser of Lovat and Glaishan Gow the blacksmith of Beauly. Usually resulted in an unbreakable bond of love and affection between the foster parents and the child.

'The Scottish Burgh' Had the right of holding a Burgh Court and burgage tenure by which every holder of land in the Burgh was relieved, on a payment, of any form of service due for his land which could be disposed of by him at will. In addition it possessed valuable trading privileges. Compared to English Boroughs, there was almost a complete absence of friction between these and the lairds or clerics on whose land they stood; in the case of Royal Burghs the land was of course a Royal demesne, and these were represented in the Estates (Parliament) of Scotland.

The following Burghs in Ross were granted Charters which transformed them into Royal Burghs: Dingwall in 1226, 1497 and again in 1589; Rosemarkie 1445; Tain 1587; Stornoway 1597; Cromarty 1662; Fortrose 1445, the last being united with Rosemarkie into one Royal Burgh 1450.

The Burghs, their codes and trading laws were based on Flemish models, and their staple was situated till the end of the 15th century at Bruges after which it moved to Middelburg and Veere. The Convention of Royal Burghs existed until 1975.

'Handfasting' Trial marriage sanctioned by Celtic law. The parties lived together for a year and a day. If there were children born as a result they were legitimate and the marriage was blessed by the Church, but if there were no children the marriage could be annulled by mutual consent after the full period of trial, though if the couple were suited the Church solemnized the contract and it became permanent—unless there was a later annulment and divorce.

Scots law has always tended to be more humane than English law.

'Outlawry' A person is 'put to the horn' or outlawed if he fails to answer a criminal charge after being lawfully cited to appear. This carries forfeiture of the outlaw's movables and deprivation of certain rights, while no warrant is needed for the apprehension of an outlaw.

'Sept' The origin of this tribal *Tuath* (Clan) division is to be found in archaic times.

Each *Tuath* formed a number of communities under a head-man the '*Ceann-fine*' consisting of his kinsmen, retainers and slaves. This *Fine* was the 'Sept' occupying a part of the tribal lands, cultivated by a system of co-tillage, the pasturage being co-grazed, both according to certain tribal laws and customs. The forests, boglands, and mountains forming the Sept marches were unrestricted common lands for that division.

The earliest and smallest Sept was formed by the village community and these early tribal colonies pushed out, settling on the tribal march lands. As time went on part of the common land was converted into estates of severalty, thus producing a new Sept from the family who had acquired the land, while a similar process could take place within an existing Sept without causing a split.

This evolution to holding land in severalty created an aristocracy as the '*Aire*' (that is the head of a homestead within the Sept, representative freeman and controller of Kinsfolk as well as his immediate family) —whose family held the same land for three generations was called a '*flath*' (lord or prince), of which there were several grades.

These chieftains owed 'Ceilsinna'—tribute in kind and service—to their Clan *Righ*, or chief, (in Gaul Rigs; Latin Rex; old Norse Rikir) while the *flath* received a similar tribute from his Sept.

The senior *Flath* was the *Maor* (Steward) to his Chief while another might hold the office of *Tòiseach* (Captain of the Clan forces).

'Wadset' The disposal of land on mortgage; introduced in the Highlands possibly in 13th certainly 14th century.

The wadsetter occupied the lands paying crown dues and ecclesiastical duties. He could sub-let or sub-divide land, allotting plots to labourers and giving them a 'souming' of cattle and sheep in return for work; they had however to build their own houses.

Arable land let to sub-tenants was held on runrig system and usually apportioned by lot. As soon as the mortgage was paid off by the superior he could resume the land.

'Tacks' During the 17th century, in order to avoid difficulty of collecting a great many very small rents, large areas were let to Tacksmen who paid 1. Grassum=Premium on entry, in cash or cattle; 2. Rental, usually in two forms: cattle, poultry, butter, cheese, fish, blankets; and money, designed tack-duty. 3. Obligation for military service.

Inverpolly was occupied by a Tacksman—John Mackenzie, during the first half of the 18th century, as was Langwell above Strath Caniard etc.

'Titles of Nobility' To the close of the 14th century only the ancient one of Earl, originally associated with administrative duties and becoming a title of honour.

Under King Robert III 1390–1406, Dukes introduced but confined to Royal House. The Writs issued after 1428 had the effect of creating a Peerage, the members of which though all landowners, attended Parliament (The Estates of Scotland) not as of old to fulfil an obligation incumbent on all tenants in chief, but in obedience to a personal summons and lordships of Parliament became hereditary.

'Land measure' In Ross as elsewhere in the Highlands, the Davoch, c. 416 acres, was the standard used in nearly all transactions: vide many Munro Writs, such as the 1299–1311 Charter by Elizabeth Byseth (Byset) relict of Sir Andrew de Bosco granting certain lands including a davoch at Glastullich, a davoch, called Cualcolli (Kilcoy) to William Earl of Ross in exchange for davochs of land at Ardtarbard, Tarbard (Tarbat), ½ davoch Byndel in Tarbard; signed by Prior of Beauly, Sir William de Fentona, Sir William de Haya, and witnessed by Martin, Abbot of New *Fearn* and others.

The Davoch was not constant as it varied according to soil and locality; it might be from one to four ploughgates—the single plough-gate=104 acres; sometimes the Davoch was known as '*Tir Unga*'= an ounceland, i.e. an ounce of silver for rent. Further divisions were penny lands, half-penny and farthing lands.

Money and Measures in Scotland.

2 Doits	......	1 Bodle.
2 Bodles	......	1 Plack or Groa.
3 Placks	......	1 Schillin (the Scots Penny)
40 Placks	......	1 Merk which=13s. 4d. Scots or 13⅓d. sterling.
20 Schillins	......	1 Pund.

Land Measure.

The Ell	1984 yards.
Mile	37.2 inches.
Acre	6150 sq. yards.

Liquid Measure.

4 Gills	1 mutchkin	modern	1 pint.
2 mutchkins	1 choppin	,,	1 quart.
2 choppins	1 pint	,,	2 quarts.
2 pints	1 quart	,,	1 gallon.
4 quarts	1 gallon	,,	4 gallons.

Badges and Slogans of the Clans of Ross or Vassals of Earldom and some of their Principal Pipe Tunes.

Clan	Badge	Slogan
Ross	Juniper	
Rose	Wild Rosemary	
Urquhart	Wallflower	
Chisholm	Fern and/or Alder	
Fraser	Yew	(1) *A Mhór-faicha* (The Great Field) later.
		(2) *Caisteal* Dhùni.
Munro	Common Club Moss and Eagles feathers.	*Caisteal* Faolais 'n a theine. (Castle Foulis ablaze.)
MacDonald	Common Heath	*Fraoch Eilean* (The Heather Isle).
MacDonell of Glengarry	do.	*Creagan an Fitheach* (The Raven's Rock).

Clan	Badge	Slogan
MacLeod of Harris and Dunvegan	Juniper	
MacLeod of Lewis	Red Whortleberry	
Mackenzie	Variegated Holly and Deer's Grass (Heath Club Rush).	*Tulach Ard.* (A mountain in Kintail).
MacRae	Club Moss	Sgur Urain (do.)
Matheson	Broom and Holly.	*Acha 'n da Tèarnadh.* (The field of the two declivities).
Maclennan	Furze	*Druim nan deur.* (The Ridge of Tears).

Clan	Pipe Tunes	
Ross	Spaidscamchd *Iarla* Rois.	The Earl of Ross's March.
Munro	*Fàilte nan Rothach.*	Munro's Salute.
	Bealach na Broige.	Munro's March.
	Cumha Fhir Fhòlais	Lament for Munro of Foulis.
MacRae	*Fàilte Loch Duthaich*	Loch Duich's Salute.
	Blar na Pàirc	Battle of Park.
	Spaidsearachd Chlann Mhicrath	The MacRae's March.
	Cumha Dhonnachaidh MhicIan	Lament for Duncan MacRae.
Mackenzie	*Fàilte* Uilleam Dubh Mhic Coinnich.	The Earl of Seaforth (Black William's) Salute.
	Fàilte Thighearna *Ghearloch*	Mackenzie of *Gairloch*'s Salute.
	Fàilte Thighearna *Comraich*	Mackenzie of Applecross's Salute.
	Co-thional Chlann Choinnich	Mackenzie's Gathering.
	Cabar Fèidh	Stag's Antlers March.
	Cumha Chailein Ruaidh Mhic Coinnich no *Cumha* Mhic Coinnich.	Lament for Colin Ray or Mackenzie's Lament.
	Cumha Thighearna Ghearloch	*Gairloch*'s Lament.
		March—Salute to the Earl of Cromartie, 1975.
MacCrimmon	*Cogadh no sith*	War or Peace.
	Cha till, cha till, cha till, MhicCruimein	MacCrimmon shall never return.
	Fhuair mi pog o làmh an Righ.	I got a kiss of the King's hand.
	Cumha na Cloinne	The Lament for the Children.
MacLeod	*Fàilte nan* Leodach	MacLeod's Salute.
	Port Iomran MhicLeoid, no *Fàilte* nan Leodach	MacLeod of MacLeod's Rowing Salute.
	Fàilte Mhic Gille Chaluim Rathasaidh	MacLeod of Raasay's Salute.
	Fàilte Ruaraidh Mhoir	Rory *Mòr*'s (of Harris) Salute.
	Iomradh Mhic Leoid	MacLeod's Praise—March.
	Cumha Cheann-cinnidh na Leodach	Lament for MacLeod of MacLeod.
	Cumha—Ruaridh Mhoir	Lament for Rory *Mòr* (Harris).
	Cuma Mhic Gille Chaluim Rathasaidh	Lament for MacLeod of Raasay.
MacDonald of the Isles	*Fàilte* Chlann Donuill	MacDonald's Salute.
	Fàilte Ridire Seumas nan *Eilean*	Sir James MacDonald of Isles' Salute.
	Fàilte na Bain—tighearna nic Dhònuill	Lady Margaret MacDonalds Salute.
	Lamh dearg Chlann Donuill	Gathering—The Red Hand of the MacDonalds.

Clan	*Pipe Tunes*	
	Spaidsearachd Mhic Dhònuill	March of the MacDonalds.
	Cumha an Ridire Seumas MacDhonuill *nan Eilean*	Lament for Sir James of the Isles.
	Cumha Bain-tighearna Mhic Dhonuill	Lament for Lady MacDonald.
	Cumha Mhorair Chlann Dhònuill	Lament for Lord MacDonald
MacDonell of Glengarry	*Fàilte* Mhic Alastair	Glengarry's Salute.
	Gille Chriosd	Gathering—Gilchrist.
	A Sheana Bhean Bhochd	Glengarry's March.
	Cumha Mhic Mhic Alastair	Glengarry's Lament.
	Cumha Alastair Dheirg	Lament for Alexander of Glengarry.
Fraser	*Fàilte* Chloinn Shimidh	The Fraser's Salute.
	Spaidsearachd Mhic Shimidh	Lovat's March.
	Cumha Mhic Shimidh	Lovat's Lament.
Davidson	*Fàilte* Thighearna Thulaich	Tulloch's Salute.
	Spaidsearachd Chaisteal Thulaich	Tulloch Castle March.
Chisholm	*Fàilte* a t-Siosalaidh	The Chisholm's Salute.
	Spaidsearachd Siosalaidh Strathghlais	Chisholm's March.
	Cumha do dh'Uilleam Siosal	Lament for William Chisholm.

Some Particulars concerning the Counties of Ross and Cromarty.

Area of Ross and Cromarty 1,970,004 acres (Lewis 770 sq. miles.) north to south 58 miles —east to west 67 miles. The island areas which include Lewis and the Summer Isles amount to 437,221 acres.

The soil of Easter Ross varies from light sandy gravel to rich deep loam; the west has only a small area of good soil.

The County of Cromarty was carved out of Ross in 1685 and 1698 by Sir George Mackenzie Viscount Tarbat, Lord MacLeod and Castlehaven, the 1st Earl of Cromartie. It was made up of the properties held by himself amounting to some 220,800 acres (c. 345 sq. miles). Cromarty consisted of eleven detached portions: 1. Kilmuir Easter, Kildary, Tarbat, Castle—later House—area; 2. S. side of Tain Firth to Moray Firth including Loch Slyn Castle; 3. Tarbat Ness, Portmahomack (Castlehaven) and Balloan Castle; 4 and 5. Two portions on the south bank of River Carron in Parish of Kincardine; 6. North west from the Royal Burgh of Dingwall comprising Parish of Fodderty—Strathpeffer—Knockfarrel—Cat's Back—Ben Wyvis, Castle Leod and Garbat; 7. Loch Fannich and area stretching north, in the Parish of Contin; 8. A triangular portion north west of Fannich to Loch Nid; 9. The south side of Little Loch Broom. 10. The district of *Coigach* which included Ullapool and a castle— Achiltibuie—Strath Caniard—Inverpolly—the mountains of Ben *Mór Coigach*—Coul *Mór*— Coul Beg—Stack Polly and the Summer Isles; 11. The original Cromarty, or Cromartie, which consisted of the Burgh of that name with its castle and a part of the Black Isle.

This odd County remained a separate entity for 200 years, but in 1891 it lost its unique position when the Boundary Commissioners brought it, for administrative purposes, under the Ross and Cromarty County Council.

In 1921, the population of Ross and Cromarty was 70,790, of them 4,860 could speak Gaelic only, a percentage of 6.87; 35,810 could speak Gaelic and English.

Farm Wages 1730.

1st Ploughman (The Big Man) . . . 40/-s. a year, and 5 ells of cloth, after 2 years a finer quality; 2 linen shirts; 2 prs. shoes; 2 prs. woollen hose; board and lodging or a house.

Young Ploughman, £11. Scots p.a.=11/4 st. (£3.=1/8 st.) and 3 to 4 ells of clothing; Board, lodging.

The Pleghan-farm boy, £5. to £6. Scots.

Maidservants, £8. Scots exclusive of Bounties—Serge or drugget gown—2 linen shirts—an apron—2 prs. shoes and stockings.

All the above would have board and lodging, the clothes being made at master's expense.

By 1760 there was a rise, but the ploughmen's wages were only £3. sterling, and women 20/- st. p.a.

Casual labour 1720–30: 5d. in Summer, in winter a groat=4d. st.

1756 : 6d. in Summer.

By 1827 the farm labourers living in cottages attached to the farm had a milch cow, grazed with the master's—a plot of land for lint (flax) or potatoes—fuel and carriage free, either peat or coal.

His wage was £5. or £6. by the half year, unmarried; £8. or £10. with 2 pecks of meal weekly, married.

The 1st Ploughman was getting £7. to £9. st.
Maidservant £3. to £4. 10. st.
Man shearer at harvest £3. 10. st.
Woman shearer at harvest. £2. 5. st.

Ross and Cromarty in 1885:

Under Crop: bare fallow and grass 134,399 acres of which, grain 47,639. Green crops 26,496 acres. Rotation grasses 40,819 acres. Permanent Pastures 19,075. Fallow 370.

Since 1857 the area under wheat had diminished from 9715 to 1185 acres. Barley increased from 6435 to 13,681 acres, and oats from 16,256 to 31,685 acres. Potatoes doubled from 4471 to 8982 acres. Turnips 12,228 to 16,557 acres. Rotation grasses 20,869 to 40,819 acres.

In 1885 horses (garrons—Clydesdales and crosses) numbered 7365. Cattle mostly Highland breeds and crosses 42,976. Sheep 309,590.

The area under wood was now only 43,201 acres, a sad retrogression since the days of the planting lairds of the 18th century, largely due to the importation of cheap foreign timber and high sporting rents, which made forestry an unprofitable pastime. Not till 1911 did any signs appear of a revival in this nationally important industry; the improvement owed nothing to the government, but was due to the Scottish Arboricultural, Highland and Agricultural Societies, and certain landowners such as Munro Fergusson (Lord Novar).

Deer Forest accounted for 719,305 acres, most of which was situated above a possible tree growing altitude, but which in the old days had provided good grazings for the hill cattle together with the deer, an altogether excellent and natural arrangement (hence the old natural fauna of deer and auroch). Both cattle and deer eat different kinds of grasses, so that a judicious mixture of both meant evenly grazed and well manured lands, with no deserts of bracken, or grass run wild.

Since the above computation of acreages the necessity to produce more food due to the war and its aftermath, a much greater acreage is under crop, while the deer forests carry such stock as is possible. New forest areas (trees) are appearing in many parts of Ross planted by the Forestry Commission, who to a great degree have taken over re-aforestation from the old owners of the land, who in the majority of cases are far too impoverished by taxation to carry out this, nowadays, very expensive job except in a minor degree.

Telford's works in Ross and Cromarty.

Bridges—surveyed and built 1806–1817.

Conon—Balnagown—Alness (Strath Rusdale)—Easter Fearn (Fearn Water)—Bonar Bridge, destroyed by flood 1890.—Altmore and Redburn—Shiel (Glen Shiel)—River Croe—Contin (Blackwater).

Harbours. Cromarty was surveyed by Telford as a Naval Base in 1801.

Piers. 1813–17.

Ballintraid—Channery—Invergordon and Inverbrickie ferry pier. Dingwall—Dornie ferry piers—Portmahomack improvements. Fortrose new pier and deepening of harbour—Avoch 2 piers—The Dingwall Canal, 2000 yards long, to connect its small port with River Conon, and harbour improvements.

Roads. 1807–90.

Loch Carron, Achnashean division—*Fearn* road—Loch Alsh—Ardelve—Loch Carron, Contin division—Loch Carron, Jeantown division—Loch Carron, Luip division—Tain road—Glen Shiel—Glen Elg—Kintail—Kishorn—Rhibuie—Kessock Ferry road.

Churches.

Loch Broom—*Croich* (Kincardine)—Poolewe—Kinloch Luichart (Contin)—Carnoch (Strathconon)—Shieldaig—Applecross—Plockton—In Lewis, Cross—Lewis and Knock.

This man engineered the Caledonian Canal, built 1000 bridges, 12,000 miles of road, harbour works in 43 places, Churches and manses in Scotland.

Proper Names, their use and their meanings, many of which appear in the text and are or were common in Ross and Cromarty.

a/. The introduction of surnames into Scotland came about during the latter half of the 11th century, and their use had become fairly common by the 13th century. Prior to this the Celt was always described by Pedigree, and of course continued to be so described in the Highlands in the majority of cases till modern times, but the Norman and Saxon was known by the name of his land.

In addition to the clan name there were the clan sept names, which included:

1. The names of those related to the chief by marriage though not blood relations of the clan.
2. Of those unconnected to the clan by blood but bound to it by a 'Bond of Manrent.' (See Glossary above).
3. Of those of clan blood who wished to be better distinguished from their namesakes in which they adopted:
   (a) A Pedigree by name, e.g. Angus MacRanald (Angus son of Ranald) though the individual's clan name might be MacDonald.
   (b) A by-name derived from profession or hereditary office.
   (c) A name already given on account of some personal peculiarity or infirmity.
   (d) The name which was retained by those of the clan who were originally known by the name of a portion of the clan territory occupied by them.
   (e) Clan names Anglicized. In addition, there were,
   (f) Various names adopted by oppressed or proscribed Clans, and
   (g) Names adopted to conceal identity during the persecutions following the 1745 Jacobite Rising.

*Mac*Domhnuill=a *son* of Donald (the fem. of *Mac* is '*nic*,' contracted to 'ni,' for '*Nighean*' daughter, & *mhic*).
MacCoinnich=son of Kenneth, i.e. Mackenzie.
The '*Mac*' was used also by both Norse and Lowland people. The *O*'=Grandson, used in the early days of Scottish history, e.g. O'Beolan, prevalent in Ireland since XIth century, A.D.

b/. '*Maol*' means the 'tonsured one' or Votary and was used as a prefix to the names of Celtic Saints, e.g. *Maol Rubha*, *Maolmuire* (Votary of the Virgin Mary); during the 10th and 11th centuries *Maol* was replaced by '*Gille*' meaning lad or servant.

c/. Only chiefs used the simple patronymic, e.g. '*Iarla* Rois agus MacDomnaill agus *Ardfhlath Innsigall*'=Earl of Ross and MacDonald and High Chief of the Isles.
Territorial designations were frequently added at a later date, probably after the 12th or 13th centuries, to the patronymic of the Chief, e.g. *MacCoinnich mór Chinn-Taile*=Great Mackenzie of Kintail.
The titles of 'Cromartie' from the town, firth and territory are a corruption of 'Crombadh'= Crooked Bay—spelt in 1257 Crumbathyn—'Tarbat' in Easter Ross (there are several others in Scotland) from 'Tairbeart'='Isthmus' or 'a place over which a boat can be drawn,' from 'Tar' across and 'bir,' bring or bear—spelt in 1226 'Arterbert'=High Tarbert, 1257 Tharberth.
The title 'Seaforth' is corrupted from 'Seafort' a great sea loch of the Island of Lewis, the word derived from old Norse 'soer'=sea and frith or fjord.

d/. Many names were derived from Scriptures:—
Aindreas, Gille Andrais=Gillanders, Mac Andrew—Anderson.
Eoin, Ian=John.
Seumas=James.
Simidh=Simon, so MacShimidh personal name of Lord Lovat.
Adamh=Adam, but sometimes from Adamnan.
Daibhidh, Clan Dàidh=the Davidsons.
Marcus=Mark, Marquis, etc.
e/. From Church Officials.
Ab=Abbot; *Mac an Aba*, MacNab.
Biocair=Vicar; *MacBhiocair*, MacVicar.
Easbuig=Bishop (episcopus); Gilleasbuig angl: to Archibald.
Sagart=Priest; *Mac an t-sagairt*, MacTaggart, etc.
Cléireach=Clerk; Mac a' Chleirich.
f/. From Saints.
Aongas=Angus.
Brandan, *MacGille* Bhrai, MacGillivray.
Briget or *Bride*, Gillebrigde, Maelbrigde, etc.
Colum, Columba, *MacGille Caluim*, MacCallum; *Maol Caluim*=Malcolm. His pet name was

Calumcille=the dove of the Church.
Find-barr, Mo-fhionn-i, from the first part Munn, MacPhunn; Barr from second (White-poll).
Finnen (fiom-shan, white and old); MacGille Fhionnain, MacLennan.
Frangas=Francis.
Gildas; Geddes.
Martin; MacGille Mhartain, Mac Martin. etc.
g/. From Kings and famous people, etc.
Colin perhaps from *Ailean*, a green, or plain.
Caimbeul—wrymouth=Campbell.
Camshron—wry nose= Cameron.
Ceanaideoh—Kennedy, *ceann-aodach*—head-protector.
Coinneach—Kenneth, Mackenzie—in Galloway MacWhinnie.
Domhnell (dubno—valdo-s world ruler) MacDonald.
Dubhgall (A black Gaul) MacDougall, MacDowel, etc.
Eachunn (equo-donn-s horse lord) Hector, Mac Echan.
Eideard—Edward; also Norse Iomhar, Mac Iamhair, angl: Edward for Ivor.
Fearchar (man-loving) MacFearchair, MacFarquhar etc.
Fionnla, *Fionnlagh* (white hero), Finlay.
Gall. 1. a Gaul. 2. a Viking. 3. a Lowlander; Galbraith etc.
Goraidh (Norse) god-fridr God's Peace—Godfrey, MacGorry.
Grannd—(Grand Eng and French)—Grant—but possibly from *Grànnda*, ugly.
Harailt. (Norse) Haraldr (Eng) Herald—Harold, MacRaild by metathesis, Walter,
MacBhaltair whence Walt, MacWattie, Watson, etc.
Mac-a-Phi, *Mac Dub shìthe* (son of the black one of peace or Fairy)
MacAmhlaidh—Mac Aulay.
Mac an Lèigh (son of the physician, *liagh*)—Mac Leay.
Mac an t-Saoir (son of the artificer) MacIntyre etc.
Mac Aidh (O.G. Éd)—MacKay—O'h Æ dha= Hay, MachAedha=MacHeth.
Mac Asgaill (N. Askell sacrificial kettle)—MacAskill (Lewis and Kerkaig. Sept of MacLeod of Lewis).
Mac Beatha (son of life), *MacBheatha*, MacBeth; with suffix 'an' makes a diminutive, *MacBeathain*, MacBean, Beaton.
MacCormaig, Cormac (corb mac' *carbadair* charioteer)—Cormack, MacCormic.
Mac Corcadail (Mac Thorketill, son of Thor's kettle—MacTorquil, Sept of MacLeods of Lewis, MacCorquodale, etc.
MacCulloch (1) (*Mac-cu-uladh*, son of the dog of Ulster) MacCulloch and (2) *MacGilleUlaidh* =MacLulaich, (the E. Ross family).
MacGilbe, MacGill are curtailments of a name, e.g. *MacGille maol* or MacMillan.
Macgille & an adjective usually colours form many names, e.g.
Bàn=white, Macbain, Bain.
Buidhe=yellow, *Macbuidhe Macgille buidhe*—Ogilvie, etc.
Dubh=Black, Doo transliterated Dove whence (*Mac Calmain*); etc.
Glas=grey or green, (MacGlashan).
Gorm=blue, (MacGorman). Also:—
Mór=great, *naomh*=holy; *odhar*=drab, sallow, e.g. Kenneth *Odhar* the Brahan Seer;
  Riabhaiche=grizzled, wizened, grey; *Ruadh*=red.
MacLèoid (Norse) Ljotr=ugly and ulf=wolf in old Scots. MacLeod; Cloud.
MacMathan, Mac a mhathain (*mathgaman*=bear) Matheson.
Mac Neacail, Nicholson, MacNicol; MacCreacail, (Knickell Isle of Man).
MacRath (son of grace) MacRae etc.
MacRaonuill (Norse) Rogn—valder god's ruler; Ranald, etc.
Mac an Rothaich (son of the Baron Munro) Munro, Monro, Roach, *Riach*.
Mac Suibhe (*an t- Suain*=Sweden) MacSween, etc.
Malcolm from *Maol-Caluim*, tonsured one of Columba=Columba's attendant.
Manus (N. & Lat) Magnus; Mac Vanish.
Moirreach (Moravia, Mor-Apia) Murray, etc.
Murchadh (mori-catu-s=sea warrior) Murchie, Murcheson.
Ruadh—(red) Roy.
Ruairidh (*ruadh-ri*) Red King Rory-Rorie. Roderick, etc.
Somhairlic (Norse) sumar-lidi summer sailor; Somerled, etc.
Torcul (N. Thorkell) Torquil.
Tormoid (N. Thormodr Thor's Wrath—mundr—protection)—Norman.
Uisdean (N. Hug-steinn, poet—Uisdean) Hugh, etc.
h/. Some often used as Christian names.
Chaluim=Malcolm. *Eachainn*=Hector. Tearlach=Charles.
Alasdair=Alexander. Seamas (Hamish)=James. *Ian*=John.

Scorus=George. Murchadh=Murdoch. Uilleam=William.
i/. The chief of certain Clans originated from places outside the Highlands—two of these were once included within the Earldom of Ross:—
   Fraser, Friseal, Frisealach—de Fresel of Touraine, France.
   Chisholm, Siosal, Siosalaich—Chisholm in Roxburghshire.

The Derivation of certain place names in Ross.

From Saints' Names.

Cladh mo Bhrigh at Lemlair from St. Briget (*Bride*) or another Saint, *Brigh*.
Portmahomack a diminutive of St. Colman, i.e. Port of my own little Colman. (At Synod of Whitby A.D. 664).
Kilchoan (Kiltearn) Church of St. Congan, Churches of St. Congan in Lochalsh and Skye. Glenshiel Churches of St. Kentigarna, Congan's sister, children of *Ceallach Cualann* a prince of Leinster who died 715.
Kilchrist (now *Muir* of Ord) Church of Christ (Christchurch).
Kilbey Head, Lewis from St. Begha, female disciple of St. Aiden and Abbess Hilda 6th century.
Kildonan Church of St. Donan—(Kintail and Lochbroom). This saint a contemporary of St. Columba, with his 52 followers was killed by pirates on the Isle of Eigg by the orders of some queen. Kel-du-nin-ach (voc. case & do)=St. Ninian, Ringan, Rynnan.
Duthach, Dubtach, Kilduich, Loch Duich and St. Duthus well Cromarty and shrine at Tain; he was martyred by Norsemen 1088.
Kilellan Loch Alsh   Church of St. Fillan.
Kilmichael Cromarty   Church of St. Michael.
Kiltearn Church of the Lord (*Tighearna*).
Killearnan (*Muir* of Ord)   St. Ernan.
Killen (Avoch) poss: cill annaidh=St. Anne.
Kilmuir   St. Mary's Church.
Loch Maree   St. *Maol Rubha*—left Ireland for Scotland 671.
Logiebride (Logie Wester)   St. *Bride* (Briget) Contemporary of St. Patrick and St. Ninian.
Flannan Islands Lewis   the Red Saint.
Teampull Frangach, Strath, Skye.   St. Francis.
Gorman Suidh—Ghuirmuin Glen Urquhart.   St. Gorman.
Kessock   St. Kessog.
Kilmoluag Skye   St. Moluag, Abbot of Lismore. d. 557.
Dochmoluag (Davochmaluach) Strathpeffer   St. Moluag.
Slios an Trinnein Glenmoriston=Slion Sanct Rinnein. The hillside of St. Ninian Ringan—Rynnan—A.D. 400.
Rona off Lewis and Ronay off Raasay.   St. Ronan.
Kiltarlity   St. Talaricanus.
Killtearn   St. *Tighernach* d. 548. Was a pupil at *Candida Casa*, Ninian's headquarters.

Other names. Unless otherwise marked are Celtic—either Pictish, ancient or later Gaelic, though in many cases spelling has become corrupted.
(N.=old Norse. Fr.=French. O.E.=Old English).
   Caledonia c. A.D. 60 mentioned in Lucan's Pharsalia.
   Albany by the Senior Pliny for Great Britain, from Celt: Alb=White or Alp=High.

Achanault—Contin=a field of the streams.
Achiltibuie=Field of the yellow haired lad.
Achnasheen=Field of the Foxgloves.
Achterneed=Upland of the Nests.
Allan=A green plain.
Alness of Ailean & Pict. ais=Green plain.
Arboll—*Fearn*. Earbil=Point of land.
Ardgay, Kincardineshire=Windy height.
Ardmeanach=Mid high land.
Ardross=High Moor.
Arpafeelie, Cromarty=Height of the Sea Gull.
Aultbea=Glen with Birches.
Avernish. N.=Oats Ness.
Avoch Pict.=River place.
Badicaul, Loch Alsh=Hazel Clump or Thicket.
Balcony=Town of Kenneth.

Balintore=Bleaching village.
Balloan=Loan, village in damp meadow.
Balloch—*Bealach*=Gap.
Balnabruaich=Village on the bank.
Balnagown=Village of Smiths.
Beallachantuie—Applecross=Pass of the Seat.
Beauly. Fr. (Beaulieu)=Lovely Spot.
Bindle. N.=Sheaf dale.
Boath=House, Bothy.
Bran R.=Raven R. or name of Fingal's Hound.
Bròn=Mourning, sorrow.
Broom. *Braon*=Drizzle.
Buillean Osgair (Loch Broom)=Oscar's Blows.
Cadboll. N.=Place of Wild Cats.
Cailleach=Point of the Old Wife.
Callernish. N.=Keel Cape.
Calrossie. N.=Hazel wood.
Carron=Bending, winding river.
Chanonry. O.E.=Rice of the Canon.
Clashmore=Hollow—Ditch.
Clay of Allan=Big clayey plain.
Clyne=Slope.
Coigach=Five Fields.
Conon=Dog River.
Contin=Confluence.
Corrie= A cauldron.
Couliss=At the back of the garden.
Cromarty—Crombadh=Crooked bay.
Culbokie=Nook of the bogie or goblin.
CulKenzie=Kenneth's Nook.
Culrain=Nook with the Ferns.
Dalgheal=The White field.
Dalnoch=Brindled field.
Loch Damph=Loch of the ox.
Davoch=Land measure c. 400 acres.
Delny=Place full of prickles and thorns.
Dibidale. N.=Deep dale.
Dingwall. N.=Meeting place of the Thing, (Norse Council or Parliament).
Dirriemore=The big climb.
Dornie=Pebble place.
Druim nam Fuath (Lochcarron)=The Spectre's Ridge.
Drumrunie=Back of the Runie.
Dunskaith=Fort of dread.
Dun Sgàthaich (Sleat)=Here Cuchullin got part of his training from *Sgàthaich* a female warrior.
Eathie Burn=Fordable stream.
Enard Bay. N.=Eyvind's fjord.
Evanton. E.=c. 1800. Evan Fraser of Balcony.
Loch Ewe=Loch of the Echo.
Edderton=Narrow Hill.
Fairburn (in Gaelic *far brasin*)=Over the wet place.
Farrer=Thick muddy water.
Ferintosh=Land of *Toiseach* or Thane.
Ferindonald=Donald's Land—anc. of Munros.
Fearn=An Alder.
Findon=Clear, white, hill.
Fodderty=Lower place.
Fortrose=Under the promontory.
Foulis (in G. is Folais=fo-glais)=Sub-stream, burn.
Gairloch=Short loch.
Garrabost. N.=Goirres farm or a triangular strip of land. (Lewis).
Garrynahine (Lewis) N. & G.=Strip of enclosed land.
Garty=Corn enclosure.
Garve=Rough.
Grimsheder. N.=Grim's sector or summer farm.
Gruinard. N.=Shallow Bay.

Guisachan=Pine forests.
Hilton. E.=Hill town.
Inchnadamph=Pasture of the ox.
Inver=Confluence.
Inveran=Little confluence.
Invergordon=1760 named after Sir Alexander Gordon, before that date Inver or Inchbreckie
    =Speckled.
Katewell. N. & G.=Fold dale.
Kenmore=Big head.
Kennetis=O. Irish ith=corn.
Killin=White Church.
Kincardine. O.G. & Pictish=Head of the wood.
Kildary=Narrow oak wood.
Kincraig=Head of the Rock.
Kinkell=At head of the wood.
Kintail=At head of the salt water.
Kirksheaf. Scots.=Land given as tribute to church.
Kishorn=Bulky cape.
Knockbain=White Hill.
Knockfarrel=Hill of high projecting stone building.
Kyle=A narrow ('Aikin' of Hakon of Norway).
Laid=Water course.
Langwell. N.=Long field.
Leckmelm=Stone of Malan which he is said to have flung across Loch Broom. Ulst. Ann.
    A.D. 677.
Letterfearn=Land on a slope, with alders.
Lochluichart=Loch of Palace or Establishment *lùchairt*.
Logie=Hollow or Pit.
Morangie=Big inch or Links-meadows.
Muirneag. G.=Diminutive of cheerfulness or joy. The Hill visible to Lewis fishermen at sea.
Navity=Church Land, hallowed meeting place.
Nigg=Bay or notch.
Nonakiln=Glebe of the church.
Novar=House of the giant.
Obsdale. N.=Bay dale.
Ord=Steep rounded height.
Orrin=Offering the Mass.
Oykell=High.
Pàirc=Enclosed field or Park.
Peffer Pict.=Fair, beautiful.
Pitfour Pict.=Pasture land.
Plockton. G. & Eng.=A large clod or turf.
Poolewe=Echo pool.
Raddery=Fallow arable land.
Rapach=Noisy, bustling place.
Rariche=Fort of scratching (brambles).
Resolis=Slope of light.
Rhidorroch=Dark slope.
Rhu=Point, cape.
Roag=Roe deer Bay.
Rosemarkie=Cape of the horse burn.
Rosehaugh=Promontory above Avoch.
L. Rosque=Loch of the crossing or pass.
Ross=From ros, a moor or rois, a promontory.
Rosskean=Pleasant dry wood.
Salen=Little arm or inlet of sea.
Scatwell. N.=Place paying tribute.
Scuir Vuillin (if Sgòrt muillinn)=Rock of the Mill.
Seaforth (Loch in Lewis)=Sith phort from Norse. Sloping county inlet, or fjord.
Shandwick. N.=Sandy Bay.
Skiach=Blackthorne.
L. *Slin*=A weaver's reed or sleay. *slinn, slige*.
Slioch=Spear. *sleagh*.
Stack=Isolated rock. *stacan*.
Stornoway. O.N.=Helm Bay.
Suainabost. N.=Swean's boy's place. (Lewis).

Tain. N.=Osier, twig.
Tarbat=Isthmus—place over which boat can be transported.
Tarradale=Bull dale. *tarbh*—a bull.
Tarrel=Over the cliff.
Teaninich=House of the market place.
Tobermory (Alness)=Well of Mary.
Tobaran Tuirc (Kintail)=The boar's well.
Tolsta. N.=Place of toll.
Tomich=Place of knolls.
Tulloch=Hill.
Tweedle (Lochcarron) G. & N.=Pasture dale.
Uig= Cove.
Ulladale. N.=Olaf's dale.
Ullapool. N.=Olaf's place (King of Norway 1015–30).
Urquhart Pict.=On a wood.
Urray=Repaired fort.
Ussie Pict. is of unknown meaning.
Wyvis Pict.=Ben of the Bogle (or Wavey Hill).
Neither in the Gaelic nor Norse names have the various evolutionary phases of the composite words been recorded here, but simply the present day method of spelling the name and the old meaning—which in some cases is doubtful.

Some Folk Tales and Kindred Subjects.

Faeries ('*Daoine Sith*,' 'The Men and Women of Peace') dwelt in the green knowes, such as Tomnahurich, occasionally they 'borrowed' human beings, pipers being especially popular. Black Mackenzie of the Pipes, disappeared into one of these hillocks, passing a year and a day dancing reels, though to him the dance seemed only to have lasted a few hours.

The silver chanter, belonging to 10 generations of the MacCrimmons who ran the great Piping College in Skye 1500–1800, was presented by the '*Daoine Sith*', with whom are connected the Brownies beneficent but touchy, the female of the species being the '*Loireag*'.

Faery dogs and cattle etc. The *Cro' Sith* or sea cows are usually of a red or dun colour, being recognizable by their notched ears, one of them was observed near *Gairloch* in 1854. Closely allied to them are the water-horses—'*Each Uisge*', to be found in many Lochs, but dangerous to ride as literally possessed of magnetic powers, as he can draw you immovably attached to his back into the Loch, where the monster can eat you at his leisure. This kelpie has the power of assuming human form, which makes him doubly dangerous; stories of this creature were very common in Skye, while something of the sort dwelt in *Loch-na-Beiste* above Achnahaird, though it may have been a somewhat similar creature the *Tarbh Uisge* or Water Bull.

One day on the moors of the Island of Lewis a herd-girl was sitting knitting when she was approached by a very handsome stranger who, taking a seat beside her, laid his head on her lap and fell asleep. Suddenly the girl observed that there were river weeds mixed up with the young man's hair, which brought the startling realization that her companion was a specimen of the *Each Uisge*. Very carefully she cut out the piece of skirt on which rested the stranger's magnetic head and fled to the village, followed by the awakened water horse which had now assumed its true form. To save the girl the village bull was liberated, the two creatures meeting in mortal combat which swayed back and forth till they reached the sea shore, then the water's edge, and finally into deep water. Nothing more was seen of the combatants until the sea washed up on the beach the horns of the bull and the liver of the water horse.

The Sea Serpent, the Seal Folk, the King Otter, and the Feolagan, the last being a super mouse, and Birds. These all appear in the rich folk lore of the North, which relates many attractive stories about our birds; one of the prettiest, telling how the Oyster Catcher came to be known in the Gaelic as *Gille-Bridean*, the servant of St. Bridget, this honour being conferred on this beautiful little sea bird for hiding Christ from some enemies, by covering him with seaweed. This bird's Gaelic cry of '*Bi glic*' means 'be wise'.

Mermaids were not uncommon, one having belonged to the Cromartie Firth, last seen early in the 18th century, but probably she resented the oil that nowadays fouls the water and moved elsewhere. Another at Kessock married Patterson, of the Kessock Ferry, who having effected her capture, hid her scales in the loft, as without these she could not return to the sea, but one day she discovered these old scales and quickly slipping them on was drawn back, in part unwillingly, into her natural element, leaving behind a sorrowing husband and family.

Of a less kindly nature are the Blue Men of the Minch and the Storm Kelpies, some of whom tired of crossing from Tain to Dornoch in cockle shells, built in one night a bridge over the Gizzen Briggs, but a passing Highlander asked God to bless the Bridge, which at once collapsed having been constructed by agencies more closely connected with 'old Hornie.' The ruins of this Brig' formed the dangerous bar across the Dornoch firth which wrecked the 'Rotterdam' owned by a wicked pirate, both ship and crew being a total loss, and till recently the ship's company could be heard singing psalms and praying under the water, a non-stop penance till the Day of Judgment.

Ghosts are very numerous, throughout Scotland, among them the *Glaisltig*—a thin grey woman with yellow hair falling to her heels, Castle *Camus* in Skye once belonging to the MacLeods and then passing to the Lords of the Isles, was inhabited by one of them. It is said that the removal of the MacDonald Lords of Sleat from the Castle of Duntulum to Armadale Castle during the 18th century was largely due to the haunting of the former by the ghost of an ancestor Donald *Gorm* who would carrouse very noisily. But as every old castle of Scotland has one or more ghosts it seems an unsatisfactory reason for moving so perhaps the story that a nurse by mistake dropped one of the children over the battlements is the real reason.

Another troublesome ghost is said to reside in the still occupied but very ancient Scandinavian Dune Tower in the Lewis.

Wells. We have already mentioned the very numerous Holy Wells, and so great was the faith reposed in their efficacy that in 1650 the Presbytery of Dingwall issued a warning against the practice of visiting Holy Wells in Wester Ross for consulting the waters.

They were credited with all kinds of powers, one in the Lewis near the 'Temple of St. Molochus' was held to cure insanity; still though we may laugh, we are told on very good authority, that faith can remove mountains.

Giants. In the hills of *Fearn* there is a cave wherein dwelt the last of the giants, his only daughter married to a normal sized man. Unfortunately giant and son in law did not get on too well together, the normal human showing a sad lack of taste and manners by mocking his giant host, who was very old and very blind, for saying that the legs of the birds consumed by the giants of old were heavier than his biggest oxen. At length the giant told his servant to take his bow and arrow, and accompany him to Balnagown Forest; first he pointed out normal birds, then others that were three times the size of eagles, and finally a lot three times bigger than oxen; telling his servant to guide his hand to the bow he shot one of the latter taking back a leg to his cave, after which one is glad to hear that his son in law treated him with more respect and kindness.

Kirk and Kirkyard have their quota of stories; the one of the tailor being common to Beauly Priory and Dornoch Cathedral; it goes as follows: a bold tailor undertook, for a consideration, to watch all night by the light of a candle within the precincts of the Priory or Cathedral. All went well till attracted by a sound he turned and saw a skeleton hand emerging from under a slab; for a time the tailor stuck to his post, but as more and more of an immense skeleton came to light so the tailor's nerve failed, till at last it broke and he fled, followed by the skeleton who all but caught the man as he crossed the threshold.

At *Clachan* Duich in the burial ground of the very old Kirk there lies a stone slab the '*Leach Chuileanach*' which commemorates an old tale.

One of the MacRaes of Inverinate was murdered in Strathglass presumably by a Chisholm, so a party from Kintail set off to collect the body, but met on the way a funeral party from Strathglass, who as well as their own corpse were carrying his grave stone. The MacRaes, not in the best of tempers, picked a quarrel with the opposing funeral party, winning the ensuing brawl, and taking the stone back home to Kintail where presumably it marks the grave of the man they had set out to collect.

The stories of witches, warlocks and the like are to be found in all quarters of Ross and Cromarty, so that we end with the old Scottish prayer:

Frae ghaesties and ghoulies and long legged beasties
And things that gang bump i' the nicht
Guid Lord, deliver us!

ACKNOWLEDGEMENTS

In a book of this nature the author is dependent on the works of a great many other people, both for facts and the 'atmosphere' of certain periods. To these many men and women I tend my sincere gratitude.

To Professor V. Gordon Childe, whose 'Prehistoric Communities of the British Isles' and 'The Prehistory of Scotland' I have used extensively, I owe special thanks. To Professors Collingwood and Myers, the authors of 'Roman Britain and the English Settlements'. To Dr. Agnes Mure Mackenzie, the authoress of: 'The Kingdom of Scotland.' 'The Foundations of Scotland.' 'Robert Bruce King of Scots.' 'The Rise of the Stewarts.' 'The Scotland of Queen Mary and the Religious Wars.' 'The Passing of the Stewarts.' 'The Foundations of Modern Scotland.' To Dr. W. M. Mackenzie: 'The Mediaeval Castle in Scotland.' To Mr. E. M. Barron: 'The Scottish War of Independence.' To Provost Norman MacRae: 'The Romance of a Royal Burgh, Dingwall's Story of a Thousand Years.' To Mr. Frank Adam: 'The Clans Septs and Regiments of the Scottish Highlands.' To Mr. George Scott Moncrieff, Editor and author of:' The Stones of Scotland.' To Professor W. J. Watson: 'History of the Celtic Place Names of Scotland.' To Dr. George Calder: 'A Gaelic Grammar.' To Mr. J. A. McCulloch: 'The Misty Isle of Skye.' To Sir Alexander Gibb: 'The Story of Telford.' To Professor James Gray: 'Sutherland and Caithness in Saga Time.' To Mr. W. D. Mackenzie: 'Andrew Fletcher of Saltoun.' To Professor J. G. Fyfe: 'Scottish Diaries and Memoirs.' 1550–1746 and 1746–1843. To Editor and Authors of 'Transactions of Gaelic Society of Inverness.' To Sir Thomas Innes of Learney: 'Scots Heraldry.' To Mr. H. F. MacClintock: 'Old Irish and Highland Dress.' To Mr. S. W. Kitchin, M.A.: 'History of France.'

INDEX

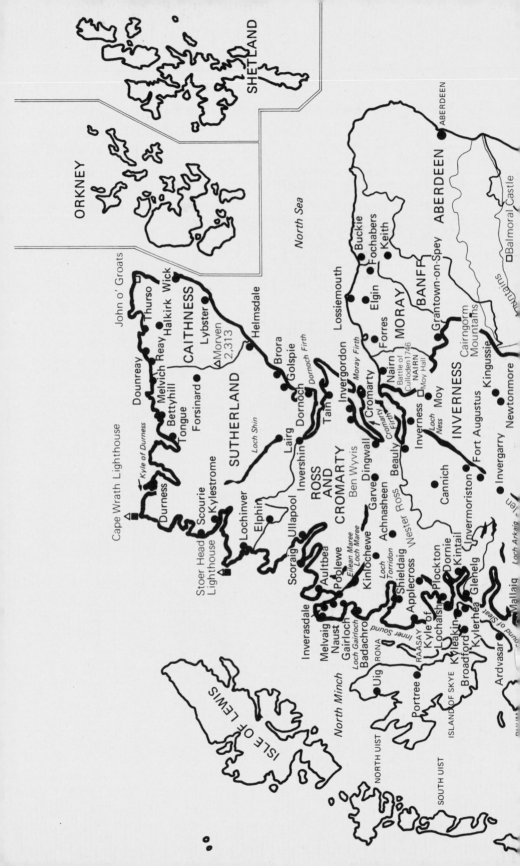